I Found a JOB!

Career Advice from Job Hunters
Who Landed on Their Feet

Marcia Heroux Pounds

jist
Works
America's Career Publisher

I Found a Job!

© 2011 by Marcia Heroux Pounds

Published by JIST Works, an imprint of JIST Publishing
7321 Shadeland Station, Suite 200
Indianapolis, IN 46256-3923
Phone: 800-648-JIST   Fax: 877-454-7839   E-mail: info@jist.com

Visit our Web site at **www.jist.com** for information on JIST, free job search tips, tables of contents, sample pages, and ordering instructions for our many products!

Quantity discounts are available for JIST books. Please call our Sales Department at 800-648-5478 for a free catalog and more information.

Trade Product Manager: Lori Cates Hand
Development Editor: Colleen Totz Diamond
Production Editor: Heather Stith
Cover Designer and Page Layout: Aleata Halbig
Interior Designer: Toi Davis
Proofreaders: Paula Lowell, Jeanne Clark
Indexer:

Printed in the United States of America
15 14 13 12 11 10   9 8 7 6 5 4 3 2 1

Library of Congress Cataloging-in-Publication Data

Pounds, Marcia Heroux, 1957-
   I found a job! : career advice from job hunters who landed on their feet / Marcia Heroux Pounds.
      p. cm.
   Includes index.
   ISBN 978-1-59357-814-5 (alk. paper)
   1. Job hunting. 2. Vocational guidance. I. Title.
   HF5382.7.P686 2011
   650.14--dc22

2010040779

ISBN 978-1-59357-814-5

ACKNOWLEDGMENTS

I want to thank all the job seekers who participated in this project, passing on their experiences and valuable lessons to others looking for work. You are the heroes of America's Great Recession:

David Adamson

Amy Babcock

Ruth Balsam

Suzanne Beard

Jeanette Benway

George Berkley

Kirsten FV Binder

Lauren Burchett

Sophie Cardona

Anthony Cortese IV

Nancy Cranford

Michael Crehan

Paola de Angeli

Mary Beth Dew

Ashley DuFrene

Rob Ewanow

Stephen Fox

John Galea

Diana Galvin

Rosanna Garofalo

Rodrigo Garrido

Christina Gleason

Lisa Godoski

Howard Goodman

Renee Govig

Maria Harkins

Hal Howard

Andrea Hubbell

Michael Hudak

Ed Humble

Alan Hunt

Kenneth Jones

Ollie Jones

Marina Konchak

Robert Kostin

Jim Kowalczyk

David Kravetz

Will Kuchera

Jenipher Lagana

George Lambros

Eric Levy

Steve Liewer

Mitch Lipka

Dane Lyons

Patricia Martinez

Robert McClure

Sondra McFarlane

Bryan McMahon

Angel Mercedes

Gordon Murray

Janet Nelson

Scott Nemeth

Michael Ni

Grace Orejas

Rodrigo Parra

Mary Pastick

Jackie Penalver

Laura Perry

Larry Petralia

Charles and Mindy Pheterson

W. Alejandro Polanco

Alex Popov

Kurt Porceng

Adam Rees

Martha Restrepo

Luis Riano

Darwin Rivera

John Rives

Alvaro Ruiz

Marian Schembari

Jessica Schmidt-Bonifant

Nicole Sheets

Nancy Sickles

Greg Siegelman

Natalie Silva

Michael Simon

Kathy Stein

Bob Struth

Layla Thomas

Mistie Thompson

David Tow

Angel Valentin

Lisa Viale

Alexa Von Staden

Scott Walsh

Terri Warren

Mary White-Cornell

Pauline Wilcox

Denise Williams

Don Winsett

I'd also like to thank the many job search experts around the nation who have helped with contacts and insight for this book: Thomas Shea, Romayne Berry, Jim DeChant, and Alan Berger of Right Management in South Florida; Diane Crompton of Your Social Media Strategist; Ellen Sautter of Right Management, Atlanta; Mason Jackson and Susan Leventhal of Broward County's Workforce One; Marilyn Durant of Durant Resources; Sam Hines and Sue Romanos of CareerXchange; Kristen Nevils of HR Broker; Jeannette Kraar of Performance Management International; Roy Lantz of American Recruiters; Kia-lee Bussey of Human Resource Association of Broward County; Marge Balcom and Janine Moon of ExecuNet; Erin Lamberti of Keystone Partners; Lisa Montagna of Robert Half International; Carlos Baldo of Asesores Balor; Ed Loucks of TMI Executive Resources; Luis Martinez of Gran Altura; Linda Van Valkenburgh of My Executive Career Coach; Kristen Bergevin of The Phelps Group; Phil Scruton of the Small Business Development Center, Palm Beach State College; Grace Totoro, career coach; and Juan Pujol, human resources executive.

Special thanks to my many good friends and family members across the nation who reached out to their networks on my behalf. I couldn't have written this book without you.

CONTENTS

INTRODUCTION

I began writing this book in the fall of 2009, when America's economy was still far from recovery. Millions of people were out of work, and many others, including myself, wondered how long they might keep their jobs. Workers faced unbelievable odds, especially those in industries or regions hurt by the housing and financial crises.

As a journalist covering unemployment in Florida, one of the hardest-hit states in the nation, I interviewed people nearly every day who couldn't seem to find work. They sent out hundreds of resumes and got few interviews. They told me, "I've never been out of work." Suddenly, they couldn't find a job.

Yet despite the challenging environment, *some* people found jobs—perhaps because they had better networks or advice, or they were more assertive than their peers. I decided to find out what was behind some people finding work while so many others continued to struggle.

I interviewed successful job hunters from across the nation, in many different professions, and I discovered that many people who found jobs share certain traits: persistence, the ability to ask for help, an open-minded and positive attitude, and a dogged will to succeed. They used every tool available for their job hunts, not just one. And when they were rejected, they learned from their mistakes and kept on going until they found a job.

I Found a Job! is your opportunity to learn from those who have found jobs in the worst economic time since the Great Depression. Even as America's economy improves, job hunting will remain highly competitive, and the pool of job seekers will become more widespread. Discouraged job hunters will re-enter the market. At the same time, employees who were afraid to leave their jobs during the recession will decide it's time to look around. The personal stories in this book will inspire you to stay motivated in this competitive environment, which is the biggest challenge during a long job search. You will see that even in the most difficult of times and circumstances, people do find jobs.

As a job hunter, you need hope, but you also need a *plan*. This book also can help you develop your own blueprint for success, no matter where you live or what industry you work in. Find the elements of *your* plan in these stories. For quick reference, you'll find a list of "streetwise strategies" for job hunting at the end of each chapter.

If you're a professional who hasn't looked for a job in 10 or 20 years, this book is especially for you. There are new ways of networking, creating and submitting resumes, and interviewing and strategizing to make you stand out from the crowd and land the job you want and deserve.

In interviewing successful job seekers for this book, I've had the opportunity to talk with some extraordinary Americans. Many have credentials that would be enviable in any time. In this recession, they've had to draw on their emotional resources and reach out to other people for help, which was uncomfortable for many. Despite obstacles and difficult times, these survivors maintained an upbeat attitude.

That healthy mindset is critical to finding a job. And *I Found a Job!* is the book that keeps you in the right frame of mind. Adapt these strategies and tactics from these inspirational Americans who have landed jobs— and perhaps you can be one of them.

CHAPTER 1

LOSE THE BITTERNESS, BUT KEEP YOUR SENSE OF HUMOR

Workers who lose their jobs often are told, "It's not personal, it's business." But a layoff *feels* personal. Still, it's critical to get past the anger and hurt in order to move on and find a job.

Software engineer Dane Lyons, 39, admits he was "freaked out" in late 2008 when his business clients were dwindling, the economy was tanking, and he needed to find a job.

Lyons had been through job loss before. Last time, "I became psychologically down about it and let that take over. I let it cripple me. All I could think about was how bad things were, and how angry and upset I was," he says. As a result, in 2001 it took Lyons about nine months to find a job.

He eventually went into business for himself and did well—until the recession hit. In late 2008, he was down to one client who hadn't paid him for three months. Finally, Lyons realized, "I'm unemployed."

"You can't change being upset," Lyons says. "I was scared." Instead of panicking, he channeled his fear into an intense job search. "This time I said, 'I'm going full guns ahead. This isn't going to be the way I did it before.' This time I didn't let it control me."

In May 2009, Lyons was hired by an information technology firm in South Florida, just four months into his job search. With many Florida workers out of a job for six months or more in this recession, that was record speed.

"You've got to be in the right frame of mind," Lyons says. Emotions run rampant after losing a job or a business, and everyone reacts to it differently, with some people moving forward more quickly than others. Some job hunters I interviewed for this book shook off the setback and launched into a rapid job search; others needed time to adjust and deal with the loss.

Yet all of the successful job hunters I interviewed for this book managed to let go of the bitterness. Most also kept their sense of humor, even during a long job search and through financial upheaval. That helped them stay emotionally intact and enabled them to reach out and expand their network, which is critical to a job search.

Embrace Change

In this uncertain job market and in the years ahead, ongoing change is something to be expected and even embraced. Many of those who landed new jobs or created their own say they're happier than they've ever been. That's probably because they examined what they really wanted in life, and then went after it.

Don Winsett, 55, had always transitioned easily from one job to another in South Florida, where he has lived for more than 30 years. He ran the landscape division of a major developer. When the division was sold in 2008, it was time for him to move on.

He took advantage of his outplacement services, part of his severance, and learned from the experts that executives tend to change jobs every four or five years. "It's not necessarily a bad thing. There's this constant flow of positions," Winsett says.

The Great Recession has changed the way many people look at work. They no longer expect, or even want, to stay with one employer for 10 or 20 years.

"Before, there was the dynamic of younger generations staying in jobs two or three years. Because of everything that has happened, that will become a reality for everyone. Understand and manage the new environment," says Martha Restrepo, 50, a human resources executive who recently landed a job with a Boston-based online job board after looking for more than a year.

Most people I interviewed who were laid off during America's recession in 2007 to 2010 went through stages of acceptance, some quicker than others. Many were stunned that they, and so many other highly qualified professionals, could be in the job market.

"Friends say it's what a divorce feels like. You feel betrayed," says Marina Konchak, who lost her job in human resources at Home Depot after 28 years. "I didn't want to give those feelings any energy. I didn't want to fall into the hole of 'woe is me.'"

Konchak, 46, avoided the doldrums by spending time out of her house and at the office, where she was given outplacement services as part of her severance. "When it happens, you go through 'why me?' But it's not you. It's a financial decision," says Konchak, who recommends spending about a day grieving and then revitalizing. "The second day, get your body healthy. Go to the gym."

She threw herself into her job search and landed a job in her field in just two months. "Don't be scared of what's to come. What's to come may be exactly what's meant to be," Konchak says.

Change is hard, especially as one gets older. But embracing change can help you reach another level in your career, learn new skills, and open yourself to opportunities. A mentor once told me, "Change is your friend." And she was right. Every time I've embraced change and adapted to a situation, I've benefited. That's especially important in my field of journalism, which is rapidly evolving into new mediums.

The world today is an environment of ongoing change, and the workplace exemplifies that. Whether you are employed or looking for a job, you want to be seen as a worker who adapts.

Move Past Anger

Anger after being laid off is not unusual. Workers who are let go from a job often feel hurt. Vent to family and friends, and then get over it. Bitterness will not help you in your job search.

"I was pissed," admits Alex Popov, 49, who was laid off on New Year's Eve 2008. Popov had been down this road before. Several years earlier, he had been downsized at a major transportation company and even though he was given outplacement assistance, it took him awhile to land a job. His heart really wasn't in it, so Popov focused on finishing his MBA.

Finally, he was hired at a finance lease company in Fort Lauderdale and worked there for three years. But then came the nation's finance and mortgage crisis, and his company's parent firm was caught up in it. "They offered me money to leave, and I took that option," Popov says.

Unlike the first downsizing when he gave into his anger, Popov poured his energy into his job search, talking with people, finding connections, and staying positive. "You treat looking for a job as a job and go to work every day," he says. It's easy to get into a funk, so watch your demeanor. "When someone has been beaten, you can see it on him. Tell yourself, 'I'm as good as it gets. I've got to put my best foot forward.'"

Popov's wife noticed the difference in him during this job hunt. "You're a lot calmer this time," she told him.

Why? Instead of focusing on the past, he turned his attention to figuring out what he really wanted to do in his career. Popov was less frustrated with his job search because he first went through the hard work of understanding himself.

With the help of job search experts, Popov recognized he was more entrepreneurial in nature than his previous jobs had allowed. That self-knowledge allowed him to entertain the idea of a job with a startup.

In May 2009, Popov was offered and took a job at Liban, a transportation-related business in Rochester, New York, where he had a commission-based salary structure. That's something he wouldn't have considered before. But he also could work out of his home— fortuitous at a time when it wasn't favorable to sell a home in South Florida's downtrodden real estate market.

"I'm making less money than I used to, but the upside is greater," Popov says. "You've got to adjust your expectations."

Lose the "Woe Is Me"

Face it: No one wants to be around someone who is a downer. Make a commitment to yourself to take pleasure in what you have—a family, good friends, an enjoyable hobby. Your positive attitude will be a magnet that draws people to you, which is what you want during a job search.

In my reporting on the unemployed, I talk with people every day who have lost their jobs and homes, and who are barely getting by with the help of friends and government assistance. Some are focused only on what they've lost; they can't see beyond that. Others manage to take even obstacles in stride.

Job hunters who participated in *I Found a Job!* managed to keep their positive attitudes even in ridiculously bad situations:

- **When it rains, it pours.** Mike Simon got laid off from a job where he often worked in China. Soon after, his South Florida home became uninhabitable due to Chinese drywall, an imported product that some believe to be a cause of ruined appliances and health problems. The situation could have been a nightmare. Fortunately, "we were just renting," he says.

- **Pay isn't all that matters.** Jeanette Benway found a great-paying job at a private equity firm, but her boss completely ignored her—for six months. "Is there something I can do for you?" she would ask. "Don't worry about it. I'll let you know," was the reply. To stay busy, she brought sewing to work and watched movies. "People would tell me, 'You have the dream job.'" But Benway was frustrated. "Week two I started job hunting," she said.

- **Don't let the door hit you in the....** Nancy Sickles loved her job in pharmaceutical sales and had been promoted several times. One day in February 2009, her team was told to call in for a teleconference. She heard something like this: "Today will be your last day of work. The last day on payroll will be February 28. If you have any questions, hit 'star pound.'"

- **Who gave you my name?** Alvaro Ruiz was comfortable making cold calls when he was in career transition. So he asked "Mike," a former vendor, if he knew anyone at a target employer. Mike suggested calling "Jack," a sales manager at the company, and gave him his cell phone number. But when Ruiz called Jack, he said he didn't know Mike and demanded to know where Alvaro had gotten his contact information. When Alvaro told Mike what had happened, he "started laughing nonstop." It turns out that Mike and Jack knew each other from Alcoholics Anonymous, and group members don't share last names. Once the situation was explained, Jack was more helpful.

You'll read more about these job seekers, and how they succeeded despite their challenges, in other chapters.

Take Time to Assess Your Life

Think of being laid-off as an opportunity to write a new script. Take the time you need to reassess your career and your goals. Consider where you've been, your skills and experience, and where you want to go. Think about what you like or dislike about the work you've done.

As the economy recovers, looking for a job will become more of a choice. Still, every worker should take some time at least once a year to think about goals, achievements, and aspirations. Besides the environment around you changing, your own life is likely to go through stages during which your priorities may change.

In a job search, it's important to know yourself, your skills, and the job you really want. I interview job hunters who tell me, "I'll take anything." Although I applaud their willingness to work, that's not usually a successful approach.

"A lot of people go in too fast. You send out resumes, and then you find an error in your resume, and you've almost shot yourself in the foot. Think through what you want to do," says Jim Kowalczyk, 37, a process improvement specialist who now works for a company in Atlanta.

So when embarking on a career transition, take some time off to breathe, talk with family and friends, review your career, and consider your future. Pick a place you enjoy to simply think about you. One job hunter meditated near a lake, which helped her slow down and think about her career. Another idea is to turn to a mentor you trust for counsel and feedback. By going through this introspective process, you'll be more likely to find the job that best suits you and one that you're passionate about—not just another job.

A classic career guidebook, such as *What Color Is Your Parachute?* (by Richard N. Bolles, Ten Speed Press), can help you with this process. John Rives, 44, who landed a job as a quality manager for a manufacturer in Columbus, Ohio, says reading that book and other job search articles helped him flush out his strengths and weaknesses. "It really helped me narrow down my transferable skills," he says.

Ask Yourself These Questions

Laura Perry, a communications professional in Los Angeles, took advantage of a voluntary severance package her employer offered in August 2008. "I thought, I'm going to take this offer and then I can be in control of my own destiny," she says.

Of course, then the economy took its dive that fall and she was out of a job for 10 months. Perry, now 54, used the time to really think what she wanted to do, asking herself:

- What do I like?

- What are my core strengths?

- What value do I bring to the table?

- What kind of organizations do I want to work for?

- What position would allow me to grow in my career?

- If I decide to move, what kind of environment and community do I want to live and work in?

Perry wanted to remain in communications but needed a new challenge. In targeting potential employers that fit her criteria, she steered clear of troubled industries. Perry ended up having two job offers. She chose the position of communications director for the School of Nursing at University of California, Los Angeles.

In deciding between jobs, go with your gut, most participants in this book say. Perry favored the UCLA position because she was immediately drawn to the director's way of thinking. "I had just one interview with him and I sat in his office, thinking, 'I like him and I want this job,'" Perry says. "He's more than advancing the school. He has this thought of advancing the profession. From a leadership standpoint, it was very exciting."

Perry approached every job interview as a quest to learn whether this was the place she wanted to work. "Listen to yourself," she says.

She learned from a few bumps early in her job search. Perry became a finalist for a few jobs but didn't get offers. The feedback from one interviewer was that the hiring manager liked her and thought she was qualified, but "there are so many qualified candidates, I'm going to talk with some more people."

In a recession, where so many qualified candidates flood the job market, the human resources director's job is to find the best candidate. Often, that results in long searches, months of interviews, and one candidate being chosen over another for a minor difference.

Still, that doesn't make anyone feel better when they lose out on a job. Perry was hurt and discouraged. That week, she shut down her computer and went to play golf with a friend. "I took a vacation without going anywhere or spending any money. Sometimes it's okay to do that," she says. "I came back refreshed."

She also balanced her job seeking with other activities. She went to a Pilates class twice a week for exercise. On Mondays and Tuesdays, she spent her time on job applications. By midweek, she moved on to other job search and social activities including an occasional lunch with a friend. She also took time to attend the Ragan Social Media Conference in Las Vegas—something she thought was important to show she was keeping up her skills.

When she returned home, she did pro bono work to practice social media, such as setting up Facebook fan pages. She also joined Twitter and started tweeting on a regular basis. And Perry wrote some articles that were published while on her job search. So when an interviewer asked her what she had been doing in her time without a job, she could point to the articles, social media learning, and pro bono work.

It was the combination of her background, skills, and passion for the work that helped her land the job at UCLA, she says. "They're going to pick people at the end of the day who are excited and engaged," Perry says. "Do whatever you have to do to keep that energy level up."

Know Your Best Fit, but Don't Limit Yourself

Some people can work through the "getting to know me" process themselves, and others need the guidance of a job search counselor. If you've been fortunate enough to receive outplacement services, take full advantage of it. If not, seek free help available through your local workforce agency, which also has career experts ready to put you on the right path.

Luis Riano, 39, considered widening his job search based on his career coach's advice. Ultimately, his opportunity was with a former competitor in his field.

"One of the key things is you need to sit down and find out exactly what it is that you want to do," says Riano, whose job in Ecuador with a U.S. telecommunications firm came to an end in August 2009.

After his Ecuador assignment, Riano was offered another job with his then-employer in South America. But he had a home in South Florida and wanted to return with his family to the United States, where he was now a citizen.

His career advisor told him, "You could probably work in another industry. You have the skills for a different environment. Don't limit yourself."

Riano agrees with his career consultant's advice. "Sometimes you get married to your job or your lifestyle and you forget to lift up your head and look at the landscape of opportunities that are out there," he says.

But he also knew his best contacts were in his telecommunications field. After losing his job, Riano reached out to a former competitor and ended up with a job interview.

Some people might hesitate to contact a competitor about a job, but what recommendation could be better? "You have to put your pride aside," Riano says. "One of the things that make you a better person is when you're humble." He got into the mindset that, "I need to find something new because I need to take care of my family."

Riano landed back in the United States on September 1 after losing his job in August. In just six weeks, he was working again at a new job in his field at a comparable salary.

Understand Your Strengths

Learn about your strengths and how to communicate them to a potential employer, says Sondra McFarlane, a marketing professional. That's what helped her land a job with a jewelry retailer in Rochester, New York.

In the summer of 2009, McFarlane and her husband, Daniel, found themselves out of work at the same time. She found emotional support for the process through a career coach and from her husband. "His words to me were 'find what you love to do.' For someone to say that to me in the midst of his own job search was unbelievable," she says.

A Type "A" personality, McFarlane says she's always planning. She needed her husband and others to tell her to take time to contemplate. Instead of rushing from place to place, she took time that summer to sit by the lake and walk along the pier.

"When you're floundering, people ask, 'What job are you looking for?' and you have this blank look. You're in such a fog. You really need to take some time to figure it out," she says.

She found out more about herself through Gallup's StrengthsFinder 2.0 test, which was suggested to her by a networking contact. McFarlane was not surprised to find that she was strategic, positive, a good communicator, and an idea person. But focusing on those qualities helped her translate them to her resume.

To tailor her resume for each application, McFarlane created a sheet of measurable accomplishments from her past employment. She then plugged the relevant highlights into her resume.

To gather information on two target employers, she posted on her Facebook wall, asking if anyone had worked for or knew the companies, and then she followed up with an offer of coffee. As a result, one woman whom she had attended high school with in Rochester offered to send her resume to people she knew in an organization.

She had a couple of interviews at nonprofits and was hoping one would offer her a job, but neither was moving along as quickly as she would like. So McFarlane contacted a woman in her network who was well-connected in the region. She told her, "One of these nonprofits would be perfect for you, but I know of this other position. They're looking for somebody with your skills to be more of a business partner and take more of a strategic view."

But when McFarlane interviewed with the owners, they weren't certain they wanted to hire a marketing director. They were considering using an agency or someone on a contract basis.

McFarlane showed them what she could accomplish for the company, a jewelry retailer. She talked about how she had overseen a product launch at a former employer, developed the marketing plan, brought the product to the Consumer Electronics Show in Las Vegas, and generated more than 1,000 leads.

She also had revamped her former employer's website using search engine optimization to increase unique visitors from 500,000 to 1.25 million a year. The company's e-commerce sales had tripled year over year. She talked about all of this during her interview and was prepared to document it. "You've got to make sure you can express what you've done in terms of accomplishments. When you do that, people understand you're the real deal," McFarlane says.

McFarlane got a job offer from her new employer in October 2009, just after her husband had found a new sales job. "It has been fabulous, one of the best jobs I've ever had," she says.

Seek Help from the Experts

I've seen too many job seekers get a late start on a search because they didn't think they needed or didn't want to go to outplacement services included in their severance package.

Recognize that you might be experiencing depression and seek mental health counseling. Do whatever it takes to put yourself in the best frame of mind to look for a job.

People who have been laid off from jobs often feel awkward about explaining their unemployment, and that makes other people uncomfortable.

"I didn't feel whole without having that piece of me," says Mary Pastick, 56, a South Florida healthcare executive who lost her job in 2008, but has since been hired for a top-level position. "When you meet new people, they ask, 'What do you do? Where do you work?'"

She learned to simply say, "I'm in transition," as many career experts recommend. "That was my tagline," Pastick says.

Develop and practice your "elevator" speech, a brief pitch to market yourself. Practice both a short and a longer version that you can roll off your tongue at any opportunity.

Some job hunters find support groups helpful during the initial search phase. You can find them through your local workforce agency as well as industry groups and networking organizations such as ExecuNet. But be careful not to get caught up in the "woe is me" syndrome. If you find yourself getting angry or depressed, maybe that group is not the best place to spend your time. Surround yourself with positive people who will help you stay on track, not just soothe your wounds.

Understand That People Want to Help

Remember that generally people want to help you. Perhaps they've faced unemployment themselves, or they make a practice of trying to connect people in their lives. Successful job hunters told me that even strangers were often willing to help them. If they didn't have a job lead, they helped connect them with someone who might, or they took time to give them valuable feedback.

"It surprised me how open people are. Everyone I reached out to for questions and contacts was very happy to help," Kowalczyk says. "I was able to create new relationships."

Rob Ewanow, 43, a marketing professional, is fortunate to live near Rochester, New York. Rochester is a city that has its act together in helping job hunters. He belongs to the American Marketing Association's local chapter, and he joined The August Group, whose motto is "networking for life." The August Group offers job postings online and holds meetings where job hunters can trade leads. "They meet multiple times a week. There are about 3,500 members, and 75 percent are employed," Ewanow says.

The strong networking culture is likely due to Rochester being home to several large corporations that have gone through massive restructurings. "We've learned," he says. "Kodak and Xerox have been downsizing for years. We're ahead of the curve in that area."

Keep on a Schedule

When you were working, you no doubt had a work routine. Suddenly, when you are unemployed, there is no structure. Think ahead each week and create a schedule for networking and other job-related activities to stay focused.

In searching for a software engineering position, Dane Lyons set up a daily routine of checking online job boards. He meticulously recorded each job, the date he applied, information supplied, his follow-up, and the response from the employer. "I made a spreadsheet. If I didn't hear from employers in a couple of days, I would contact them," he says.

When he attended a networking event, Lyons would take the business cards of those he met and input the information to his spreadsheet. Within a few days of meeting people, "I made it a point to call them," he says.

Lyons took the same systematic approach with recruiters, seeking to work with many different ones. "A recruiter wants an exclusive relationship so he can make an easy process of a match. That's for their benefit. You have to talk with every single recruiter," he says.

This job search was resolved more quickly than a previous job search for Lyons because of his direct approach. "I felt all the same things but I didn't react in the same way," he says. "You have to attack it head on. It's like diving in the deep end when the water's cold."

Be Proactive to Keep Up Your Spirits

David Kravetz watched as his technology company went through cutbacks and wondered when his time was up. He lost his job just before Thanksgiving 2007. "It was devastating. I always had excellent performance reviews, won awards, worked hard," says Kravetz, 53.

Kravetz found an interim contract job as a Japanese translator in Ontario, a nine-hour commute from his Lexington, Kentucky, home. He made the best of it by taking photographs along the way and posting them on his blog, sumoflam.biz. "I used that as one of my escapes to get my mind off the dilemmas," he says.

He lost the contract job after three months and turned to his church for help. With no new job in sight, he took a $10-an-hour call center job that his minister arranged. "It was the closest thing to working in a sweatshop. It was a demoralizing job. But I hung in there. I had perfect attendance," Kravetz says.

Kravetz had other pressures as well: His two daughters were about to be married. At a time when he was supposed to be basking in his daughters' happiness, Kravetz was feeling depressed. So he reached out to friends to keep him sane. "I used my five close friends as sounding boards to talk through my depression," he says.

Ultimately, his wife Julianne also was let go from her job, but soon found another as an administrative assistant with a firm that promotes high school athletes. Kravetz's two sons had played high school football and his two daughters, high school basketball. So when a marketing job came open at his wife's employer, Kravetz wanted to apply. His wife of 30 years wasn't sure it was a good idea.

"She has never worked with me before, and I'm very passionate about everything I do. Even though I hated the call center job, I still strived to be the best of anybody there," he says.

Kravetz got the job, and he loves the company's entrepreneurial culture. "They recognize I have other skills that can help this company as it grows. My time isn't being micromanaged. They're treating me as an individual," he says.

He marked six months at his job by writing this in his blog:

> *I have found enjoyment and fulfillment in a job more than I have enjoyed since my days as a tour guide in Flagstaff, Arizona, from 1981–1984. This fulfillment doesn't come from the money I make. I have discovered that I am happy as can be with my job because every day brings me a new example of fulfillment and meaning. These two things are so much more valuable than any financial compensation....*

> *As I look back over the years in my various jobs, I can see that in a sense I was prepared for this job. I have done Web design and support, video production and editing, customer support, tech support, and project management...I honestly believe this is the perfect job for me. And I love it.*

Exude Confidence, but Be Honest

At the time when you've lost a job, you may not feel at your best, so fake it. Learn to boost your morale, repeating mantras that work for you, and surround yourself with can-do people. You don't need people feeling sorry for you.

I've talked with many job hunters during the recession who blame their age for not being able to find a job. While I have no doubt that there is some age discrimination, you can't go through life expecting it. Instead, focus on improving your energy level and updating your skills. Exercising and staying fit is especially important in keeping up your energy for a job search. If you don't have a regular exercise routine, get one. You'll lose a few pounds and feel more youthful. When you interview, mention how you jog or play tennis or golf; it illustrates your vibrancy, which is what employers want in a hire.

Youth has the advantage in computer skills; if yours are lacking, it's time to get some training. Still, experienced workers need to remember what they bring to the table is a wealth of experience that it would take years of training and investing in a young graduate to attain.

Larry Petralia, 59, had those concerns as an experienced worker suddenly looking for a job in technology. Petralia thought he had a lifelong job with Anheuser-Busch, once St. Louis's largest employer. When the maker of Budweiser beer was acquired in 2008 by InBev, a Belgium beer company, Petralia and other long-time brewery workers couldn't believe it. Large downsizings began. At Anheuser-Busch, Petralia often attended lavish parties, and benefits were top-notch: Employees didn't even have to pay a premium for health insurance until recent times.

"Anheuser-Bush was such a nice place to work," he says. With the acquisition, "the glory days were over," says Petralia, who thought it best to take an early retirement package offered to him in December 2008. "I felt I was going to lose my job eventually," he says.

Petralia had worked his way up at the brewery, not obtaining his college degree until he was 39. He worked in such a specialized area for the brewery that he was concerned about his competitiveness in the job market. "I'm an old dog, and IT is ever-changing. Some of my skills were not easily transferable," he says.

But he did have people skills, which are also valued in technology departments. After about five months of unemployment, he got an interview at a St. Louis healthcare company.

"I'm a pretty good listener, and I have good communication skills," Petralia says. As it turned out, the healthcare company was looking for someone who had basic technology skills but who also could work well with customers. Petralia thinks his description of handling customer concerns in his former job may have given him an edge.

When asked to give an example of when a customer was unhappy with the product or service, he relayed a particular incident when he made a mistake fixing a program. "When the customer found out, she was mad that now there was a bigger problem than before," Petralia says. So he enlisted his team of experts and came up with a new solution. "I spoke honestly with my team to admit the mistakes. I then e-mailed my customer admitting my mistakes, apologizing, and committing to do whatever it took to fix the new problem," he told his interviewer.

Petralia's integrity in handling a tough situation may have been one factor that got him his new job. "You have to think on your feet and have a good answer for them," he says. "I was ready and on the ball."

Stay Motivated

When a job search lasts for months and even to a year or more, as many did during the recession, it can be difficult to stay motivated. Here's what successful job candidates did to stay up and at their best for that opportunity that was around the corner:

- **Cross off items on your to-do list.** "I found myself becoming my own personal assistant. I sewed on buttons that had been missing from my dress clothes, I organized every closet and drawer in the house, I painted my bathroom ... I always looked forward to crossing an item off the list. It gave me a sense of accomplishment." —Kathy Stein, Florida

- **Become a volunteer.** "I kept myself busy with volunteering and pro bono projects, which was a great way to keep on developing my skills, while at the same time building confidence." —Sophie Cardona, New York

- **Recognize that a little fear is a good thing.** "I was motivated by the fact that my husband and I really couldn't afford to take a cut in our income." —Andrea Hubbell, Virginia

- **Seek a support group that keeps you accountable.** "People who go into these networking groups are not victims. You have to report to this group how many letters you sent, phone calls you made. It keeps you moving forward. It keeps you off of the dark side." —Nancy Sickles, New York

- **Return to your roots.** One job hunter became active in his alumni association, and when he was vying for a job, an old MBA classmate became his advocate. "I got involved in social event planning: breakfasts and after-work drinks. I used those vehicles to network." —Ken Jones, North Carolina

Learn the Art of Cold Calling

Like many in the financial world, Gordon Murray was stunned and worried when he was laid off in October 2008 from his 16 years of work as a municipal bond trader in New York City. He and his wife have 12-year-old twins and had a big mortgage on their house that they bought in 2006.

"Our company was very successful in 2008, and I enjoyed what I was doing. I felt I had good experience to offer. It was misplaced, but I was hopeful," says Murray, 49.

It took Murray 11 months to find a job, and he was one of the lucky ones. He has former colleagues and friends who are still looking for work. In his affluent neighborhood in Maplewood, New Jersey, many families were affected by the recession's layoffs in a wide variety of industries, including finance, pharmaceuticals, and advertising.

The evening after Murray lost his job, he and his wife went to the cell phone store to replace his company BlackBerry, and he printed business cards on his computer. "I had an identity," Murray says.

He thought, for a bit, about transferring his skills or changing careers, but soon realized his years of experience in bonds were more likely to help him land a job quickly. *The Bond Buyer,* a public finance newspaper, offered six months free access to its website, which Murray took advantage of to keep up professionally. He did some freelance work to have something new to show his competencies. And he attended a securities industries conference that invited people in transition to attend certain sessions for free.

"You have to overcome your shyness," Murray says. "You can't feel sorry for yourself that you lost your job. You had nothing to do with it."

So he got on the phone and started calling all the people he knew and many he didn't who were in the industry. He would see an article in the newspaper that a company was expanding in the area and then go on LinkedIn, an online professional networking site, to see if he recognized a name. "I did a lot of cold calling with people I was acquainted with," he says. "I would say, 'Hi, we know someone in common....'"

He preferred calling or e-mailing to meetings over coffee. "With the layoffs there came a lot more busywork for people still working. You called people, and a lot were nervous about their own jobs," Murray says.

Murray also jumped at the chance for any social opportunity, such as drinks with former colleagues, which helped keep up his spirits. When a manager bought him lunch in Manhattan, he returned the favor by looking up credit reference materials for his sales team. "I asked him to keep me in mind if he heard anything," he says. "I would look forward to those things. It got me back in the swing."

"You're always going from beacon to beacon of hope. You work on a lead. You think of something new to try, new people to contact," he says.

Finally, he had lunch with his former boss who told him about an opportunity at a credit fund manager in Westchester, New York. A friend of his was quitting the job. "You should go for it," he told Murray.

Murray did follow up on the lead. He later learned that the company had cancelled its ad for the position after being inundated with applications. But with a recommendation from his former boss, he got an interview.

At the interview, he instantly hit it off with the management team. "I thought it would be an hour, and it stretched to two and a half hours. I was enjoying myself. These guys were very bright. I said, 'Here are the things I think I can do for you.'"

Murray was offered the job in August 2009 and has been working there for more than seven months. "I think I understood what they wanted," he says.

Gain New Perspective

Job hunting can be a time to explore new options and to re-examine what you want to do with your life. While you're going through it, the path may not be clear, and you may feel scared and frustrated. But many job seekers who found jobs say they look back on this period and realize how much they've learned about themselves, their work, and what's important to them in their lives.

Eric Levy, strategist for a financial services company in Boston, had been through a layoff in 2004. He was out of work for 14 months. In early 2010, he was happily employed when he was recruited for a similar position with another company. He took the opportunity. Being out of work a few years earlier had changed the way he looked at his life and work.

"It gave me a very different perspective. It was probably one of the best things that ever happened to me. It provided me with an opportunity to spend more time with my family, try some entrepreneurial activities, some consulting. I wrote a book for a research company. And got a chance to go skiing, bicycling, and play golf," Levy says.

"As difficult as it is, think about it in terms of 'it won't last forever.'" says Levy, 45.

"I was 40 years old at the time. It was like a midcareer sabbatical. It lets you step outside your business and see other businesses and network in different ways."

Levy ended up working for a division of his former employer after his 2004 layoff. Returning to a former employer—even your last—will be more typical as the recession moves through the recovery cycle. Many businesses cut too deeply, and as they begin to grow again, they will need to hire. Someone who already has knowledge of the business has a competitive edge over others. So keep in touch and continue on good terms—because needs change.

"If I knew how it was going to end, I would have enjoyed it even more," says Levy of his 14-month job search. "There *are* other opportunities."

Leave on Good Terms and with a Game Plan

Whether you leave a long-time employer by choice or not, doing so can be a traumatic event, as many participants in this book will attest. But try to control your emotions and think about what you gained from the job experience.

John Galea, 52, of West Hollywood, California, knew he was ready to leave his nearly 13-year employer in 2008, but he didn't give voice to it until one day when he had a performance review. "My boss was talking with me, and I said, 'I think it's time for me to leave.' I had wanted to leave, but I didn't have a game plan. Luckily, I had a job within an hour of my last day."

Still, he thought it was important not to burn bridges, so Galea took care to write his boss a letter thanking him for how much he learned in the job. "When you leave, be gracious about it," he says.

Galea says he should have left his former employer earlier than he did. "My greatest fear was that I was going to be unemployed. When I found myself unemployed, I realized that I not only survived, but I also did better."

He left his job for an opportunity in advertising sales for an interior design magazine. But when the housing industry fell on hard times, Galea was laid off in January 2009, just short of a year's employment. He then was looking for work for more than eight months.

"I was hitting the job boards and meeting with headhunters. It always seemed promising, but nothing ever came of it. I sent out maybe 1,500 resumes. In the beginning, I was getting interviews, but then the economy really tanked," he says.

Galea reached out to his network in the professional beauty industry, where he had worked for more than a decade, and heard about a job through a former client. "A friend of mine worked with a woman who used to work at the company I'm at now. I reached out with an e-mail to her," he says.

He got an interview at Orly International in Los Angeles, which makes products for manicures and pedicures. "I knew all the players in the industry, and I was able to talk about people they knew. I tried to show not only that I was interested, but also that I'm valuable," Galea says.

Instead of checking back with them over the following weeks, Galea became proactive. He saw on a website, Help A Reporter Out (www.helpareporter.com), that a writer was looking for sources for a story about how women change their beauty routines during pregnancy. "I said I'd like to pitch this. And I worked on it with my dermatologist, who contacted her obstetrician. I showed them I was connected," he says.

"I was trying to think of creative ways to keep in touch other than, 'Hey, have you decided yet?'" Galea says. It must have worked because he was offered the job of communications manager at Orly International in October 2009.

Galea says if he had to do it all over again, he would still quit a job where he was unhappy. "When you come home and you just feel exhausted, when you're not getting enjoyment out of it, then maybe it's time to make a change instead of waiting it out," he says. "It chips away at your well-being and self-esteem." But next time, he would have a game plan.

Streetwise Strategies for Maintaining a Healthy Frame of Mind

- Allow yourself time to vent and then start working on your plan.
- Assess where you've been in your career and where you want to go.
- Surround yourself with positive, upbeat people.
- Schedule daily job search activities.
- Forget about your age; it's your energy and experience that counts.
- Do pro bono work to stay active in your industry.
- Keep balanced by socializing and doing hobbies you enjoy.
- Appear confident, even if you don't feel it all the time.
- Take a job search break when feeling particularly discouraged.
- Consider the soft skills you have to offer as well as the technical.
- Know your strengths, but don't limit your possibilities.
- Stay in touch with your former employer for new opportunities.
- Think of creative ways to stay in touch with a potential employer.

CHAPTER 2

PUT ON YOUR BEST PROFESSIONAL FACE

The job candidate looked sullen. He was dressed too casually for a job search, and he was slumped in his chair. He didn't feel like a success, and it showed.

Thankfully, the job hunter was sitting in a career counselor's office, not at an interview. The counselor made him aware of his demeanor and urged him to think about how he was feeling and how he was dressed before taking another step.

I followed this job candidate, as a reporter covering unemployment, and I watched over the months as he transformed into a viable job candidate and found work. It took a concentrated effort on his part and being open to advice from others.

Before you send out even *one* resume or go on an interview, you need to put on your best professional face. This includes your appearance, your presentation, and your attitude.

Prepare for Career Transition

There are many signs that it's time to leave a job, and many of us ignore them. We have a natural tendency to cling to what we know. But keeping your eyes open to what's going on around you can help you both mentally and financially through a career transition.

Stay tuned to what's happening with your employer. If your employer is going through a period of belt-tightening or a structural change, there will be staff reductions or reassignments. Do you suddenly have a new supervisor? Is there a merger pending?

This can be a difficult time to figure out which way the wind is blowing—toward you or against you. Keep in close contact with associates to stay on top of changes. Long before these events take place in the form of a reduction in force or consolidation of departments, there will subtle signs of impending change.

This is not a time to freeze in fear. It's a time to explore options, expand contacts, and consider opportunities internally and externally that could arise. If job hunters have learned anything in this recession, it is to always be looking for their next opportunity.

Ideally, your job search work should begin well before you leave an employer. Here are ways you can start preparing:

- Sock away money in an emergency fund. Each payday, put aside money in a special fund for your transition time. Financial advisers used to recommend six months' worth of expenses. Now nine months to a year is a better goal. Review your living expenses and reduce or drop those you don't need.

- Join new industry and community groups. Volunteer for activities and become involved in the group's leadership.

- Take career and personality assessment tests to better know your strengths and style. You can take Gallup's Strengthsfinder 2.0 by purchasing the book *StrengthsFinder 2.0* by Tom Rath (Gallup Press, 2007).

- Begin assembling a portfolio or "brag book," as some call it, to help you talk about sales goals you met and other quantifiable accomplishments during an interview.

- Take a class or study for a certification that will give you any missing skills you may need to get to the next level and set you apart from the competition.

- Try a job or new career on for size by doing a freelance project or other moonlighting, as long as there is no conflict with your current job.

The following sections describe other things you can do to prepare yourself for job changes.

Make the Most of LinkedIn

LinkedIn (www.linkedin.com), an online networking site, provides a place for you to post your accomplishments along with recommendations from others in your industry. It also makes it easier to build your network of professional contacts. You should build a profile on LinkedIn if you don't already have one and keep it updated.

Will updating your LinkedIn profile send a red flag to your current employer that you're looking around? Perhaps, but don't be overly concerned. LinkedIn is viewed as a necessary tool for any professional. (Chapter 3 has more tips about using online networking sites to help your job search.)

When Angel Mercedes knew his telecommunications company was merging with another and he would likely be out of a job, he moved fast. Mercedes sent an e-mail message to key people at his firm, saying simply, "I'm looking for a change and I need your recommendation." For recruiters and potential employers browsing LinkedIn, seeing recommendations by former colleagues is critical, he says. Mercedes soon found a new telecom job without having to move from his home near Richmond, Virginia, which was important to him.

Line Up Trusted References

Jessica Schmidt-Bonifant, 26, of Baltimore knew in late 2009 that the nonprofit she was working for was struggling. She started looking for a new job in October and found a position by December. She even used her boss as a reference—a risky move—with another nonprofit, a student scholarship organization where she was hired as business development director.

Using her boss as a reference could have backfired. But she had a good relationship with her and, in a sense, was protecting her boss from having to make a difficult decision. Although some businesses certainly have used the recession as an excuse to reduce labor costs permanently, many small businesses owners and company managers don't like to have to let people go. It's difficult for them, as well.

"My boss knew that there was a possibility that I might leave," Schmidt-Bonifant says. "I think she was genuinely happy for me when I got the new job." If there is no one at your current employer who could serve quietly as a reference for you, turn to former colleagues and bosses who are no longer with the company.

Use Outplacement Services

Seek out others who can guide and support you. If you're fortunate enough to be given outplacement services in your severance package, use them to the fullest. Everyone I interviewed who worked with either outplacement or free career services said once they found the right people to help them, everything turned around.

Steer away from groups or agencies that require big bucks upfront to "place" you in a job. Whether you decide to hire a career coach for assistance or find free guidance, you need to be part of the job search process.

Mike Simon, who was downsized from the automotive industry, knew he didn't know enough about looking for a job, so he hired a career coach. "You have to go to the people who are experts, and don't wait. I just assumed I would be able to find a job the way I always did, but 2009 was completely different, and the world is a lot different," he says.

His coach called him every morning at 7 a.m. for six months. "She called me to keep me motivated and critiqued me on what I did. She was continually monitoring my progress," he says.

When Simon didn't get calls returned from a potential employer, she assured him he was doing everything he could. "You really start to get depressed, to second guess yourself. She's the expert, so therefore you know you've done everything," he says.

When Nancy Sickles lost her pharmaceutical sales job, she was entitled to outplacement help; but because she was applying for similar jobs, she didn't seek help right away. After hearing several times that she was "overqualified"—in other words, her base pay was too high—she checked out the outplacement services offered by her severance package.

But Sickles didn't "connect" with her assigned job counselor. Then she noticed bulletin board postings about the successful job candidates who had worked with a different counselor. She asked to work with her, and soon everything began to turn around.

"She made changes in my resume and brag book that made a difference," Sickles says. Her resume needed to be more quantitative, pointing to her top successes. The counselor edited the brag book Sickles took to interviews to include her stellar sales numbers, letters of recommendation, and performance reviews, which showed she was highly rated and had been promoted several times.

Most important, the counselor was available when Sickles needed her. "I could e-mail or call, and she would get back to me right away. She was fantastic. She had a handle on the industry and what my challenges were," Sickles says.

Avoid Job Search Firms That Charge Upfront Fees

Never pay someone else to find a job for you. Although there are career coaches who can guide you and outplacement firms that are paid by your former employer, a company that claims to find "hidden" jobs and contacts for a fee is a red flag.

At least two job candidates I interviewed put their trust and money in the hands of such firms, only to be disappointed and to have their job search delayed. Often, these firms offer minimal help with a resume or predictable contacts that any job hunter could find with a little effort. As a result, people who pay someone to find them a job waste money and lose valuable time in their job search.

Bob Struth, a former Navy pilot who has worked in private industry, ultimately landed a job through networking. He now knows networking is the best way to find that hidden job market. But initially Struth paid nearly $5,000 to a job search firm. "They provided a database and rewrote my resume, and I didn't get one single interview," he says. "Stay away from firms that tell you they're going to rewrite your resume and send it out to a bunch of companies. You want personal contact and personal referrals."

He complained, but his money was not refundable. The firm would agree only to start the process over again. It had been 10 months of futility.

Struth then turned to a career consulting service that emphasizes networking, and he met just the right person who would lead to his new job. At his first meeting with other executives in transition, Struth told one of them about his background as a Navy pilot. "He knew this retired general, and he said, 'You've got to meet him.'"

Struth's new friend set up a phone call, and he chatted with the retired general, who now worked in a Department of Defense consultancy. They spoke the same military language. "The phone call lasted about an hour, and then he invited me to his office," Struth says.

Over lunch with another executive, they talked about the company's work on a new generation of more fuel-efficient military jet engines. "The engine is very exciting to me. It's going to be in so many different airplanes in the Navy and Air Force," Struth says.

Struth started his new job working in the jet engine program in March 2010 and likes the way the company operates. At orientation, he learned his new employer is all about networking, a strategy in which he has become a true believer. "It just felt right," he says.

Check the references of any firm or counselor you choose and be aware of the real services being offered. A simple check of the Internet or with the state attorney's office can help you avoid those who prey on the unemployed.

There is plenty of free and low-cost guidance available to help you develop your own job search game plan. Do the work to find the right job for you.

Update Your Appearance and Make Over Your Attitude

You may need a makeover before you look for a job, and it may not be just a physical one. Take a good look in the mirror and ask family and friends' opinions: Do you need to update your hairstyle or dress? Do it, but not to extremes.

Some job hunters overreach by trying to look substantially younger in their hair color or style of dress. It's good to update, but is this the time to undergo plastic surgery? That's probably not necessary and certainly not viable for many unemployed workers who can't even afford to retain health insurance. Instead, your goal should be to look and act like a "professional," whether you're applying for a customer service job at a retail store or a top accounting position at a Fortune 500 firm. In addition, dressing well just makes you feel better, and you need to be at your best for any interview.

More important than your clothes or hairstyle is your attitude and your energy level. In this aspect, you definitely want to be seen as youthful— that is, energetic, enthusiastic, and flexible. An "old" attitude is acting weary or being negative or stubborn. Who would *you* hire?

Jenipher Lagana, 46, of Brookfield, Connecticut, had the right attitude for job hunting, but had trouble accepting the professional dress requirement. Lagana used to work in a T-shirt and jeans for a music wholesaler. When she started looking for a new job, she saw no reason to change her style. "They should want me on my merit," she told her career coach, who convinced her that she could get passed over for an opportunity just because her look was too casual.

Although she resisted, Lagana says she finally "did see the merit of getting a nice briefcase and a pantsuit. I grew my hair out a bit. I picked up shoes I wouldn't normally wear." After extensive networking, Lagana eventually found a job in sales for an energy management company. She now wears business casual, but steps it up to a suit for important business meetings.

In addition to not being too casual, you also should avoid dressing too provocatively in a short skirt or tight pants when you're in a professional situation. You want the attention to be on what you're saying, not what you're wearing. Women should avoid low-cut tops and opt for low heels instead of stilettos. Men should generally wear a suit or sports jacket and make sure their hair is neatly cut and groomed. Keep the jewelry to a minimum.

You can have a bit of flair or style, especially if applying for a creative job. Just make sure when you check yourself in the mirror that the reflection says, "I'm a professional worthy of hiring."

Be Aware of the Undercover Interview

Another reason to dress well is that sometimes you are being interviewed and you may not realize it. This could happen at a networking function or professional association meeting when someone in a hiring position is mentally "filing away" information about how you handle yourself. What you consider an informal lunch or coffee could actually be one step in an interview. So always strive to be at your best.

Rochester marketing professional Rob Ewanow had no idea that when he was making a pitch as a consultant, he was actually auditioning for a job. Ewanow gave a presentation to the person who is now his boss. A short time later he got a call from the executive asking, "Would you like to work for me?"

"It was the second job in a row that I've been hired like that," Ewanow says. He reasons that some managers have little patience for the red tape it often takes to hire someone. The benefit to Ewanow was that while he was prepared to make a pitch for consulting work, he didn't have to sweat it as a job applicant. It was a more relaxed situation, and he tends to do better in conversational situations, he says. The lesson here is to treat any encounter as a potential interview.

Present Yourself Professionally

Your "professional face" also includes how you present yourself on the telephone, in e-mail, and on your business card. Review these items to ensure that you're the total package:

- **Voicemail greeting.** Being professional means your voicemail on your cell phone and answering machine should be in your voice, clear and concise. Delete the voicemail with the joke or your kids' greeting that you thought was clever or cute.

- **E-mail account.** Set up an e-mail just for your job search. If you've been using Hotmail for your e-mail, change to a Gmail account from Google. Just use your name in your address: MarciaPounds@gmail.com, for example. Do not use the sexy e-mail name you created for dating site Match.com when you apply for jobs.

Lagana, who favored her jeans to a suit, also didn't see a reason to change her e-mail address, which is named for her pet Yorkies. Again, her career counselor reminded her of the purpose of her e-mail address. "Wouldn't you rather have the employers see *your* name in front of them?" she asked her.

- **Profile photos.** If you post a photo on Facebook or LinkedIn, make sure you use a good, clear photo of you, not your favorite celebrity. A pleasant, smiling recent headshot works—no funny faces or shots on your motorcycle.

- **Business cards.** Print business cards with your contact information on it; you will need them for networking meetings. Consider including your photo on your business card to help new contacts remember you.

Upgrade Your Resume

Your resume most likely needs a makeover. Take your resume to an expert at a recruiting or employment agency; he or she may recommend hiring a resume writer, but it's not necessary. Like writing a business plan, it's a better strategy to go through the process yourself—only you know what you've really accomplished. But you may need someone to coach you on arriving at the quantifiable results employers are seeking and point you toward the keywords needed to attract recruiters.

Some experts argue that companies still want a chronological resume, so do one, just in case. But more often, employers are looking at skills, so you want to emphasize your overall experience and certifications.

Developing the best resume takes time. Get several opinions and then settle on a format that is pleasing in appearance (avoid multiple typefaces) and can be e-mailed without a hitch. Lines and special characters can get in the way of clean electronic transmission of resumes, so test the template by sending it to a friend before you e-mail it to a prospective employer.

Use Keywords

Find keywords for your industry and the particular job you are targeting. That can help send your resume to the top of the pile. This is especially important when a resume is electronically scanned, which is typical these days. Recruiters also look for keywords when they search LinkedIn for potential hires.

Jim Kowalczyk, a senior manager, identified the right keywords to plug into his resume and found a new job in July 2009. Here's what he advises:

- Research the typical words used in your industry by looking at other resumes on LinkedIn. What keywords are job competitors using?

- Find keywords by researching target employers' websites and press releases.

- Check a public company's annual reports (on the U.S. Securities and Exchange Commission's website at www.sec.gov) and do a search for articles written about the employer and industry.

"I put those keywords everywhere, on my resume, cover letter, and social networking sites," Kowalczyk says.

Get a Second Set of Eyes

When your resume is ready, ask several friends and experts to review your resume for typos or errors. It's easy to overlook a typo, even if you've looked at a resume again and again.

In the process of rewriting my resume, I asked a friend who places high-level executives to review it. I had written several versions and reviewed my current "masterpiece" dozens of times. "What's this date?" he asked, after a quick look. I had written an incorrect start date for a job. I was appalled: How could I have made such an error? But mistakes can happen, and such sloppiness can keep you from being considered for a job.

Quantify Your Successes

Software engineer Dane Lyons kept his resume short and concise in the beginning of his career. But when he was looking for a job in 2009, he added detail to his resume that quantified his successes. "What I found this time around is if the resume was one page, they thought it was light," he said.

If you have 10 or more years in your profession, your resume should probably be two or more pages in length. But more important, it should contain quantifiable accomplishments. How did you contribute to the bottom line of your former employers? That's what future employers want to know. Some experts say the bigger the numbers on your resume the better, but make sure they're based on fact. You want to impress potential employers, but don't ever lie.

Consider Hiring a Resume Writer

Plenty of resume experts are available who can help you craft a good resume, and you'll probably find as many opinions as experts. If you're not getting results, you may want to seek a strong resume writer who can package what you have with more winning results.

Laura Perry, 54, of Los Angeles, wasn't happy with the interviews she was getting in her job search for a communications management job. She met a resume expert at a networking meeting and decided to hire her to revise her resume. After she sent out the new resume, "I almost immediately started getting calls from the companies that I wanted," she says.

The resume expert had crafted a strong brand statement to lead off the resume, using keywords. "Some job descriptions have keywords at the bottom," she says.

The expert also helped her better define her experience, not just naming her former employer but describing it as a "Fortune 500 company," for example. That shows that she understands what it means to work in that size organization. The resume writer also helped her quantify her experience, such as results from an employee satisfaction survey she conducted for a company.

Perry was instructed to condense experience, such as movie production credits early in her career that were not relevant to the job she was seeking. The new resume made her look like more of a strategist, she says, which was important for the communications manager jobs for which she was applying.

Against most advice, she didn't hide her age on her resume by dropping off graduation dates. Job applications "always ask when you graduated from college, anyway," she reasons.

Her work experience, which comes with age, helped her land a job as communications manager at UCLA's School of Nursing. "I just had the right resume and the right experience," she says.

Smooth Employment Gaps

If you have employment gaps in your resume, fill them with other work that you've been doing that's relevant to the position for which you're applying. You could point to volunteer work or additional job training. Or you could show how you've used your skills in other ways during the hiatus.

After being out of the job market for five years because of his daughter's illness, David Adamson had gaps in his resume. "I had to explain a big absence and with a resume, you only have so much time to make your impact. I had been out of the workforce because my daughter had cancer. You can't lead off with that," he says.

Adamson, 45, hired a professional resume writer to help him transform his resume. The resume writer also helped the South Florida resident uncover his achievements. "Tell me about your mortgage company," he prompted Adamson.

"When it was sold, it was worth over $10 million," Adamson told him. The resume expert led him to think about his achievements, something many professionals don't tend to keep track of or don't tout as they should on their resumes. Now Adamson's advice to job hunters is: Imagine you're a professional athlete and create your own stats card.

"To this day, every month when we get a sales report, I think about what I can use out of it," he says. Then he files it away for updating his resume. If he ever has to look for a job again, Adamson will be ready to toot his own horn: "The first month I achieved 122 percent of my quota" or "I was No. 1 in chemicals sold."

Keeping a record of your achievements also helps to keep you motivated in those times when life just isn't going your way.

Tailor Your Resume

Think of your resume as a template that you alter for each job application. Look at the job description for the position you're applying for and mirror those keywords in your resume and cover letter. Describe in your cover letter how you fit each qualification requirement listed in the job description. You also may want to develop a few different resumes, each focusing on expertise in a particular area.

When Scott Nemeth was laid off from his job in Detroit, he was not particularly upset. He was expecting it; as part of human resources, he had been in on the plans for the downsizing. Nemeth and his wife saw the layoff as an opportunity to move with their two young daughters to Columbus, Ohio, where they had family.

At first, Nemeth sent out resumes that focused on his corporate strategy background, but he wasn't getting responses. Then he tailored a resume to his workforce planning background and struck gold: For every resume he sent out, he got a call and an interview.

But it was the new friends he made in networking groups who made the difference. Nemeth didn't know people in Columbus except his family, so he began joining networking groups, both online and in-person. He made friends with his brother-in-law's friends on Facebook, many of whom were in human resources. And he joined three networking groups: ExecuNet, for community members and those in transition; Scioto Ridge Network, a faith-based networking group; and Getdot, which stands for "Good Excuse to Drink on Thursday," but is really about making new connections. Nemeth made new friends in the groups and still attends some functions.

At an ExecuNet meeting, he met someone who worked for the insurance company he was targeting for employment. That contact was intrigued with Nemeth's experience in workforce analysis and said he would set up a lunch meeting for him. Nemeth called to remind him of his offer, and his friend brought along two colleagues, one of whom was a hiring manager.

Nemeth gave her a portfolio he had prepared for another interview. "She looked through it, and about one and a half hours later, she called me, saying, 'I want you to have this job,'" he says.

The formal interview was nearly as quick, with an offer by the time he arrived home. Nemeth attributes his hire to his workforce specialization, which is a mix of knowing demographics; figuring out how many workers are needed for a job; establishing who will be leaving, retiring, or quitting; and identifying how many people will be needed to fill the gaps.

His circle of networking friends who worked for the insurance firm coached him on answering potential interview questions. One even called during the interview to see how it was going.

Nemeth's job search was relatively short: He left his old job on September 15, 2009, and started his new job on February 15, 2010—just one day after his severance ended. Nemeth says he trusted in his faith that he was on the right path to employment. After leaving Detroit, Nemeth says he only doubted once—when he was having a bad day—that he shouldn't have moved to Columbus to look for a job. When he didn't get a job, his wife would tell him, "That wasn't the job you were *supposed* to have."

Looking for a Job Is a Job

Maybe you've been a workaholic and hardly took vacation. Now you've been laid off and perhaps you have severance and unemployment and savings. Isn't this the time to take that well-earned trip to Europe? Unfortunately, it's not. Looking for a job requires your full-time attention. A good rule of thumb is to spend as much time looking for a job each day as you did working at your former job.

"I've told other people who have lost their jobs: You need to turn off the TV and not read the doom and gloom in the paper. You have to make your own options," says Don Winsett, 55, who was laid off from a landscape company in South Florida, but found another management position with a security firm within a couple of months.

Find a place you can really work. It might be your home office, but that may come with too many interruptions, especially if you have children underfoot. Getting out of the house was better for George Lambros, 48, now working as a corporate controller. He went to his outplacement firm or to a buddy's office to work on his job search. "The first couple of months I was at the house. That didn't work for me. I would make calls, set up breakfasts, lunches, and coffees. If I went to an office, I would spend four or five hours working. I'd be much more effective getting out of the house," he says.

Do whatever you can to get into a professional, "I'm working" frame of mind.

Brand Yourself for Your Job Hunt

To make yourself stand out, develop a brand to market yourself while you're in career transition. But just creating a brand isn't enough. You need to use it in everything you do.

As a marketing executive, Greg Siegelman, 52, would be expected to present himself well. So in designing a marketing campaign for his job hunt in 2009, he created his own brand with the catchphrase, "A Swiss Army Knife with a Marketing Blade." Siegelman put that phrase on his business card, resume, e-mail, and LinkedIn profile. Some people thought it was corny; others said it was cool. "But they never forgot it. You've got to put yourself out there," he says.

Each week, Siegelman would peruse the list of networking opportunities in Rochester, New York, where he then lived. He chose events he had to pay for because there were likely to be more employed people at them. And since he was paying, he made sure he was interested in at least one topic.

Once at the event, he would make it his goal to ask two good questions. "I wasn't shy about asking them, and people noticed me. If I asked one, that was too few. If I asked three, that was too many. I can't tell you how many people came up to me and said, 'You ask good questions.' You can't be a wallflower." He also tried to show high energy and a positive attitude at such meetings. "You're always being interviewed. You've got to look at it that way."

Was it his brand or his go-getter attitude that ultimately helped Siegelman find a job? Probably both. Still, the brand made him memorable. A couple months after he found his new marketing job, he went back to the networking group, and people still remembered him for his catchphrase. "I think that's the ultimate power of a brand," he says.

New Grad? Get Experience in Your Field

Young people ages 16 to 24 have the highest rate of unemployment in the nation. As a result, many college graduates have been staying in school through the recession, earning graduate degrees, instead of facing a difficult job market. Some young graduates have moved back in with their parents or are working outside their field.

These aren't the best strategies. If you're still in college or a young college graduate, get whatever experience you can in your field. It won't be easy, but employers are more likely to hire someone who has been hustling to get experience than someone who has not.

My son, Christopher Pounds, 24, graduated with a degree in architecture from New York City's Cooper Union in May 2009—the only worse job market was perhaps a year earlier. But he had spent his summers gaining experience in his field, from working in construction to internships with New York City architecture firms. He was hired within weeks of his graduation by one of those firms. Now he's laying the foundation he needs as an architect to eventually obtain his license.

Another young graduate, Alexa Von Staden, also took the path of building experience throughout her high school and college years. During the summers, she was a lifeguard working for the Pompano Beach, Florida, parks system and a camp counselor overseeing 50 children when she was only 19. She graduated with a bachelor's degree in parks recreation and tourism from the University of Florida in May 2008 and went on to get her master's degree in tourism and commercial recreation, which she was scheduled to complete in the spring of 2010.

Her plan was to go into events planning or hospitality, but she enjoyed working as an assistant in the alumni affairs office at University of Florida while getting her graduate degree. "I found my niche," she says.

Von Staden, now 22, was visiting a friend at Florida State University in Tallahassee and decided to look at its website for potential jobs. She spotted a posting for alumni affairs and decided to apply for, if nothing else, the interview experience. Because of her early work experience, she had references for university managers to call.

After she interviewed with the communications director, Von Staden was offered the job on her Christmas break while she was visiting her family in South Florida—a happy time to share that she had employment.

"A lot had to do with my position at UF. I had one year of on-the-job training. I could start this job and know what I was doing," Von

Staden says. Her new job, which she started in February 2010, is alumni affairs and special events coordinator for FSU's College of Medicine. At University of Florida, she had worked in alumni affairs for the pharmacy school, so she had that related experience as well.

Von Staden also came to the interview with ideas, such as using social media, on how FSU could engage alumni in the school. She is developing the College of Medicine's Facebook page, for example, and creating more reasons than football games for alumni to come back to the school.

Young workers are learning that persistence is important to getting what they want. Some give up too easily.

Jackie Penalver, 23, was no stranger to working. The first college graduate in her family, Penalver helped support herself while taking classes at Florida International University in Miami while working in a doctor's office.

But that wasn't relevant to what she wanted to do, which was work in politics. She caught the "political bug" by getting involved in student government. When an internship opened in the university's federal relations office in Washington, D.C., she applied. Penalver didn't get it, so she tried again. Finally, in the spring of 2010 she went to the nation's capital for the semester.

The position proved to be a springboard to a job. Penalver says she worked hard to prove herself to her boss. "I kept up with current events. Whatever task I was given, I always gave my best," she says.

Penalver got to know the legislative staff of a Florida representative who was involved with the Congressional Hispanic Leadership Institute, a nonprofit that promotes the interests and views of Hispanic-Americans. When an opening for an executive staff assistant came open at the Institute, Penalver was recommended by a staffer with the Florida representative's office as well as her boss at the university's federal relations office.

She is off to a promising start to her career, with dual bachelor's degrees in international business and finance and a certificate in international bank management. Better yet, she has a job.

Stay Active and Keep Your Skills Fresh

Lisa Godoski, 47, wasn't supposed to be let go: She was a Web producer for STLtoday.com, the online product of the *St. Louis Post-Dispatch*. Isn't online the future of journalism? But like many media organizations, her company was undergoing rapid change and the introduction of new technology, and she lost her 12-year job at the newspaper company.

Godoski immediately became active as a volunteer in Businesspersons Between Jobs, a St. Louis nonprofit organization that helps people find jobs. With her online skills, she developed a website for the organization. She also used the time to update her skills, taking design classes at the local career center that were available for free through government training grants. She helped other job searchers learn about LinkedIn and Twitter and found freelance photographers to take head shots of the job hunters for their social media profiles.

"It's how you use your time. You can network with a bicycle group or a reading group, but if you're not networking with people who are in the industry you want to work in, you're spinning your wheels," she says.

She kept in touch with coworkers at the *Post* through Facebook. "By June and July, the job market was getting very bleak. There seemed to be nothing in St. Louis," Godoski says. "The hardest part is keeping the right attitude."

Volunteering with Businesspersons Between Jobs helped her stay upbeat and focused. "I had a reason to get up in the morning," she says. Spending her time at the career center was better than "sitting on the couch staring at the TV."

About 10 months into her job search, Godoski saw an online ad for a job at a medical publishing company in St. Louis. She interviewed and didn't get the job, but then another job opened and the publisher asked her to come back in to talk with the hiring manager. Godoski was offered the job at a comparable salary to her former position at the *Post*, a pleasant surprise. "I thought I was going to have to work a full-time job and a part-time job," she says.

Staying active and keeping your skills fresh while job hunting can score points with a potential employer. When Godoski interviewed for her current publishing job, she was able to talk about how she continually updated her technology skills. Her positive attitude toward change was no doubt appealing to her new employer. In today's environment of ongoing technological improvements, being open and willing to learn is attractive to any employer.

Be Part of the Community

Terri Warren had worked in South Florida banking for 35 years. Despite the many mergers and acquisitions in her field, she had long tenures at three banks. In March 2009 she was laid off for the first time in her life. She had broad experience in banking, working as a branch manager and loan officer, and in training. Unfortunately, when the bank was downsizing, she was doing training—something the bank didn't need when they weren't hiring new employees.

"This was the year I was going to retire," says Warren, 55, looking back to earlier plans. But in 2006, her husband was in a boating accident and was no longer able to work. With the family depending primarily on her income, Warren was taken aback when she was laid off and didn't immediately have an offer from another bank.

Warren has friends and knows former colleagues at nearly every banking institution in South Florida. She has been involved in Women in Distress, United Way, and other community organizations. "I do a lot of community service because I love it. It's not just something I picked up. It was such a wonderful opportunity to meet people from all different industries," Warren says.

Shortly after being laid off, she contacted a friend in banking whom she had gotten to know by serving on community boards. "For years she had told me, 'You should really come to work for us,'" Warren recalls.

But there were changes going on at the bank and people were being shifted around. Warren got outplacement services with her severance package, so she enrolled in the program where counselors confirmed her theory about job hunting, telling her to get off the computer and in front of people. "It's all about who you know. I strongly believe that. Even other positions in the past, somebody called me. They knew me or I knew someone," she says.

Yet here she was networking all the time and being involved in the community, and she still couldn't seem to land a job. Warren soon learned that it had very little to do with her. Banks were telling her they had hundreds of applications for every job opening. "It was sheer numbers for recruiters. They would pick out the top 30 and start reading from there. They never had to get to the rest," she says.

But Warren thinks the combination of her banking experience and community involvement, and having inside contacts, eventually helped her get a job at a new bank. Involvement in community organizations is especially valued at financial institutions because they have a responsibility to serve a community they take money from—when they don't, it can jeopardize the bank's opportunity to open new branches.

In four months, Warren did get a job offer as a branch manager from a Fort Lauderdale–area bank as the result of personnel changes. A woman she had worked with at her previous employer left before the downsizing and got a job with her target employer. When her former colleague was promoted, Warren got *her* job.

Streetwise Strategies for Professionalism

- Aim to save nine months to a year's living expenses before launching your job hunt.

- Create a portfolio or brag book to illustrate and quantify your accomplishments.

- Improve your appearance, energy, and attitude.

- Dress as if you are always ready for an interview. Any encounter with a potential employer can be an informal interview.

- Keep your e-mail and cell phone messages professional.

- Rework your resume as long as it takes to develop a basic resume. Then tailor it with keywords to fit each application.

- Hire a resume writer if needed. Quantify your accomplishments: the bigger the numbers, the better.

- Ask a friend to proofread your resume before you send it anywhere.

- Get focused: Looking for a job is a job.

- Develop your own brand, and use it in your business cards, LinkedIn profile, and cover letters.

- Ask good questions to get noticed at networking events.

- Upgrade your skills, obtaining a certification that could give you the edge in a job hunt.

- Volunteer for community activities that will be an asset to your job hunt.

CHAPTER 3

EXPAND YOUR NETWORK: IN PERSON AND ONLINE

Tell everyone, I mean everyone, that you're job hunting.

When you hesitate, think about David Adamson's story. He was with his young daughter MaryGrace at a birthday party and started chatting with another father. The inevitable "What do you do?" arose, and Adamson responded, "I'm in the all-American job search!"

"I made that my catchphrase," says Adamson, 45, of South Florida. He always got a laugh and that relieved any uneasiness.

Within days, his new friend was talking with a neighbor who is an area manager for a food-safety company based in St. Paul, Minnesota. He mentioned Adamson to the neighbor. Three months later, Adamson had a job as sales manager for the multinational company.

"That position would have never come to be if I hadn't admitted I was out of work," Adamson says.

Nearly everyone I've interviewed who has landed a job found it through a connection with someone he or she knew. Your best contacts are the colleague or boss you worked with at a former company, the person you've come to know in your trade organization, or the family member who tells everyone about you.

Put Your Pride Aside

It's important to get over any embarrassment about being unemployed and to reach out to everyone you know, using every available tool. Get out and talk to people face to face at industry meetings, networking groups, and social events.

People want to help; it's human nature. But they don't want to feel cornered or put in an awkward situation. So play the reporter. Ask questions and be interested in them. You'll soon make a connection, and that person is more likely to take action that could lead you to a job.

Sometimes, networking may be the last thing you feel like doing. Adamson was looking for a job after a time of personal tragedy: His three-year-old daughter Emily (MaryGrace's twin) was diagnosed with cancer. So David sold his $10 million mortgage banking business in South Florida and devoted himself to his daughter. His wife had to continue working because she carried the family's health insurance. The journey ended sadly in May 2008 when Emily died at age seven.

Then Adamson had to pick himself up and look for a job. At first, he took on the role of consultant, doing contract work in TV sales. But it wasn't until he attended classes for professionals at his local career center that he changed his approach. Adamson realized he had lots of company searching for jobs: Mortgage and finance professionals, accountants, and even lawyers were in the same boat. When Florida's real estate market tanked in 2008, many with jobs related to the industry found themselves out of work or out of business.

"People knew of me as a well-to-do mortgage banker. I employed over 30 people. How could I tell them I was unemployed?" Adamson says. "You have to say you need work, and you're going to have to tell people that."

"The biggest lesson I've taken out of this is being able to drop the pride around your friends and acquaintances, to drop all your shields whether you're broke or going broke," he says.

To find a job, he began talking openly with his inner circle: doctors and other health professionals he had come to know, his church pastor, friends, and neighbors. It was then that the interview opportunities started coming his way. "Once I made it known, everyone wanted to step up and offer some help," he says.

That's why, at a child's birthday party, he was able to tell another father he was looking for work and make the connection that led him to a new job. He had gotten through the emotional trauma, perhaps because he knew there were worse things in life than losing a job.

Get Your Family Involved

When my brother-in-law Mark was looking for a job after getting his bachelor's degree in information technology, my sister Marijean told everyone about him. It worked: One day she was chatting with a client, and it happened that the client's husband worked for a technology company. One thing led to another and my brother-in-law got an interview and landed the job.

W. Alejandro Polanco's new job opportunity also came as a result of his wife telling someone about his job search. "You don't look for a job— you network for a job," says Polanco, 36, who had three job offers in early 2010, within a few months of losing his technology job based in Baltimore. "The minute I stop 'looking' and am more about networking and talking with people, the exact right opportunity surfaces right in my face."

Polanco has built an extensive network in technology and related industries through LinkedIn. But it was his wife's chatting with a friend whose husband happened to work at Kaplan, a private university in Fort Lauderdale, Florida, that led to the job he now has: senior manager, strategic alliances with Kaplan.

"It's being out there, having lunch, having coffee, meeting for drinks, talking to people, and getting your name out there. That's network marketing—getting other people talking about you," he says.

So involve everyone in your family in your job search. They can help spread the word. The job search then becomes a team effort, which pulls family members closer together, instead of apart, in a time of stress.

Find Jobs Before They're Posted

Ideally, you want to learn about job opportunities before they appear on the online job boards. As soon as a job is posted, an employer is flooded with resumes. Networking in person and online can help you find the hidden job openings and make connections that can lead to being in position for a job before most people know about it.

As the economy recovers and employers have more flexibility in hiring, a position might even be created just for you, if an employer values and wants to hire you badly enough. Lay the foundation for that potential job opportunity by getting involved in industry organizations and adding to your professional education.

Get Involved in Networking Organizations

Don't just join networking organizations; get involved in them. Look for networking groups that have a broader membership than those in career transition: ExecuNet, which has chapters across the country, is a group that brings executives, recruiters, and business leaders together for discussion in-person and online.

John Rives, a quality manager in manufacturing, took advantage of the resources available at ExecuNet in Columbus, Ohio, for coaching, learning about job hunting, interviewing, and networking. But Rives, 44, made his job connection through an industry group, American Society for Quality, where he signed up for an e-mail listing of available jobs. That's how he found a posting for his new quality manager position. As a result, he was able to e-mail his resume directly to the contact for the job, instead of applying online and hoping the right person saw his application. "It's nice to get to the hiring manager," Rives says.

Leadership organizations also can be great networking groups for job hunters. For example, Toastmasters, which helps people become comfortable with public speaking, is a way to meet people from many different industries in your community.

Instead of dwelling on her job loss in late 2008, Patricia Martinez, 50, of South Florida became active in Toastmasters, which kept her presentation skills sharp while looking for a new sales position. She became an officer of the local chapter and organized an event for 350 people, which broadened her networking contacts and raised her profile in the community.

"I had heard about Toastmasters for years and just started to go. I became the treasurer, then the secretary...It's great for networking and helping your communication skills and leadership skills," Martinez says. When she interviewed for her job with a financial services firm, Martinez was able to point to what she accomplished for the group during her job search. That made her stand out as someone who had community connections, which made her more attractive as a financial services representative.

Use Your Alumni Network

The term *alumni* can apply to different groups: your college, high school, sorority or fraternity, or people you worked with at a former employer. Mobilize them all.

Michael Crehan, then 53, didn't know he would be joining a unique club in March 10, 2008, when he was laid off by Lehman Brothers, the Wall Street firm that later declared bankruptcy, triggering a panic in the financial markets. As the Wall Street debacle grew in 2008–2009, thousands of people were out of work, suddenly unable to find jobs in investment banking, where they had spent most of their careers.

Crehan was a research analyst for Lehman Brothers. When his boss asked him to come into his office one day and close the door, he knew it was not good news. He had plans with his wife Joanne for dinner that night. It was her birthday. He didn't want to spoil it, so he waited until dinner was over to tell her he had lost his job.

"The good news was her reaction was pretty good," says Crehan, who has two adult children. Crehan decided to hit the ground running, telling people he was looking for work. "You *want* people to know. That's what you have to do. I held my head up high," he says.

Two research analyst opportunities came pretty quickly—one in Atlanta and another in Connecticut, where he and his wife had a home. Neither one resulted in an offer. It seemed Crehan would get close to a job and then the company would decide to hold off on hiring until the economy picked up.

Crehan had been touching base with his network, from old Wall Street buddies to alumni at Notre Dame and Babson College, where he went to undergraduate school and graduate school, respectively. Still, it was a long, quiet summer, and the holidays were even worse. In the spring of 2009, he went to Notre Dame to apply for a position. It didn't work out, either, but "it opened the door to start thinking about other options," Crehan says.

He made it a habit to check Notre Dame's website for jobs and saw one for a career adviser. It so happened that the person hiring for the job was looking for someone like himself, who came from a background where he had recruiting contracts. In his previous jobs, Crehan had done a fair amount of recruiting. He figured going back to Notre Dame was a "way of giving back." Some of his friends thought he was crazy to exchange a Wall Street salary for a nonprofit educational organization's pay. But, so far, he is pleased with his choice.

Crehan now works with finance majors, advising them on their career paths. Working at a university has unique benefits, such as access to concerts and events. "On a bad day, you walk around the campus, go for a run around the lake. I commute 6 miles instead of 60," he says.

Mitch Lipka, 47, turned to his alumni network at Northwestern University's Medill School of Journalism in Chicago. Lipka was laid off from two jobs in two years during the recession. With a young family to support, Lipka recognized he couldn't rely on traditional job search techniques to find a job.

Lipka, a journalist whose "Consumer Alert" column appears in the Sunday *Boston Globe*, had hoped to parlay his freelance column into full-time work. But with newspapers making budget cuts and laying off reporters, he switched gears.

He found a job for AOL posted in LinkedIn Groups by his alma mater, Medill School of Journalism at Northwestern University. The editor hiring for the job also went to the journalism school.

Lipka began freelancing for AOL and within a few months was offered a full-time job with benefits. Though he is now working for an online product, Lipka says he is doing much of the same type of reporting he once did as a consumer reporter for the South Florida *Sun Sentinel*, *Philadelphia Inquirer*, and *Consumer Reports*. "I do virtually nothing different than I would have as a newspaper person—other than a different platform," he says.

Lipka says he has learned that "you need to look proactively, as opposed to waiting for something to find you." He also urges job hunters to apply for an opportunity, even if it's past the deadline. Because the job search process is often slow, a selection may not have been made even if the posting has expired.

Alumni associations can provide a wealth of contacts and resources for job hunters. Have you caught up with a college roommate lately? Use LinkedIn or Facebook to find out how they are and where they're working. You could find a potential advocate for a target employer. If not, you've at least reconnected with an old friend.

Remember It's a Small World

With so many people in so many industries displaced in the recession, it's highly likely you will know people at potential employers. Previous work experience with someone on the inside can be a major advantage.

Michael Hudak, 44, was laid off from his job as human resources director for a South Florida manufacturer in December 2008 and couldn't seem to find employment. Moreover, his wife had lost her job in October.

With top human resources jobs in scarce supply, Hudak started exploring other possibilities, including working as a restaurant manager and training to become a policeman. "It's talking to people who are employed and being open to any opportunity. You want to try and stay in your career field but it comes to a point when the mortgage needs to get paid. You're an HR professional, but you also can do spreadsheets and be a manager. You have to keep your options open," Hudak says.

He was invited by a friend to an ExecuNet networking meeting. There he met another HR manager who had landed a job some months earlier. "We kept in contact throughout my ordeal. She sent me jobs she found," Hudak says.

Then in September 2009, his friend became aware of an HR director job for a Fort Lauderdale law firm. Hudak lucked out again when he was interviewing for the job and bumped into someone he formerly worked with who was the payroll manager.

When it came down to choosing between Hudak and another candidate, the law firm went with Hudak, who came highly recommended by his former coworker. "That helped me," Hudak says. "She actually works for me now."

Hudak's experience is a lesson for any worker: Be kind and respectful to those you work with because you never know when someone might become a reference, your team member at a new employer, or even your boss.

Be Curious Wherever You Go

As you're networking or just running errands, be aware of what's going on around you and ask questions. You never know where it might lead.

Curiosity worked for public relations professional Scott Walsh, 47, of Vista, California. Walsh had been a manager of public relations for a golf equipment company and previously had more than 10 years of experience in media relations and corporate communications.

After his job was eliminated in late 2007, he was getting a haircut one day at Supercuts. He noticed a short-haired man also getting a trim and struck up a friendly conversation. The customer turned out to be from Chicago, where Walsh was once a sports journalist, and now headed a large healthcare group in northern California.

"I told him I was looking for a marketing opportunity and followed up with him," Walsh says. In searching for work, Walsh made it a habit to call new contacts three times and then stop. He didn't even have to make that effort with the healthcare executive. After three weeks, the executive asked Walsh to put together a marketing proposal. Walsh made a presentation and the company became his first client of his new business, Aslan Communications.

Curiosity usually leads to discovery, and for the job seeker, that can mean meeting someone who will lead you to a potential job. For those shy about touting themselves, asking people about their jobs, careers, or interests can be a way to expand a network in new and surprising ways. As a journalist, I've learned that people like to talk about themselves; better yet, they like people who listen.

Volunteer Your Expertise

Use your knowledge in a field to help others, and it can benefit you in your job search.

Pauline Wilcox, a human resources professional, volunteered at a local job search organization to teach people about networking. She also put it into practice herself by serving as a speaker for a professional organization, which led to a new job.

Wilcox has been on both sides of the job-hunting equation. After working for Eastman Kodak in Rochester, New York, for 34 years, she was part of a major downsizing in 2006. The well-known camera company was making its transition from film to the digital world. Wilcox, 56, found a human resources contractor job. But it turned out to be a position in which she was asked to hire 500 contractors and then lay them all off. And then she had to fire herself.

Before starting her own job search, Wilcox decided to take time to give back. She presented a weeklong boot camp called "Career Navigator," supported through a grant with RochesterWorks!, an organization that counsels the unemployed.

She taught the job seekers to "strive for five," setting up five informational chats a week. Networking, she told the class, was really about "information gathering."

"When you were dating, did you go out with the intention of 'I want to marry this person?' You're gathering information to see if this person is even of interest. You don't go on a first date and say, 'I want to have three kids.'"

What her class didn't know was that she was going through emotionally difficult times as well. Her husband Stephen, a mystery writer and former journalist, also was looking for work. And there were bills to pay for her son's college. "We were three people living on one unemployment check," she says.

Wilcox's volunteer work and networking helped her stay upbeat and motivated during her own job hunt. "What helps is to have a good support system—friends who have worked with you and know your capability, a loving supportive husband, people who remind you that it's tough right now—but hang in there," she says.

Wilcox volunteered as a speaker for a newly formed human resources networking group, HR Quest, whose members met regularly to keep their skills sharp. At one meeting she talked about coaching and effectively managing performance. "It's important to give back to people and to show them your capability," she says.

One audience member, a human resources director for a local company, was impressed by her presentation. After they got to know one another better through the group, the HR director told Wilcox, "If I ever leave, you should have my job."

One day when she was at her son's college, Wilcox got a call from this HR director: "I got another job. Before I post my current job, I wanted you to know about it," she told Wilcox. By networking, Wilcox had found an advocate inside a potential employer, and she was well-positioned to get the job, which she did. She is now human resources director at Catalyst Direct, a marketing company.

By volunteering her expertise as a coach and for her professional organization, Wilcox made herself stand out in her industry. Employers want to hire people who are highly regarded in their fields. For the professional, volunteering provides the opportunity to build a reputation in an industry while making key contacts.

Develop Yourself and Make New Contacts

Never stop learning. In today's job market and in the future, staying updated in your field and adding to your skills through continuing education and new certifications are the keys to getting jobs. Jobs are becoming more technical. For example, healthcare, which is the primary sector adding jobs nationwide, now requires a combination of medical and technology skills. Whatever your field, relevant certifications and specializations can make your resume stand out.

Sometimes, you can be ahead of your industry, which was the case for general contractor Layla Thomas. Thomas, 36, moved from North Carolina to work with a large residential builder in South Florida. But then came the residential housing bust, and Thomas was out of a job. She eventually found work with a commercial builder, which soon saw its business squeezed. Thomas was laid off again in late 2008.

In this job and in prior ones, Thomas had pursued special certifications in her field in both energy and construction. Each year she attended the invitation-only Building Science Symposium, an annual event where experts in construction science and analysis gather. "I started to look at sustainability, not just conventional construction," Thomas says.

Her then-employers weren't quite on board with her attending the conferences. "Neither company I worked for would pay for it. I took my own vacation time and savings, and I went. I made some of the best contacts," says Thomas, 36. "My passion wasn't shared by any of my employers. But I tried to stick with what I knew I wanted to do."

By the time she lost the commercial building job, Thomas had gained her LEED AP certification—an accredited professional in environmental building design—and was a certified energy rater. Because of these qualifications, she was approached to operate an energy services franchise by a professional colleague she had met at the symposium. "The symposium is a relatively small group of people. Everyone gathers at the host's house and eats and drinks and gets to know each other. You really develop friendships. We share a passion for a pretty obscure field," she says.

As a mother of four who had already spent much of her savings, retirement income, and unemployment benefits on living expenses, Thomas couldn't invest in a franchise at the time. Yet the Texas-based energy services firm still wanted her expertise and offered her a temporary job. Now she has started her own company, Sustainabuild.

Thomas says her certification as an energy rater is something that's only going to increase in value as builders emerge from the slump. With homeowners getting burned with mold problems, Chinese drywall, and shoddy building practices, "there's going to be higher expectations from consumers," Thomas says.

Be tenacious about your self-development, even if your employer isn't paying for it. Look for skills you can update and certifications that will make you stand out from the competition. But before you pay for expensive schooling or training, do your homework to make sure there are jobs at the end of your journey. It's best to update your skills before you lose a job, but after a layoff, there also may be federal or state money available for training. Check with your local career center or state workforce agency.

Open New Doors with Online Networks

Become active in online social and professional networking on LinkedIn, Facebook, Twitter, and other online social networks. Reconnect with former colleagues and old friends, and make them aware of the opportunity you're seeking. Find emotional support during this time through your network of friends online and offline.

You may or may not like posting on Facebook or tweeting, but do master the possibilities of LinkedIn, the online professional networking site. LinkedIn is the most powerful tool of our time for job hunters. Although many professionals have profiles on LinkedIn, few pay much attention to improving and updating them.

Jim Kowalczyk, 37, made the most of his LinkedIn profile. A specialist in the process management technique Six Sigma, Kowalczyk scoped out his competition for job openings through LinkedIn and compared key industry words they were using in their profiles. When recruiters did a Google search, he made sure it was his LinkedIn profile that came up first.

"Once a week, do something to your profile, such as 'here's what I'm working on or information I've found,'" he recommends. "Bring value to the reader, not 'I'm having a ham sandwich today.'"

Kowalczyk joined LinkedIn groups and participated in online discussions on Six Sigma. When he met people at networking functions, he later connected with them on LinkedIn. With this method, "you're not just a name on a computer. They had actually met you and you had some kind of conversation," Kowalczyk says.

He took the approach when connecting with people on LinkedIn that he wanted to learn more about the company. "You try not to scare people off. You don't want to say, 'Could you hand my resume to this VP?'" Kowalczyk says. "You want to say, 'Could you put me in touch with this person?' Most people are willing to do that. Sometimes they'll offer, 'If you send me your resume, I'll pass it on.'"

Ultimately, it was through LinkedIn that his new employer, GSI Commerce in Atlanta, found him. GSI Commerce's hiring manager was searching online for someone with both call center and Six Sigma experience—that was Kowalczyk and four other candidates. Kowalczyk won out and has been working for his new employer, an e-commerce solutions company, since July 2009.

Kristen Binder, 35, of Chicago found two jobs through connections on LinkedIn. The first was in November 2008 when a recruiter contacted her friend Woody on LinkedIn and found Kristen. "It wouldn't have worked if it hadn't been for the relationship between Woody and me, and Woody and the recruiter. LinkedIn was the medium," Binder says.

LinkedIn worked again for Binder a year later. Her husband, who is in construction, had been laid off in the spring of 2009 and was looking for a new job. So Binder wasn't about to jump into the job market even though she didn't think her current job was a perfect fit.

Binder says that in a more robust market, she might have tried to talk with her supervisors to change her job, but in the shaky economic climate of 2009, "I was head down. Glad to have a job." Still, she put the word out to a couple of close friends: "If you hear of anything, let me know."

Then Binder attended a professional conference. After meeting people at conferences, she often invites them to join her LinkedIn network. One such invitation laid the groundwork for her next job offer.

At this conference, she met the office director for a Chicago architecture and engineering firm. He was with a group of professionals she had dinner with one evening at the conference. Meeting people at a conference can be a great way to find new job connections: "It's far more relaxed. Compared with a cold interview, you're miles ahead," she says.

She soon connected on LinkedIn with the office director. "Even though the relationship existed without LinkedIn, I'm not sure he would have thought to contact me," Binder says.

Extending a LinkedIn invitation is a professional courtesy that often gets returned. Getting an e-mail from LinkedIn can pave the way for a conversation that might not have happened through a regular e-mail that may be ignored or discarded. It gives you legitimacy.

Binder is choosey about who she invites on LinkedIn because she considers her connections a reflection of her professional reputation. "I don't invite people out of the blue. And I don't accept invitations without at least a few e-mails," she says.

The office director later reached out to Binder on LinkedIn saying, "I have this business development position. I'm wondering if you are interested or if you know someone who might be."

Binder was excited about the position, which she thought was a better fit for her skills than her current job. "I zipped over on the lunch hour and sent my resume. I had a conversation that evening and arranged an interview later that week." She was soon hired as the director of business development for the Chicago architecture firm.

As these job hunters found, LinkedIn is a critical tool in today's job hunt. It's easy to use, and the more you use it and learn about connecting on groups and reaching out to new contacts, the more comfortable you will be with it. Recruiters and employers are using the website, so your activity might catch their attention, particularly if you exhibit knowledge about their business or industry.

Play the Numbers Game

Persistence in networking pays off. Like dating, networking is a numbers game. The more people you can meet who connect you to a potential employer, the more likely you'll find a job.

But it's *how* you network that can make the difference. The more targeted you are in your job goal, the better you can choose networking online and in person that will lead you to the job opportunity that's the right fit.

Rob Ewanow, a marketing professional who lives near Rochester, New York, found the numbers game to be true after going through layoffs before in his career. "One of the perils of being in marketing is that you're usually the first to be let go," he says.

Ewanow, 43, was the global communications manager for an international manufacturing firm and was laid off in December 2008. It was the third time he had been laid off in 16 years after working in marketing roles in a variety of industries: banking, healthcare, and manufacturing.

Because he had been through this before, he had worked to keep his network alive, attending the local chapter of the American Marketing Association and The August Group, a local networking group that met several times a week and included both job hunters and community members. "I was really trying to find that next hidden job," he says.

But a friend of his who founded The August Group counseled him about his job search. "He told me 'you're not doing as much as you think.'"

So on his friend's advice, he began setting up meetings with 8 to 10 people a week. He searched for people who were at his target companies, those in his profession and people in human resources who were in the know about jobs now and those coming down the pipe. "The way the economy was going, HR people were looking to be more networked as well," he says.

Ewanow asked for a meeting, usually through an e-mail, saying someone they both knew had referred him. "I would say, 'I'll keep it brief. I understand you're working.'" If he didn't hear from the person, he politely followed up until he secured an appointment.

He set up mainly morning meetings. "I'm at my best in the morning. It was either coffee or an occasional lunch. A fair amount said, 'come into the office and we'll talk a while,'" he says.

Ewanow's break came pretty quickly, within a few weeks of doing one-on-one meetings. He was invited to make a presentation as a consultant and that led to his job today, marketing for Retrotech, an engineering consulting firm. The job is only a three-mile commute from his home and pays at a higher rate.

Generate as much networking activity as possible each week during your job hunt. Odds are you eventually will have coffee or lunch with someone who makes the difference for your next career opportunity.

Learn How to Set Up Informational Meetings

LinkedIn has made life easier for most job hunters because people generally welcome a message through the website. It also has made it easier to find contacts at potential employers. But you don't want to rely only on LinkedIn or other online services to develop your network. Connect the dots of networking tools by using whatever is comfortable for you, from cold calling to a LinkedIn message, to approach a contact.

Marketing manager Robert Kostin of Rochester used cold calling combined with in-person networking after he left Xerox after 17 years in May 2008. At the time, Kostin, 48, thought networking was about attending cocktail parties.

"It's the one-to-one meeting you learn how to set up and how to conduct. That is the core of networking," Kostin says. He learned how to call someone he didn't know, mention a common contact, and ask for an educational meeting over coffee.

Kostin learned these techniques through Rochester's networking organizations, which include Getting There Executive Network (GTEN), The August Group, and Digital Rochester. Through these groups, Kostin says it took him three months to understand networking and then only two months to land a job once he did.

It's the executives who are often willing to meet with you, not the lower-level employees who may feel you're after their job, Kostin says. "The higher level will understand that you're just networking."

Approach them with a *warm* referral, someone you know or a mutual contact through LinkedIn or an industry association. Then cater to the person's timeframe, Kostin says. When you sit down with them, talk about their favorite subject—themselves. "You barely say a thing. They think you're their best friend. It's just like dating," says Kostin, who is married with two teenaged children.

The mission is to learn about their company or industry and walk away with at least two names to meet with next, Kostin says. "I don't think anyone said, 'I don't want to meet with you,' or 'I'm too busy.' Keep on them in a nonaggressive way. Never say you're looking for a job, but 'I'm looking to learn more.'" At the high point of his networking, he had 10 such meetings a week. "That's more or less your target if you're not working," he says.

When Kostin planned to attend a Digital Rochester presentation, he prepared ahead of time by finding out who he wanted to meet. One person was a CEO of a telecommunications company. Kostin found out through LinkedIn that they went to the same high school. When he and the CEO talked, Kostin dropped his alma mater's name, and soon they were talking about Kostin working for the company.

"Networking is a leap of faith. You're not filling out applications or giving out your resume. You're getting to know people. You learn more about the industry you're targeting," Kostin says.

Kostin found his latest job through his GTEN networking connection. He hired a career coach to help him uncover the job that best suited him. He also got to know the coach's wife, who heads the marketing department at the University of Rochester Medical Center. When she was looking for someone to do Web development, Kostin came to mind. "Because she already knew who I was and knew something about me, my resume jumped to the top of the pile," he says.

Networking also helped Kostin learn what he really wanted to do. He never thought of himself as a marketing manager even when he was doing tasks that might be considered that at Xerox. He earned his master's in technology while working at Xerox and later went to work for two smaller firms. Each time, he got a little closer to the right job for him. At networking events, Kostin was more engaged when talking with Web developers than with information technology managers or support. He finally realized that Web development is what he really wanted to do. His current job at the medical center is a blend of what he loves to do: marketing and Web development.

Now Kostin advises friends who are looking for jobs to take a dual approach. "You can network in a particular direction. In parallel, do a traditional job search," Kostin recommends. While looking for job postings online and sending resumes, he also sought to get ahead of the postings by finding contacts who could lead him to a Web development job. Without the dual approach, even if you see a job description that seems like your dream job, "the odds are you won't get it because it's too late to start networking your way in," he says.

Incidentally, Kostin's wife Linda didn't have to work nearly as hard to find her job match. After eight years of caring for their son Michael and daughter Julia, Linda decided to go back to work to help the family out financially when Kostin was out of a job. A lawyer, Linda Kostin hadn't practiced for several years but kept her license active. She went to a job fair (against her husband's advice), met a recruiter, and within two weeks landed a job doing promotions for a legal service. "She talks with one headhunter, who sets her up with one interview, and she lands the job of her dreams!" Kostin says.

But most people don't have it that easy. So learn the art of setting up an informational meeting. Target your networking toward your job goal so that when you spot a job description that fits, you have the inside contacts in place to pursue it.

Be Proactive and Seize Opportunities

Opportunities for potential jobs are everywhere. When you see one, seize it. Your opportunity could come when meeting with other professionals in your field, when volunteering for a community organization, or when attending a social event. Be proactive by seeking new activities, ways to meet people in your field, and learning opportunities to advance your career.

Like many of this recession's young college graduates, Ashley DuFrene had a rough entry into the job market. DuFrene, now 23, found a job at a television production company in Fort Lauderdale, Florida, almost immediately after graduating from the University of Florida in May 2008. But five months after being hired, she was laid off. She had already started looking for work because she felt her job was in jeopardy. DuFrene landed a job at an advertising agency only two weeks later.

But then the agency hit slow times, and she was let go just nine months later in May 2009. "I loved it so much. They had to let me go, and it was very upsetting to me. It crushed my morale a little bit," she says.

In the next four months, she sent out about 100 resumes but got only one call. When her roommate decided to move out of town, she suggested DuFrene apply for her job as an assistant to a consultant. It paid the bills, but DuFrene's heart wasn't in it.

"I'm a people person. I like being in an office environment. It was just me and the CEO, Monday through Friday. I was in 600-square-foot office by myself. It was pretty much driving me insane," she says.

DuFrene went to a meeting of Six Degrees, a young professionals group that's part of Big Brothers/Big Sisters. She was inspired by the speaker, Jaynie Smith, who talked about her rise from flight attendant to author, international speaker, and business consultant. "She said to make sure what you did in life was fulfilling and to take risks," DuFrene says.

At Smith's book signing after her presentation, DuFrene asked for her advice. "I started talking with her about my situation, that I was an independent contractor and that I wasn't happy. I said I would love to talk with her."

DuFrene mentioned that she had website experience, and Smith said she might be able to use her part time. She later had lunch with Smith and her business partner and was offered a job in November 2009.

She now is a project manager at Smart Advantage, a business consulting firm in Fort Lauderdale. She manages the firm's websites, keeps track of projects, organizes seminars, writes press releases, creates fliers, and works with social media. DuFrene has taken on more and more responsibility so that her part-time job has turned into a full-time one.

"It's all about timing. You never know what might happen," DuFrene says. When she lost her advertising job, she "wondered what she did wrong. But I didn't do anything wrong. It's just because of the economy."

DuFrene was proactive in approaching Smith, and it paid off. Smart managers are always looking for talent and might even create a job for you. Even if an employer can't immediately hire you, developing relationships with people you admire and want to learn from is always a great idea. They could refer you for another job, or their needs could change and you'll be on their list.

Keep Doors Open

When you leave a job, the conventional wisdom is "don't burn bridges." That's solid advice, especially in these times when business needs are constantly changing.

So in your job search, remember to reach out to a former employer with whom you left on good terms or the employer of your spouse, partner, extended family member, or friend who can give you a referral. Many people hesitate to reconnect, but you can sell yourself as a known quantity who will take less time to train if your former employer rehires you.

Mary Beth Dew, 49, of Charleston, South Carolina, spent only *four hours* unemployed after she lost her job in the spring of 2009. After working for 20 years in an administrative assistant position for AC Controls, a utility supply company, Dew was hired away by a customer for a marketing job. After she worked four years with the firm, the troubled economy hit, and layoffs began; she lasted until the third round.

She immediately called her former employer to ask for a letter of recommendation. The owner agreed to recommend her but asked: "Why aren't you asking for your job back?" They started negotiations for her re-employment.

Dew, who had been the business owner's personal assistant before she was promoted to office manager, was comfortable enough to hold her ground. "I needed him to know how much I had grown when I was away," she says.

The business owner matched her new salary, restored her vacation time, and gave her 12 years of credit toward the company's incentive program. After 15 years, employees at AC Controls get a week's vacation with $6,000 to spend. (Now there's an incentive to stay around!)

Back since March 2009, Dew still makes time to have lunch with former colleagues where she was downsized. The biggest lesson from her story, she says, is "not burning bridges. When I was furloughed, I handled myself very well, and I've supported them since I've been gone." As Dew recognized, it's important to stay in touch with former employers and other contacts on an ongoing basis.

Reach Out to Former Colleagues

Think about all the people you've worked with during the years and contact them. Why not? It's fun to catch up, and easy to do so with online tools like Facebook and LinkedIn.

Marina Konchak found out how critical her connections to former colleagues were when she was let go in April 2009 from Home Depot, where she worked for 28 years. Konchak started working for the home supply retail chain when she was just 17, and she kept in touch with many of those who passed through.

When she was laid off, she called friends at retailers, including Best Buy and Toys "R" Us. One was the former president of Toys "R" Us, who put in a call to the current president. She also talked with a well-connected contractor at Home Depot who recommended her to the executive team at Best Buy.

Konchak, now 46, also made new contacts by volunteering at human resources association events and coaching others on resume-writing. "Volunteering gives you an open door to talk with people," she says. "You must love to talk with people, not just in your inner circle. Get out of your comfort zone."

Finally, she was weighing jobs at Toys "R" Us and Best Buy when she was offered the position of human resources director at Catholic Hospice, a nonprofit organization in the Miami area. Although the retail jobs paid more, they involved travel, and she wanted to stay near her daughters' schools. Konchak is happy in her new job, but "I've kept my doors open with them," she says of the retailers.

So reconnect with colleagues and expand your network. Those connections will increase your chances of finding opportunities that suit you. You also will be better prepared to get another job in the future.

Find Insiders at Your Ideal Employer

Your long-lost colleagues and friends may be job hunting as well. You can help each other. Perhaps you don't have job leads for others, but you can guide them with what you do know about an industry or a potential employer. Introduce them to a professional who works for a targeted employer. Or offer to attend a networking meeting with the job hunter and introduce him or her around. For many job hunters I interviewed, their network of former colleagues and bosses turned out to be the most lucrative for a job search.

Steve Fox, 48, was determined to work at a federal agency, but he couldn't seem to get his foot in the door. He had moved from Florida to Virginia after being laid off in the summer of 2008 from an international transportation company, where he had been a vice president of product marketing and e-commerce. He also had previous experience with major companies, including AOL and General Mills. But Fox had no government background, and that matters in Washington, D.C.

Have you ever counted how many people you know? Fox put together an Excel spreadsheet with the names and contact information for peers, former bosses and headhunters—a total of about 250 people. In a moment of "six degrees of separation," Fox contacted a former colleague from AOL who also was looking for a new job and had recently called his mentor—who happens to work for a federal agency. After being hired at the agency, the AOL colleague began promoting his buddy Fox as the right person for a job. Fox was hired in June 2009 to head business development.

Fox is convinced he wouldn't have his job without his friend's help. "Even if I had made it through to the other side, I don't think I would have been taken seriously," he says.

Referrals can make a huge difference. Our trust level rises when we know our friend or colleague is recommending someone for a job. We pay more attention because we value our friends and colleagues, and we know they wouldn't steer us in the wrong direction. So serve as a reference for other job hunters, as well as looking for recommendations for yourself.

Check In with Former Customers and Suppliers

Other sources of networking are former customers and suppliers. You've spent a career building relationships with people in your industry. Make them advocates in your job search.

In running a landscape division for a corporation, Don Winsett had always treated his customers right. That paid off when he started looking for a new job. Winsett, 55, made it a habit to take clients to lunch and was available when there was a problem or question. "I made it a personal rule to get back with them within 24 hours with a response. I had confidence and trust with them," he said.

When his employer merged with another company, he was offered a job, but decided the corporate life wasn't the right fit. He was used to an entrepreneurial style of business.

So Winsett reached out to his network of former customers, colleagues, and other relationships he built over 35 years. In January, he had lunch with a former customer with the hope he might refer him to a landscape company.

Instead, the business owner told him: "We need someone to head our security division. I'll make you president of the division."

"What do I know about security?" Winsett responded. The customer reminded him that he had successfully operated a landscape business in South Florida, a service business that was actually similar to running a security firm. Wanting to stay in the region, Winsett took the job, turning down two offers that would have required him and his wife to move.

Sometimes, it takes someone else to remind us about our own talents and skills. By reaching out to the customers he serviced so well, Winsett realized that his skills and experience were valued in industries beyond the one he left.

Help Others and You'll Help Yourself

Your demeanor can go a long way in whether people put themselves out to help you in your job search. Even when you're feeling frustrated about the job search, try to adopt a friendly, pleasant attitude.

If there ever was a nice guy, it was my friend Angel Mercedes. I got to know Angel when we were in an executive MBA program together at Florida Atlantic University in Boca Raton. When we went to Spain for international studies, Mercedes took care of the group by translating for those who didn't speak Spanish. I remember a fantastic nightclub that wouldn't have admitted a group of Americans if Angel hadn't charmed them. As an executive with a telecommunications company, he was more traveled than many of us.

In May, Mercedes' then-employer was in the process of being acquired by another firm. Mercedes knew the team at his company probably wouldn't survive. So he sprang into action, reaching out to his contacts and going to trade shows to increase his visibility. "I was talking to anyone," Mercedes says.

At one trade show, he offered to stay around and help a marketing manager close down the company's booth. The marketing manager soon returned the favor when she got a call from a hiring manager at T-Mobile asking if she could recommend anyone for a position. Guess who came to mind?

So instead of being out of a job for several months, Mercedes made a smooth transition to a new job at T-Mobile. Now he never stops networking. "I should have done this before," he says.

Treat Your Coworkers Well

We all have our buddies at work. But sometimes you clash with a coworker. Perhaps you just have different personalities or work styles. To work effectively with colleagues, it's important to find some aspect of that person that you can relate to or like, even if he or she is never going to be your best friend. Getting along with coworkers can mean the difference between someone giving you a great recommendation and losing out on a job.

Anthony Cortese, 26, made it a practice to get along with people at work. But at his former workplace, one person used to drive him crazy. This coworker was overbearing, always in his face. "So many times I would bite my tongue," Cortese says.

Then in 2009, he and his colleague were both laid off. Cortese went on his way looking for a job. One day, Cortese got a call and saw it was his former coworker. He let his cell phone go to voicemail, but it began ringing again within 10 minutes. While interviewing for a job, the former colleague had recommended Cortese to the employer and was calling to let him know about it.

Cortese specializes in sourcing potential candidates for recruiters—just what the company was looking for. "I know somebody who did this at my last company," the former coworker piped up. Cortese soon had an interview and was offered a job in November 2009 at a South Florida security firm. "That's pretty much how I got in the door there," Cortese says.

Cortese is thankful for his former coworker's recommendation and is grateful that he never made a big deal over their past petty differences. "She is a nice person," he says.

Hang Out at Starbucks

When all else fails, hang out at Starbucks or anywhere business professionals tend to gather in the morning. That's what Jenipher Lagana did in her early mornings to get out of the house and meet people.

After losing the job she had for 15 years in October 2008, Lagana printed a business card for job-hunting purposes and gave it to everyone she met. She started her day at her local Starbucks in Brookfield, Connecticut.

"I told everyone I knew I had been laid off. People I know only peripherally—I would tell them, as well," she says. Lagana, 46, went to classes and support groups at her local workforce agency, "but the bulk of my leads came from Starbucks," she says.

One day she met the president of an energy services company. Lagana had her two Yorkies with her that day and they talked about dogs. She told him she was looking for work, giving him her business card. "I'm a people-oriented person. I'm pro-employee and pro-customer. I'm very open. I will talk about anything," Lagana says.

Lagana soon got a call from a finance executive with the energy services firm and she recognized him immediately—he had worked at her former employer, a wholesale DVD company. But the firm couldn't offer her a job at that time, so Lagana continued her Starbucks habit and pursued other leads.

"I got so much grief from so many people telling me, 'You can't be going to Starbucks. It's too much money,'" says Lagana, who doesn't even like coffee and instead sips a Chai tea while networking. "But Starbucks got me out of bed every day. I would get up, take a shower, and start my day there. I got a ton of support from these people."

In December 2009 at her favorite coffeehouse, Lagana bumped into the energy services firm president again, and he set up another interview. She was offered the position of sales administrator, a job she started in January 2010.

"There's nothing bad about being unemployed. Hold your head up high and tell everyone your circumstances. Because you never know," Lagana says.

Streetwise Strategies for Effective Networking

- Tell everyone you know and meet that you're looking for a new job.

- Use good-natured humor to put people at ease.

- Be curious about what's going on around you.

- Develop yourself through continuing education and certifications.

- Target potential employers and find inside advocates.

- Tap your alumni networks.

- Get to know a potential employer through informational interviews with current and former employees.

- Make new contacts in person and then connect on LinkedIn.

- Update your LinkedIn profile once a week. Look for jobs posted only on the website by members.

- Play the numbers game: Set up 8 to 10 one-on-one meetings every week.

- Network outside your comfort zone by joining industry and social groups.

- Stay in contact with former bosses and colleagues.

- Help others and you'll help yourself.

- Be nice to your colleagues; they may refer you to a potential employer.

- Find a local morning hangout like Starbucks to meet businesspeople.

CHAPTER 4

DO YOUR HOMEWORK ON POTENTIAL EMPLOYERS

W hen people lose jobs, they often feel they've lost control. Take it back: After you figure out what job you want, research employers to decide where you want to work. *You* decide.

Most people pursue a job the other way around by just looking at jobs being advertised online. They spend their days browsing Monster, CareerBuilder, and other online job boards. You should spend some of your time doing that, but you can also keep up with new job postings through alerts on most online job boards or an aggregator such as Indeed.

You also should make time to research which employer fits you:

- Target the potential employers in your field and geographic area where you want to work.

- Drive around your area, through industrial parks, to see what businesses are near you. You may not even realize certain companies are nearby because you've been working for one company for 10 or 20 years.

- Look at lists of companies in your field and those that are considered "best" employers. *Fortune* magazine compiles an annual list of "Best Companies to Work For," and regional publications often emulate the list.

- Ask friends and acquaintances who work at target companies what they like or dislike about their employers to get a sense of the culture.

Think about looking for a new employer as an upgrade. A new company may offer benefits, such as on-site child care or profit-sharing, and that could make your life easier and work more rewarding. Perhaps your faith is important to you, and you want to be around others who share it. Maybe you're a parent or caregiver who needs flexible hours. Or you want to work at a place that is innovative and allows you to take risks. Consider what is really important to you at work, where you will spend most of your waking hours.

As the economy recovers, workers will be able to be more choosey about where they work. Employers will have to respond with more incentives to attract and retain talent.

Look at everything you can find out about the company on the Internet, but don't stop there. Make connections on LinkedIn and in-person networking to find people who have either previously worked for the company or, better yet, still work there. That inside contact is what can ultimately get you noticed and considered for a job at the company.

Create Your Own Marketing Plan

Jim Kowalczyk, a process improvement specialist, wrote his own marketing plan and brought it to networking events so that people he met would know exactly the job he was seeking.

"You almost look at yourself as a product, defining your target market, even to the zip code," he says. Kowalczyck, 37, assembled his list of target employers, researching which companies had branch managers or headquarters within 50 miles of his then-home in Florida. Still, he kept an open mind about where he might find a job. He ended up taking a job with a firm in Atlanta.

The marketing plan helped him define the job he wanted and where he could find it. You can take a cue from his marketing plan by considering the following questions:

- Are you willing to travel? How far are you willing to drive?

- What's your job search objective?

- What specific job titles are you seeking?

"It's a good tool to hand out to people without giving your resume away," Kowalczyck says. "If you state your objective and give people a clear picture of what you're looking for, it makes them more apt to help you."

His one-page marketing plan included the following:

- **Description of his professional qualifications:** Six Sigma Black Belt Operations and Account Management Professional.

- **A positioning statement:** Black-Belt Certified Operations Management Professional with 12+ years of proven success in the insurance and financial services industries.

- **Potential job titles:** Process Improvement Manager, Operations Manager, Account Manager, Six Sigma Black Belt, Process Leader, Implementation Manager, Project Manager, Operational Excellence Manager, Business Process Analyst, or Customer Service Manager.

- **Core competencies:** Strategic and tactical business planning, key account management, financial analysis and reporting, conflict management and resolution, technical and customer support implementations, and contract negotiations

- **Target market:** He included his preferences of geographic area, industry type, and size of organization.

- **Target companies:** He listed 21 target employers.

Using his marketing plan, Kowalczyck found a job that was pretty close to his target—one that combined his process improvement and call center experience.

Gather Intelligence on Target Employers

Michael Simon became a sleuth to find a job. After Simon, 48, lost his job in the automotive industry in February 2009, he worked as a consultant in process improvement. He found he could generate a good income from his secondary skills in lean manufacturing.

After he was contacted by a recruiter for job with an Indianapolis-based automotive parts business, Simon went into his network to gather intelligence. By the time he interviewed, Simon was able to talk with inside knowledge about the industry and business, strengths and weaknesses he saw, and what customers wanted. He knew, for example, that his target employer saw its growth in hybrid vehicles. So Simon called a friend in the tire business to ask if he had any customers who owned hybrid trucks. By talking to customers, "I was able to give the hiring managers information they didn't have about customer perception," he says.

Being a consultant gave him the entrance to asking questions in the industry without revealing that he was building a case to sell himself to a potential employer. The consulting also helped Simon realize that he was versatile and could offer extra skills in improving processes and efficiencies—something many employers look for in a recession. With U.S. sales shrinking and China's market reaching new heights, his experience working in China for his former automotive employer was an asset.

A recruiter spied him on LinkedIn in July 2009, but was having a hard time juggling his schedule to meet Simon. When the recruiter said he was going to be in Vero Beach, Florida—a 100-mile drive from Simon's home in Boca Raton—Simon offered to drive up the coast to meet him. The recruiter couldn't even promise lunch he was so busy, but after an initial chat with Simon, they ended up talking through lunch and afterward. "He realized I was someone he needed to know better," he says.

Simon's experience is a lesson in patience. Often, the job search process doesn't move as quickly as we would like. In fact, it can be painfully slow. After meeting with the recruiter, Simon didn't have a telephone interview with the company's director of human resources for another month. "I thought they had given up on me," he says. But when Simon contacted the recruiter, he said, "They're still interested."

Finally, in September 2009, Simon was called in for an interview—two rounds of three hours with top executives. "Another two months go by. It was November, and I get a call from the vice president of human resources."

By this time, the company had narrowed the field to 12 candidates. His final interview was the week before Christmas 2009, and—Happy Holidays—Simon learned he was the last one standing.

Be Proactive While Still Employed

Everyone knows that it's best to look for a new job while you still have one. Most people in the recession have not had that luxury. Either they were laid off with little notice, or it didn't make sense to walk away from a 20-year job without a severance package.

But in the recovery, more people will be looking for new jobs while still employed. One way to prepare is to make sure you have the qualifications that employers seek in the job you want. Browse online postings to check the list of requirements in job descriptions: How well does yours match? If not, you may be able to earn a certification or add other skills while still employed.

Will Kuchera, 31, took his skills and found a nearly exact match in a job description online. Kuchera started looking for a new job, even though he had one, because he was concerned his employment could fade away. It was a valid concern in his home state of Michigan, which had a double-digit unemployment rate.

Another sign was the housing market. Kuchera and his wife bought a home in Ann Arbor, Michigan, in 2003. "We bought it on the way down," he says. Unfortunately, it kept going down in value.

At first, he just looked at job boards to gather information. He browsed Craigslist and Monster as well as the websites of potential employers to check the type of jobs being posted in his field. He looked regularly for four to five months, noticing the special expertise and certifications being required.

Finally, there was a posting he noticed that "I had almost every job requirement the employer was looking for—four-years-plus experience working in Web development and Flash," Kuchera says.

He tailored his resume to those job requirements and applied online. His resume must have immediately made the cut because he was called for an interview directly by the hiring manager, not human resources or an internal recruiter.

Kuchera says he thinks his resume worked because it is clean and succinct. In his own experience hiring people, he has found technology workers tend to cram their resumes with certifications of every kind. His conclusion: "If this person is doing a little bit of everything, there's not one thing he has expertise in."

Although his target employer was in a different field than Kuchera had experience, the technical skills needed were the same. Kuchera was able to show that through his resume and at his interview. "I was lucky in the respect that I had pretty much the identical experience the employer was looking for," he says.

Was it luck? Perhaps, but Kuchera's browsing through job postings and focusing on the qualifications employers were seeking helped him better position himself for success.

Find an Inside Advocate

Someone already working for your target employer can be a huge asset in researching, interviewing, and landing a job.

Ken Jones knew he wanted to remain in the Raleigh-Durham, North Carolina, area, where he and his wife Liz reside with their two children. So when Jones was laid off in March 2009 from Nortel Networks Corp., where he had been a product manager, he considered which regional employers best fit his experience and ambitions.

Jones, 43, had worked in several areas: information technology, software development, program management, and product management. "I felt I had a good, well-rounded set of experiences. The question was, 'How do I aggregate this into something better?'"

Many of his former colleagues had moved to other large telecommunications companies such as Cisco or Lucent. But Jones decided to take a different approach. He targeted innovative companies, including Elster Solutions, the smart energy company where he now works. Jones soon found an advocate within Elster—a former MBA classmate from the University of North Carolina.

"I sent him a note, 'I'm interested in Elster, something in product management or business development,'" he says. Jones also reached deeper within Elster to connect with other people in the organization who might be involved in its growth. He used LinkedIn to learn about the backgrounds of leaders at the company through the profiles they had posted.

By the summer, Jones realized that the company was actively looking to expand its product management team. Through learning what he could externally and then checking its accuracy with his advocate, he understood the company's mission and what it needed. "You're ready to go in, and you know how to position yourself. It's a sales activity. I'm presenting myself as a solution for a series of problems," Jones says. In August 2009, he interviewed on a Monday and had an offer by that Friday.

Research the People, Too

Know the background and experience of top managers at your target employer. By doing this research, Marina Konchak was able to tailor her answers during her interview for a human resources position to the executives' expertise.

Konchak, 46, of Miami had spent more than half her life at Home Depot, working her way up to a human resources position before she was laid off in 2009. She started looking for a new job by targeting the industries she wanted to work for, based on personal preference and industries showing stability or growth in the economic climate. "I was very selective about companies I sent my resume to," she says.

Konchak researched the organizations using the Internet and reports available from Dun & Bradstreet. "I wanted to make sure they were not only financially stable, but also organizationally strong," she says. She found out about the company's leadership and then dug deeper to learn about their backgrounds.

"Know who the number one players are in the organization and read everything you can get your hands on," says Konchak, who took a human resources director job with Miami's Catholic Hospice, one of three job offers she had. She found through her research that the CEO of Catholic Hospice had come from a marketing background. That gave her a clue about how to approach him in her first interview: "I did my homework, and I was prepared. It was quite comfortable," she says.

When she entered the board room for her second interview, Konchak already knew all of the senior management team's names and their backgrounds. "I broke the ice by looking at each person and addressing them by their first name...It was an immediate hit. The body language from the executive team changed to a more relaxed tone," she says.

During the interview, she made a point to address important aspects of each person's background when sharing personal experiences relevant to his or her questions.

Konchak says it's important to know your preferences before seeking a job. "The other two jobs were more money, but more travel. This is really the job that I wanted," she says. "Catholic Hospice is right here in Miami Lakes. I've gained quality of life."

Check the Employer's Financial Stability

Before seriously considering a new job—especially if you are leaving a job, learn everything you can about the company's financial condition. Many job seekers in this recession have found a job, only to be laid off again. Sometimes, it was avoidable with a bit of research that pointed to red flags.

Aim for an employer that is profitable and has a solid strategy for future growth. Many businesses have gotten off track during the recession; make sure you align yourself with an employer that is poised to take you to new levels in your career.

With some 20 years of experience in finance, Kurt Porceng of Coral Springs, Florida, wanted to make sure he joined a company that was on solid financial footing. He interviewed with an asphalt and oil industry firm in nearby Fort Lauderdale. Because it is a private company, the firm doesn't make its financial information public. But Porceng, 42, asked the owner direct questions about revenue and year-over-year growth, which he was proud to share because the company was doing well.

Such questions are certainly expected of a candidate applying for a controller position, but any job hunter should be aware of a potential employer's financial stability as part of research about the organization.

Many people feel uncomfortable asking such questions, but as long as you ask them diplomatically, an upfront business owner or manager will credit you for being thorough.

Here are some other ways to get the information you need:

- For public companies, you can get a snapshot of financials through their required filings with the U.S. Securities and Exchange Commission at www.sec.gov. Look at the company's revenues and earnings, and compare them with a year earlier. Look at the trend over five years. Recognize, of course, that nearly every company took a hit in the recession in 2008–2009. Has the company started to recover since then? Ask what the company's strategy has been to weather the recession.

- Do an Internet search to see what has been written about the company, especially in the archives of your local newspaper, which may offer more detail.

- Is the potential employer in acquisition mode? That could be a good sign, showing the company is positioned to take advantage of opportunities in the marketplace. But acquisitions and mergers also mean the company will likely be reorganizing certain departments for "synergies," which usually results in layoffs somewhere in the combined companies.

Before accepting his current job, Porceng also interviewed with a startup company. He found them hesitant to answer his financial questions and decided it was not the place for him.

Still, a startup company may be just where *you* want to be—a place where you can get in on the ground floor and grow with the company. But it also comes with risks because the company may not yet be profitable or be stable enough to overcome financing troubles or the sudden loss of a major client. As frustrated entrepreneurs leave the workforce in the recovery and start businesses, there are likely to be more opportunities at startups. Weigh the benefits and the risks before you jump.

Work with a Recruiter Who Has Inside Knowledge

When starting your job search, seek recruiters in your field. Let them work for you, but don't rely only on them to find you a job.

Rodrigo Parra, 36, works as a recruiter in Tampa, Florida, and landed a new job in early 2010. He says the best way to find a staffing company or recruiter is to call the human resources office of your target employer. "Ask, 'Who do you use?' Then call that recruiter and say, 'I'd like to work with you.'"

That recruiter will have the inside line on the company and know who and how they tend to hire. You also can find a recruiter through an Internet search or on LinkedIn. You're likely to come up with names when you search online for the type job you're looking for and location, such as "sales, marketing, Philadelphia" with "recruiter" or "staffing," Parra suggests.

Interview recruiters as you would any potential employer, says Kathy Stein, 48, national sales director for a GPS tracking company near Fort Lauderdale. She found the job through a local recruiter after being laid off from an automotive leasing company. "It doesn't cost you anything. Recruiters have jobs that aren't on Monster. It's working all the angles," she says.

A recruiter who is being paid by the employer can get you through what seems a closed door. "They know the decision makers. It's as if you're in Hollywood and you're hiring an agent," Stein says.

Here is Stein's advice on finding a recruiter:

- Find someone who specializes in your industry and knows the companies you're targeting as employers.

- Talk with the recruiter's former clients to see how hard he or she worked for them.

- Check the history of the recruiting firm. Has it been around awhile and do its employees know the players in your industry and region?

Last, make sure you have a good gut feeling about the recruiter, Stein says. You have to like the person, she says.

Give the recruiter your specifications for a job. "When you go to a Realtor, you say, this is a list of what I'm looking for in a house. It's the same thing when looking for a job: 'I need benefits and to work out of my home,'" she says. And it's okay to work with more than one recruiter in your job search, Stein adds.

After you have an interview with a potential employer, a recruiter can give you honest feedback after talking with the potential employer. Recruiters also can be helpful in getting you what you want when it comes down to negotiating salary and benefits, Stein says.

Stein's job connection came when her recruiter was at a networking dinner with the president of her current employer. In the course of conversation, the recruiter talked about Stein, and she soon had an interview. "When you find good recruiters, stay in touch with them," she says. "They become your friends."

Still, process improvement specialist Jim Kowalczyk cautions that while recruiters may seem like your best buddies, remember that they're working for the company. Don't give too much away in information about your previous salary and benefits. "I would recommend handling a recruiter just like you were talking with a company," he says.

Volunteer Your Services to Become Known

If you take a temporary or freelance job with a potential employer, do more than is expected: Work longer than the hours assigned, show you're willing to learn and be a team player. Volunteer your services where needed. You'll get to know people and become thought of as "one of them."

David Tow of San Diego, California, always knew he wanted to be a teacher. He spent seven years working in the retail industry during undergraduate and graduate school. Like many school systems in the country, the Southern California school system was downsizing jobs, not hiring more teachers.

Tow, 27, offered his flexibility to get his first teaching job. "A lot of teachers are not willing to drive and change neighborhoods. They want to teach where they live. I was able to drive 30 minutes to an hour to get there. And I was one of the only candidates who were willing to teach less than full time."

After that job ended, Tow was offered a one-year contract. Still, Tow has found from year to year that he has no assurance of being employed as a teacher. Instead of worrying about having a job, Tow immerses himself in the educational community.

His credentials in several different areas give him an edge. "If I only had my English credential, I wouldn't be back this year," says Tow, who is in his second year of teaching in 2010. "They were looking for someone to teach speech and debate. That's more on the nights and weekends than most people were willing to do."

He also has credentials in and enjoys teaching history, social science, and philosophy. "Even a certification in studio art or cooking or drama can separate you from others," Tow says.

Teachers also should recognize that their clients are the students as well as the school system, and their opinions count, Tow says.

"You have to make yourself part of the environment," he says. He did so in his first year by becoming involved with the high school's improvisational comedy team. "It's not how I preferred to spend my evenings, but kids on campus saw me. The kids are the clientele. Teachers like every other profession are involved in the service industry."

Tow also regularly surveys his classes to get their feedback on how well he has taught the course and what he could improve, something he learned from his retail background. "I remember when I was in school and I had very good teachers and very bad teachers," he says.

He was offered a full-time teaching position at a time when public schools were downsizing in California. He continues to work under the philosophy that volunteering strengthens his position in the school system. Any additional credentials also ready him for a new opportunity, if needed.

Be Savvy with Online Job Boards

It's easy to sit at the computer and browse online job boards, and think you've looked for a job. Expand your online job search beyond the obvious.

Online job boards such as CareerBuilder (www.careerbuilder.com) and Monster (www.monster.com) are useful tools, but don't focus exclusively on them. The successful job candidates I interviewed saw opportunities on online job boards, and then made a connection for the job through a recruiter, LinkedIn, or their industry or personal network. If you've done your homework, you've already made that inside connection before you ever see the job posting.

Pay special attention to industry groups and their online sites or e-mail lists and the websites of the employers you're targeting.

George Lambros, now a financial controller for a Kuwait conglomerate, used TheLadders (www.theladders.com) to select filters and receive daily updates of relevant job postings. RiteSite (www.ritesite.com) also has a feature that sends an e-mail blast to hundreds of recruiters. "That was helpful in quickly establishing some new relationships and generating a few opportunities," he says. Lambros, 48, also used Financial Executive Networking Group, which issues a daily newsletter containing articles, tips, and a list of senior-level finance opportunities.

Michael Crehan, 54, who was formerly a research analyst on Wall Street, turned to eFinancialcareers (www.efinancialcareers.com). "It was helpful with ideas and leads, not so much with concrete opportunities. Too many job boards have dated positions that have been filled," he says.

Michael Ni, a 27-year-old public relations professional in San Francisco, found his best job listings on PR News and the Public Relations Society of America Job Center. Sophie Cardona, 38, of New York recommends Indeed (www.indeed.com), which pulls job listings from all the search engines. "Setting up alerts is also extremely useful. That way you're not wasting your time surfing the Net all day," she says.

Cardona, who is an environmental building specialist, also went to GreenBiz (www.greenbiz.com), a website that posts green-related jobs. Process improvement specialist Jim Kowalczyk used local

networking boards in Atlanta, including CobbWorks (www.
cobbworks.org), Atlanta Linking (a LinkedIn group), and RE:FOCUS
ON CAREERS (www.refocusoncareers.com). But he found specialty
job boards—including iSixSigma (www.isixsigma.com), the Project
Management Institute, and International Customer Management
Institute—most effective. "The paid job boards are overcrowded," he
says.

Don't forget Craigslist (www.craigslist.org). It isn't just for restaurant or
retail jobs. All kinds of jobs, even professional positions, are listed on this
free site, but be cautious about listings that ask for personal information
or don't specify the job opportunity.

Nicole Sheets, 34, used Craigslist to search for a job after she was laid
off from a manufacturer in South Florida. "Craigslist is where I had the
most success," says Sheets, who now works as office manager for an
environmental consulting firm in Fort Lauderdale. Nearly every ad she
responded to on Craigslist resulted in an interview, and she had three
offers at the same time in early 2010.

While she ultimately found her job through a Craigslist posting, Sheets
replied to the ads with caution. "I was inundated with recruiters," she
says. She had concerns about identity theft in sending information to an
unidentified employer.

She recommends avoiding postings that are vague, where there's no
specific person to contact. "You send your resume and you get some
guy from South Africa who wants your money in his bank account and
wants you to be his personal assistant," Sheets says.

Also don't forget government employment websites, such as USAJOBS
(www.usajobs.gov). The federal government under the Obama administration in particular has been hiring, and the salaries are comparable
and often even better than the private sector.

Consider a Temporary or Contract Job

A temporary job gives you and the employer the opportunity to try
each other out. You get to experience the environment and meet the
people, which can help you decide whether this is a workplace where
you can excel and be happy. The employer observes your skills and
decides whether you're a good addition to the team.

After being laid off in April 2009, Diana Galvin didn't waste time browsing job listings online; she went right to placement agencies that specialize in accountants. She worked in two temporary accounting jobs. The second job, which she began in August 2009, was temporary for two months, then moved into part-time, and finally, full-time by January 2010.

"I would recommend temp-to-full-time to anybody. When you're a temp, you don't have to stay forever. If personalities don't mesh, you still have the ability to walk away," Galvin says.

After spending time as a temp at the CPA firm of Conrad & Co, Galvin knew it was a good fit. The office environment had none of the political tension she once experienced, and she liked that many of the colleagues shared her religious faith.

So Galvin, a 51-year-old staff accountant, looked for ways she could be helpful. With 20 years of experience in the field, she could anticipate what the firm needed for its growth. "If the trash needs to be taken out, you just do what you can to help. Make yourself a team player and they appreciate that," she says.

Galvin did much more than take out the trash. She

- Set up a system to keep track of the client's tax returns throughout the process to ensure that no one fell through any cracks and the work was done timely.

- Organized a centralized binder documenting clients, work accomplished, tax adviser, and amount charged. That helped the firm's employees "make better informed decisions about the type of services they need to offer each client and what the price of those services should be."

- Set up binders to track work deadlines.

- Did research and put together a professional website for the firm in about 30 days.

But Galvin really sold her coworkers when she took the initiative to clean out and organize the supply closet. "Apparently, it hadn't been done for a while. They've all really liked that part."

Conrad & Co. paid her more money as a temp than she was getting in her last job, and the firm just extended the pay when she became full-time. Though Galvin now commutes about an hour to work at Conrad's office in Spartanburg, South Carolina, she thinks the job is worth the drive.

Even if her temp job hadn't turned into full-time, she could have asked the firm for recommendations to get hired somewhere else.

Now that Galvin is happier at work, her 18-year-old daughter has noticed a difference in her mother. "My daughter says I am a much nicer person," she says.

Know When It's Time to Go, and Plan

Determine what you want, plan for it, and go for it. It was nearly that simple for Lauren Burchett, 32, of Los Angeles.

Burchett was doing the work she loved in advertising sales, but in the summer of 2008 her employer went through a restructuring, and her job changed. During the recession, she was happy to have a job, but then as the pressure mounted, she began thinking, "What kind of job do I *have*?"

"As soon as I accepted that my old company was going to be the way it was going to be and I could only go along with it, then all of a sudden things started to come my way," Burchett says.

She stuck it out until the economy seemed to be picking up and began looking around for new opportunities in late 2009. Burchett quietly put out the word to trusted friends, colleagues, and family and contacted a recruiter who specializes in the advertising industry: She was looking for a change.

"You never want your boss to know you're looking for work. It makes it a little easier when your boss is in New York," Burchett says.

Burchett didn't post anything on the Internet that would let her then-employer know she was looking. She had already built her LinkedIn profile, including recommendations from colleagues.

After the reorganization, she paid off her credit card debt and began stashing away commission checks and extra cash when she could. Burchett had a year's worth of salary socked away by the time she launched her job search.

In January 2010, she began looking earnestly for a new job and had an offer about three months later. The key, Burchett says, was being clear on what she was looking for in a new job: Growth opportunities and lifestyle were important to her. "I wanted to be part of a company that values an employee having a personal life, a company that treats you like an adult, where you can work hard and play hard. I was looking for balance," she says.

So in her off time, she spent time doing her homework on potential employers. She collected job opportunities through Indeed alerts and went on interviews set up by her recruiter.

The Los Angeles sales job for a magazine publisher came to her almost simultaneously through her recruiter, a colleague, and a posting she saw on LinkedIn. She called her existing clients to find out how the publisher was regarded, and it got rave reviews.

When she interviewed, Burchett says she knew it was the right job for her. "I really loved the publisher from the first meeting. It was completely comfortable," she says.

When the publisher asked her in the interview to describe a "big win," she told him how she went after a magazine ad from a major motion picture for six months. When she was told it was going to fall through for budget reasons, Burchett persisted, and, because she had built a relationship with the clients, they found money for the ad.

She had two interviews: one with the publisher and the other with the president of the firm. She e-mailed thank-you notes after each interview and updated the publisher on her interview with the president. She also kept her recruiter in the loop.

Burchett was offered a sales position. "On my first day, the president of the company called me to welcome me to the team and the company," she says. "He didn't have to call me—he could have shot me an e-mail. That speaks volumes to me."

With careful planning and clear goals, Burchett was able to make a smooth transition from a job that was not working for her to one that was more promising. She went about her job hunt quietly, systematically, and with determination until she zoned in on her best opportunity. Today, she feels valued and is happier at work as a result.

Streetwise Strategies
for Researching Target Employers

- Identify companies in your area that have branches and divisions as well as headquarters.

- Target about six employers of your choice for in-depth research.

- Create a marketing plan and use it for networking.

- Review qualifications in job postings for the job you want; make sure you have them.

- Know your potential manager's career experience before your interview.

- Investigate the company's financial stability.

- Find a recruiter to represent you and give you the inside track.

- Ask target employers which recruiters they use.

- Consider a temporary or contract job to try out an employer.

- Be the flexible job candidate.

- Immerse yourself in the community of your potential employer.

- Get prepared financially to leave a job.

CHAPTER 5

KEEP YOUR PERSPECTIVE DURING FINANCIAL TURMOIL

You've been laid off or fear you soon will be because your company has just announced a merger with another firm. Acquisitions and mergers and the resulting personnel changes are all part of the recession and the recovery cycle. Or perhaps you just *want* to look for a new job: It's time to move on, and you've been waiting until the economy picks up.

Finances often are the biggest obstacle to changing jobs. You probably have a mortgage or rent to pay and family to feed, as well as college tuitions, credit cards, or car loans. A layoff affecting you or your partner will prompt an emergency financial review, but it's always better to know where you stand and prepare for a transition to another job.

If you get a sizeable severance package, you may feel rich and start thinking about a trip to Europe now that you have the time. After all, you'll land on your feet soon, or so you think. The recovery may speed up your job search, but don't count on it. Prepare a budget to stretch that severance over six or more months with unemployment insurance benefits until your next paycheck is rolling in.

During the recession, the Obama administration extended unemployment insurance up to 99 weeks in some states. The deadline for eligibility ended on November 30, 2010, though payments continue through April 30, 2011. Benefit payments will likely go back to the standard 26 weeks as the economy recovers.

How long might you be out of work? The lengthy period of joblessness has surprised many people in this recession. In a normal job market, the estimate is one month of unemployment for every $10,000 in salary you need to replace. However, job seekers who have been through the experience in this economy say it's wise to figure double, so that someone who is trying to replace a $70,000 salary should be prepared to be out of work for 14 months. And in this economic downturn, the higher the salary, the tougher it has been to find a job with comparable compensation.

Before you leave your job voluntarily, structure your financial life in terms of survival, figuring on little income. "If your search time calculation is greater than your survive time calculation, do not quit your job," warns Alan Hunt, 51, a San Diego finance executive who did just that for another job that didn't pan out.

For high-unemployment states such as Florida, California, Michigan, and Ohio, no savings, severance, or government help has gone far enough to cushion most people from a year or more out of work in this recession. Some have had to move in with a friend or family member and apply for food stamps. Many have had to let their homes go into foreclosure. It's hard not to get depressed when the very things you've worked for most of your life are evaporating.

But job hunters I've interviewed who have survived this difficult time tell me they now realize it was temporary. Many have gained a new perspective. They've come to recognize what really matters: their family, friends, and health—not stuff.

File for Unemployment Benefits

The day after you are laid off, file for unemployment benefits. There's usually a waiting period while your claim is verified, so you want to apply as soon as possible. Then make up a new budget to stretch your unemployment compensation, severance, and savings as far as possible.

In reporting on unemployment, I've met many people who made the mistake of not filing or delaying unemployment benefits. Your employer has paid into the state insurance system, so that weekly income—no matter how meager—is available to many laid-off employees. The system is in place to get you over the hump until you find a new job.

Besides, it's not as if you have to stand in the "unemployment line" any more; most states' unemployment insurance systems are online.

I remember meeting an elderly lawyer who hadn't filed for unemployment benefits after his firm let him go. He thought surely he would be picked up by another firm soon—he already had a job lead. But the economy was at its worst, and even law firms were downsizing, especially those in Florida that handled real estate transactions. Leave the unemployment benefits for someone else, the lawyer and his wife decided. But a year later, he still didn't have a job. He had drained his lifelong savings and was about to lose his home. And it was too late to file for unemployment benefits.

Not every layoff situation is so drastic, but even when you are getting ready to look for a job, it's good to get your financial house in order and trim expenses.

Plan Ahead

Lisa Godoski, 47, was laid off from her 12-year job at a St. Louis newspaper. Fortunately, she had planned ahead, saving more than six months' salary. She also paid off her car loan to free up almost $400 a month. "I was a little miser for two to three years," she says.

"I lived on the severance package and unemployment for quite a while before I had to dig into savings. Because the *Post* had four previous rounds of layoffs, I started watching my spending and paying off debts long before I was actually let go," she says.

Godoski had that savings, her three-month severance, four weeks of vacation owed to her, and unemployment benefits to pay her mortgage and living expenses for the 10 months she was unemployed. Still, unemployment benefits in Missouri are only $325 a week, and her severance package was taxed at 25 percent by the federal government and 6 percent by Missouri. "The city of St. Louis has an earnings tax as well. So I paid almost 41 percent in taxes on my severance package," she says.

She paid for necessities first and looked for deals. "You focus on the things you can control," Godoski says. "You pay for what you can pay for." She took advantage of free offers by her cable and Internet provider, which upgraded her services for six months.

"Otherwise, I lived very sparingly. I didn't go to movies or such, only bought food I needed, and skipped the extras. I always pay my credit card off every month, so no running debt there," she says.

Godoski chose to stay in St. Louis and look for a job. She had friends in Chicago, Los Angeles, and New York, but decided the cost of living was too high in those cities.

Her careful planning and stretching of her dollars paid off. "I didn't miss a payment on anything," she says. Godoski found a job in September 2009 at a medical publishing firm for a salary comparable to what she had been making at the newspaper.

Be Honest with the Kids

Ken Jones, 43, was laid off from his management job at telecommunications firm Nortel Networks in March 2009. Soon after, Jones and his wife Liz addressed the family's new financial situation with their two children, then eight and nine. "We sat down and talked to them about it: 'I don't have a job. Mom is going back to work. You guys don't need to be scared, but you do need to understand it. I want you to ask as many questions as you want.'"

The kids had a few moments of "Why can't we do this or that?" But mostly, transparency worked for the Jones family. "We're just going to have to pull together, and everything is going to be fine," he told them.

"I wanted this to be serious, but I didn't want it to be something that colors their outlook on their lives," Jones says. He assured his children that, "America and the world will come back."

Jones had no severance because his former employer Nortel had entered bankruptcy. His wife picked up more hours at her job, and Jones took over her previous duties with the children during the summer. "I did a top-to-bottom review of financials," he says. "Here's what we have in reserve. Here's the mortgage, utilities, food, and living expenses."

They changed their lifestyle a bit, and even though Jones was looking for a job for seven months, the couple didn't have to dip into their long-term savings or retirement accounts. "We really got ourselves down to a pretty simple existence," Jones says.

Kathy and Brandt Stein of Fort Lauderdale used her job hunt in 2009 as a personal finance lesson for their son. They stopped going out to dinner and prepared meals with friends and family. "We call it our village. We all have to take care of each other," says Kathy Stein, 48. The Steins let a friend whose home was foreclosed stay with them for a while, for example.

The Steins got rid of their leased car and bought a used one. They held garage sales to generate cash from the extra stuff they decided they didn't need. Most important, Stein says they were teaching their eight-year-old son the value of money by urging him to save his allowance if he wanted to buy something.

Learn Financial Survival Techniques

Scott and Monica Walsh's story is familiar to any American who got caught in the housing squeeze. When Scott Walsh lost his job in public relations in November of 2007, the couple didn't have a safety net. Monica doesn't work outside the home because she homeschools their nine-year-old son. The Walshes also had never built up the six to nine months of expenses that most experts recommend.

"We relied on the value of our house. I was let go right when the economy was starting to go down and real estate started to collapse," Walsh says. The couple bought their house near San Diego in April 2003 for $300,000. It was appraised in 2007 for about $475,000. It currently is worth about $220,000.

They tried to short-sell their home but couldn't come to an agreement with their lender. A year later, the couple's home was in foreclosure. Because the courts were so backed up with foreclosures, the Walshes were able to live in their home for about two years.

Walsh has since started Aslan Communications, a public relations business, but as in any young venture, it takes time to build a client base. They've moved from their home into a rental. "We knew this was coming, and we're better prepared for it now than a year ago," he says. The Walshes cut every expense they could and sold some of their accumulated belongings to stay afloat.

The couple's more frugal lifestyle has now become a way of life. Monica trims her son's hair, and she and Scott go longer between haircuts than they once did. They use coupons and shop at discount stores such as the 99 Cents store and Dollar Tree.

They trade babysitting with friends. With one family, Monica tutors and in exchange receives child care. They sign up for birthday clubs and e-mail lists that offer free meals.

The Walshes are careful to reconcile their "explanation of benefits" from their health insurance carrier with the actual bill from the doctor. They pay auto insurance in one lump sum to avoid monthly interest payments. They dropped collision coverage on their old vehicles.

The Walshes unplug their washer, dryer, and other appliances when not in use to reduce energy use and decrease the electric bill. They close heating vents in bedrooms and bathrooms that are not in use, forcing heat into the common areas.

The couple spends more time with each other, taking walks, playing board games, and watching TV programs such as *24,* which they both enjoy. This resulted in more bonding and less need for things, the Walshes say.

So, instead of tearing them apart, the financial struggles brought Scott and Monica closer together. Walsh says he and his wife are opposites in strengths and personality: She's more analytical and athletic; he's more emotive and goes with his gut. "She likes to do sports; I watch sports," he says.

In their first years of marriage, their differences would often result in them "butting heads," Walsh says. During their financial and job troubles since 2007, "it has really changed," he says. "Our situation presented us with a common enemy. We both recognized that we had to start doing something to change our situation. We started working together better than we had."

They needed each other more emotionally, so instead of the financial turmoil pulling them apart, Walsh says he and Monica turned toward each other and their faith. "We were very blessed. We've never gone without a roof over our heads. We've never missed a meal. What do I have to complain about? My life could be so much worse," he says.

Walsh tells others who are going through similar financial difficulties due to unemployment: "Don't be afraid to reach out to people, your family, coworkers, and neighbors. People have a tendency to want to help each other, especially when there is a relationship or a friendship. It's not a bad thing to ask for help."

Trim Your Costs in Tough Times

Here are some ideas for cutting expenses from the Walshes and others who participated in this book:

- **Cut your cable.** They dropped it until Scott Walsh needed it for his business, and then they paid only for basic cable.

- **Drop your land line,** which comes with heavy taxes, and use your cell phone. Check whether bundling your phone, cable, and Internet connection costs through one company will save you money. Some say it's important to have a land line so your calls are not dropped, but you also need a cell phone to receive that important job call wherever you may be job hunting.

- **Ask creditors for a discount.** You'll be surprised at what some companies are doing to keep customers during the economic downtown. That includes freezing credit card interest, cutting credit card rates, and offering a service at a lower price for six months.

- **Stop going out for dinner.** Budgeting for groceries and planning meals can save you money. "A nice dinner out was Starbucks," says Walsh, during his transition from layoff to starting his business.

- **Use coupons clipped** from the newspaper and found online to trim your grocery and pharmacy bills.

- **Join the Facebook fan pages of favorite eating spots.** Restaurants often give away free offers to fans.

- **Consider public school for your children if they're in private.**

(CONTINUED)

(CONTINUED)

- **If you're still paying on a student loan, request a deferment online at salliemae.com.** Deferments are commonly given for unemployment, but note that interest continues accruing on unsubsidized loans such as Parent Plus or Graduate Plus.

- **Take a leave of absence from your gym membership.** But exercise at home or in the great outdoors to relieve stress.

- **Move in with family or friends if need be.** Consider it a temporary situation until you get back on your feet and consider yourself fortunate to have someone to live with; many people do not. The Walshes, for example, moved in with Monica's parents temporarily.

- **Use the free Internet access at your public library.** You can spend your days applying for jobs, without the monthly bill.

- **Ask your church or a community group if a senior citizen needs help at home or transportation to the doctor.** One job hunter helped a 92-year-old blind woman with buying groceries and an 84-year-old woman with packing. They both insisted on paying her, which helped supplement her unemployment compensation.

- **Create a cash flow model** in an Excel spreadsheet that details expenses and then determine what needs to be paid with cash and what can be paid with credit. This will maximize your survival time, although it also will drive up your debt.

- **Apply for food stamps.** Although not many people with income or assets qualify, you have nothing to lose by applying online.

- **If you're faced with homelessness or urgent issues, seek help from your community crisis line.** Be persistent. Community services are overwhelmed, but they may be able to arrange a month's rent, a utility bill, or other measures. If you belong to a church or synagogue, there may be help there as well.

Prioritize When Living on Less

Robert Kostin, 48, once had a six-figure income from his job at Xerox in Rochester, New York, where he was a marketing manager for 17 years. When Xerox was downsizing, Robert decided in May 2008 that it was time to take a severance package.

He later found a job to transfer his marketing skills and try Web development. But Robert's new salary was about half of his previous income. His wife Linda took a part-time job for an organization that provides free legal assistance to low-income residents.

Even though their household income dropped substantially, the family still lives comfortably. They're even keeping up with flying lessons for their 16-year-old son, Michael, a passion that costs at least $200 a month, and Girl Scouts for 13-year-old daughter Julia.

The couple made a commitment to continue their children's activities and to cut back on other items. "We made the kids' activities our highest priority. Our kids were aware of our change in cash flow—and we used it as a learning opportunity for them—but that was the extent we wanted to let it impact their lives," Kostin says.

The Kostins embraced the philosophy that "you can have anything you want, but you have to wait a week." They found that a week later, they either wouldn't want the item anymore or could buy it at a cheaper price.

Holiday presents were reduced, and major purchases were deferred. Kostin was let go just before the summer of 2009, and the $400-a-week summer camp that Julia favored had to go. Linda found less expensive camps with outdoor activities, which Julia graciously accepted, her father says.

Now the Kostins are looking toward colleges for their children, and, as luck would have it, Robert is employed by the University of Rochester, which has a generous family tuition benefit. Although that may not fit Michael's goal to be a pilot, the Kostins are hoping Julia will consider the university or its affiliates for college.

"We think we made the right choice by focusing on their development during our times of financial insecurity," Kostin says. "We're proud of them and happy with ourselves."

Remember, It's a Temporary Situation

The financial squeeze after losing a job hopefully will be temporary. So even if you have to leave your house and move in with family and friends, say to yourself, "I can do this for a little while. It's temporary."

Scott Nemeth, 39, took residence in his sister-in-law's basement with his wife and daughters ages six and two. They had moved from Detroit after Scott was laid off and wanted to be closer to family.

Instead of this being a painful time, the Nemeths looked on their basement "home" as an adventure. The girls loved running around the basement. Scott was fine with it as well, except for his sister-in-law's cat. He's allergic to cats.

But Scott dealt with it by getting dressed and leaving each day as if he were going to a job. He had outplacement services and was able to use that as his office to look for work. He also joined multiple networking groups and had several meetings a week. It was through one of those, ExecuNet, that he made his contact for his new job.

"It was only a month living together in the basement. When I look back on that, it was fun," he says.

Embrace Your New Lifestyle

Michael Crehan, 55, was laid off from Wall Street before his former employer, Lehman Brothers, filed for bankruptcy protection. Crehan, a former research analyst, endured a 17-month job search.

As the government moved to bail out Wall Street, Crehan recognized that empathy would not be on his side. Some people even took their anger out on him in comments on a blog he participated in for the *Wall Street Journal* online.

When Lehman fell apart, employees who had held onto their incentive compensation in Lehman stock saw their nest eggs disappear. "Think of the guy who had been there 8 to 15 years, had maybe a few hundred thousand dollars, and now that's gone," Crehan says.

Crehan, an eight-year Lehman veteran, wasn't quite in the same financial boat. He had always been thrifty, the type who would "walk three blocks to save 25 cents on a tuna sandwich to take my family on vacation," he says.

Still, Crehan went through his severance and was soon digging into savings, even with his wife Joanne working part-time. A surprise stock distribution from Lehman came through and that paid for a couple months' mortgage payments. He cashed in a life insurance policy. They paid the final installments on their children's college education.

When he finally found a career development job at his alma mater, Notre Dame, the Crehans sold their Connecticut home and were able to buy a more affordable home in Indiana. Their lifestyle is more conservative than it once was, but they're comfortable.

"For years and years, we had some good vacations. We've been to a lot of countries overseas," Crehan says. Now the couple is happy to take the occasional trip to visit their daughter, who is working in another state. "We won't be going to Paris this year," he says.

A lifestyle that involves fewer expenses can have the extra benefit of alleviating stress over financial commitments. Consider whether you can live on less. Involve your partner or family in the discussion. Then accept your choices. You may find a simpler life more satisfying than your previous struggle to pay for big houses and expensive toys.

Streetwise Strategies for Keeping Financial Perspective

- Apply for unemployment benefits right away if you've been laid off.

- Draw up a budget to stretch your benefits and severance over six months or more.

- Change your lifestyle to a more frugal one.

- Prioritize your bills. Pay necessities such as mortgage and utilities first.

(CONTINUED)

(CONTINUED)

- Ask every creditor for a discount or extended payment plan.

- Sell unneeded items at a garage sale, on eBay, or on Craigslist.

- Defer your student loan if you have one.

- Consider selling your house or condo.

- Move in with a relative or friend if you must; it's temporary.

- Continue your more frugal lifestyle, even when you find a job.

CHAPTER 6

ADJUST YOUR MINDSET AND EXPECTATIONS

C onsider how you can solve an employer's problem, and you could create a win-win proposition. Think about what you do best and how that might be advantageous to a target employer. Find out what the employer needs and how you can be the solution: Is the company trying to expand its geographic market? Do you have the contacts to attract new business?

At the same time, as a job candidate you need to be open to new possibilities. You don't want to be so narrow in your job search that you dismiss potential opportunities. You could take a road that leads to a new job that you never considered. So while working toward a certain job goal, you also want to keep an open mind.

Pursue Employers That Are Expanding Their Reach

Consider looking for employment with a business that is expanding its presence nationally or even internationally. With your experience and contacts, you could be that organization's ticket to new business while securing a job for yourself. That was the case for Rosanna Garofalo, who ended up working for a New York firm from her Chicago-area residence.

When the stock market took its dive in late 2008, Garofalo was working for a shareholder services firm in Chicago. She loved the job, but as a condition of her severance, Garofalo had signed an agreement that she couldn't join a competitor for six months.

So after a 25-year career in shareholder services, Garofalo, 52, had to think how she could transfer her skills to another business. She reached out to her large Chicago network and applied to many large banking and financial institutions in the region. She landed several interviews, but just as she seemed close to an offer, the job would be frozen.

She knew of an opportunity in New York, but didn't want to leave her home in Chicago. Her noncompete agreement also was a problem because the firm was in the same business as she had left. Still, she kept in touch with the New York firm.

Around Thanksgiving, Garofalo got a call from the hiring manager at the New York firm saying that she was making up her 2010 budget: Should she include her? Her noncompete agreement was expiring, and she had been out of work for nine months, but Garofalo still didn't want to leave Chicago. So she asked the firm's managers if they would be willing to let her work remotely. They agreed, not for her convenience, but because they knew Garofalo could bring in clients from the region.

"I know the business, I know the process. If it works out, I will be able to call on contacts in the Chicago area," she told her future bosses. "My relationships were stellar and they had been trying to win business from those accounts," she explains.

Garofalo offered her potential employer a solution to its problem. The firm was looking to expand its business and generate revenue; Garofalo convinced the firm's managers she could accomplish that best from her Chicago home where she had a strong network.

So think beyond an employer's geographic location: It could be an effective strategy for residents of Florida, California, or Nevada who are looking for work but can't sell their homes until the housing market recovers.

Take a Contract Job

Consider a contract job in your search for full-time employment. It allows a potential employer to get to know you and gives you a glimpse into working for the company or organization. Even if employment with that firm doesn't become permanent, you'll likely make new contacts that could lead to a job.

That's how Suzanne Beard, 49, of Miami found a new job with a Seattle firm that needed an East Coast representative. She didn't start her job search with that in mind, but she stayed open to new ideas, which worked in her favor.

When Beard got laid off in August 2009, she took it hard. "I had worked for the company for 14 years," she says. "You've got to take care of yourself. It's real emotional. After working weekends, giving up vacation, and working late nights, your number comes up, and it's very painful. You have to be around people who love you and support you."

To "shake it off," Beard and her husband took some time to drive around Florida. She worked on house and yard projects she had been meaning to do and regularly exercised at the gym. "I actually wrote Christmas cards last year," Beard says.

When she was ready, Beard began attending career transition meetings at the outplacement service she was given by her former employer. "You get to hear other people's stories. It really helps to put things in perspective. It's not anything you did. You have to understand it's not you and stay positive."

She learned that networking was the best strategy, so she began reaching out to former colleagues and friends across the country. She sent an e-mail about the downsizing to a former colleague in Seattle. He had a new venture in freight forwarding and thought Beard's experience in logistics would be perfect. But he didn't have a full-time job to offer. He asked whether she would like to do a couple of projects on a consulting basis.

"When you're unemployed, anything sounds great," Beard says.

While Beard was working on the project, her friend also asked her to talk with an executive from a software company that provides operating systems for freight-forwarding companies. Beard agreed to meet him on his travel route through Miami. "We met in the rental car lot and talked for 30 minutes before I drove him to the gate," she says.

After the discussion, the executive wanted to set up another meeting with Beard. That following week, they had a three-hour conversation, with Beard asking a lot of questions. Finally, he said, "Do you want to work for me?"

The following Monday, he made her a formal offer. "I was a good fit for the company," Beard says. "It is a Seattle-based company and has sales offices all over the world, but it didn't have any representation on the East Coast."

Beard was hired as implementations and customer support for the software company, working from her Miami home, where she can easily travel to Europe or South America if needed. Although her background is not in software, Beard brings her understanding about customers in the sector from spending 25 years in the field.

Like many workers who have been laid off, Beard had moments of uncertainty. "I occasionally kept dwelling on the whole situation. It really hangs over you. But you've got to let it go and look forward," she says.

Realize that you may not land the same job, but that a different experience, people, and venue can be re-energizing, Beard says. "You have to be open to all possibilities. You've got to be excited about what could happen. Something positive will happen, and there's no way to predict what it will be. You just have to be open to everything," she says.

Transfer Your Skills

Sometimes, you have no choice but to transfer your skills to another industry. In 2007–2009, millions of workers in construction; business and professional services; retail; and banking and finance were displaced from their jobs. When your industry is not expected to recover anytime soon, look at your strengths and technical skills and consider how you could use them in another field, perhaps a related industry.

David Adamson, 45, entered the job market in mid-2008, a time when his home state of Florida already was in a housing crisis and the nation's bank and financial rescue was around the corner. Adamson had 15 years of experience in mortgage banking, but he knew that was a futile pursuit for work. He also had sales and management experience.

So he applied for sales jobs outside the industry. To get a job, Adamson had to convince his interviewer that his people and sales skills transferred easily to the new industry, in this case, selling restaurant cleaning products.

Adamson pointed out how he grew a two-person mortgage business into one with $10 million of annual revenue. His business depended on referrals, which demonstrated his people skills. "Give me an opportunity, and I'll take these people skills to your industry," he told the hiring manager. It took patience, but after three months of interviews, he was offered the job.

In transferring your skills to another industry, it's important to be realistic. Look at who is being hired for the jobs. Sometimes, employers feel comfortable hiring younger people for a job because they fit in with colleagues, work for lower salaries, and are less costly in benefits. Although there are laws against age discrimination, violations of these laws are often difficult to prove.

When Kathy Stein of Fort Lauderdale, Florida, was laid off from a job selling automotive leases, she was in her mid-40s. Stein initially focused on the medical and pharmaceutical industries to transfer her skills, but she soon found she wasn't seen as a good candidate. "Typically a medical rep is 20 to 25 years old, just out of college. It was very eye-opening. I've never been faced with a stereotype. I realized this is something I couldn't do," she says.

But Stein did have success transferring her sales skills to a business that was related to the automotive industry: a GPS tracking company. Though she knew little about the field when she interviewed for the job, she peppered the company president with intelligent questions. She was enthusiastic and engaged, and he soon was introducing her to the CEO.

"We discussed the learning curve," Stein says. Although she didn't know the GPS industry, Stein knew the players in the automotive industry. "The hardest part is getting the right contact information. I already had that: a whole list of contact names and decision makers." She was offered a job the day after her interview.

Combine Your Skills with Your Passion

"Sometimes in the winds of change we find our true direction."
—author unknown

Maria Harkins of Greensboro, North Carolina, uses that quote in her e-mail signature. Harkins, 55, followed the wind by reaching out to friends after losing her job in legal services in October 2009. She told them the job she was seeking, and they sent her information and leads. Ultimately, Harkins found her true direction by applying her legal skills to help women in troubled domestic situations.

Initially, she looked at opportunities at other law firms, but also pursued informational interviews—coffees with people at local nonprofit organizations, hospitals, and other employers she was targeting for work. "I went through somebody I knew. 'Who can I talk with about a job here?'" she says.

The informational interviews were good practice. She always followed up with a handwritten thank-you note, asking if she could call them back occasionally to see if they had any leads.

It was through this networking that she found her job lead. A friend let her know an agency was looking for someone with a legal background who was bilingual, and Harkins is fluent in Spanish. She also speaks a bit of Portuguese and Italian.

In February 2010, she had an interview with Family Service of the Piedmont, a nonprofit organization that helps protect women against domestic violence—a cause about which Harkins is passionate. "Being a parent and a woman, I see what happens, especially to Hispanic women who don't know the law. They're stuck with an abuser, and they don't know what to do," she says.

Although Harkins had no experience as a case worker, the nonprofit organization valued her legal background, and she was hired. She's making more money and getting health benefits, which she didn't have previously. That was especially important to her as the mother of a 19-year-old daughter and a 16-year-old son.

Show Your Versatility

If you don't have years of experience in the industry, show your versatility in the job experience you do have. For Bryan McMahon of Chicago, connecting with friends and emphasizing his diversity of skills helped him land a job.

Fresh out of college, McMahon didn't know a lot about job hunting. But the 23-year-old was lucky at first. He found a job after his May 2009 graduation at an advertising agency in Chicago, exactly what he wanted to do. Then he was laid off in February. "I had been out of school all of seven or eight months. It was surprising, and I didn't know what I was supposed to do or feel," he says.

After talking with his mother, who had gone through a similar experience in her career, he realized that layoffs happen to many people, often at the worst times in their lives. "There was some comfort in having it happen this early in life. I don't have a mortgage. I don't have a wife and two kids. I'm not trying to put a kid through college. I'm learning early how to hit the ground running and overcome it," McMahon says.

His first reaction was to look for another ad agency job in Chicago, and he launched into applying for advertising jobs posted on online job boards. That didn't pan out, so he broadened his search "to get a paycheck until things got better."

For a while, McMahon did whatever he could just to pay the rent: He tried a week of training for a door-to-door sales job selling office supplies to small companies. "It was a horrible job," he says. "It was not even going to big companies, but small businesses with maybe 10 or 20 employees: 'What are you paying for paper? Do you need ink cartridges?'

"Even before that I didn't want to get into sales. This confirmed every fear that I had," says McMahon, who jokes that he gave up watching the TV show *The Office* for a few weeks.

When his friends in marketing had promotional gigs, McMahon helped them out to earn a little money. At a wedding expo, he handed out protein bars to promote a company. "We spent the entire time switching off so we could get cake samples and other fancy desserts. Not a bad way to spend the afternoon," he says.

While fun for a day, handing out samples was not what McMahon wanted to do in his career. But such activities helped him keep in touch with people he knew at his former ad agency and friends in the business. One friend, who had been hired at the outplacement firm Right Management in Chicago, recommended McMahon to her boss for a freelance marketing project. "Why don't you give Bryan a call? Let me get you his resume," she said, taking the initiative to get her friend considered.

When he interviewed for the job, McMahon tried to show his versatility despite his young age: "I was bringing up all the things I had done in school and in previous jobs."

For example, at DePaul University, where he earned his bachelor's degree, McMahon was on the planning board and organized events. He worked in the career center, something that appealed to Right, which works with people in career transition. It also helped, he found, that he knew Microsoft Office Suite and could put together an Excel spreadsheet and create a PowerPoint presentation. He was originally hired for a marketing project but now is working for the firm full-time. "It was the connection and my background," he says.

McMahon, who has been working for Right since July 2009, also has learned a few things about job hunting by this point. Looking back at his job search, he would have focused on networking—not blasting out resumes like he did. "I could have been better with the follow-up, really hammering my name home. I hate to admit how many times I sent out my resume and never followed up," he says. "You're never going to get anything out of that."

Now he tells friends who are looking for jobs, "just keep in touch with people. The whole reason my name was passed along was that I was checking in. Just keep talking with people and putting yourself out there," McMahon says.

Get Out of Your Comfort Zone

Broaden your thinking about the type of work you can do, even if you think you may not be immediately comfortable with it. Sophie Cardona, 39, of Brooklyn, New York, had never considered a sales job in her industry. But she opened herself up to new possibilities when, due to the economy, she lost the job she had been searching for her entire career.

Cardona spent her academic years and early career trying to figure out exactly what she wanted to do. She had graduated from Columbia University's Barnard College in economics and psychology and from Parsons School of Design in Manhattan where she earned a degree in interior design. After working in that field for about seven years, she returned to graduate school at Johns Hopkins University to study economic development and sustainable development.

"I eventually came to the realization I wanted to combine interior design with economic development and green building. All the pieces of the puzzle came together," Cardona says. "Then the economy hit rock bottom."

She found a job as a green consultant in New York, but within months of her employment, the company was on the brink of collapse. She jumped to a contract job that she hoped would lead to full-time work, but it didn't. Back in the job market again, Cardona volunteered for a nonprofit organization that wanted its building to become LEED-certified, the rating for a green building.

"I learned a lot. I was doing it three days a week, which helped me to have structure," Cardona says. "The rest of time I was on my job search. If you're at home every day, it's a little depressing."

Then she found a job posted on SustainLane (www.sustainlane.com), an environmental job board. It was an advertisement for a sales position at an energy services firm in New Jersey. "I had no interest in doing sales, but I applied anyway," Cardona says. "I had nothing to lose."

She was called for an interview at the firm. Her open-minded attitude worked in her favor: "It made me more confident. I said to myself, 'this will be very good practice.'"

When she was asked why she applied, Cardona said although she had never worked in sales, she had been in a consulting role and in communications. "I talked about my background in psychology since selling has to do with convincing people. I weaved in all the things I had done in the past," she says.

Cardona was offered the job in January 2010, and she's enjoying it. The experience has taught her that it's important to "get out of your comfort zone," she says. By being flexible, she opened herself up to a new dynamic. "If I hadn't done that, I probably still would be unemployed, looking for the 'ideal' job," she says.

Consider Your Entrepreneurial Side

Are you meant for the corporate life or are you really an entrepreneur? Are you a person who likes structure and following the rules? Or do you like to make up the rules and tend to go your own way? Perhaps starting your own business is a better option, if you have the financial resources. If not, look for an employer that wants workers who are independent-minded and driven by rewards for generating business.

Alex Popov, 49, found his employment opportunity through LinkedIn, but credits his new mindset with landing him a job. Popov, now living in Boynton Beach, Florida, had worked for big companies in the transportation sector around the country: UPS, Ryder Systems, and Waste Management. But in 2008, he was working for the finance arm of a mortgage company in Fort Lauderdale when the nation's financial crisis took hold.

He had been through corporate restructuring before and knew the economy was bad. So Popov jumped into his job search by connecting with people on LinkedIn. One day he was scrolling through jobs on the site—many listings are exclusive to LinkedIn—and a position called out to him. "There was everything but my name on it," Popov says.

Still, the job would be a huge change from the corporate life: The potential employer was a startup and was asking him to work on 100 percent commission. In weighing the decision, he talked over the job opportunity with a career counselor who confirmed what he already knew deep inside: "You don't want to go back into corporate life. You want to be an entrepreneur." A few years earlier, earning his MBA had given him his first inkling he might be best suited for an entrepreneurial venture.

Popov took the job at Liban, Inc., a fleet management firm based in Rochester, New York, after negotiating a base salary schedule that scales down as his commissions rise. "I'm making less money than I used to, but the upside is greater," he says.

He wouldn't trade it for the corporate ladder. "I like the freedom, the ability to move without looking over my shoulder." What about corporate America? "I don't think I want to go back there."

Stretch Yourself to Think Differently

Do something different—this is your opportunity. After a decade or more in a certain job or career, we start to define ourselves by what we do. Think beyond your last job title or job description. Keep your strengths and skills in mind, but consider using them for a different industry, type of business, or role.

When Paola de Angeli of Miami found herself without a job in November 2009, she stopped to think about where she had been in her career. "What do I do now?" she asked herself, a question many people have been challenged with in the recession.

So she reviewed her career path. Her first job out of college was in the textile industry in South Carolina. She worked for the same company for nine years, eventually working out of Miami. When her employer wanted her to return to South Carolina, she headed back to school for her master's degree, studying energy relations and international policy. De Angeli was hired as an energy consultant, often traveling back to her home country of Brazil, for research. Then oil prices plunged, and she was again looking for a job.

While job hunting, de Angeli took a trip to Rio and bumped into a friend of a friend she had met a few months before during a holiday visit with family. De Angeli, 46, told him she was looking for a new job and they talked about his new venture as distributor of a new green window treatment product from Germany. "I was giving him ideas: 'Have you thought about this and have you thought about that?'"

She also sent him a magazine article about green fabrics. A job wasn't her intention: "He was a really nice guy, and I wanted him to do well," she says.

But soon de Angeli was engaged in a conversation with her new friend and his Washington, D.C., partner about working for the distributor. She's now selling in Miami for the textile distributor, Green America Design Group, a job that combines her work experience with her interest in green products.

De Angeli says she wasn't finding any such jobs on online job boards. It took a personal connection, reaching out to others to let them know she was seeking work, and a different way at looking at work that led her to a new opportunity. "The importance of who you know is huge," says de Angeli as she looks back at the people she has come to know through family and friends.

Stay open to new people and ventures, she advises. "Forget the regular paycheck and do something different from what you've been doing." The positive part of a poor economy is that "more people are stretching themselves," she adds.

Pitch Your Skills to Uncle Sam

Look where the jobs are and how your experience might fit. Every month, the Bureau of Labor Statistics reports new information about the industries adding jobs. Certain industries have been consistent: healthcare, private education, and federal government jobs.

So when Steve Liewer decided it was time to look for a new job, he thought, "What looks good right now?" The answer was federal jobs.

Liewer already had what he considered an ideal job: reporting on the military for a newspaper in San Diego. Liewer had spent six and a half years working for *Stars and Stripes*, the military's newspaper, becoming a war correspondent with tours in Iraq and Afghanistan. "It was hard on my wife, and I was tired of the tempo," Liewer says.

He heard about an opening for a military reporter at the *San Diego Union-Tribune*. "It was a great place to be a reporter. I had the kind of editor you always dream about having," says Liewer, now 49.

But then, like many newspapers across the country, the company cut costs due to shrinking advertising, and there were several rounds of layoffs. In the summer of 2009, the paper was sold to a private equity firm.

"After maybe two years of not being able to sleep nights," he sought advice from mentors who urged him to look around while he was still employed.

Liewer was already perusing USAJOBS (www.usajobs.gov), a site run by the U.S. Office of Personnel Management to list government jobs, when he got an e-mail from an old friend from his *Stars and Stripes* days whom he had connected with on LinkedIn.

"There was a former Army officer who was in public affairs in Germany. We had worked together for a couple of years. We e-mailed once in a while. Last year I was building my LinkedIn network, and I found him and we reconnected," Liewer says.

The officer was involved in creating an advanced media training program and contacted Liewer. "You probably don't want to leave San Diego, but we're creating this position and we'll keep you posted," he wrote in an e-mail to Liewer.

By late summer 2009, Liewer got the heads up from his old friend that the job would be posted in September. Liewer applied and was called for a phone interview. "I figured it was a preliminary interview," he says. "I interviewed on Thursday, and they called me on Monday and offered me the job."

Though his wife was aware of the phone interview, she was in Japan when Liewer got the job offer. After she returned, the couple flew to Leavenworth, Kansas, where the job would be located. They decided Steve should take the position, which was a media training instructor, at comparable pay to what he was making at the newspaper. The only problem was their home in San Diego, which they couldn't sell in the current housing market. So they rented out their home and moved to Kansas, where they were able to buy a house twice as big at half the price of their California home, Liewer says.

Like the Liewers, other successful job candidates and their spouses or partners found that moving from a big-city job market to a smaller town made a significant difference in their cost of living and helped them recover financially from a layoff. But the salaries are often lower, too. (You should also check state and local taxes before considering a major move.)

In February 2009, Liewer began teaching a seminar in advanced media training at the Army Command and General Staff College at Fort Leavenworth. "They told me later they liked that I seemed very down to earth. They already knew they wanted one broadcast person and one print person. The other guy had no military experience, so they liked the fact I had that," he says.

The position also required a master's degree, which Liewer had earned on a special program for journalists at Ohio State University, before joining *Stars and Stripes*.

For others interested in a federal government job, Liewer suggests trying to find someone in the government agency where you want to work to learn more about it. And review USAJOBS without putting limits on what you can do. "You'd be surprised what you're qualified for," he says.

Think Out of the Country

Job seekers usually set out to find a job in a certain geographic area, but keeping an open mind about location can pay off in an interesting opportunity.

George Lambros, 48, had spent time as an ex-pat, working more than three years in Mexico as finance director for a company's subsidiary. His resume includes experience with NCR Corp., Ryder Systems, BAX Global, and Tyco International.

In his last position, he found his responsibilities narrowing as the company went through structural changes. It was time for him to look for a job. Lambros received outplacement services, and his job counselor urged him to launch a broad, geographic search. "Despite repeated suggestions, I confined my search to South Florida," he says.

After working in locations including upstate New York, Ohio, California, and Mexico, Lambros and his family were content living in Weston, Florida, near Fort Lauderdale. "My wife and I felt we'd finally put roots down in one place," he says. So he began his job search by targeting chief financial officer positions with small-to-medium companies in South Florida.

He left his employer in August 2008 when job prospects were still good. Soon after, the global economy screeched to a near halt, beginning with the Lehman Bros. collapse in September. But Lambros had interviewed for a chief financial officer position and had another opportunity in the pipeline as vice president of finance for a large multinational company. He was confident he would land a job by the end of the year—he didn't.

"Two hot opportunities all of a sudden went cold. December and January were tough months. I was doing a lot of coffees and not much was happening," Lambros recalls.

"In early January, I decided that given the state of the economy and the job market, I needed to be open to opportunities outside of South Florida," he says. By March, a manager he had worked with at his previous employer called him with an opportunity in Kuwait.

Though they had been determined to stay in South Florida, Lambros and his wife, Michelle, decided that a move to Kuwait could be a great educational experience for their three sons, ages 6 to 11.

Lambros also adjusted his expectations in terms of the job opportunity, which was a controller position with a multi-industry company based in Kuwait. "I wouldn't have naturally gravitated towards a corporate controller role. Now I realize it will provide me with the experiences that I'll need to advance to a CFO position with a large organization."

He was fortunate that his wife was enthusiastic about the move, despite having to leave her South Florida wine business for others to manage. "Anyone who is married or has a significant other has to make sure both parties are on board," Lambros advises.

Open a New Door: Shanghai Adventure

Adventure-seekers have the world to find a new job. My good friends Howard and Ellen Goodman found themselves faced with a choice: Wait out the U.S. economy and hope for a rebound in the media industry, or sign up for a year in Shanghai, China.

I worked with Howard Goodman for several years at the *Sun Sentinel* newspaper in Fort Lauderdale. He came to the paper with big-city experience, including being a staff writer at the *Philadelphia Inquirer* and Bloomberg in New York City. After serving as an editor and columnist for the *Sun Sentinel*, he was enthusiastic about an opportunity to work on the interactive side, helping reporters develop blogs. But changing times bring changing staff needs, and, despite his varied experience, Goodman was tapped in a layoff in spring of 2009.

Goodman, 60, immediately began reconnecting with the people he knew throughout his journalism career to let them know he was available. But with the economy tanking and advertising shrinking at newspapers, Goodman soon realized he had to stop thinking about working at other publications. He then focused on his new digital media skills and on think-tank and speech-writing job possibilities, but there were many people who already had that experience lined up ahead of him. "They could always find someone who fit their qualifications perfectly," Goodman says.

When job opportunities are scarce in a recession, workers are urged to focus on their job experience, instead of changing careers. But what do you do when work in your field seems to be disappearing? For Goodman, the answer was, "Go abroad."

After making connections with former colleagues, Goodman was suddenly presented with an opportunity to work for the *Shanghai Daily* newspaper. "It was really sheer luck. It was the one time I wasn't looking for it," he says.

In talking with former colleagues, he went all the way back to the 1980s when he first graduated from the University of California at Berkeley and took a job on the copy desk at the *Oregon Statesman*. The editor he had worked for at the time was now retired; he didn't expect him to know about a job opportunity.

But when Goodman told him he was unemployed, the former editor contacted Sue, a reporter that Goodman had worked with at the Oregon paper. Sue had moved on to have a career in Asia, working for the *Wall Street Journal* and Bloomberg News, and was the Western adviser for an English language newspaper in Beijing.

Goodman e-mailed Sue that he was interested in a possible job in Shanghai and was shocked at her quick and confident response. "All right, I'm going to get you in," she told him. "I know the people there, and personal relationships are everything."

"You hear that a lot in the States. It's the cliché of job hunting. But in China, it's really true," Goodman says. "It's the ancient system of *gwangi* or 'who you know.'" His friend Sue talked with the editor at the *Shanghai Daily* who told her, "Yes, I could use him right away."

"That was before I had sent off a resume, and she was letting me know I was hired!" he says. Goodman did finally submit his resume and received a note from his future editor: "We at the *Shanghai Daily* should thank the economic situation in the United States for being able to send us journalists of your caliber."

"It was so nice," Goodman says. Still, with his wife Ellen's real estate business and a house in South Florida, he wasn't convinced he should pick up and move to China. "I didn't think she would want to leave that and our grandkids. But she said, 'not so fast, you know I have always wanted to live abroad.'" Ellen soon made arrangements to turn her business over to her partner.

Goodman committed to work at the *Shanghai Daily* for a year, editing Chinese reporters' copy into understandable English. Meanwhile, he and Ellen are fascinated with the culture and the excitement of Shanghai's booming climate. They're writing a blog, *Shanghai'd: Our year in China,* to keep friends updated on their adventure.

After Goodman started working at the Shanghai newspaper, his son Ben was offered an internship at the *Daily*. A Florida college student, Ben had been studying Mandarin long before moving to Shanghai was even a thought for his parents. "In our case the *gwangi* system is working tremendously," Goodman says.

"There are days I just thank the *Sun Sentinel* for laying me off. Walking down the street and seeing people on bicycles and selling steamed rolls on the street—so many exotic things, and none of this would have happened," he says.

Streetwise Strategies for Thinking Out of the Box

- Think how you can be a solution to an employer's problem.

- Look for businesses that are expanding nationally and internationally—perhaps they need a representative in your geographic area.

- Combine your talents with your passion.

- Transfer your skills to another industry. Consider employers that are related to the one you left.

- Do contract work; it could lead to a permanent job or put you in touch with an important job contact.

- Consider whether you're more suited for an entrepreneurial position.

- Open yourself to potential work outside your comfort zone.

- Explore a federal government job.

- Consider opportunities outside the country.

CHAPTER 7

SNAG THE INTERVIEW AND THE OFFER

Job seekers often tell me they have

- Lots of job interviews, but never seem to get the job.

- No interviews and they can't understand why—after all, they're perfect for the job.

- Two or more interviews for a job, but always come in second place.

What's the magic formula for attracting an employer's attention, getting an interview, and becoming the winning candidate? Job seekers say you have to stand out from the crowd, understand what the employer is really seeking, practice potential interview questions, look sharp for the big day, provide solutions to the employer, and create a connection with the interviewer. This chapter shows how some job hunters got that crucial interview and made sure they were the ones left standing.

Get Noticed by Your Target Employer

Do you feel like your resume goes into a black hole? You e-mail your resume or apply online and you never hear from the potential employer. How do you get it into a human being's hands?

One strategy is to dress in your best interview suit and hand-deliver your resume to an employment prospect you've targeted. Adam Rees, 25, wasn't in a suit but he dressed nicely to find a job as a personal trainer: "Decent shoes, leather; a pair of jeans; and blue buttoned shirt. I took my earrings out. I looked very classic and clean, but not preppy and over the top," he says.

Rees, a former football player who had just graduated from college, followed a girl to Minneapolis and he needed a job—fast. So he found the locations of all the fitness centers in the region through a search engine and went to them.

"Who is your top personal trainer? Who is your department manager?" he would ask at each fitness center, handing his resume to the receptionist. "This is me," Rees would say, pointing to his resume. "And I'd like a job."

Every time, the tactic got him talking with someone who was in a hiring position. Showing up in person instead of e-mailing a resume made a huge difference, Rees says. "They saw my face, shook my hand. I'm 6'4" and 230 pounds. I look like an athlete." In person, interviewers also could see that he is well-spoken.

Rees didn't even have experience being a personal trainer. Still, he was hired at a fitness center he visited in Minneapolis, worked there for a year, and then returned home to Iowa City, Iowa, where he used the same strategy to find another job. This time, Rees only had to visit one fitness center to get hired. He has been working there as a performance trainer for high school athletes since March 2009.

Mary White-Cornell, 51, of Seattle used a similar tactic. She had recently moved to Seattle from Denver, not expecting it to be difficult to find a job. White-Cornell had once operated a restaurant and had 15 years of experience in marketing local restaurants.

But the months were ticking by after her move and an opportunity wasn't presenting itself. "After a couple of months of sending out a lot of resumes and not one response from anybody, I thought, 'Maybe, I'd better change my approach.' I had to find a way to separate myself from the pack, instead of waiting for a job to be posted," White-Cornell says.

She started contacting people through LinkedIn and asked to meet them for a cup of coffee to learn more about Seattle's restaurant industry. It worked about 50 percent of the time, but still she wasn't getting interviews. She kept at it, trying to build her network. "If I found an interesting article or something they would enjoy, I would send it—so I was contributing to them as well," White-Cornell says.

Then one day, White-Cornell saw an ad on Craigslist for a local restaurant marketing position. "Here was this perfect job. I wanted to work for this company," she says.

She knew someone through LinkedIn who once worked for her target employer. He introduced her via e-mail to people he still knew at the business and coached her about talking with management and on potential interview questions. "That gave me the confidence to go in there," White-Cornell says.

White-Cornell understood by now that she was up against stiff competition for a job, and she was determined not to lose this one. So instead of waiting for an interview, she put together a gift basket with her resume attached, and arrived at the company's office in the early morning. She asked for the hiring manager, who came out to meet her, and she introduced herself, giving her 30-second elevator speech and handing him the basket.

The theme of the basket was "everything you need to market your restaurant," she says. It contained a light bulb, symbolizing bright ideas; a heart, illustrating the desire to build sales; a wind-up monkey clanging cymbals for "never-ending enthusiasm," a ruler to measure results, and duct tape "to fix anything." It was an attention-getter, but the gimmick also illustrated that she knows what it takes to run a successful restaurant marketing campaign.

White-Cornell didn't hear from the company right away and thought she had blown it. But, about a week later, she was called for an interview. She was hired and started her new job in November 2009. "The lesson is to be tenacious. You have to do something different from everybody else," she says.

Stress Your Social Media Know-How

Social media is something many small-to-medium-sized companies do not yet understand. If you've had experience using Twitter or Facebook, that can give you the edge in an interview or even get you the job.

Jessica Schmidt-Bonifant, 26, knew she wanted to continue working in the nonprofit sector after she decided it was time to leave her Baltimore employer of two and a half years. So she posted her resume and looked for jobs on industry sites specifically for her profession: Maryland's Association of Nonprofits website, the Association of Fundraising Executives, and Idealist (www.Idealist.org).

Schmidt-Bonifant applied for a job posting for a business development director at a student scholarship organization in Baltimore and was called in for an interview. In interviewing for the job, she focused on the solutions she could provide the employer, such as enhancing the organization's visibility through social media. Schmidt-Bonifant suggested using Facebook and Twitter to connect donors as well as students.

Beyond social media skills, Schmidt-Bonifant had the traditional background the association sought. Fund-raising is important to a nonprofit, so she detailed her quantifiable results: percentage increases over time for campaigns she previously managed.

Social media may not be your bailiwick, but consider what other cutting-edge skill you could bring to the table. That's what could make you stand out among equally qualified applicants.

Prepare for Interviews like an Exam

You can't prepare too much for a job interview. Spend the time doing research and practicing interview questions. It will make you feel comfortable and more confident in the interview simply knowing you've done your homework and are ready to answer questions.

Dane Lyons, 39, approached his job interviews like he was studying for the bar exam. Lyons, a software engineer, used the Internet to find the likely questions he would be asked by his interviewers.

"Take those questions and make sure you have the answers. Copy them to a place where you can refer to them again and again. After you've got a bank of questions prepared, take the questions and answer them out loud. Speak them as if you were on the interview," Lyons recommends.

For general interview questions, Lyons searched in Google for "basic interview questions" and "first interview questions" to come up with samples. For technical interview questions, he searched for "C# interview questions," "SQL Server interview questions," "ASP.NET interview questions," and "WCF or WPF interview questions," all referring to technology in which he has experience.

"You can refine it a little by adding more keywords, technology versions, dates, and years. For instance: '.NET Framework 3.5 interview questions most asked in 2009,'" Lyons says. "You have to use your knowledge about whatever profession you're in to get the questions that you'll be asked."

Then practice your answers. Particularly when answering technical questions, it's important to practice so you don't fumble under pressure, Lyons says. "Explaining it and knowing it are two different things," he says. The ability to communicate what you know "is the difference between getting a job and sitting home."

For any industry, a typical interview question is "What do you need to improve?" Prepare an innocuous answer, such as "I'm not a morning person, so I have to work at being energized. Exercise helps." Lyons says interviewers are looking for an answer about how you've addressed a weakness.

Know enough about the company to be able to have more than a rudimentary conversation, he says. "Everything's available online. You've got no excuses."

Before an interview, Lyons would work for hours figuring out what he would say when asked a certain question. "Have a plan so you can lead the conversation to things that make you look good," he says. "You can't dictate the interview to them, but you can influence them."

Take a Plant or Office Tour

If it is not offered, ask for a tour of the workplace before or during your interview. You can gather clues about the operation, people, and culture that could be useful.

When John Rives, 44, interviewed for a quality manager job at a manufacturer, it was the plant tour that gave him the opportunity to gather information and present potential solutions to the hiring manager.

"If you have the opportunity, do that first. Make as many observations as you can so you can really directly tell managers how you can fix their problems for them," Rives says.

Rives had no doubt he had the technical background for the job: He has a master's degree in ceramics engineering. In his interview, he was able to draw parallels between the processes at the plant and those at a previous employer in Pittsburgh.

He also stressed how he is a "hands-on" floor manager who communicates with workers. "It's important how you get along with people in the plant because you're going to be with them every day," Rives says.

"I have the knowledge, the energy, and the experience. And I don't mind getting my hands dirty," he told his interviewer at the manufacturing plant near Columbus, Ohio.

Rives demonstrated confidence, presented solutions, and expressed enthusiasm for the job. He was offered the quality manager position in March 2010, within a couple weeks of his interview.

Demonstrate How Your Personality Is a Good Fit

Some companies use personality tests or include interview questions to find out whether you are a good fit for the job and with the culture of the organization. Personality tests can be challenging because you may be tempted to answer questions based on what you think the potential employer wants to hear. It's best to be true to yourself, however, because your goal isn't only to get a job but to find a job that works for you.

Also be aware that a test's purpose may not be what it seems, says Patricia Martinez of Boca Raton, Florida, who had that experience in her job search. Martinez, 50, was making a switch from retail sales to financial investment sales in 2009. She navigated several types of tests designed to see whether she could sell.

Martinez took four written personality tests in the course of interviewing with several financial services companies. Questions on the tests were along the lines of the following:

- "If you were at a party, would you introduce yourself to someone?"

- "Would you feel comfortable in a mansion?"

- "Could you sell a product to someone you don't like?"

At two potential employers, she was given the same assessment test. The second time she took the test, she was told it revealed something about her that "could be interpreted as negative." That turned out not to be true, the interviewer later admitted.

"That wasn't what the test showed, but they used the test to see how I responded to feedback," Martinez says. Responding with curiosity, instead of anger or dismay, seemed to work in her favor.

Another potential employer gave her a test where she was asked to pick out a certain number of words from a long list. She chose words that were "nonthreatening but assertive." The point of that test also was to test her reaction.

Martinez says she was simply honest in her answers on the test. In October 2009, she was hired by as a financial investment representative, has earned certifications in financial planning, and now is well on her way to building her client base.

Look Local, Even If You're from Out of Town

When applying for a job long distance, it can be helpful to appear to be local or at least to show knowledge of the geographic area where you are seeking a job. A company may be considering only local candidates because it is not providing relocation. If you're prepared to relocate at your own expense, you don't want to be eliminated before you're really considered for the position.

Michael Ni, 27, of Hawaii wanted to work in San Francisco. So he borrowed a friend's address for his resume and job applications so that his Hawaii residence wouldn't be an obstacle. But in interviews, he was upfront with employers that he was trying to relocate from Hawaii.

Ni, who was looking for a public relations job in the restaurant or hospitality industry, also became familiar with the restaurants in San Francisco. Ni is a self-described "foodie" who enjoys cooking Japanese and Thai dishes. For his research, Ni regularly read the *San Francisco Chronicle* online and browsed industry and regional publications including *7x7 Magazine, San Francisco Magazine,* and "Urban Daddy," an online newsletter.

While still working at a public relations job in Hawaii in August 2009, he called potential employers seeking informational interviews: "Hey, I'll be in town. Can I stop in?" Ni also prepared by saving money for his move because he knew it wasn't likely in the current economy that any employer would relocate him from Hawaii.

When he landed an interview with Andrew Freeman & Co., which specializes in restaurant public relations, he showed his enthusiasm by being persistent and involved. The firm was hosting a webinar about restaurant trends and Ni joined the call and e-mailed his feedback. The agency asked Ni to produce a sample public relations plan for a client. "I did it in less than a week to show them I'm on board," he says.

After each interview, he e-mailed participants thank-you notes. If he didn't hear from an employer after an interview, he called to check in. "I think persistence is key in this day and age," says Ni, who was offered an account manager position at Andrew Freeman & Co. in November 2009, after about six weeks of follow-ups.

Watch Your Interview Etiquette

Dressing well for an interview shouldn't have to be said, but it does. Jeans, shirts flopping outside pants, or shorts are not acceptable dress for an interview. Expenses may be tight, but there are ways around that, as well. Borrow a jacket from a friend or go to Goodwill or Dress for Success, an organization that helps outfit women in transition for interviews and even initial employment.

Even if the dress at your potential workplace is casual business, you always want to be dressed a bit better for the interview. That says you care what the interviewers think about you and that you want the job.

Dane Lyons, the software engineer, wore a suit to his interview. His interviewer was wearing shorts. "Technical people don't always wear suits. I came wearing a suit and a tie," he says. "They're expecting technical people to walk in business casual." But Lyons, 39, donned his suit because he was trying to make a good first impression. "Get your hair cut, shine your shoes," he says. At the same time, he let his interviewer-in-shorts know that he liked business casual for everyday wear. "Hopefully, this is the last time you'll ever see me in a suit," Lyons told him.

When former mortgage banker David Adamson dressed for an interview, he wore a double-breasted suit and tie. That was even when he was applying to drive a pesticide truck.

Adamson says it doesn't matter what job you're applying for: Err on the side of overdressing for an interview. "I've been to so many interviews with other people dressed in khakis and a polo shirt," he says. "When [hiring managers] look into a room of applicants, and one is in a suit, he stands out."

Women should wear a suit with a skirt or pants or a dress with a tailored jacket, and low heels. In northern states, hose for women is protocol, but most women simply don't wear them in humid Florida. Consider the environment and office culture, but remember you always feel more confident when you look your best.

You may also want to videotape yourself, or ask a friend to tape you, while you practice answering interview questions. Facial expressions and body language communicate as loudly as what you say in an interview. Be careful not to slump in your seat. Instead, lean forward a bit to indicate your interest in what the interviewer is saying or asking.

More interview tips:

- Get to the interview in plenty of time to feel relaxed and not rushed.

- Turn off your cell phone so you are not interrupted.

- Be prepared with extra resumes to hand out in case you are interviewed by more than one person.

- Be nice to everyone in the office, from the receptionist to anyone else you may come across.

You also should carry a portfolio of extra materials to use in the interview as evidence of your brilliant strategy or solution to a problem for a former employer. Lyons calls this portfolio his "brag book." It contains information on special projects, highlighting financial results, with a few charts thrown in for appearance. "Toward the end of an interview or whenever I feel there's a shot, I say 'here's more detail about what I've done,'" Lyons says. "If it's appropriate, I'll open it up while in discussion and say, 'This is the project that replies to your question.'"

Negotiate the Job Description

Who says a job has to be exactly as written? Bring your strengths and creativity to an opportunity like Natalie Silva did.

Silva, a public relations professional in San Antonio, Texas, spends about $25 on each portfolio she creates of her work, updating it for each job she has had. She leaves the portfolio with the potential employer, never asking for it back, despite the expense. "I consider it an investment," says Silva, 36, now media and community relations manager for Whataburger, a family-owned hamburger restaurant chain based in Texas.

Her portfolio includes sections for each job with writing samples and results of media campaigns, speeches she has written for executives, and community brochures. She uses a printing store to add color and a professional-looking cover.

Silva got her foot in the door for a job at Whataburger as a consultant. She had left her job at a petroleum company in early 2008 to start her own public relations firm. For six months, the business was going well—and then the economy hit the skids. "I got to the point where I was in a panic. I was terrified because we were in the middle of the recession," she says.

She knew that Whataburger was moving to San Antonio from Houston, so she called to offer her public relations services in the transition. The group director for communications asked her if she knew anyone for either of the two lower-level internal public relations jobs she needed to fill.

"I was overqualified for the jobs," Silva says, adding that neither one paid enough. So she made a proposal to combine the two jobs: "Spend the same amount and hire me," was her reasoning. Whataburger did, and as a result, Silva says, the company got her wealth of public relations' experience in one job.

Before starting her own business, Silva had worked in public relations for Tesoro Corp., a petroleum company, and was an account supervisor at Fleishman-Hillard. Despite her experience, Silva tried to avoid acting like a know-it-all during her interview. "I approached it in a collaborative way," she says.

Silva later asked her boss what it was that prompted her to hire her. "You had the guts to call me and then had the foresight to say, 'Let's look at what you're offering and position it this way so it would work for me,'" her boss told her.

Be Likeable: Master Small Talk

Your social skills come into play during an interview. An employer wants to know how you'll fit in with the team. So be friendly and interested in the people and environment around you.

After earning his MBA, Rodrigo Garrido's goal was to get to the next level in his profession as an accountant. But he also was realistic about South Florida's challenging job market. So he focused on his strengths and his experience and touted that in his job search.

Garrido, 34, says he was hired for two reasons: He was a good fit for the work, and he hit it off with the managers at his new employer. He had been an accountant for construction projects for a local retailer, and that type of experience was exactly what his new employer was seeking.

His interviewer—now his boss—was responding well to what he was saying in the interview. He asked about Garrido's typical day at his former job and began nodding his head as Garrido filled him in. "In those couple of minutes, you have to be able to communicate with that person," he says.

He soon realized that he and the hiring manager had similar personalities. They both liked to crack jokes. "I was just being myself," Garrido says. Although you don't want to pretend to be something you're not, pick up on any interests you may connect on. Remember the manager is selecting someone he or she can work with for up to 10 hours a day, Garrido says.

Garrido saw the fishing pictures on his future boss's wall and recounted how he fished with his father. Soon they were talking about snook, boats, and trips to Costa Rica. "You've got to be able to talk with interviewers," he says.

Scott Nemeth, 39, also had clues on how to relate in his interview, literally in front of him on an office wall.

When Nemeth was laid off from his job in Detroit, he and his wife decided to move to Columbus, Ohio, to be near family. His wife grew up in an Ohio family that breeds horses to become trotters and pacers at the racetrack. "My wife's dad is sixth generation," Nemeth says.

So when he walked into his interview with a senior vice president at an insurance firm, he knew just how to connect with his interviewer. "That person had horse pictures all over his wall!" Nemeth says. Although it was his experience in workforce planning that ultimately got Nemeth the job, being able to talk about horses "didn't hurt," he says.

When Kurt Porceng, 42, interviewed for a financial controller position at a Fort Lauderdale asphalt company, he had two interviews at the office. But the final interview was a dinner at his employer's home. In a small or family firm, it can be particularly important to be regarded as someone who fits into the company culture.

"It was very easy-going—a normal Sunday night family dinner," says Porceng, who was invited to the dinner with his wife. The business owner's wife, mother-in-law, and four children were there, as well as the company's vice president of operations.

"They were trying to get a feel from me—how I would react under a looser situation," he says. Afterwards, the business owner asked him to step into his home office, and Porceng knew he had passed the test. "I gave my wife a wink," he recalls. He was offered the job that evening and has been with the company since February 2009.

Still, although you want to be personable, avoid getting too personal in an interview situation. David Adamson, who made his initial job connection at a birthday party his child was attending, ended up interviewing with a neighbor.

So it might have seemed natural to say, "How is your kid doing in the new school?" But an interview is not a social situation, Adamson reminds job seekers. "Keep it professional."

Push Back a Little

Don't agree with everything an interviewer suggests. By pushing back a bit, some job seekers found that they made an impression. The strategy also helped them determine whether the job was a good fit.

When human resources executive Pauline Wilcox interviewed for her job at Catalyst Direct in Rochester, New York, she had the dream setup. The professional in the position knew her through an HR networking group and recommended her for the job.

Still, it was up to Wilcox, 56, to land the job. "You never want to come across as sounding desperate. There's got to be a level of confidence in yourself without being cocky. In this case, I was really genuine. I was confident in things I truly knew about, and I questioned some things," she says.

Wilcox even went so far as to tell the owners, "If this line of questioning doesn't work for you, I'm probably not the right person for the job." At the time, Wilcox was questioning the company's use of job descriptions. "I was pushing back on it a bit. We laugh about that today. I didn't even have the job and I'm pushing back," she says.

By asking such questions, Wilcox learned whether the employer was right for *her*. "If it doesn't feel like a good fit, there will be a level of discomfort," she says.

You may need to shift your approach in a new job, but if the movement is too far afield of your values or style, it may not be the right job for you. Some people find themselves leaving a job quickly "because they haven't done their homework or listened to their gut," she says.

Present Yourself as You Are

Greg Siegelman, 52, also was brutally honest in interviews. He suggests job seekers go on any interview to get practice, even if the job isn't right. And don't overanalyze your presentation, says Siegelman, who found a job as marketing director with a high-tech firm in Dayton, Ohio. "That's what hamstrings people," he says. "I did that to myself."

His motto became, "it is what it is." If an employer didn't like him, then he probably wasn't the right choice, Siegelman decided.

"It's important to really know the position you want. I wasn't going to settle for a manager position. I was willing to wait for a director, vice president, or chief marketing officer position."

The price was a long time out of work: He was laid off from a job in Rochester, New York, in February 2009, and didn't find what he was looking for until spring 2010.

"There has to be a level of patience. I've known people who have jumped on jobs and four months later, they're out looking again," he says.

Fortunately, Siegelman and his family had always lived frugally, so he was prepared financially for a long time out of work. "I don't have any credit card debt. I pay cash for everything except for the house. I always try to live below my means," he says.

His goal was to take the right job, even if he had to move from Rochester, New York, where he and his wife have family.

"My wife was very positive. The only comment was, 'Maybe you're trying for too high a position.' She never got on my case. She said, 'I know you have to go where there's a job.' It's really important that you've got that support from your friends and family," Siegelman says.

So in his interview for the Dayton job, Siegelman says he was straightforward in answering questions about how he would approach his job. "The president debated me on a couple of answers," he says. "He liked the fact that I had a different point of view than he did, but that I could rationally explain my answers."

He got the job and the marketing director position he wanted. "Some people would say I was lucky, but I worked the process. I was disciplined," he says.

Interview the Interviewer

Typically, the interviewer asks the job candidate questions. But Denise Williams, 57, of Bronx, New York, an organizational development trainer who often does interviews herself, had the tables turned on her in a job interview. She was told to ask the questions, and it enabled her to direct the interview, presenting herself as the best candidate for the job.

The recession's impact on jobs was nothing new to Williams. As an organizational development specialist and trainer, she has been through layoffs four times since 1992.

"One door closes, another one opens. Training is one of the first departments to get hit. I've had family members tell me, 'You need to get in another profession.' But I really love it," Williams says.

Williams was never unemployed for long and added new credentials to her resume. But in 2008, she quit a job for what she thought was a better opportunity and was laid off after just 15 weeks. It was October 2008, the height of the financial meltdown. This time Williams searched for five months before finding work in her field.

"You have to keep going even when you don't feel like it," Williams says. "You try to keep a routine for yourself. Get up in the morning like you're going to work. It may feel like an exercise in futility, but it really keeps you going."

Williams spotted her opportunity on an industry organization website in February 2009, and she knew there would be a lot of competition. She immediately applied for the job, a training position, through the American Society for Training & Development, as well as Monster—just to make sure her resume arrived.

She scoured the company's website for information to be prepared with knowledge about the organization for the interview. But when she interviewed at the company, the hiring manager turned the tables on her.

"He said, 'I want you to interview me.' I asked him what type of person he was looking for and what type of skills," Williams says. By listening to what he described, Williams was able to share her applicable experiences, such as creating interactive training classes and training different levels of managers. "I was able to say to him, 'It sounds like you need someone who can hit the ground running. I can do that,'" she says.

As a trainer, Williams teaches behavioral interviewing skills. "I do believe the past is a good indicator of performance," she says.

Be prepared for behavioral interview questions, ready to draw on your experience. They may include: "How did you handle a difficult situation? What was the outcome?" Or the typical question, "What are your strengths and weaknesses?" Williams says to pick a weakness that you've addressed, such as, "I wish I had more knowledge of how to use Excel in my work, so I took a class and now I'm using the program to track my training programs."

Williams was hired for the job in April 2009 and had just celebrated her anniversary when I interviewed her. She has never been happier. "I'm being allowed to spread my wings and be creative. I love the people," she says.

Understand What the Job Entails

It sounds simple: Read the job description or talk with the hiring manager, and you get the gist of what the job is all about. But some people have found that the job they apply for isn't what they anticipated. And, often, they find that out too late.

Kristen Binder, 35, had a job that unexpectedly became more of a marketing position than business development, which is her forte. So when she went looking for a job again, Binder made sure she had an understanding of the expected responsibilities for the job, a business development position in Chicago for a national architecture and engineering firm.

Here are some of the questions she asked in her interview, which could be adapted to any job:

- What do you expect my typical day or week to include?

- How much time would I spend in the office as opposed to out?

- At what point in the business development process would you expect to be brought in?

As a result, Binder says she had a better understanding of the expectations for this job than her previous one.

Ask for the Job

Sometimes, job candidates forget to show that they really want a job. Act too blasé and you might give the impression that you are not fully engaged by the job.

Ruth Balsam had worked in accounting for 30 years when her employer closed its doors and she was let go in June 2009. At age 75, Balsam still wanted and needed to work. "I was terrified. My stocks had gone into the garbage," says Balsam, who had long been a self-supporting, independent woman.

She worked temporarily for a firm, but it was not a place she felt comfortable. So she started looking at listings on Craigslist.

Balsam answered an ad for a TV production company in Boca Raton, Florida, and was brought in for an interview. She immediately liked the atmosphere. "I just wanted to go to a job with happy people. They were young and exciting."

There was the typical concern of her being "overqualified," but Balsam dismissed it with her upbeat attitude: "Yes, I probably am, but I still would very much like to work here."

As her boss-to-be took her around the office to introduce her, Balsam would shake hands and say, "I'm trying to get a job here, and I hope I get it." Balsam reasoned that if she didn't stand out during her interview, she would be passed over. "If I had just gone in and answered questions, I would have just been someone else applying for the job."

Recognizing that mostly younger people worked at the company, Balsam was upfront about her age. "I put it right on the table. I'm bringing to them years of experience and a work ethic they won't get from a younger crowd."

Know What *Not* to Do on an Interview

For those who have gone on one interview after another, only not to get an offer, starting over again can be frustrating and difficult. But it's important not to take this process personally. It may feel good to vent your hurt or angry feelings, but you never know who is connected with whom in your industry, and it could come back to haunt you.

New Jersey sales professional Nancy Sickles shares her story of blowing any chance she might have had with a certain employer. When Sickles was passed over for a job in favor of another candidate, she called the hiring manager: "I wonder if you could give me feedback as to why you didn't select me?" The hiring manager mentioned being impressed that the other candidate had called the company's customers and done some "unofficial" selling.

Sickles, 46, pressed forward: "I would still really like to work with your company." When a new job opened up, she did get another interview, but it was clear to her from the outset that she wasn't being seriously considered. Instead of interviewing with the hiring manager, she was being asked questions by a newly promoted manager.

One question the interviewer asked her was, "What gets you out of bed in the morning?" Sickles was feeling frustrated with the situation, so she replied with a sassy, "I have a three year old."

On the way out the door, she stopped to see the hiring manager. "I was disappointed that when it was down to one or two candidates that you didn't call me to let me know I wasn't selected. I would appreciate a phone call from you if you decide not to proceed with me," she told him.

Sickles didn't get the job—big surprise. But after months of applying for jobs and rarely hearing back, she didn't particularly regret her outburst. "It felt very good. In hindsight, was it the smartest thing to do? Of course not, I burned a bridge," she said.

Fortunately, another employer appreciated Sickles' selling experience and assertiveness and hired her soon afterward.

Unfortunately, there is no guarantee that you're going to be treated as you think you should be during the job interview process. But always take the high road. If you feel yourself getting angry, take a deep yoga breath, excuse yourself to go to the restroom, and collect yourself. In the end, you may decide the job or workplace isn't for you. But never say or do anything that would immediately take you out of the running for the job at hand, or one in the future.

Get a Little Help from Your Friends

Ask your friends to help you prepare and become better at interviews. They can be honest with you without, hopefully, hurting your self-esteem. It can help you see how you're perceived and improve your presentation.

Lisa Viale, 47, had no trouble getting interviews. With a background in technology and finance and a sharp resume, Viale was getting plenty of calls. But she would never get past the first interview and she didn't know why.

Viale turned to one of her best friends, Beth, who was a presentation coach. Beth videotaped her answering typical interview questions.

"I always looked to the right when answering a question," Viale says. "It made it seem like I was making it up." Beth also told her to avoid fidgeting in order to come across as confident and capable.

Viale also needed help communicating her message. She had been at her previous technology job for 12 years and was comfortable talking with her coworkers. But in an interview, she felt under pressure. "It's very personal. You're trying to tell people you're good at your job."

With the help of her friend, she came up with 8-second, 30-second, and 2-minute "elevator" speeches—a quick memorable introduction in the time it might take to ride an elevator.

"I am an IT professional who is first and foremost dedicated to problem solving for the customer," is an example of her 8-second statement. She then expanded on that, sharing a story about what was important to customers in the business and how she rose to the challenge.

She also created a "values statement," which is a guideline for that perennial interview question, "Tell me a little bit about yourself." The values statement details her philosophy about understanding a customer's business before she can solve its problems.

Viale also gives examples about how she goes the extra mile to solve problems when a request went beyond her IT duties. "People know they can come to me and their problem will be resolved," she would tell the hiring manager.

Everywhere Viale went, she asked friends to drill her with interview questions until she felt more comfortable.

Viale sought friends' help because she had a bad first interview experience after being laid off in February 2009. She was asked a simple technology question, and she froze. "This internal clock is ticking in my head: Say something, say anything." She didn't get the job, but she learned from the experience.

Besides reworking her presentation style, Viale went to the new chief technology officer of her former employer and asked for his help. "You're hiring all these people. Would you look at my resume and compare it to what you're seeing?" she asked the CTO. He did, telling her she needed to better quantify her work on her resume. Ask yourself, he says, "How did it help them? How do you put numbers behind that?"

He advised her to bring samples of her work, so she put together reports she had done with talking points and diagrams that showed the impact of her work. Showing her work made her feel more comfortable, so she was more natural in her presentation.

Viale also learned how to stay on message. "I watch politicians, and no matter what you ask them, they answer the question they want to answer. They have a message, and they don't want to get distracted. They want to get to the point."

It's the same with a job interview, she says. You want to keep coming back to your message so that the interviewer knows, "If you hire me, this is what you're going to get," Viale says.

Then in August, a recruiter called her out of the blue—she had put in her resume with several recruiters back in February. The recruiter wanted to talk with her about a job at the same company she had interviewed with in February.

"If you get me back in there, I'm very confident, and I'll be much better at interviewing," she told the recruiter. And the second interview did go much, much better. She was prepared: Viale knew the company and she had her message ready and her samples to illustrate what she knew.

Viale interviewed for the job on a Monday, and by Saturday she had an offer. By reaching out to her former colleagues and friends, she improved her job hunting techniques. And because she had their support, Viale wasn't about to let them down. "Once they help you, they feel invested in you," she says.

Streetwise Strategies for Interviewing

- Hand-deliver your resume to get it noticed.

- Consider what cutting-edge skills, such as social media, could make you stand out from other candidates.

- Prepare for the interview like you would for an exam. Start by searching for typical and industry interview questions on the Internet.

- Look local when applying, even when you're not from the area.

- Dress in your best suit for the interview. If applying at a business casual workplace, still dress a bit better than the staff.

- Negotiate the job description to better suit you and the company.

- Make sure the job is right for you as well as you being right for the job.

- Ask for the job. Be enthusiastic and tell your interviewers you really want the job, without sounding desperate.

- Practice your interview answers out loud and with friends.

- Videotape yourself to check your interview presence.

- Stay on message like a politician would.

CHAPTER 8

PICK YOURSELF UP, AGAIN AND AGAIN

Just when you think you've found the right job, circumstances can change: the job is not what you were told, the company does more restructuring and you're let go, or you find you can't work for the supervisor to whom you've been assigned. There may be nothing harder to face than another job search after you've been through financial upheaval and a long struggle to find a job. How do you remotivate yourself and move on?

Job seekers I interviewed who were faced with this extra challenge suddenly had a sharper picture of what they wanted in life and in work. And that was to their benefit in finding a new job.

Know the Job You Want

Although you have to market yourself for a job, don't lose sight of what you want in the process. Before healthcare executive Mary Pastick accepted her new job, she made certain her role was clearly defined.

Pastick never thought she'd have trouble finding a job. Her three-page resume lists top positions at major hospitals and healthcare companies. Her previous job was director of internal medicine for a South Florida hospital, where she was hired to start a residency program. But after six months, her job abruptly ended when an agreement couldn't be reached on implementing the program.

The timing for her departure couldn't have been worse. It was late 2008, and the U.S. economy was in a tailspin. As a result, it took her a year to find a new job. "I now would count to 10 before I would say, 'I'm done' and think of the circumstances as well," says Pastick, 56.

She immediately contacted people she knew in healthcare across the country about potential job openings. "These were connections I had had for years and years, and they would say to me, 'I'll see what I can do.' But nobody was hiring at an intermediate level, and I didn't want to move out of Florida."

Pastick got a few leads, but kept hearing from potential employers that she was "overqualified." Once earning a six-figure salary, she found herself in danger of losing the home she had owned for 17 years.

Her fortunes turned when she saw a job posted on CareerBuilder. It was for a chief operating officer position for Eye Physicians of Florida, a group of doctors in Sunrise, Florida. It was immediately clear to her that she was the perfect fit for the job. "I think it was the right place and right time," Pastick says. "My skill set was exactly what they wanted." She had an interview within two weeks of applying and an offer within another two weeks, starting work in December 2009.

But after her last position took its unexpected turn, Pastick wanted to make sure she would be allowed to do the job she was hired to do. When the physicians' group made her an offer, she was upfront. "Here's the deal if you want me to come work with you: You need not tell me how to run the business, and I won't tell you how to practice medicine."

The doctors had no problem with that, and because she was transparent about her own requirements, Pastick made a better job choice as well. In her first board meeting after being hired, "I had two rounds of applause," she says. "They told me that in six weeks I had done more than my two previous predecessors."

Learn from Each Job Experience

Sometimes, an organization makes changes, and you're not part of the new plan. Then it's time to review your strengths, consider what's important to you, and develop a new plan on how to achieve it.

Alvaro Ruiz, 41, spied an opportunity to change his hectic travel schedule at a Chicago-area company where he had worked for two years. Ruiz had been traveling heavily, and he missed his wife Lori and his three daughters, ages 5 to 13. "I was a road warrior. I would only see my family on Saturday or Sunday," he says.

So when a job opened in marketing at his firm, he moved to that department to reduce his travel. But then there was some restructuring, and Ruiz found himself out of a job.

Unfortunately, he hadn't seen it coming, and the Ruizes had purchased property to build a home near his then-job. They had to sell the property at a loss and trim family expenses as well.

Ruiz says he has learned from the experience to pay closer attention to the political situation at work. At his former employer, he was assigned to a new supervisor, someone he often disagreed with on work issues. When the supervisor needed to make some cuts, Ruiz was an easy target.

He also realized that in searching for a new job he should better define what he was seeking. Ruiz wanted to be recognized for his achievements and spend more time with his family.

He spent time trading job leads with former colleagues and Kevin, a soccer dad from his daughter's team. "Kevin and I used to get together on Mondays for coffee to motivate and sometimes coach each other. We had a couple of other dads from soccer who joined us. It was a good way to jump-start our job hunting efforts on Mondays," Ruiz says. "With the tough job market, as it was in February 2009, there was no time to waste on self-pity or to feel depressed after losing our jobs."

Kevin referred Ruiz to a recruiter, and that recruiter came to him with a job opportunity with The Wood Group, an energy services company based in Houston. After a screening call, Ruiz had a five-minute interview with the company's hiring manager, who happened to be from Colombia. The Latin connection made Ruiz, who is originally from Mexico, immediately feel comfortable talking with the manager.

Ruiz told the manager what he could provide him, including his Portuguese and Spanish language skills, and that he wanted to be measured by his results. He was offered the job, and in his first five months, Ruiz made sales that substantially exceeded plan.

He now travels about half the time he once did, and he's happier in his work environment: Many of his new colleagues are originally from Latin America, and they get his sense of humor. "My jokes in English sometimes work and sometimes they don't," he says.

Shortly after Ruiz got the job, his wife told him they were expecting another child. Since he travels less, he has more time with his wife and daughters—and their first son, born in March 2010.

Ruiz eventually will be based in Houston and thinks that will position him for more opportunities at the global company. "This time, I will definitely keep my eyes open for something that fits my family and career," he says.

Find the Right Job for You

In a difficult job market, most job experts advise looking for work in the field where you have experience. It may be tempting to try something new, but you're more likely to get hired when your background closely matches the job description.

Nancy Cranford worked for a major retailer for nearly 30 years, never having a Christmas off. When she lost her job in a downsizing in February 2008, she decided to look outside the retail field for a change of pace and a chance to be home for the holidays. After six months of job searching, Cranford took a human resources position in another industry near Atlanta. But about two months into the job, she realized it wasn't the job for her. "I didn't see myself there long term," she says.

Cranford, 52, doesn't regret taking the first job. "In this economy, it doesn't hurt to get back in the game," she says. However, when she started her search again in November 2009, she focused on a human resources job in retail because she realized the economic downturn was not the time to change fields.

She reinvested in her profession by increasing her education and participation. She completed her certification as a senior professional in human resources. Cranford also became deeply involved with her local chapter of The Society for Human Resource Management and other industry groups, spending time at events and participating in online seminars. "I wanted to keep my pulse on the ever-changing laws, learn more about benefits, legal changes. It helped me keep in the game," she says.

She made great contacts, including an executive who would later interview her. About a month after they met, Cranford spotted a human resources job at that executive's employer. She liked the job description because it would make use of her varied skills in human resources. "Without ever having to move, I can go into so many roles," she says.

In again looking for a job, Cranford also changed her approach in interviewing to make sure that she was getting the information she needed to make a good decision. Cranford finds interviews fun, so she tends to be chatty and passionate about her work. Her husband Frank observed that while she was great at interviews, she had trouble closing the deal.

To guide herself, she wrote out answers to possible interview questions to refine key points she wanted to make. "I found I had to keep people on track. Otherwise, I went away with 'They liked me, but were they sure I could do the job?'"

Her new approach must have worked. She was offered the job in March 2010, a day after her interview with the executive she had met while networking. Although the job search process can sometimes feel discouraging, she says, "When it's right, it will happen."

Gain New Perspective

As businesses recover from the downturn, hiring will pick up. Don't rule out a former employer that knows your work and appreciates your skills just because the company is already on your resume.

Ed Humble, 40, loved his work at Hydromat, a rotary and machine manufacturer in St. Louis. But after seven years he felt burned out, and the mechanical engineer started looking around for a new position. He found a new job pretty easily and decided to make the leap in July 2007.

Everything was going smoothly at his new employer until about September 2008 when America's financial crisis froze capital markets and stalled projects. The machine his team was designing was used to make ducts for air conditioning and heating systems in the building industry. "The sales just disappeared, and they started laying people off," Humble says.

He and his coworkers were expecting furloughs, but what they didn't anticipate is that the entire plant would close down. July 1, 2009, was the last day for the operation.

Humble didn't feel so bad. Between severance and vacation owed him, he had seven weeks of pay coming. He also had been given a retention bonus to stay until the plant closed. So he and his fiancé took a week's vacation and visited friends. Humble took time to ride his bike and go to the St. Louis Rams football team's training camp—something he always wanted to do. "I wasn't financially strapped. I had socked some money away for a rainy day," he says.

He applied for unemployment compensation and went online to look at jobs posted on the state site. Almost immediately he recognized a position at his old employer, Hydromat. That night, he had a call from Rob, an old friend who was the company's project manager.

"Are you calling me to offer me that job I saw?" Humble asked him.

"No, I'm calling to offer you a *different* one," Rob told him. (This is another example of why it's a good idea to always keep in touch with past employers and colleagues.)

Humble had lunch with Rob and another top manager and openly talked about the reason he left Hydromat: Departments often had worked at cross-purposes, and he had become tired of it. "We discussed the issues I had and what was different," he says.

He accepted the Hydromat job in September 2009 and now works across the room from where he once did. After pointing out the two raises he got from his former employer, Humble was even offered a slightly higher salary than when he left.

By working for another employer, Humble had gained a fresh perspective. "There's going to be a certain amount of tension at work. The job is going to be demanding. You have to be able to back off from the grind," he says. Small things become magnified when a person is under stress, and Humble had reacted by changing jobs. Now, he recognizes, "some of that pressure may have been self-inflicted."

Go Back to Your Roots

When a job doesn't work out as expected, perhaps it's time to go back to something reliable: yourself. For Amy Babcock, 43, that meant reviving her business in 2009. And that eventually led to a telecommuting job that suits all her needs.

With her expertise in technology, marketing, and alternative energy, Babcock had some high-powered clients. But it was getting hard to compete with larger agencies that were entering her field. "I was very tired of the fluctuation, the ups and downs, making payroll, and paying subcontractors," she says. After 10 years of being in business for herself, she accepted a job offer from a local marketing group in Rochester in 2008.

She liked her new job and the reliability of a regular paycheck. After 18 months, she was given a promotion and Babcock happily went on vacation. But when she came back, she found they had eliminated her position. "It gave me quite a financial shock," she says.

Babcock was still winding down her business at the time, so she reversed course to generate income. She had a 14-year-old daughter to support. She also owns a 32-acre horse farm where she boards horses and gives riding lessons.

At the same time, she looked for a new job. To get her search off to the right start, she joined Getting There Executive Network, a local networking group for C-level executives in Rochester known as GTEN. "It was a key to feeling that I wasn't alone and that I'm a bright, worthy person," Babcock says. "On the other hand, it was a little scary. There were so many brilliant, talented people out of work." Members of the group traded leads and practiced their elevator speeches (30-second to 2-minute speeches to pitch themselves to employers).

At the same time, Babcock started to rebuild her client base for her business. She reached out to an association she had worked with in the past to see what she could do for them in business development or marketing. Soon Babcock was put on retainer to help the Electric Drive Transportation Association in Washington, D.C., build its membership in a challenging economy.

Meanwhile, she was interviewing for other jobs, and she started to get offers. But Babcock really wanted to work for the association. "I have quite a quandary," she told the association president. "I need a full-time job, and I've got to let this company know if I'm interested. I would like to propose to you that you hire me full-time."

"Let me see what I can do," the association president said, going back to his board. The association found money in its budget, creating a business development and marketing position for her in February 2010.

Now Babcock telecommutes from her Bloomfield, New York, home where she also can oversee her horse farm. She travels to Washington, D.C., about once a month. "I would be on the phone anyway and when I need to visit a potential client, I can do that from Rochester as well as D.C.," she says.

Learn to Communicate What You Can Do

Veteran Darwin Rivera, 33, recognizes the importance of education, communication skills, and presentation in achieving success. That foundation has guided him through many obstacles.

After serving eight years in the Air Force with 13 months in Iraq, Rivera said goodbye to the military life in June 2007, ready to embrace a new career. He had earned the rank of sergeant in the Air Force. He had management and technology experience and had earned his bachelor's degree and master's in business administration while in the military. "I did half my MBA while deployed in Iraq," Rivera says.

But when the highly trained Rivera went to his local employment office to find out what jobs might be available, he was shocked at the suggestions. "I walked in with my resume. I was nicely dressed in a jacket and tie. I had a two-page resume with credible skills in management and an MBA. The person didn't even look at my resume and starting talking about jobs they had at Macy's and hotels. 'You should consider coming here next Tuesday,' the job counselor told him. 'The school district is going to have a career fair. They're going to be hiring bus drivers.'" Wondering what alternative universe he had stepped into that day, Rivera told the counselor, "Uh, I'm looking for something more in the computer field."

Rivera turned his attention to networking, and through someone he knew, he found a job at a bank. Two years later, his branch was sold to another bank, and he was out of a job.

To look for a new position, Rivera posted a notice on the job board of the National Society for Hispanic MBAs. Rivera got a call from a national tax and audit firm in Alexandria, Virginia, that was looking to hire someone with technology credentials who also understood business.

A recruiter later told him his resume was picked from the pile because he was able to tie his skills to his experience and communicate that in his resume. To do that, he used the STAR method, an interviewing technique to present a **s**ituation, the **t**asks involved, **a**ction taken, and the **r**esult. He used this method to describe his skills both on his resume and in his interview.

Through his networking contacts, he was able to find out that his potential employer "wanted someone with deep technical skills who also could sit down at the table with senior executives and navigate problems," Rivera says. "For the position of consultant, you need to have a good grasp of business as well as be able to talk technology, not only with the techies and geeks, but also to nontechnical people."

Rivera was able to show the interviewer he had the required skills through the experience and accomplishments listed on his resume. "You have to be prepared. When I was a sergeant in the Air Force, we used to say 'life is 95 percent appearances, 3 percent sweat, 1 percent intelligence, and 1 percent dumb luck,'" he says.

He also found positive comments on his past performance reviews helpful, using relevant information both on his resume and during the interview. "I understood the most significant experiences I could bring to the table. I went over how I was able to break barriers and get everybody's buy-in," Rivera says. He was offered and accepted the technology consultant position at the audit firm.

He now offers this advice to others who may soon leave the military and enter or re-enter the job market: "It doesn't matter how much experience you may bring to the table. If you're not able to communicate it, you're going to have a real hard time," Rivera says.

Keep Your Faith in Better Times Ahead

When the life's challenges seemed insurmountable, several job hunters turned to their faith, trusting that eventually everything would work out.

Renee Govig, 43, of Delray Beach, Florida, was laid off from her human resources director position in July 2007, at a time when her husband Michael couldn't work because he was recovering from a car accident and back surgery. The day she lost her job also happened to be her fifth wedding anniversary.

With her husband unable to work, Govig needed a job—fast. "The second half of 2007 was about him and my emotional meltdown. I needed to take care of him. I was very depressed and questioning, 'Do I even want to go back into this field?'" she says.

When she was offered a contract human resources job in August 2009, she took it. A lower-level position with less responsibility was just what Govig thought she needed: Her husband was just returning to work, and they were juggling care for their daughter, Gabrielle, who was not yet two.

But she kept looking for a new job, and it was a good thing she did. Govig soon found that "the more I produced, the more they expected." There was enormous paperwork, and she found herself working more than 50 hours a week for bargain-basement pay. She couldn't pick up her daughter from school after-care, and her husband had to change his work schedule to do that.

She also could tell that the company's culture was not for her. "Every single employee at this company had a red Swingline stapler," Govig says with a laugh, referring to the movie *Office Space,* which spoofed fed-up software workers. In this classic comedy, mistreated worker Milton is continually asked to move his desk. He does so reluctantly, clinging to his one prize, a red Swingline stapler. But when the boss takes his stapler and fails to pay him, Milton can't take it anymore and sets the office on fire. The movie is a great rental for a sick day.

While working at the contract job, Govig found a posting for a human resources director position on her industry chapter website. In October 2009, she was called for interview for the job with Searcy, Denney, Scarola, Barnhart & Shipley law firm in West Palm Beach, Florida.

Her first interview was with a firm partner, who had just flown in from Europe and had a terrible head cold, and a hiring consultant who kept disputing her answers. "I thought I would never hear from them. I thought I had completely bombed it," she says.

The consultant "started role-playing with me," Govig says, giving her human-resources challenges such as, "What would you do if a high performer took too many breaks?" When Govig gave what she thought was the appropriate answer, the consultant would say, "Nope!"

Because the situation was out of her control, she turned to prayer: "Lord, you're going to put me where you want me to be, and that's where I'll be."

Then during her interview, Govig discovered she had a personal connection. She mentioned to the law firm partner that she drops off her daughter at a local private school. "Oh, my sister is the librarian there," the partner told her.

Govig knew the school librarian through volunteering at the school and called her after the interview, asking for a recommendation to her brother. But Govig said she felt awkward asking, and thought she had fumbled that, too.

Govig also e-mailed the partner thanking him for the interview, saying "whatever it takes to make the team successful, I'll do it. I've plunged a toilet before, and I've waited with a man who had a heart attack for the ambulance." The partner apparently liked her get-it-done attitude, she was later told.

She was called back for a second interview and was offered the job in mid-November. Her work and personal life have never been better, she says. Govig now works a 35-hour week and is able to pick up her daughter after school. She has 15 paid holidays and 2 weeks of vacation to start, plus 6 personal days. Each year, employees get two months' salary as a bonus. For the holidays, the partners hand out cards with two crisp $100 bills to employees.

Now as human resources director, Govig says, "My challenge is what *more* can we do for employees? We do everything."

As a result of her job search experiences, Govig says, "I don't take things for granted. Every day I get to take Gabby to school and pick her up. The people I work with are genuinely good people. All the partners are involved in the community. I'm in the green grass.

"Every morning when I'm driving to work, I say, 'Thank you, Lord, I'm so grateful.'"

Streetwise Strategies for Starting Over

- Don't waste time on a bad job situation; move on.

- Be clear upfront about your expectations for the job.

- Learn from past mistakes and apply them to your new job search.

- Gain perspective about what you want from work and life from each new job.

- Keep in touch with former employers; new opportunities may arise at old workplaces.

- Turn contract work for a client into a full-time job.

- Learn how to communicate your skills and background to the potential employer.

- Have faith you'll find the right job, despite life's twists and turns.

CHAPTER 9

ACCEPT THE RIGHT OFFER

When a job offer is before you, jumping at it is natural, especially if you've had a long job search. But make sure you've done your homework, especially before uprooting your family or putting your home on the market.

Alan Hunt, 51, left a job at a nonprofit in Miami for another in New York. He packed up his family's belongings and moved to what seemed like a promising position at another nonprofit organization.

"My first day on the job, one of my lowest-level employees walks into my office with so much bravado and leans across my desk, 'I give you two months,' she said. That's a very interesting thing to say to your boss on the first day," Hunt says.

It turned out there had been five people in five years in the chief financial officer job for which Hunt had been hired. He had been told the job was a new position. Hunt soon learned that they had created a new title, but someone had always been in the job. He also soon realized he couldn't work with top management.

"There was an office pool for how long I would last," he says. "I will never jump at a job offer again. I'll let someone make an offer, go back home, and do my research."

If he had only spent some time doing an Internet search of the organization and the management, Hunt may have been spared the costly moves. Hunt left after two months and moved with his family to San Diego where he started his job search again. But California's job market proved too challenging. So 10 months later, he accepted a position as a chief financial officer for a nonprofit educational institute in Boston.

To research a potential employer, look for news and feature stories on a potential employer and top management through Google and local media outlets; check for mentions in blogs through Technorati.com; ask those who might be in the know on LinkedIn about their experience with the company. Ultimately, go with your gut; it's often right.

That's a difficult choice, of course, when you've gone through your severance and unemployment benefits, and no other jobs are beckoning. But you might be better off taking a contract job or consulting than making the wrong move.

In this chapter, successful job candidates recommend how to find the right job and negotiate an employment package that works for you.

Remember Your Values

Before accepting a new job, think about whether it matches your values. What's important to you and does the employer live up to *your* standards?

Martha Restrepo had just about everything bad in life happen to her at once. But it made her recognize what is important to her and look for those qualities in a new job.

After her mother had a stroke, Restrepo booked a flight out of Miami for Colombia, her parents' home. At the airport, she got a call from work: She was being laid off. It was October 2008, and her husband was already out of work. The couple also was in the middle of a divorce. Meanwhile, Restrepo's children were leaving their Coral Springs, Florida, home. Her son, 23, was working, and her daughter, 18, was attending college. Life as she knew it was already changing—now this.

Restrepo, 50, had to take care of her mother, and that's all she could think about for several months. When her mother recovered, Restrepo had to face the reality of the 2008–2009 job market. "I had worked straight for almost 31 years, no stops. I moved to other positions because they were better opportunities. I began working in December of 1977. All of a sudden, in October 2008, it was over," she says.

For almost three years, she had been the human resources director for the Latin American division of a personal care products retailer. The company filed for Chapter 11 reorganization and had to downsize and sell off assets. Her division was to be sold, but the sale fell through, and it was shut down instead.

This time, Restrepo was the job hunter, not the human resources person delivering severance packages. At first, she used the tried-and-true formula to find a job: contacting everyone she knew in human resources, seeking out recruiters in her field, selecting target companies, and finding connections within those companies. But she soon found it wasn't enough. "You have to sell yourself, market yourself," Restrepo says. "To me, that was a very new concept."

While caring for her mother in Colombia, she had time to think about her body of work during her career and the type of company she wanted to work for as a human resources professional. "I had to have a clear understanding of who I am, what I bring to the table, and what I expect from an employer," Restrepo says.

Restrepo determined that she wanted to be part of an innovative workplace, perhaps in another field than consumer products. She also keyed in on her values: She wanted to work for a company that was straightforward: "I like to work in a place that what you say, you say; what you do, you do. If results trump everything else, I wasn't looking for that. I wanted to work for a place where results and behaviors are important," she says.

In December 2009, she had a breakfast scheduled with a recruiter to talk about a potential job. He came instead with a lead on a human resources position for an online job board based in Boston. "This is a great opportunity for you," he told her, sending her resume to the recruiter handling the job.

It wasn't easy: "Fourteen interviews later, I got the job," she says. Restrepo had a phone screen with the recruiter, a videoconference with the recruiter, two phone interviews with the internal recruiter, and phone interviews with the senior vice president of human resources. Then she was flown to Boston headquarters for in-person interviews— she had about six the first day. She came back for two more rounds.

But Restrepo says she didn't mind the intense interview process. "At the end of the day, I liked it. It allowed for both parties to really dig deep."

In the interviews, Restrepo was able to communicate how her experience and skills in human resources for consumer products business were transferable to a technology company. Job hunters often limit themselves on potential opportunities, she says, because they don't have an understanding of how their skills can translate to other industries. "That allowed me to be much more flexible," she says.

After more than 15 months out of work—many of them caring for her mother before she could even look for a job—Restrepo also had to fight off depression and anxiety. "You have to look at your strengths and what you bring to the table. That allows you not to spiral down in a sea of fear," she says.

Restrepo was offered the job at a better-than-comparable salary than she once made. She's selling her Florida home and moving to Boston to start her new life. Although the past two years have been stressful, she sees the good that has come out of this period in her family's life. "It was a great opportunity for the kids to step out," she says. Her son found a paying internship; her daughter applied for and was awarded college scholarships and also got a job.

"They discovered a lot about themselves that they didn't know," she says. "As difficult days as they were, we've come out the better for it."

The career transition will forever change Restrepo's perspective on her work in human resources. "Companies need people who are engaged. They need to have people come to work to be fulfilled, not because they have to go to work," she says. "They're energized, engaged, and they understand the business. There's an understanding about what employers and employees both get out of the relationship."

Go with Your Gut

How do you know a job is a good fit? You can rely on your research, but often it comes down to a gut feeling.

Marina Konchak, 46, of Miami knew her new job was right for her. She had worked for nearly 30 years for Home Depot and could have easily found work with another retailer in her specialty, human resources. But after her interview with Catholic Hospice in South Florida, she knew it was meant to be. "I felt this overwhelming sense of spirituality, a sense of 'I belong here,'" she says.

She also wanted a challenge and going back into retail would have been more of the same type of work. At Home Depot, she worked most Saturdays and always six days a week.

But her daughters were growing up fast, and she wanted to be near them. One retailer presented her with a great offer, but she would have had to travel every week. The other jobs also offered more money, but she chose quality of life over salary. "Be flexible, but know what your preferences are," Konchak says.

Take the Long View

When considering a job offer, take the long view. Will you have to take a pay cut? Many successful job candidates I interviewed accepted a job with a lower salary than they had earned before their job loss. But consider the whole compensation package being offered: Are there health benefits, a 401(k), or other retirement plans? Can you expect an annual bonus or earn extra compensation for meeting sales goals? Relative cost of living in different parts of the country and state taxes should all figure into your compensation analysis.

And don't forget your personal lifestyle and your family's well-being and happiness. Steve Fox, 48, was thrilled to accept a job as head of business development for a federal agency because it was in his field and gave him a foothold in the Washington, D.C., job market. Still, Fox took a sizeable pay cut from his former position at a major transportation company where he had been vice president of product marketing and e-commerce.

But compensation isn't the only consideration in accepting a job offer. Where do you want to live? As young executives have families and older employees near retirement, that becomes a larger concern.

Fox, for example, had moved his family from Virginia to Florida for his former job. When he was laid off, they decided to move back to Virginia, and he was determined to find a job in nearby Washington, D.C.

"It was really hard on my family to move to Florida, and moving back to Virginia was almost as traumatic," says Fox, who has three sons ages 8, 11, and 17. His third-grader had changed schools every year. "I'm going to stay here a while and build up my credentials. That will make me more marketable in Washington," he says.

Despite taking a pay cut, Fox was able to move forward in his career goals without uprooting his family again. And those factors were ultimately more important than a slightly lower paycheck.

Be Assertive About Your Value

When you get the job offer—not before—is the time to discuss salary and other compensation. Workers who are still employed naturally have more leverage than the unemployed in compensation negotiation. Workers in transition have to work harder at showing their value.

Despite being laid off, Mary Beth Dew, 49, knew she was in a good negotiating position when she rejoined her former employer, AC Controls Co. in Charlotte, North Carolina. Four years ago, she had been recruited away by a customer. Then came the economic downturn and she was laid off. That would have seemed to put her in a weaker position to negotiate a return to her former employer, but Dew stood her ground.

"My mother was saying, 'What are you doing? You don't have a job. Take anything,'" Dew says. But Dew wanted to make sure the experience she had gained while away was recognized by the CEO. "It was the potential. That's why I didn't jump on it immediately," she says. "I got all my vacation back and sick and personal time. And he matched my salary." Dew, who is now in sales, also asked to work out of her home, near Charleston, South Carolina, and the company provided office furniture and equipment to make it happen.

Leverage usually helps when negotiating a salary, but you have to be careful how to use it. Quality manager John Rives, 44, didn't plan to reveal the fact that he was also talking with another manufacturer about a job when he was offered a position at a plant near Columbus, Ohio. But when asked if he had any other offers, Rives was truthful that he had a tentative offer on the table. "I wasn't going to bring that up, but he opened the door," he says.

Rives is unsure whether the competing offer snagged him a better compensation package. But when he mentioned a family obligation that required a week of vacation soon after his start, the hiring manager "didn't even blink," he says.

Check Your Attitude

The recession has been a buyers' market for employers. That will start to change in the recovery, but remember there are still many people who are unemployed and competing for jobs. As the economy recovers, more workers will enter the job market as well. For the long-term unemployed, it will be even more challenging to compete for jobs.

Although it's important to be confident, people who come across as arrogant, unflexible, and know-it-alls often lose out. Why would an employer offer a job to someone who might be difficult when there were so many choices of applicants?

Check your attitude by doing the following:

- Listen completely to what an interviewer has to say about the job requirements and compensation before you rush to judgment, declaring a job offer "unacceptable." There are always items you can negotiate.

- Keep an open mind about compensation until the employer gets to know you and decides to hire you.

- Expect to make some concessions, but know your bottom line.

When Kurt Porceng, 42, was negotiating compensation for his new job as a financial controller in 2009, the South Florida resident decided the humble approach was the smart move in the economic downturn. "You start a little lower and you work your way back up," he says.

Luis Riano, 39, saw that the salary range for a potential telecommunications job in Miami was lower than he knew he was worth. It was the fall of 2009, and Riano had recently lost his job.

Riano pushed on through the interview process because, as a hiring manager himself, he knew there could be no real salary discussion until the potential employer got to know him and what he could do for the firm. "I didn't get discouraged when I saw the base salary on paper. You can close the door on yourself," he says.

Riano was used to facing obstacles. He immigrated to the United States with his parents when he was 15 years old and had to learn English and find opportunities for himself as a young man. He joined the Navy and obtained his bachelor's degree in electronics by taking classes offered on base.

"Consistency, flexibility, and execution are my three core foundations," Riano says. "When you show consistency in your actions, it creates credibility. Flexibility shows you can adapt to a situation. You develop trust with your boss, coworkers, and customers. Execution is when you say you're going to do something, you get it done. When you execute on your promises, you build a stronger image." Those values were engrained in him during his Navy years and have served him well in his career.

So when compensation was brought up during his final interview with the new employer, Riano told his hiring manager: "I think the opportunity is great, and I want to be a part of your team. What I'm looking for is 'this price range....' " The manager told him he would try his best to get it. He came back with a compensation offer comparable to Riano's former job. Six weeks after losing his previous job, Riano was again employed.

Ask for Severance

Consider this twist in negotiating compensation: Ask for severance upfront from a potential employer. That may seem like a doomsday proposition, but it's happening more as people go through layoffs and know the probability of divorce from a job.

Greg Siegelman, a marketing executive in upstate New York, always asks for a severance package when he's being *offered* a job. "The worst they can say is no," he reasons.

After going through layoffs twice in his career, he wanted to protect his family. "Surviving a layoff begins in advance," says Siegelman, 52. The first time he asked for severance to be included in his offer, the employer was reluctant but acquiesced.

Siegelman did end up being part of a downsizing from that company and had the severance (in addition to unemployment compensation and a "rainy day" fund) to tide over his family during the time it took him to find a new job. "I thank my lucky stars I had asked for it," he says. "I took the worry about the financial side out of the picture."

He asked again for severance in spring 2010, when he was offered a marketing director position for a high-tech firm in Dayton, Ohio. The tactic didn't work this time, but Siegelman was pleased with the overall compensation package and the position level and took the job.

Don't Get Too Comfortable

Perhaps you've landed a job; that doesn't mean you should stop looking. Job hopping is more frequent these days and doesn't carry the stigma it once did. If a better opportunity presents itself, it may be time to move again, even you have worked only a few months at a new job.

Human resources executive Grace Orejas, 43, was happy to have a job at a South Florida law firm after being out of work for four months. She had worked for her former employer, an international communications company, for nine years and was surprised when her job was cut.

Being in the industry, "I knew what I had to do," Orejas says. She launched an aggressive job search, connecting with industry colleagues on LinkedIn and at local chapters of The Society for Human Resource Management. But she was among many colleagues in transition, and it seemed like there were no jobs.

She regularly attended a "coffee break" series of discussions between human resources executives, many of whom traded job search tips and leads on jobs. One woman who worked for an employment agency decided to help her out and sent her resume to a local payroll organization. That organization passed it on to a client, a law firm.

Orejas was offered the job in November and took it, because she was grateful to have a job. But the employer wasn't in her field of expertise; she had previously worked in hospitality and communications and preferred those industries. "I didn't really think I was going to be there for many years, but I said while I'm here I'm going to dedicate myself totally," she says.

Meanwhile, Orejas was receiving job leads from a vice president of human resources for another local employer, a property management company. Orejas had once interviewed with the hiring manager, and they immediately connected, but the right opportunity wasn't available. Still, the executive kept in touch with Orejas.

Then in the spring of 2010, Orejas got a call from the executive about an opening for director of benefits at the property management firm. Orejas hesitated, "but not too much," she says, because it was the job she really wanted.

Because she had career consistency behind her, Orejas didn't think that jumping from one job to another in a short time was significant. It was more important to be in the right job.

"You should never disconnect from your network. We tend to get comfortable when we're working and with an employer for many years. You should always be open to opportunities," she says.

Do Your Compensation Homework

Use your connections at the employer to find out the salary range and other compensation they may be willing to negotiate. Don't be afraid to ask about benefits, but also get a sense of what is *not* negotiable, advises Terri Warren, now a branch manager for a South Florida bank.

"I already had an officer title. I had been a vice president. In some institutions the title goes with a certain position. I did mention that to the recruiter: 'Since this is a large office and I've been a VP in the past, doesn't that title come with the position?'" The internal recruiter said she would put in that request.

Warren also asked about vacation and was assured she would still have four weeks as she did in her last job. "If you can't find out the benefits ahead of time, you have to ask," she says.

Asked about salary almost immediately when she began talking with the bank's recruiter, Warren begged off with "I'm uncomfortable talking about salary until you find out more about me." The recruiter was upfront about the range the bank could offer, and Warren later found out one candidate flatly refused to take less than he was previously making.

Warren was more flexible. "Well, let's see what the opportunities are," she said when the recruiter asked her about salary requirements. "At this time, with the benefit package, I'm willing to continue interviewing with the company."

When the offer came in lower than she would have liked, Warren's husband put it in perspective for her: "Right now your salary is zero." Warren took a realistic approach, and today she's working instead of still looking for a job.

Negotiate What Matters

Two books, *Secrets of Power Salary Negotiating* by Roger Dawson and *Get Paid What You're Worth* by Robin L. Pinkley, were recommended by job hunters. Some used Salary.com (www.salary.com), PayScale (www.payscale.com), or the Bureau of Labor Statistics (www.bls.gov) to check salary ranges for a certain job. Glassdoor (www.glassdoor.com) gives anonymous salary information and reviews from current and former employees.

Most negotiation experts advise never to take the first offer. "I've never taken the first offer because I'm a salesperson," says Kathy Stein, a Fort Lauderdale sales director. She worked with a recruiter and that helped ease the way to ask for the salary and benefits she wanted. "It makes people feel uncomfortable discussing money," she says.

Stein was pleased with the job offer from a GPS tracking company, but she was concerned about her health insurance taking too long to kick in. Her husband is an independent contractor who doesn't have insurance. Through her recruiter, she was able to negotiate a "no waiting" period for insurance, an increased percentage on commissions, a car allowance, and the ability to work from home. "I got everything but a 401(k), because they didn't have one," she says.

Relocation and travel expenses were the primary concerns for Jim Kowalczyk, 37, who found a job as a process improvement specialist in Atlanta after first searching near his home in northern Florida. In his negotiations, he got moving expenses covered and a signing bonus to cover incidental expenses. "We went back and forth two or three times and ended up coming to a happy medium," he says.

Consider Your Stage in Life

Your circumstances in life are a major consideration for the salary you require. You may have a partner with whom you share expenses. You may have a family or care for an aging parent. You may be in your 20s with fewer of life's responsibilities. Or you may be what some consider "retirement age," but you want or need to keep working.

Ruth Balsam, a 75-year-old accountant in Boca Raton, Florida, was happy and willing to take a job that paid less than she was accustomed to making. At this stage in her life, she is more interested in a good work environment and she liked the young, energetic culture at Information Television Network, a TV production company that hired her in January 2010.

"You can't go for a job that's slightly above your abilities; too many people are taking jobs below their abilities. You have to take less money and hope the economy turns around," Balsam says. Besides, Balsam is confident that she'll win them over: "I start off with the first offer, and if they love me, I can get a little more."

Talk It Over with Family or Friends

Discuss the job offer with your spouse, partner, parents, mentor, or good friends to get their perspectives. You can be too close to the situation or too emotional and may not think of asking for something doable in the compensation package.

Mike Simon had been out of work for 11 months when he got an offer from an automotive-related firm in Indianapolis. Simon was making a good income as a process management consultant. Still, it had been nearly a year since he had a full-time level salary and benefits.

The search to fill the job at the firm had come down to 12 candidates, and then 2, and then Simon. When asked what his salary requirements were, Simon said, "Here's where I was, and here's what I think I'm worth."

Some job hunters are so eager to work that they don't risk asking for more when they are finally offered a job. But an improving economy will give job hunters more leverage in negotiating compensation.

"My wife had to help me. She was much more objective than I was," Simon says. "At the point where you've gone through a layoff and you're collecting a drawer full of rejection letters, you're pretty desperate when a job offer finally comes along."

Simon's wife was able to reassure him of his worth in the market, and he negotiated a signing bonus, a larger base than he had previously, a bonus plan, and a moving budget.

Choose the Job That Will Make You Happy

Sometimes the stars align in a job search and you have to weigh offers from two or more employers. How do you choose?

W. Alejandro Polanco was the casualty of a downsizing in late 2009, but within a few months, he had job offers from three employers. Polanco, 36, who has technology skills such as building databases and automating systems, was a man in demand after losing his job with a Baltimore technology firm. He began an aggressive search on January 1, 2010, relying heavily on his extensive LinkedIn network. He had been building contacts over time with people at former employers where he had worked in marketing, product management, and technology roles.

He found two opportunities through LinkedIn contacts. One firm paid well, but he didn't see potential for future growth. The other firm was offering too-low pay. Then a third opportunity developed at Kaplan Inc., a private education company with a large presence in South Florida.

Polanco researched all the companies, checking their financial outlook and management, and found connections inside to invite for coffee and get more information. "At least get a sense of how happy people are.

Do you truly believe the company is going places? How do you feel about the culture? The dress code? Many people are happy to divulge that information," he says.

When he interviewed with Kaplan, the company didn't even have an open position. "They said 'Come in here and build your own position,'" Polanco says. As a result, "I'm having a blast. I have so many ideas."

But, when he went to interview, Polanco admits he was a bit uncomfortable because there was no job description. "I felt a little skeptical about the whole thing. I didn't know what kind of angle I was going to be able to approach them with," he says.

So Polanco just decided not to make a pitch, but to be himself. He went in with the attitude of: "These are my quantifiable skills and this is what I've been able to do to prove myself. No sales pitch, just what I had done in the past and what I'm really good at doing. If they like that, then they're going to give me a call."

Polanco was told at the outset that the company wouldn't be able to move much on pay, so he negotiated other parts of his compensation package and job. He got a higher title than originally proposed, a commitment to have his salary reviewed at earlier than the standard year, more vacation, and flex time so he could work at home at least once a week.

"I had a list of things I was keeping in my back pocket," he says. "Most companies are very willing and able to negotiate things other than actual salary." Propose any negotiation as a "win-win," Polanco suggests.

Polanco had three job choices, but compensation was not the driving reason for picking the Kaplan job. "Always go for the job you know you're going to be happy in," he says. "A lot of people will take an opportunity based strictly on the money. I took Kaplan because I liked the culture. I had a good feeling that I was going to be happy."

Streetwise Strategies for Accepting the Offer

- Do Internet and other research on the employer to spot any red flags before you accept the job.

- Make sure the employer's priorities are the same as yours.

- Take a long view on compensation when times are tough. Your flexibility may win you the job.

- Be assertive about your value, especially if you've added skills.

- Put off a salary discussion until the employer gets to know your background and skills.

- Research the typical salary range for the job. Find out what is and isn't negotiable with that employer.

- Consider the total compensation package. Vacation or perks may be negotiable.

- Consider cost of living and state and local taxes when comparing offers in different locations.

- Ask for a severance package upfront; all they can say is "no."

- Know what you want to negotiate and go back to ask only once.

- Factor in the economic reality and your needs at this stage in life.

- Ask for the opinion of an objective friend or your spouse before accepting an offer.

- Multiple job offers? Choose what makes you happy.

CHAPTER 10

CREATE YOUR OWN JOB

If you can't find a job that suits you, why not create your own? Some professionals have decided that they don't want all of their income coming from one source. Others have found they prefer working for themselves.

Some people who have been laid off have found work as freelancers, contractors, or consultants. Others have bought franchises or existing businesses, and some have started their own ventures.

Use Your Skills in Multiple Jobs

Working three jobs is not what Andrea Hubbell pictured when she finished her architecture studies. "I thought I would come out of school and get a really good job and study for my exams and climb the ladder," she says. But when Hubbell graduated with a master's degree in architecture from the University of Virginia in 2008, she couldn't immediately find a job in her field in Charlottesville, Virginia, where she and her husband wanted to stay.

She later found work with a landscape architecture firm, but nine months later, she was laid off because business was slow. Fortunately, she quickly found work with a firm she had worked for part-time during graduate school. They hired her to work on a large housing project they were designing. Just five months later, the project ran into financial trouble. One worker was let go, and the rest took a 20 percent pay cut. Hubbell also had her work hours reduced to part-time.

Her husband Brian, who was working for the same firm, took a leave of absence to renovate houses. That helped the firm reduce staff temporarily.

But Hubbell, 28, needed more money than her part-time job paid, so she put her talent and skills to use in other ways. A friend owned a paper shop, and she went to work there part-time doing custom design. She also began a photography business specializing in architectural photos. She essentially created her own full-time job with three part-time ones.

Hubbell is earning what she once did six years ago when she was just out of undergraduate school working for a homebuilder. She and Brian also are working more hours. But even when the industry recovers, she's not sure she will return to architecture. Hubbell likes doing different types of work, especially photography, and plans to develop that as a business. "It has actually been fun to have a little extra time to enjoy other things I'm interested in doing," she says.

To tap into your skills to create a job, follow these guidelines:

- Consider how else you can use your skills, besides your profession.

- Think about the work you enjoy doing most and focus on that.

- Diversify your sources of income: a part-time job with a side business and a teaching gig, for example.

- Determine how much money you need to cover living expenses and how many hours you need to work.

- Consider whether this is going to be temporary or you're really creating a business.

Parlay Your Skills into Your Own Business

Some professions lend themselves more than others to starting a business or consulting firm. Public relations work is one area where a professional can hang a shingle and start working for clients as a self-employed individual.

Scott Walsh, 47, was laid off in late 2007 from his corporate communications position at a golf manufacturer near his home in San Diego.

"I looked long and hard for a corporate opportunity. I couldn't find anything. I conservatively sent out probably 500 resumes," Walsh says. He even expanded his search to other parts of the country, although his wife didn't want to leave her family in Southern California.

Walsh was trying to pick up contract work when he met a healthcare executive at a barber shop. Their casual conversation resulted in his first contract for his public relations business, Aslan Communications. Walsh then began expanding his network and adding other clients. He also has broadened the services to corporate communications, business writing, media relations, and cowriting books.

In St. Louis, Mistie Thompson found out in the summer of 2009 that her public relations firm was laying her off. She received six weeks' notice. During that time, her doctor called for advice on public relations for his new office, asking if Thompson could recommend someone.

"You can hire me in two weeks," Thompson told the obstetrician who was opening a new fertility clinic.

So Thompson, 39, secured her first client before leaving her old job and she has been busy ever since. An hour after she was laid off, Thompson came up with a name for her business, Sweet Tea Communications, drawn from her Southern roots. She immediately reserved the URL.

"I never in a million years thought I was the entrepreneurial type. I'm too much of a chicken. I have small children. It takes a special way of thinking and attitude about risk. You sink or swim," Thompson says. It helped that she didn't have to worry about health benefits, which she gets through her husband's job.

Thompson mobilized her existing network to keep costs down. She reached out to friends who were business owners to answer her questions about setting up and operating a business. She decided not to be a freelancer, but to set up a company and develop a personal brand for her communications business.

She looked into the best way to set up her business. Her accountant recommended an S-corporation so that any corporate income or losses flow through her personal income tax return and are assessed at individual income tax rates. Thompson also has set up a Roth IRA, which allows money for retirement to grow tax-free.

To distinguish her business from others, Thompson offers clients a short- and long-term marketing plan. She works mostly with small business clients who can't afford the fees of a large public relations or marketing firm and like the personal attention she can provide. An admitted "Twitterholic," Thompson uses social media as a major component of her work for a client.

She kept startup costs in check, partly by using barter. "I have a friend who is a fantastic graphic designer who designed a logo and website for me," she says. She traded her writing services for the designer's help.

Thompson bought new office equipment only when needed. "My laptop is old but serviceable. I invested in a Mac mini, so I can switch back and forth from a PC to a Mac," she says. She worked for a while on a table, and only when cash flow improved did she buy a desk.

A mother to two young daughters, Thompson likes the flexibility of her own business, so she can pick up her daughters after school and spend time with them before dinner. At night, when the girls go to sleep, she is often back tapping on her keyboard. "The only downside is you really can never turn it off," she says. "I try to take Friday nights off. But when the kids are asleep, I'll go online. There's always something to be done."

Although the business is just starting out, Thompson says she has already more than replaced her former salary. Often, she needs to hire others to help out.

If you're considering starting your own business in your field, keep the following things in mind:

- Consider where you will find clients. A noncompete agreement with your former employer could be a concern in recruiting clients.

- Offer a broad array of services. Tap your experience in the field and be flexible in the work you do.

- Partner or align with other professionals in your industry and with those who can offer additional services to your clients.

- Understand your competitive stance. What can you offer clients the competition can't? A more favorable price? Quick turn-around?

- Seek expertise from business owners you know.

- Establish a brand for your business.

- Look professional. Get help with designing a logo and setting up a website.

- Seek professional advice on the best corporate structure for your business, based on taxes, liability, and other considerations.

- Use barter to keep your expenses low. Barter your services for other professionals' work.

- Set up a Roth IRA or other savings vehicle for your retirement.

Offer Your Consultant Services

So you've decided to become a consultant. One decent-sized client will get you started, but you'll want to work to diversify your client base.

Janet Nelson of Rochester, New York, started her consulting business with a Japanese firm that needed help with a project. Soon, she was offered a second project and then a retainer for her services.

Nelson, 57, had worked for more than 25 years for Xerox, and then was recruited by Kodak, two major businesses in Rochester. When Kodak cut staff in her unit by 40 percent, she decided to take the severance package and go out on her own in 2004.

Consulting is "one of the few places where age is a benefit, where expe-rience helps," Nelson says. But she cautions that being a consultant is risky for those who have worked for only one company. "Their breadth of experience is very narrow. You have to have a broad toolkit from which to draw," she says.

After a few years working solo, Nelson missed the camaraderie of an office. So in 2009, she founded The Workout Consortium, made up of consultants who provide senior-level expertise in sales, marketing, information technology, finance, and operations. Their work ranges from turning around a company in financial distress to helping a business move in the right direction and expand.

Recently, Nelson has been finding a lot more interest from corporations in her consortium's services. Emerging from the depths of the recession, some companies are turning to consultants and contractors as a cheaper option than rehiring workers and providing 401(k) matches, health insurance, and other benefits. "They're recognizing they need the skills they shed earlier," she says.

For Nelson, working on several business projects at a time is the kind of multitasking she craves. "It's so much fun, and it's so exciting. I enjoy the diversity of it."

Nelson gives the following advice to those thinking about operating a consulting firm or business:

- Avoid a single client providing a disproportionate amount of your income. "The risk is that when that client stops doing business with you, you're sunk," she says.

- Make sure you and your family are comfortable with risk and the ebb and flow of income. "If you don't view it as part of the chase, don't do it," Nelson says.

- Do a financial spreadsheet to find out what you need to make. Nelson didn't count her husband's income in determining how much she needed to generate from her business. "I need to make this much a year before Social Security kicks in so as not to dip into the money already saved [for retirement]," she reasoned.

- Approach it as a business, and not as an interim job. If you view consulting as temporary and you're looking for a full-time job, "your mind is not really there. You can't serve your clients and take on a long-term project if you might find a job somewhere else," she says.

- Invest in a good website. That's your calling card so make sure it works and is easy to navigate.

- Learn how to manage your time well. You have to manage your calendar, follow up with clients, and always be marketing the business.

Follow Your Quest for Independence

Technology-savvy workers are making income from social media and online writing. Businesses and professionals are finding that social media is a must for their marketing, but many don't have the time, or desire, to spend their waking hours on Twitter. Younger workers who grew up on computers and text-messaging are finding that their social media skills are in demand.

Marian Schembari, 22, has journalism in her blood. Her father is a long-time writer for *The New York Times*. But Schembari couldn't see herself sitting behind a desk, at least not for someone else.

After graduating from Davidson College in North Carolina in May 2009, Schembari decided she wanted to work for a publishing house. She wasn't getting any bites from sending out resumes, so in July she took out an ad on Facebook to market her talents to publishers. "I got 100 different responses. They all said, 'This is awesome, but I'm not hiring,'" she says.

Schembari did get some freelance work, and one new contact referred her to a previous employer. She was soon hired in September as an associate book publicist, but she quit after a few months.

"I'm not equipped to work in an office. I don't like 9 to 5," she says. Schembari also soon realized that she could make a better living freelancing in social media. "I'd gotten really good at it, and that's what people were hiring me to do," she says.

Now Schembari helps publishers with authors' blogs, often writing blog posts for other people. She also works part-time in a museum to make ends meet, but thinks she'll soon be able to give that up with the income she's making from social media. She's a contributing editor for Digital Book World's website and does Twitter consulting and ghost tweeting.

Social media "is really time-consuming. You have to do it all day, every day. That's why I get hired. It's a time sucker," Schembari says. She charges $500 a month for her social media services. She also has taught a social media tools workshop at Barnard College.

Being self-employed suits her, Schembari says. "Most of my friends are independent and don't want to work for the Man. Two of my friends already have started their own business." She has been helping them develop a Web presence for their brand.

"If it weren't for the economy, I probably would be working at some office like a good little girl. Freelancing is more lucrative and significantly more fun. I really, really love what I do," she says.

After Christina Gleason, 31, was laid off in February 2009 from an Internet marketing firm, she took the contacts she had made and started her own business, Phenomenal Content LLC. She also writes a blog, where she markets herself as an "exceptional editor, rock star writer, and founder of Phenomenal Content."

With a master's degree in psychology and experience working with children in a psychiatric hospital and as a front-desk supervisor at a hotel, Gleason isn't your usual suspect going into online writing. She gained experience as an online message board moderator. Then she joined an Internet marketing firm, managing a team of writers.

After being laid off, she immediately got on Twitter to let people know. The clients then started coming to her, asking her what she would charge to write for them. Gleason charges $40 or more, depending on the length of the article or blog post.

The business, based in her home in Clifton Park, New York, is also more flexible than her previous job, allowing her time with her four-year-old son. She started out by creating content for marketers working on client websites. Today she mainly serves as an editor, maintaining quality control, and has hired two writers. She also makes sure the articles have the right keywords to get traffic from search engines.

After a year in her own business, Gleason earns double the salary she used to make at the Internet marketing firm. "Betcha you wish you didn't let me go now," she says with a laugh.

Working in her own business initially was "outside my comfort zone," she admits. "I was quite happy working for other people." But now, Gleason can't see why she would ever work for someone else.

Is going solo for you? Ask yourself these questions:

- Are you an independent worker? Do you enjoy working alone or prefer being among people?

- Can you work out of your home? If you have children, consider how you would handle both your work and their needs.

- Do you have sufficient skills? Are you up-to-date on Web content creation, search engine optimization, software-based design, online writing, social media, and other computer-based skills?

- Do you have the necessary tools? Compared with most businesses, the initial cost is low but there are basic computer, software, and office requirements.

- Can you hire others for overflow work? If you're not getting enough work, do you have other options for income? Will you be in a good position to apply for a regular job, if need be?

Buy a Business or Franchise

In past recessions, experienced workers who could not find jobs in their field often opted to buy a business or franchise. People once used their home equity or retirement savings to finance a business, but the U.S. housing and financial crises eliminated that option for many.

But for those with the money to invest, buying an existing business or franchise could be the way to go after losing a job. Just make sure it's a business you really want to work in, and weigh the financial risks.

George Berkeley opted for a franchise after being laid off. He spent 23 years as a computer engineer on Wall Street, supporting brokerage networks including the New York Stock Exchange. "In a six-year period, I was downsized four times. That bugs you after a while," he says.

By late 2008, when Wall Street was in turmoil, Berkeley was getting ready to open his UPS franchise in South Orange, New Jersey. He got the idea from his own experience. When his wife used to give him packages to mail, he'd have to take them from his New Jersey home, carry them on the subway, and mail them in Manhattan. There was nowhere along the way to easily drop them off.

Later, when he was managing apartments for a friend, he found clients also worried about package deliveries. "I was constantly getting calls from tenants, 'I'm at work, and I have an important package coming. Can you be there to meet the driver?' " He suggested that tenants consider a post office box, but found that none were available in the area.

"I realized I lived in a town in need of a UPS store. I started looking at franchises in general and decided of all the options, UPS was the best option for me," Berkeley says.

He did his homework, contacting 27 store owners and asking them the same list of questions: Why did they buy the franchise? Were they happy with their decision? Would they do it again?

"Most everybody said they would *not* do it again. The main reason was they never get time off," Berkeley says. Many of the stores were run by husband-and-wife partners who switched off working at the store.

But as he asked more questions, Berkeley found all the store owners had renewed their franchise with UPS. That's partly because the contracts stipulated that franchisees could renew or sell their franchises after five years, but the location had to continue as a UPS store.

Berkeley, 59, wasn't bothered by long hours: He worked late and on weekends on Wall Street. And he saw opportunity in customer service. As a corporate engineer, he had turned disgruntled clients into multimillion-dollar contracts. At UPS, "it's the same thing. My customer who walks in the door may not be a multimillion-dollar contract, but I treat him like he is," Berkeley says.

He took about two years to secure what he thought was the right location, directly across from the train station where people waited to go into Manhattan every day. Berkeley opened the doors of his store in February 2009. To market the business, he stands on the train platform and hands out fliers.

Recently, he has added other services for clients, such as printing for next-day delivery.

"'Can you handle 25 briefs by the morning?' a customer will ask. 'Sure. Could I get you a cup of coffee, too?'" he says.

Services beyond package delivery now bring in 15 percent of the revenues. "I started making money the third month I was here," Berkeley says. "I haven't recovered my capital expenses, but I would be surprised if that takes more than two years."

Franchises come in all sizes and costs. Berkeley paid an initial $4,000 franchise fee. But the real expense came in starting the store: leasing the space and equipping it cost about $350,000. He pays UPS about 7 percent of sales in monthly royalties, which goes mainly to marketing and advertising. He's happy to pay the fees for the ample advertising that UPS provides.

"My wife and I went to an event and flashing on the big screen were the UPS shield and stores. I said, 'Look at that, I paid for it!' But I don't have to *do* it. I could watch Letterman and see advertising for my store," Berkeley says.

Companies that sell franchisees often tout a relatively quick ramp up to profitability if owners follow the playbook. But make sure a new franchisee can't locate within a certain geographic region of your store—such competition could hurt your ability to succeed and has been known to end in a lawsuit. Berkeley says he bought a specified territory, and his franchise documents spell that out. "I can open as many stores as I want within my territory, but nobody can open a store in mine without my permission," he says.

If you choose to buy a franchise, make sure you get all the training you can. Even with his business and technology background, Berkeley says, "I've had a steep learning curve." He found that even with training, every customer who entered the store in the first week presented a new challenge.

He also spends a great deal of time working with new employees. "That's the hardest part of my job. I get some pretty smart young adults in here, but I have to train them for customer service."

It also pays to keep in close touch with franchise headquarters. But after spending two decades in the corporate world, Berkeley says he won't be a "corporate lackey." When he disagrees or has a problem with the way franchise headquarters is handling something, he writes to the company president. "I'm going to write him and tell him a better way to do it," he says.

For anyone considering a franchise purchase, there are plenty of online resources available. Visit the Federal Trade Commission online at ftc.gov, the Small Business Administration at sba.gov, and the International Franchise Association at franchise.org. But, like Berkeley did, visiting different franchisees and talking with them about their experiences is your best research tool.

Before you buy a franchise, consider the following:

- Consider whether it's a business you want to spend most of your time doing. You will spend the good part of your weekdays and weekends working on the business until you're able to afford help.

- Visit multiple franchise owners and ask the same questions to find out if they would go into the business all over again.

- Look at lawsuits and other legal problems that may have arisen with other franchisees or the franchise company.

- Check the location of the same or similar businesses in your demographic area. Are they too close for both businesses to succeed?

- Make sure you understand the total expense: The cost to build, franchise fees, royalties owed to the franchise company, and any other costs should be detailed in the franchise disclosure document.

- Consider whether you can tolerate the rules of a franchise. If not, you may be more of an entrepreneur.

- Understand the daily manpower needed to operate the business. If it's a family business, make sure your spouse or other family members are on board. Divide duties and responsibilities upfront so no one feels overburdened.

- Check the typical time it takes to make a profit and for the owner to take a salary. Prepare to have enough income to sustain the business during the ramp-up, which could be years—not months.

- Know your exit strategy. What if the franchise isn't profitable? Are there provisions about when you can sell it?

Start a Business Doing What You Enjoy

Husband and wife Chuck and Mindy Pheterson, both professionals in their mid-50s, opted for starting a business after they became unemployed around the same time in 2009. The company where Chuck worked as a vice president of product development was sold. Mindy was laid off from her work in software processing, began teaching, and lost her job again because of school cutbacks.

Chuck figured he could parlay his skills into a business. He knew a recession was no time to develop new high-tech, expensive products. So he thought, "What would be a good product in this economy?" He decided the answer was "comfort food." One of his favorite treats was a chocolate-covered banana at a local candy store. He didn't think twice about paying $6 for one when he was employed.

"I could do a better job and sell it for half the price," Chuck Pheterson reasoned.

The couple agreed that they they'd live off Chuck's severance pay while developing the company and not touch their retirement funds. But Chuck had stock options from his former employer, so he exercised them and used the proceeds to launch their Fort Lauderdale–based business, Totally Bananas.

"I probably went through a hundred names. You come up with something that clicks. I wanted something that's lighthearted, and I wanted it to be a fun product. Totally Bananas kind of made me smile," Chuck Pheterson says.

The Phetersons incorporated the business in June 2009, and Chuck began doing research on product development. He used frequent-flier miles accumulated from his previous job to fly to Wisconsin to talk with a chocolate manufacturer. He used his engineering skills to design equipment to wrap the bananas and also for packaging and marketing materials.

By the summer, the Phetersons bought storage freezers and in September, they rented a commercial kitchen from a restaurant owner who was not yet ready to open. They decided to start selling the bananas immediately, even though the printed packages weren't available. They hoped to build clientele, get cash flow, and obtain feedback. "We sold it where we could with generic packaging, at festivals and through home delivery," Chuck Pheterson says.

Originally, Chuck planned to develop the business alone, while Mindy got a job elsewhere. But Mindy decided to help out with bookkeeping, networking, and social media to ramp up the company faster. Their Facebook page now has more than 400 fans. Chuck focuses on growing the business through new sales, currently at 30 local ice cream, gelato, and other stores.

For further help, Chuck and Mindy turned to SCORE, a national organization of retired executives who help startup businesses navigate financing and other issues. By creating the business in phases, the Phetersons are being careful not to spend more than they really can afford. But growth takes capital. They are seeking funding either from a bank or private investors for their next phase, which includes new equipment with increased capacity. They also plan to hire a few employees with the help of a federal stimulus program.

There are many considerations before anyone should invest in starting a business. The Phetersons asked themselves:

- Who is our target market?

- What are customers willing to pay for this product?

- What's the cost of making the product?

- What's the cost of getting customers?

- How many products can we make in a day?

On a frugal business budget, they've had to learn to do everything themselves. But Pheterson wanted to make sure he did everything by the book so he eventually can sell the business: Their product manufacturing process is FDA-inspected, for example. Chuck did the research on nutritional information for the packaging instead of outsourcing it.

When you start a new business, it's also important to expect problems and not to get discouraged, he says. "No matter how well you plan, things happen. If you order something, it's going to arrive late or be broken or wrong. It's not the world conspiring against you. You learn to double-check everything," Pheterson says.

Pheterson says he thinks many people stop themselves from going into business because they can't envision themselves selling. "I never thought of myself as a salesperson. It's like any other talent, you just learn it," he says. Practice on potential customers who are not the core ones you hope to sign, Pheterson advises.

Working together as a couple is another consideration for business success. As an independent-minded professional, Mindy Pheterson says it took some getting used to for her to be taking orders from her husband at work. Now they've divided duties so they don't get in each other's way.

The Phetersons were not yet taking a salary, but that's typical for a startup business. Any money they make is being reinvested in the business to expand it. Chuck hopes he can work for three to five years, and then sell the company and retire.

"You have to have a lot of money upfront," Mindy Pheterson says. "If we didn't have Chuck's severance money, and our house and cars were not paid off, we wouldn't have considered it."

To start a business unrelated to your profession, follow these guidelines:

- Use your skills from your work experience, such as product design, for your own business.

- Total your startup costs, leaving room for unforeseen expenses.

- Make sure you have enough money to operate the business through at least the early stage.

- Have another source of income to live on while building your business.

- Understand what you don't know and need to learn about the business.

- Seek help from small business centers, SCORE, and other entrepreneurial resources.

- Make sure there's a market for your business in good times and in bad.

- Plan how you're going to finance the next stage of your business growth.

- Determine an exit strategy. Could you sell the business? Bring in a partner?

Update from Traditional to Digital

Another option to traditional jobs is to create a nonprofit organization. Those starting a tax-exempt organization may be able to tap grants from foundations, the government, or wealthy individuals to fund their operations and salaries. More journalism ventures are moving in this direction.

In Seattle, Robert McClure was pursuing his passion: environmental watchdog journalism. But then the Pulitzer Prize finalist and more than 100 journalists at the *Seattle Post-Intelligencer* found out in March 2009 that the publication was going completely online. That meant the print journalists were out of jobs.

"It's got to be wrong," McClure says he first thought when he heard a TV report that the paper was up for sale. But it didn't sell, and publication ceased.

McClure, 50, immediately decided to launch a digital news service to continue his work in environmental journalism. In his former newsroom, "I was one of the first one to say 'this is what I'm going to do,'" he says.

He held an organizational meeting and nearly 45 people showed up. "We realized that if we were going to be a nonprofit, we couldn't have 45 people." So he started the news agency with just six partners.

He and his partners began blogging daily, and in July 2009, they launched InvestigateWest, a news agency for environmental and social issues, primarily in the West. They set up the organization as a nonprofit organization so they could apply for grants and get support from individual donors interested in keeping environmental journalism alive.

They bought audio and video equipment and went to industry conferences, including Investigative Reporters and Editors, to make contacts—all on their own dime. "Financially, it was not a very smart thing to do. Everybody has incurred a lot of expenses," he says. McClure refinanced his house and lived off his severance and savings.

To cut outlays, the startup looked to local incubators and business groups. McClure and his partners found help writing a business plan through Point B Solutions Group, consultants who work with startups. They also secured pro bono help from a local law firm to set up their nonprofit. "It's an amazing amount of work to set up a nonprofit," McClure says.

The nonprofit's lucky break came in February 2010 when it was awarded a $100,000 grant from the Ethics and Excellence in Journalism Foundation. InvestigateWest now is pulling in revenues for articles it produces and sells to national and regional websites. It also hopes to raise money through website membership.

McClure writes confidential white papers for business and trade groups to help pay the bills, but the nonprofit's primary mission is environmental journalism. "We have to be open to opportunities. But we don't want to alter what we do so much that we're not doing journalism," McClure says.

If you want to make a job from your passion, consider the following:

- Are there others as passionate who will support your business or organization?

- Consult a lawyer about setting up a nonprofit corporation. As a nonprofit, you will be able to apply for government grants, seek support from foundations, and ask for donations.

- Plan on an initial investment from you and other founders. Have other income to rely on until you can draw a salary.

- Identify sources of revenue: Beyond your mission, what side activities could generate revenue?

- Consider ways you can keep expenses low. Do you need an office or can you work from home?

- Create a plan for donations: Who is your target donor? Are there wealthy individuals, corporations, or foundations that would share your passion?

- Remember the mission of your organization. Stay true to your intentions while being flexible enough to welcome new opportunities.

Move to Where You Want to Be

Sometimes, starting a business may be your best option when relocating. If work won't come to you in your city, then you can create your own venture where you want to be.

That's what long-time news photographer Angel Valentin decided to do. He and his wife Isaida Ortiz were living in Miami and dreamed of moving to their native Puerto Rico to be closer to family.

So in 2008 when Valentin, 43, was offered a management job at a Puerto Rico newspaper, he was thrilled. The money was good, and he was excited about the job. They decided Isaida would stay in Miami until Angel could get settled.

But Angel was laid off from the job after about a year. And Isaida was still in Miami, working. To make ends meet on one salary, the couple rented out their South Florida home, and Isaida moved in with relatives. Valentin commuted back and forth, when there was work in Miami, but still wanted to make his living in Puerto Rico.

The transition was tough. "I wasn't really getting any work. Every two months I would fly to Florida and shoot assignments," Valentin says. His unemployment check in Puerto Rico was barely enough to feed his dog. "I would eat at my parents and in-laws. My social life disappeared," he says.

Still, it was easy to forget his predicament when he lived 200 steps from the ocean. One day he playfully sent his wife a photo of him and his dog on the beach, saying, "Hey baby, look I'm on the beach again."

He soon realized he needed to do more if his wife was going to be able to join him in Puerto Rico. So Valentin opted to build a business in wedding photography, work he had done previously as a freelancer.

There were obstacles: Valentin no longer had the photo equipment he needed because he had to give it back to his former employer. And he knew little about starting a business. He bought second-hand equipment from other photographers. He also spent money on a website and hired a search engine optimization expert to make sure it placed high on Google and other search engines.

His business, Island Wedding Fotos, has a niche: documentary wedding photography where Valentin captures the moments of a wedding day naturally as they happen, rather than traditional wedding portraits and group photos. He specializes in destination weddings.

Valentin had to learn how to market his business and himself. "As a photojournalist, I was always trying to be invisible, never really selling myself. As a wedding photographer, I have to tell people how good I am, how much better I am than the other guys. Clients need to be reassured that you're confident in your ability and experience and you can do your job."

He has learned that getting a photography business off the ground is a lot of work. "You have to have money or access to money, a decent website, and samples of your work. You have to know your market and your competition," Valentin says. By mid-2010, he was starting to make a good income and was planning for his wife to finally join him in Puerto Rico.

Even though operating his own business has been challenging, Valentin says he wouldn't go back to news photography, which was his passion for 18 years. He has grown as a professional and sees potential in documentary wedding photography. Valentin enjoys his new work, especially when a couple appreciates his brand of photography. "You can get over a bad cake or a DJ. The photographs you have to live with for a long time," he says.

Before you try to start a business where you want to live, think about the following:

- Choose a location with the business in mind. Is there a market?

- Consider the family and other emotional and financial support you have in the location.

- Who is your competition? Is there room for your business in this location, even if you're the best?

- Invest in a website, business cards, fliers, and other items to promote the business.

- Learn social media to market your business.

Seek a Partnership

A partnership is a vehicle to start or join a business. But choose your business partners with care. When partners can't work together, a business can suffer or even fail.

Hal Howard, 49, became partners with someone he knew and trusted after closing his Chrysler Dodge dealership in Goldsboro, North Carolina, in 2008. He had thought he would own the dealership the rest of his life. "My dealership was number one in customer satisfaction, sales, and profit for seven and one-half years. We saw a turn in the market around 2008 and our client base declined. Then General Motors filed for bankruptcy. That devastated the small dealer," Howard says.

He had hoped to pass on the wealth he built to his two children. But that plan screeched to a halt, and Howard made the difficult decision to close his dealership. Meanwhile, he had to figure out what to do next. Howard had owned the dealership for 10 years and had made many friends in the industry and outside it. One customer was a successful investment manager who Howard had known since he was a kid.

When that customer wanted a new car, Howard used to personally deliver it, and the two would chat about business and life. Howard made it a practice to keep in touch with people he met in many different industries over the years. "Ultimately, that's what bridged the gap for me," he says.

He began his new career raising capital for the investment firm and buying distressed properties, including auto dealerships, hotels, casinos, and restaurants for eventual resale. A car dealership, for example, is selling for 20 to 30 cents on the dollar.

"It satisfies both my needs: to be able to eat and maintain my lifestyle and to build generational wealth," Howard says.

From his upbringing, Howard says it is important to him to leave money someday to his two children, now both in college. "It goes back to my mother and father...I had two younger brothers and, if they were outside and they ran into a tree—that was my fault. I should have been watching them." His mother would say, "There are no excuses."

"When I had to close the dealership, I said, 'There are no excuses.' You've got to do something else," Howard says. Fortunately, Howard had skills that were transferable to a new business. He had worked for Fortune 500 companies before becoming an auto retailer. "I started off in engineering and manufacturing, so I understood the operational perspective. Then I went into marketing and sales, so I understood the customers," he says.

To take advantage of new opportunities, Howard says it's key to anticipate change. "You can sit there and cry, but this is a period of tremendous opportunity," he tells former colleagues. "If you have a strong belief in who you are and what you can do, this is a big time in history for a lot of people. It's all about transitioning yourself."

If you are considering a partnership, keep the following in mind:

- Make sure the partner is someone you know well and who has a solid reputation.

- Think about the benefits as well as the drawbacks to partnership versus going solo.

- Seek a lawyer specializing in contracts and partnerships to draw up a contract specifying each partner's equity and responsibilities.

- Have an exit strategy in your contract.

Use Your Skills for Others

Engineers are problem solvers. Ollie Jones, 48, once used his engineering skills on state-of-the-art transportation systems. Today, he is the inventor of physical therapy equipment for special-needs children in his own business, Janae's Designs. The inspiration for the business was his daughter, Janae Hope, who has cerebral palsy.

Early in his career, Jones was on the move, working on projects for different employers in New York, Pennsylvania, and Florida. When in New York, he married Tracy and they had a daughter, Nya Faith, now 11. A couple of years later, the young family decided to move to a community outside Philadelphia. They also discovered that Tracy was pregnant.

Through an ultrasound, the couple found out the baby had a rare condition called arterial venous malformation. Simply put, too much blood was going to the baby's brain. After Janae Hope was born, she endured seven brain surgeries. "In the meantime, she developed cerebral palsy," Jones says. "It was a very tough period in our lives."

The Joneses later moved to South Florida so that Ollie could take an engineering job. But in 2006, he was laid off. Jones had a tempting offer to work overseas, but there was no assurance he could find the services abroad that he needed for Janae. "My daughter has special needs, and I just can't pick up and leave like that," he says. "She can't eat or walk by herself. We have to feed and dress her."

Jones was asked by the physical therapist at Janae's school if he could use his engineering skills to fashion equipment that would be helpful to Janae's progress. "They do offer therapy on site, but it is not enough. And there's a constant fight with insurance companies to pay for what she needs," he explains.

Children with cerebral palsy need one to two hours of stretching a day, so he designed the Wedgster, a seat that children can watch TV, eat, or read in and get the therapy they need at the same time.

When Janae again had surgery and her leg was in a cast, Jones came up with the Legster, which attaches to a wheelchair and provides a platform for prolonged stretching. Janae, now 8, also now uses the Walkster, a physical therapy device Jones developed to enable a child to stand independently and perform leg-strengthening exercises. "We're trying to strengthen her to walk some day. That's one of my goals with the equipment," he says.

Now several special-needs children use Jones' equipment at the Potentials charter school in South Florida. Jones officially launched Janae's Designs in late 2008 and rented an office near his home in Wellington, Florida, to build the equipment. Each device sells for $500 to $1,200, depending on materials cost and labor for the custom design.

There is other equipment available, but it is often cost prohibitive for parents. "And it's not exactly tailored to each child's needs," says Mary Pengelley, the therapist at Janae's school who first broached the possibility of Jones designing special devices.

As a result, Janae has progressed from a four-year-old whose legs were not able to bear weight to an eight-year-old who can walk with the help of equipment, and whose legs are getting stronger everyday. Jones is "innovative, very perceptive, and he knows his daughter very well," Pengelley says.

To help other special-needs children, Jones is applying for federal government grants to do further research, hire some employees, and provide equipment for free or at a reduced cost. But he also believes Janae's Designs is a viable business. He has turned to the local Small Business Development Center for guidance. On advice from a counselor, Jones took time to secure provisional patents for his equipment. He also has been trying to conserve cash, negotiating a deal on his office space and looking for bargains on wood and other materials for the equipment.

Meanwhile, Ollie and Tracy recently had a third child, a healthy son they named Jadon Niles. The couple hopes their experience can inspire others who have suffered hardships to pursue their dreams. "Never give up. Just apply the skills you have to improve the life of your child and make a life for your family," Jones says.

"Tap into all your resources, your skills, all the things you've learned over the years. There is a wealth of resources out there for people who want to start their own business."

To turn an invention into a business, follow these guidelines:

- Consider the size of the target market for your product. Is it large enough to attract a retailer or consumer company?

- Apply for a provisional patent on your invention. It costs less to apply for a provisional patent and gives an inventor time to test an invention before investing in a regular patent.

- Test the product, following government regulations and protocol.

- Determine the lowest cost of making a good product: What materials can be bought in bulk? Can you make a large volume for less?

- Consider how you can market the product and grow sales. Will you need employees or can you outsource production?

Streetwise Strategies for Creating Your Own Job

- Use your skills for a different type of work.

- Capitalize on your established network.

- Consider whether the work suits your lifestyle.

- Follow your passion, but develop a business plan.

- Think seriously about your capital investment and risk.

- Seek grants to finance your work.

- Do your due diligence if buying a business or franchise.

- Prepare financially to start a business. Do you have other income to rely on for several years?

- Create a business in phases to test if it works.

- Buy a franchise for the brand, but know that generating sales is your job.

- Consider a partnership with someone you trust in business.

- Use your skills to help others and make a living from it.

EPILOGUE: KEEP LOOKING, NEVER STOP

I began this project in September 2009, with the bulk of my reporting occurring between December 2009 and May 2010. Although America's recovery was underway, most economists were expecting a bumpy ride.

Case in point: Of the 90 successful job candidates I interviewed for this book, four lost their jobs again in late 2009 or early 2010. By the time this book was going to press, three had already found new jobs. In mid-2010, the speed at which people were finding work seemed to be picking up.

People who have been through the job search process are forever changed in how they approach their careers. They learn to constantly add to and broaden their networks. They keep their skills fresh by earning new certifications or mastering the latest tools in their field. They regularly update their resumes and portfolios.

If there's one thing California teacher David Tow has learned, it's always to be looking for his next job. With state budget cuts, he never knows from one school year to the next whether he's going to have a job. "I hope my job sticks around, but I prepare for it *not* to be around," Tow says. "That's the only way I can ensure I'll have a job."

Once you land a job, it's natural to want to relax, enjoy your new income, and start planning a vacation. That's okay, but remember to keep your eye out for new opportunities, network on a continual basis, and invest in updating your skills. Act as if you are always job hunting because you never know when life is going to throw you another curve.

Being unemployed was an "eye opener," says Jim Kowalczyk, the Atlanta process improvement expert. "Don't get too comfortable," he advises. "Don't let your network start to fizzle. Stay involved in professional organizations and attend one a month."

Layla Thomas, the South Florida green energy specialist, continues to update her skills and stretch in new ways. She is teaching at a local college and recently received her residential contractor license.

Chicago-area sales manager Alvaro Ruiz is more attuned to his work environment since he found a new job. "I'm more cognizant I need to work really hard so my boss understands my value," he says. Ruiz makes a point to talk about his sales results in Monday conference calls with his boss. It has made a difference in his confidence. "When you're delivering results, it feels good to say, 'This is what I did,'" he says. Those results will come in handy for a future job search.

While being ever-mindful of the new job search reality, the successful job candidates I interviewed are doing what they can to help others who are in career transition. They're also offering their services to the outplacement or job search organizations that guided them.

North Carolina product manager Ken Jones, grateful for the career resources he found through his MBA alma mater, University of North Carolina, now serves on career panels at the school to relay his job search experience and advice. In South Florida, sales manager Luis Riano mentors students who are looking for their first jobs after college.

Natalie Silva, whose snazzy portfolio helped her get hired as media director for a San Antonio hamburger chain, has been guiding an administrative assistant who is looking for work. Silva helped her create a similar portfolio and accompanies her to mixers and business functions. "Every person I introduce her to is blown away," she says. "You have to pay it forward."

Grateful for her new job, human resources professional Nancy Cranford has joined a formal organization in Atlanta where volunteers introduce professionals who would benefit from knowing each other. A new business venture, client, or a job could result.

So once you find a job, don't stop looking for your own sake. But also remember to pay it forward. Your job lead could result in someone else being able to say, "I found a job!"

INDEX

Catching Trophy Salmon and Trout

Secrets of a Great Lakes Pro

Gerry Wolfram

Stackpole Books

Published by
STACKPOLE BOOKS
Cameron and Kelker Streets
P. O. Box 1831
Harrisburg, PA 17105

Photographs are by the author unless otherwise credited.

Printed in the U.S.A.

Library of Congress Cataloging-in-Publication Data

Wolfram, Gerry.
    Catching trophy salmon and trout.

    Bibliography: p.
    Includes index.
    1. Salmon fishing—Great Lakes.   2. Trout
fishing—Great Lakes.   I. Title.
SH684.W65 1986   799.1′755   85-17249
ISBN 0-8117-2011-X

This book is dedicated to Gwynne, certainly the finest catch I ever made, who as my wife and ever helpful first mate has a priceless ability to add humor and charm to any outdoor endeavor.

Contents

Acknowledgments

The acquisition of any angling knowledge and the writing of any book invariably involve many people, who, through friendship or common interests, play a variety of special roles in completing a project such as this one. Angling clients who have shared so many exciting fishing adventures over the years have unquestionably done most to help weave together whatever depth and color this book might possess. If the tapestry wears thin in spots, or if the fishing falls off, the fault is mine.

Special thanks also go to hard-working charterboat skippers Bill Thede of Sebewaing, Michigan, and Bill Smith of Henderson Harbor, New York, to name only two, who today explore the vast Great Lakes system in a unique and delightful style. Their sharing of charterboating information and comradeship both on and off the water form the basis of strong, greatly appreciated, friendships.

There are also biologists such as Richard Hess of the Illinois Department of Conservation, John Spurrier of the Minnesota Department of

Natural Resources, Michael Hansen of Wisconsin, Ned Fogle of Michigan, Robert Koch of Indiana, Art Holder of Ontario, and many other dedicated Great Lakes fishery specialists who deserve recognition.

In addition, this book owes a heavy debt to scientists such as Dr. Jim Tibbles of the Great Lakes Sea Lamprey Control Centre, Sault Ste. Marie; Professor Peter Larkin of the Institute of Animal Resource Ecology, University of British Columbia, Vancouver; Dr. J. M. Cooley of the Great Lakes Fishery Research Branch, Burlington, Ontario; Dr. Jimmy Winter, Associate Director of the Environmental Resources Center, State University of New York, Fredonia, on Lake Erie, and his Lake Ontario counterparts, Dr. Michael Voiland and Dr. James Haynes of State University of New York at Brockport. These men are only a few of many scholars throughout North America who graciously shared valuable knowledge gained from long years of specialized work.

Thanks too to Lowrance sonar specialist Charles Ramsay of Tulsa, Oklahoma and Bob Knopf of Berkley/Trilene in Spirit Lake, Iowa, for filling in some high-tech blanks.

Last on this vastly incomplete list are two people who should be at the top: Chet Fish and Peggy Senko of Stackpole Books.

1

Welcome Aboard

It is from this point of view . . . that every epoch requires to say its own say, that the writing of a new book on fishing is not only justified, but may be valuable.

—*John Waller Hills,* A Summer on the Test

Want to get rich? Have more fun than anyone else? It's easy. Just never, but never, go into the Great Lakes salmon fishing charterboat business. Any charterboater who has pumped enough bilge water will tell you the one secret of longevity in this wacky business is being able to tap a deep inner well of bright, inextinguishable optimism during moments of black stress. He won't put it exactly that way, of course, but that's what he'll mean.

To give you an idea of the laughs you'd live with: You suddenly discover early some morning that one of your boat's twin outboard motors won't start. It's seemingly unfixable—at least not at the dock. Your anglers, who should have shown up an hour ago, are either lost or not coming. And you're standing there, idle, probably facing a big repair bill and without an advance payment jingling in your jeans. In addition, adding to the fun, marina flags snapping against an ominous, cloud-filled sky promise a faceful of five-foot waves as soon as you do clear the harbor breakwall. So who's worried?

On the other hand, to be realistic about the whole thing, you can't do anything but keep smiling anyway. Consider the alternatives. One route, which most of us have taken at one time or another, is fist-clenching, obscenity-shouting defiance of the elements, which doesn't help digestion in any way, although you do get rid of some frustration if you scream loudly enough. Or you could take the opposite tack, I suppose, although I haven't tried it yet, of holding dawn worship services to the sun and the wind on the bow of the boat. Have the salmon magically disappeared? Try deliberately dropping costly fishing lures into the lake while murmuring incantations. Who knows? It'd probably work as well as any other method to placate fickle angling spirits.

What really keeps you going, though, is remembering the good days, which always outnumber the bad. The blacker the present situation, the brighter the memories of other outings when the water was reasonably calm and the fish came easy.

What also helps are the other attractions of big water. The basic, age-old fascination of the sea itself is still an enjoyable reality, although the sense of adventure is obviously lessened by knowing, unlike early oceanic explorers, there is no danger of sailing off the edge of a flat earth. Yet the freedom of the sea, its challenges and mysteries, still exists. The independence and responsibility of being alone in a vast expanse of water and sky are still worthwhile. What better way to greet a rising sun, or feel the wind in your face, than running a midlake course toward an empty horizon, the wake of your passage cutting a sharp, clean trail in the water behind you, its crests slowly dissolving far astern like the trailing plume of a jet aircraft passing high overhead.

Additional bonuses abound. For example, what monetary value can be placed on the pride, or sense of personal worth, gained from even minor navigational or rough water accomplishments? A good skipper delights in handling a boat well in a difficult sea. He knows how his craft will behave in a storm. He can feel it beneath him, almost alive, and by anticipating its actions, as in riding a spirited horse, he can make the boat an extension of himself. Hours later, under such conditions, as the crest of one last big wave sweeps the boat safely into harbor, who can hold back a tiny grin of satisfaction?

Pleasures? Our inland oceans are full of them. As a birdwatcher I have an unscientific tendency to humanize wildlife behavior. Scientists have a dirty word for us. They call us anthropomorphists on paper—in conversation it's even worse. But I would still like to know what goes on in the head of a lone herring gull riding a small floating plank so far from

Fishing far offshore on the Great Lakes provides a wide variety of outdoor experiences as well as superlative fishing. (*Photo courtesy of Mercury Marine*)

shore. Why is it there? Is it enjoying the ride so much it abandoned its companions? Possibly it just wanted to stay dry while resting en route to some distant sea gull rendezvous. Being in a major shipping lane, it might only be waiting for a passing freighter to dump another meal overboard. But it is clear from the gull's cold stare I am an unwelcome intruder.

There is no Great Lakes angler who doesn't pause in his or her activities to look skyward when a flight of giant Canada geese noisily honks its way shoreward or whenever a flock of goldeneye ducks whistles by above the wave tops. In the heavy fogs of September an offshore boat is often used as a stopover by various migrating land birds and, occasionally, even big, orange-and-black-winged monarch butterflies heading to Mexican wintering grounds. Our last visitors of note were two tiny chestnut-sided warblers, beautiful but rarely seen multicolored birds obviously confused by fog. Both stayed with us, only inches away at times, until I brought them back within scent, if not sight, of land.

While clients who return year after year invariably remember the fish they caught, and assume you have the same recall, I must confess it doesn't work that way. The fish that are netted day after day during a normal six-month angling season, unless extremely large or caught under unusual circumstances, tend to blur together in a wild kaleidoscope of flapping tails, flying silver scales, and whooping fishermen. You remember the anglers, not the fish.

Adding interest to outings over the years is the amazingly wide diversity of client backgrounds and interests: Merchant princes, factory workers, doctors, lawyers, dentists, engineers, bankers, entertainers, businessmen, teachers, writers, farmers, housewives. We've enjoyed having them all on board. We talk of many things, of course: of fish caught and fish lost, of past days, future plans, what our families are doing. A charterboater comes to know his anglers well. Among those who return year after year, the shared experiences of earlier trips often help turn such associations into lasting friendships that carry over into other areas.

All conversations, whether with first-time clients or old friends, have a common starting point. Once tackle is rigged and the battery of rods is set up across the stern, novice anglers invariably ask, "What happens if we get fish on all the rods at once?" My answer, made in jest, is always the same: "That's when I go lock myself in the cabin. You just let me know when it's all over." More experienced anglers start the day by asking, with good reason, "How's the fishing been?" Those who ask such questions know there is no way to guarantee catches, no matter how well our boat did the day before. But it is still good for anglers to know fish have been consistently boated and, with any luck, are still there to be caught that day.

Anglers obviously want to catch fish. They're paying good money for that purpose. But from a charterman's viewpoint, a day's success is measured by clients' reactions as much as by the number of fish caught. If it seems anglers weren't happily relaxed or didn't enjoy themselves— whether because of weather, fewer cooperative fish than expected, or simple incompatibility because we all woke up with migraine headaches that day—the outing has been a total waste of time and effort. But, thankfully, those days are rare.

Oddly enough, for the male chauvinists among us, female groups— many of whom have never really fished before in their lives—often provide the most satisfying days on the lake. Women seem to watch the rods more closely, to listen to instruction better, and thus are the most fun to take out, possibly because of the total joy in their reactions to a brand new experience. Youngsters are equally enjoyable for the same reasons. True happiness is never more highly concentrated, or sparkles more clearly, than in the beaming face of a ten- or twelve-year-old, freckle-faced kid who has just "whipped" the biggest fish of his life.

I'll never forget one such boy. His mother, a divorcee, was obviously

Paying anglers expect to catch big fish, such as this chinook salmon, when they venture out onto the lakes with a charterboater. (*Photo courtesy of Ontario Federation of Anglers and Hunters*)

Youngsters enjoying their first taste of Great Lakes fishing add fun to any charterboater's day.

determined to expose the fatherless youngster to what she considered "manly pursuits." It was a cold, windy, rough-water day in spring. Before we left the dock, the boy's mother calmly predicted she would get seasick, which she did within thirty minutes of getting out on the lake. I lifted newly set tackle and returned to harbor, suggesting she stay on shore to recuperate while my wife Gwynne and I took the boy out on his own.

"Fine," she said. Both Gwynne and I had visions of the boy, a chubby kid, spending the whole time worrying about his sick, loving mother.

As it turned out, the youngster was a ready-made angling fanatic. "You want to go back in and make sure your mother is all right?" Gwynne asked several times during the day. No way. He knew his mother was safe on shore. He was there to fish. We quickly took a 2½-pound coho, a happy way to start the day for a bright-eyed kid who previously had never caught anything larger than six-inch perch and small bass from a pond near home. After another hour or so of bouncing around in three- to four-foot waves, he was slammed hard by an eleven-pound rainbow trout, a strong, big-running, deep-bellied fish that came close to beating him. "My arms hurt," he kept complaining after the fish had made its fourth or fifth run. He wanted to quit. I talked him out of it. Bullied might be a truer word. "Do it one more time. You get him anywhere near the boat and I'll net him," I promised. "You can't quit now." He did stay with the fish. We did boat it. And I like to think that boy's recollection of a difficult fish, and the obvious pride he took in it and in discovering he could be a winner, will be a bright memory the rest of his life.

Near the other end of the angling spectrum of joy, now that we've started talking about such things, are the big-money wheelers and dealers of high finance whose only angling experiences are sporadic trips to the Arctic or other remote, expensive places where fish line up to strike any kind of lure, no matter how poorly presented. Such success makes them angling experts, of course, and because of their egos (largely based on the size of their bank accounts) and their inability to admit they really know little, if anything, about real fishing, they tend to break tackle and lose a lot of fish.

Least enjoyable of all are clients (one-time clients, I might add) who equate a good time with exploring various levels of unconsciousness. One never-to-be-forgotten outing involved a young, attractive bride who booked a honeymoon charter as a surprise for her husband. It was a surprise all right. Fishing was obviously not one of her new husband's strong points. He began the day drinking beer, switched to wine, and then his own special brand of roll-your-own cigarettes. He eventually collapsed, lying on the bow deck, propped up against a cabin window where I could watch him. "You know, that's one really nice thing about George," his loving wife suddenly announced proudly, watching her husband's inert form from the mate's seat beside me, "He has a good time no matter where he goes." I admitted that was true. Smiling George was so zonked I could have put a hangman's noose around his neck and dragged him around Lake Ontario off an outrigger and he wouldn't have remembered it.

But, as I noted before, it's the good times, the fun times, you remember. Gwynne and I do a lot of experimental work, sometimes for fishing tackle manufacturers, other times for ourselves. In fact, if you want to know what a charterboater does in his free time, he normally goes fishing. Gwynne has her own special technique for catching fish on the days we're relaxing together on the water. As a native of British Columbia, and having grown up around salmon, Gwynne demands fast, West Coast–style action when she's fishing. She also has the knack of taking the largest fish. But given a slow day, when the sun is hot overhead and the fish are trying to prove still another angling theory is best forgotten, she'll often fall asleep, which is easy to do in a comfortable chair on a gently rocking boat. What puzzles me, watching her wake up to the sound of a screaming reel when a fish hits, is how she instinctively grabs the right rod. You'd think in her drowsiness she'd make a mistake once in a while but, so far at least, her record is perfect. Just luck? Maybe. Luck is certainly a big factor all anglers live with, whether they admit it or not.

The luckiest fish I've ever boated was a six-pound rainbow trout that not only saved a day but, in a sense, an entire angling year. Two years ago, I had gone close to six months without having a charter "skunked" and, by early September, was starting to think about going an entire season without a fishless day. On Lake Ontario that's comparable to a baseball pitcher hurling a perfect game or a golfer scoring nothing but par or better. Maybe it was thinking about a perfect year that did it. In many games once you start keeping score you're in trouble. But the day started well. Weather and water conditions were perfect: we had a slight chop and bright sun. It was going to be easy. Or so I thought.

Five hours later, with no fish in the boat, I could feel a cloud of doom forming overhead. I'd tried everything. I have one of the larger tackle boxes around, about the size of a trunk, and I'd worked my way through the whole thing. We stayed out a half-hour past normal quitting time, knowing, or hoping, there had to be a hungry fish out there somewhere, but finally I admitted defeat. As often happens in early September, the fish were widely scattered just prior to congregating for their spawning runs. Disconsolately, I lifted a rod out of its downrigger holder and snapped the line free of the cable release, forty feet down, preparing for the run back to port. As the lure fluttered upward, freed from the weight of the cannonball, a rainbow trout smashed it as though the lure was the last meal in the lake. I could have kissed that silly, perfect, stupendous fish. I didn't. But I could have.

The quickest fish I ever caught, high on any list of "lucky fish," won one of my anglers, Todd Besch of Cleveland, Ohio, a writer with *Walleye* magazine, a valuable prize for the first fish of the day in an invitational

Lake Ontario tournament. The tourney was held about four years ago by a major lure manufacturer to introduce a series of salmon spoons to United States and Canadian outdoor writers. The competition began with a Monte Carlo–style racing start with all boats, except mine, rushing off on signal toward the Niagara River. One of my writer/anglers had delayed our departure by disappearing in search of a last-minute cup of coffee. As a result, the other five boats in the tournament had lures in the water before we even arrived. They had started fishing well west of the river, not where the fish were most heavily congregated, so I just zipped in front of the lead boat, dropped the first cannonball, and had an obviously half-starved six-pound brown trout hit the trailing lure no more than fifteen feet below the boat while the ball was still dropping. The fish was hooked up within four seconds of the lure disappearing into the water. What the boat skipper behind us was thinking when he saw us take that brown out almost from under his bow is best not known. But the incident may prove that when you're lucky you might as well push it a bit.

An even more unusual trophy was a 12½-inch lamprey eel that hit a deeply trolled silver-blue spoon so hard it knocked the rod line free of its cannonball release. The angler involved, John Dolan, a well-known Canadian broadcaster, has never let me forget the freakish catch. A Great Lakes lamprey control official later informed me a similar lamprey attack had happened on the lakes only once before to his knowledge. As I write this, above my head on the wall over my desk is an impressive-looking plaque bearing a close-up photo of myself and the lamprey, still attached to the lure. The brass plate inscription reads: "The first (and last) annual lamprey eel tournament—Presented to Gerry Wolfram in perpetuity—1983."

Any discussion of luck inevitably raises the question, Can luck be controlled? At the risk of being accused of spending too much time chasing salmon too far from shore and coming down with a watery form of bush fever, I can only say I have seen far too many instances of mental attitudes—optimism, superstition, call it what you will—paying off in spectacular fashion to discount the possibility. Many other professional anglers, charterboaters, and tournament anglers feel the same way. They've all had similar experiences. Controlling luck and the factors of luck are quietly talked about, wondered about, and often laughed about at the end of the day when angling pros get together to share a whiskey or beer, but the subject is rarely discussed in public. Just putting such thoughts on paper makes the idea look sillier than it sounds. It's bad enough to talk about psychic matters in half-kidding fashion. But there are lucky boats and there are unlucky boats. Some anglers are lucky. Some aren't. Why? How do you define the difference?

Having happy, confident, interested anglers on board seems to be part of this indefinable magic. In fact, from a charterboating viewpoint, one of the skipper's biggest jobs is to maintain angling interest when the hours between strikes start to drag. Once anglers lose interest because of boredom you're in trouble—luck can disappear completely. So I do rather weird and wacky things occasionally to turn things around. Even stranger, they sometimes work.

I remember, as just one example, abruptly ending a fishless afternoon by telling my clients, a husband and wife, the reason they hadn't been catching fish was because they had been placing far too much attention on tackle. For what seemed like hours, they had been sitting and staring at the rods arced over in downriggers. "The best thing you can do is ignore the fish. Turn your back on them," I declared. They were ready for a seventh-inning stretch anyway. We stood up and solemnly turned our back on the fish, literally thumbing our collective noses at all personal angling gods. All of a sudden, Gwynne, who was on the wheel laughing at us, hollered "Fish on!" One rod had busted loose from its cannonball release and was bucking up and down against a running fish, its reel singing a high-pitched banshee wail of success. It was that quick. We ended the day with three coho salmon. Bang! Bang! Bang! Just like that. But I've been reluctant to tap such obviously strong powers too often. Only when I'm truly desperate. (I also know the odds of successfully repeating that little gambit.)

Fellow charterboat skipper Bruce Campbell has devised another interesting method of challenging fate. One extremely quiet day off the Niagara Peninsula, a day when any sensible angler would have gone home, Bruce, fishing alone, hung in long enough to have to use the head ("toilet" to you landlubbers). You can guess the rest. He was no sooner sitting on the ship's throne, contemplating the evils and joys of charterboating, when a rod released and a big chinook salmon attempted to make a nonstop trip back to the peace and quiet of the Pacific Ocean. Bruce instinctively jumped to his feet and started running, which is extremely difficult with underwear and trousers draped around your ankles. Dressed like the fabled nude emperor, bare butt and all, he made it to the rod and whomped that luckless fish into the boat in near record time. Lucky coincidence? Charterboater Ray Nicol, who also works the south shore of Lake Ontario, duplicated the feat the very next weekend. The only difference was that Ray managed to get his trousers back on in rather loose fashion before he got to the rod.

A sonargraph unit is another great help in keeping everyone happily fishing on a slow day. It's the equivalent of color TV. A few blips on paper, even if they're only silver bass, are almost as satisfying as catching fish at times. On quiet days, when the lake seems empty, who can really say what those occasional marks are on sonar paper? I can't. Not with any certainty. Not in summer. I also suspect that some of those big crescent-shaped readouts we get of bottom-hugging fish that seemingly can't be caught off river mouths or harbors can be king-sized carp just as easily as chinook salmon. But we optimistically drag lures through them anyway, hoping for the best, while everyone on board tightens up, bracing themselves like sprinters on a starting line as they wait for a jumping rod to signal a hooked fish.

Inexperience really shows at this time. Anglers out for the first time invariably hold back when a fish does release a rod, doing the "After you Alphonse" routine no matter how often they're told not to wait. After they've taken a few fish you see an interesting transformation. Once they know what to expect, and gain needed confidence, they'll plunge for that rod with the hell-for-leather approach of a football lineman blitzing a quarterback. Get in their way and you're liable to be knocked overboard.

I confess that even though no one should take any form of angling superstition too seriously (unless you successfully play the stock market with the help of a ouija board), any onboard antic has an extremely positive value. It might only be a "net-wetting ceremony," one I perform every day (what fish wants to be touched by a dry net?), or the use of a "fish whistle" to call big salmon to the boat. Whatever you do, no matter how crazy, helps to keep everyone psyched up. Experience has proven that anglers who have lost their enthusiasm will rarely, if ever, take as many fish as a boatload of optimists, if only because the optimists will fish harder and longer.

2

Great Lakes Fishing Myths

Even the most orthodox fisher may profitably temper the rigidity
of his beliefs with a little spontaneous heresy at times.
    —W. A. Adamson, The Enterprising Angler

Sooner or later, anyone spending time on the Great Lakes with precon-
ceived ideas about salmon fishing will discover that most so-called angling facts have a surprising habit of turning into myths. These contrary,
unpredictable fish will cross you up every time. Enjoy three or four days
of superlative fishing in a row, or whatever it takes to convince yourself
you have finally mastered the game and, whammo, the wind will change,
the fish will move, and you're back to Square One, playing a brand new
game with a completely different set of rules.

Fishing tackle manufacturer Bud Williams of Williams Wabler fame
probably summed the situation up as well as anyone. He had hefted the
fourth Lake Ontario coho of the day—all caught on a yellow-spotted,
frog-green imitation wabler fished forty feet down—and had snorted in
disgust. "This is ridiculous," he said. "These crazy fish have never seen
a frog before in their lives." We just grinned. Great Lakes salmon will
do that to you. Every outing is a learning experience.

Take the time we were experimenting with dodgers—big, brightly painted wobbler-shaped metal plates that zap a trailing lure back and forth behind them. In theory, the action and color of a dodger will draw fish a much greater distance than will a lure by itself. It also adds needed action to flies or squid imitations. The fish, in turn, if all goes well, then snap up the erratically moving, meal-sized lure behind it. Now if there's one thing every Great Lakes salmon fisherman knows, just as sure as unwrapping a sandwich or pouring a coffee will almost guarantee a hungry fish popping a rod out of a downrigger, the color of the dodger is as important as the color of the trailing lure. CB radio calls stress this point all the time. "What'd you catch it on?" a successful angler is asked. "Red and green," may come back as the answer. So everybody within radio listening distance immediately hauls up tackle and puts a red dodger in front of a green squid (or whatever the lucky angler was using).

The only trouble, and we might as well start sorting out a little bit of angling chaff right here, is that those experimental dodgers I was using were clear plastic, no color at all. Our primary interest at the time was shape and resultant lure action. Apply some heat to the plastic with a cigarette lighter and I could bend the dodgers like pretzels. The surprise was that the almost invisible dodgers drew as many fish as metal dodgers dragging the same lures in similar fashion at identical depths. The answer? I don't really know. I have to assume the real attraction of a dodger to salmon is not color but the underwater shock waves created by the dodger flipping back and forth, simulating tail-beat vibrations of moving forage fish. Those messages carry a long way, certainly well beyond sight range. And salmon, like most ocean fish, obviously know how to read them well.

British Columbia filmmaker Charlie White partially reinforces my opinion with some of his findings gained through underwater videotapes of fish reacting to lures. Only instead of dodgers, he was experimenting with vibrating spinners. "They make a dramatic difference," he says. "In one test, we were catching fish consistently on a large herring bait. When we put a fly and spinner beside it, the salmon moved immediately to the new lure, completely ignoring. . .the herring. When we matched identical lures (one with a spinner and one without), the salmon invariably went for the lure behind the spinner."

I've found over the years that water disturbance of any kind, including that created by the boat hull and engine props, may draw coho salmon, in particular, up surprising distances. An otherwise sane angling crony, who has a lot of world saltwater fishing experience behind him, insists one particular brand of outboard motor will attract fish better than any other. He swears every motor sings a different tune, or vibrates a

different way. Shiny prop blades also seem to help. Right or wrong—
and I think my friend, who has spent too many hours bareheaded under
a hot tropical sun, is carrying things to extremes—I am convinced an old
Pacific Ocean commercial angling "trick" of running a shallow lure in
the wash of a boat can pay off with extra coho salmon on the Great
Lakes, especially in flat water. I've never caught anything huge using this
technique, mainly year-old, three- to five-pounders. But on a hot, slow
midsummer day, even a silvery five-pounder can look good in the boat.

The importance of vibrations from any kind of water disturbance is
supported by the success I've had running lures at much faster than normal
trolling speeds. It seems the faster the lure goes the harder it wiggles,
and the stronger the signal it sends out to foraging salmon. Of course, it
can be argued that a faster-moving lure covers more water and is seen
by more fish. That's quite true. In fact, covering water quickly was my
initial reason for increasing trolling speed. As far as that goes, we could
safely claim that, theoretically at least, a stubby wide spoon should emit
more shock waves because of its wider side-to-side wobble, and thus

**Norm Newman of Riviera (Downriggers) Manufacturing nets salmon for author while fast
trolling hard-wiggling lures. (*Photo by Jack Davis*)**

catch more fish, than a long narrow spoon that moves less erratically through the water. Or so it seems to me. Unfortunately, my experiences don't prove that point, although I've never deliberately gone out of my way to test it in any meaningful fashion. But even if I had, there are simply too many unknown factors involved. We can only guess about such things.

An even greater Great Lakes salmon-fishing myth is the widely accepted belief that once the water is stratified, and a thermocline established, you simply find the desired temperature depth (in the case of salmon, about fifty-two degrees), lower your downrigger cannonballs to that depth, and you're in business. But if you've spent any time watching sonar, you can't help but discover salmon too often place less importance on so-called water temperature "comfort zones" than we do. The reason might be location of forage fish. It could be, at times, that some fish are pushed out of preferred water levels by other, more competitive fish species. I suspect most of this underwater conflict, if it occurs, takes place between salmon and rainbow trout. Temperature preferences, largely based on hatchery tests involving young fish, likely change, or become less important, as fish grow larger. Whatever is going on, one undisputed fact is that every king-sized chinook we've taken on our boat, and I'm talking twenty-five pounds and up, was taken underneath the thermocline—or at least what we had accepted as the thermocline.

Which gets us into another interesting angling problem. That same thermocline is up and down like a yo-yo. Water temperature levels can vary greatly in very short distances for no obvious reason. (The villain, undersurface currents, will be discussed in a later chapter.) If you mark an abrupt bottom contour change, however, or if you're offshore from a river, especially the mighty Niagara River where we spend a lot of time, you can expect it. So, lacking a temperature sensor on a cannonball that provides a continuous readout up top, about all you can do is make sure your lures are well staggered. And even with a sensor, you should run different lures at different depths. I've boated many salmon out of places the books tell us they had no reason to be, especially in the fall when fish are truly where you find them. The present Great Lakes record salmon, for example, a forty-seven-pound September fish out of Lake Ontario, was caught by a New York angler flatlining shallow water for brown trout.

Still another Great Lakes salmon fishing myth is the widely accepted belief that springtime shallow-water fishing is best done with long flatlines, or just by trolling a lure behind a boat without any special equipment such as downriggers. Casual small-boat anglers certainly take a good share of spring salmon by trolling close to shore with nothing more than bass or walleye tackle. But I guarantee that you will vastly increase both the number and size of your fish by running lures five to ten feet down off downriggers.

As often happens, this discovery resulted from no real intelligence on my part. I started using downriggers in springtime only to get a few surface lines out of the way to make it easier to zigzag through crowds of boats without tangling lines. I quickly discovered that salmon are truly phototropic, avoiding hard sunlight by holding deeper in the water. The higher the sun, the flatter the water, the deeper you will find them. Most of our midday spring fish are now caught well down in twenty to thirty feet of water, while almost everyone else is trolling just under the surface in five to ten feet of water. Lacking a downrigger, at least add an extra sinker in front of your lure. It'll help.

Downriggers, sideplaning boards, and many of the other forms of specialized equipment most of us now use on the Great Lakes also have a few mythical labels attached to them. Ask ten anglers, for example, where and when downriggers were created and all ten are almost certain to reply "Michigan, a few years back." Ditto with sideplaners. In reality, both have been around longer than I have, which certainly takes any aspect of "newness" away from them.

Deep trolling with breakaway lines rigged to heavy sinkers on wire cables controlled by winches—in other words, downriggers—has been used by saltwater anglers since the early 1900s, possibly earlier. Sideplaners were being used off California even before that. Harlan Major, author of *Salt Water Fishing Tackle*, published in 1939, notes that "the fishing sled [ancestor of the modern sideplaner] came into use on our West Coast before the kite or the outrigger and was the first method of keeping the trolled bait out of the wake of the boat . . . . In use, the sled is pulled by a line to the mast, to which the fishing line is connected by a breaking line or a clothespin." So what else is new? Very little, it turns out. Sonar has been available for many years but, like downriggers and planing boards, the only real difference between old and new units is that the early ones were not as compact or as sophisticated as those we now use on the Great Lakes.

Another widespread Great Lakes fishing myth is that charterboaters invariably catch bulging boatloads of fish, day after day after day. It's always wonderful, of course, to be credited with such overwhelming success. Charterboat industry promotions have obviously succeeded. It's very easy as well to bask in the related belief, sometimes stated, sometimes not, that charterboaters are always successful because they are better anglers, or smarter anglers. But if they are so smart, they'd also win all the big-money fishing derbies. We rarely do.

Not that charterboaters don't have an advantage at times, particularly in midsummer when salmon and rainbow trout are scattered far offshore. Most of us are out there looking and experimenting day after day, so with that kind of time and effort involved we should catch extra fish eventually. The biggest reason we generally take more fish than sport anglers is much simpler. Charterboats normally run more lines than anyone else. The more lures you have spread around in the water, the more fish you will catch. A boat with only two rods out will have to work four times as hard, spend four times as much time on the water, or be four times as lucky, as a boat with eight rods trailing lures. Give me eight rods and I can scatter those lures around like an underwater Christmas tree. With only two rods, I know I'm facing a long, hard day, the same as any small-boat angler.

Another big whopper, as far as angling myths go, is that no secrecy exists in the brotherhood of Great Lakes anglers. This is true up to a point, but only when fish are easy to find close to shore and their location and methods of catching them are common knowledge. When fish are scattered spottily hither and yon near the middle of the lake, however, there is an apparent, sometimes humorous tendency amongst some anglers to become slightly evasive, if not downright untruthful.

The most obvious offenders, certainly the tellers of the tallest, most transparent tales, are novice sport anglers still burdened with inland-pond fishing mentalities. You protect your top fishing hole, it seems, even if fifty other guys are also dragging lures through the same water. Second worst offenders are (sigh, you had to guess) charterboat operators, at least in my part of the world and, unless human nature varies greatly from region to region, which I doubt, the same situation exists elsewhere. It must be stressed, of course, that there is nothing mean or villainous about charterboat secrecy. It's simply good business. It's also another reason why charterboats are generally more successful than noncommercial boats. Who tells their competitors everything they know?

When fishing is difficult, the normal situation is for two or three charterboaters to work together, slicing up the lake in geographic chunks, each going a different way and agreeing to keep each other informed of any finds. Also agreed in advance is use of a specific, little-used VHF radio channel, which might change periodically, and codes such as *"We're just making tea. C'mon over"* (meaning fish are being caught), just in case someone else is listening. Outside of violating federal radio regulations by not continually monitoring Channel 16 for distress calls—making a brief contact on 16 and then switching to an open talk channel, after which you are supposed to again monitor Channel 16—it's a harmless business arrangement. The problem with mentioning a talk channel number on 16, of course, is that you're inviting anyone listening to make the same switch to hear what you might have to say. But as you will discover, the lakes are big enough, and there are enough fish out there to allow everyone to go their own way successfully if they wish. You don't need to run with a pack.

The biggest Great Lakes salmon fishing myth of all is the almost psychotic importance most of us place on having the "right" lure in the water. The specific lure normally changes from day to day, depending on who catches what and first announces it on CB radio. And even the lure name alone isn't enough. You also must have the identical size and color. I remember a few years ago the manufacturer of a popular Michigan lure started painting his lures a darker color, probably the result of his paint supplier not quite matching the earlier shade of light green. By coincidence, that same light green lure had been the "hot" one when the darker lures first appeared in local retail outlets. Anglers seeking replacements almost panicked. But I couldn't see the difference in terms of fish in the boat. In fact I liked the darker lure better. Fish lures deep enough and they all turn black anyway.

The subject of color opens another Pandora's box of angling puzzles. What do fish really see? Not too many years ago you could start an evening-long argument in any fishing camp by asking whether fish can see color at all. Now, most anglers accept the fact that fish can differentiate between colors quite well. Most fish that is. Deep-water ocean creatures such as tuna and marlin are technically color blind, their eye receptor cells best absorbing only blues. Shallow-water fish such as bass see reds and yellows best. But the question I have yet to hear answered by any scientist is, although the eyes of many fish are physically similar to human eyes in terms of sensory cells, what makes anyone think fish and humans see anything the same way?

Eyes are nothing more than receptor organs. What we actually see depends not just on our eyes but on the capability of our brains to interpret the visual signals sent to them. Our brains compose the information into visual images. Human brains are capable of storing and recalling a lifetime of visual memories that aid in comparative identification of anything we see. And I am not convinced that the tiny brain of a fish is capable of operating at the same level as a human brain. Why should we think fish see the same way we do? Why should we think they see colors as we do? Or see the same amount of detail? In fact, there are reasons to believe, according to some scientific experiments, that fish not only see color differently than we do, but are capable of seeing ranges of color spectrums or wavelengths that we don't. That isn't too surprising, I guess. My bird dog, a German shorthair (which isn't noted for its massive brain either), can hear high-pitched sound waves I can't hear. So why can't fish see things we can't see? Or at least see them in a completely different fashion?

Making this situation even more complicated is the rapid dissipation of light in water; what we see ten feet below the surface is a completely different color than the same lure at, say, fifty or one hundred feet down. In reasonably clear water, reds and yellows disappear first. Only blues and greens are visible as blues and greens in deeper water. What is happening, so better brains than mine tell me, is that daylight, or white light, is composed of all colors in the spectrum. If you hold a red lure in your hands it appears red only because its surface has absorbed the other colors. Because water also absorbs or filters light waves, some more rapidly than others, that same red lure turns a different color—black— when trolled deep behind your boat. Because red is a good "turn-on" color seemingly triggering aggression in fish as well as humans or Spanish fighting bulls, we can create the same visual effect in deeper water by using an orange or a red-orange colored lure. Orange apparently holds

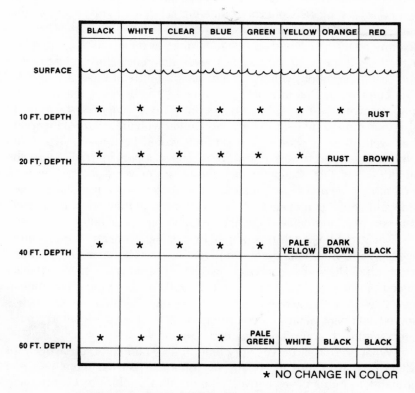

	BLACK	WHITE	CLEAR	BLUE	GREEN	YELLOW	ORANGE	RED
SURFACE								
10 FT. DEPTH	★	★	★	★	★	★	★	RUST
20 FT. DEPTH	★	★	★	★	★	★	RUST	BROWN
40 FT. DEPTH	★	★	★	★	★	PALE YELLOW	DARK BROWN	BLACK
60 FT. DEPTH	★	★	★	★	PALE GREEN	WHITE	BLACK	BLACK

★ NO CHANGE IN COLOR

Color change by depth. (*Drawing courtesy of Berkley/Trilene*)

its color in deep water much better than straight red. But as most experienced salmon anglers have discovered through experimentation and
counting fish in the boat, blues and greens are the lure colors to use
when fishing deep midsummer thermoclines. The only color as good, if
not better, is black. But up until 1984, when I first heard black lures
being touted by other anglers over CB radio, black was rarely used. Black
lures aren't "pretty" and still don't sell well.

Laboratory experiments proving fish can see colors have literally
been worked to death. Such experiments are easy and cheap. All you
need is an aquarium and some colored tubes. Some of the tubes hold
food. Others don't. Sooner or later, hungry fish will pick out the specifically colored tubes holding food and learn to ignore all other colors. As
anglers, however, what we really want to know, and the only thing that
counts, is whether or not color distinctions are made by wild, free-
swimming fish in natural surroundings.

The only work I know of in this area was accomplished by Jacob
Reighard while with the Carnegie Institute laboratory at Tortugas Islands,
Florida. His subjects were three different schools of gray snappers that
hung around different docks about a quarter of a mile apart. Once he
determined the fish would take dead sardines as readily as live ones (their
natural food), he dyed the sardines seven different colors: bright vermilion, deep vermilion, yellow, green, dark blue, light blue, and purple.
One color was tested at a time, the tinted sardines being thrown to the
snappers with normal fish. This continued, the snappers showing no
discrimination, until the fish became familiar with the color. At that point
they were given a choice. Ten sardines would be thrown, five of the
familiar color and five of a new color. The snappers invariably took the
familiar color first. Reighard then asked, Is hunger a factor? He tried
preliminary feeding before testing color choices. The fish still proved,
time and time again at each of the locations, that they could distinguish
between blue and white, blue and red, and blue and yellow.

The experiment gets much more interesting, however. Sardines were
dyed red and laced with quinine and red pepper. The snappers took them
without hesitation—but only once. Red bait became untouchable, whether
spiced or not. They wouldn't even look at them. Even more fascinating,
the fish were not shown red bait for twenty days. When tried again, they
proved not only that they could distinguish color (they still wouldn't touch
a red sardine) but also that they had a memory.

What does it all prove? Very little. If a certain color lure works, for
whatever reason, use it. As any fly fisherman knows, there's no real
similarity to human eyes between the dry flies used for brook trout and
the natural stream insects they are supposed to represent. But I think we

can assume (we have to believe in something) that a lure approximately the same size, shape, and color of alewife or smelt will always be an acceptable imitation in the eyes of Great Lakes salmon. I think we can also assume that fish perception is concerned more with one or two key features of an object rather than with detail. Whether a lure is dark green or a medium dark green with purple-pink spots probably isn't too important. (If this wasn't true, what fish would touch any kind of lure trailing one or more huge, highly visible steel hooks behind it?) But, if salmon are feeding on forage fish which, because of depth or light, show an occasional flash of silver as they move, it would make little sense to fish with a gold-colored lure.

I've proven time and time again that active offshore salmon, who seem always ready to eat, will take a swipe at anything if it appears to be the only readily available meal around. Of course, some lures will draw fish better than others on some days. Where the situation gets tricky is in choice of lures which, from a salmon's viewpoint, varies widely. On a normal day fishing, say, six different lures, you'll catch fish on three, sometimes four, of the original half-dozen lures. I have yet to encounter a true selectivity where salmon would take only one specific lure. It might appear that way at times, but only because of anglers loading lines with the same lures. It always pays to experiment. In fact, it could be argued that when everybody else seems to be fishing a specific lure is the time you should be fishing something completely different. Not that you ignore success completely. If you're out on the lake almost every day, if you know where the fish were yesterday and what they were hitting, you have a logical starting point. If a red-dotted yellow superbait was yesterday's killer, I'm naturally going to have one or two of these lures in the water. But I'll also be running a wide variety of other lures, the number of these depending on the number of anglers in the boat. (Ontario has a one-rod-per-angler rule, although we can stack up to four single-hooked lures on one line by using releases and sliding snaps.)

If the first fish of the day hits, say, a silver and blue lure, then some extra silver-blues will get wet. But I'll always run one or two oddball lures, something completely different. And as you might have guessed, considering the built-in contrariness of salmon, I would estimate that sixty percent of our biggest fish, the kind paying anglers remember and talk about, were taken on the oddball lures no one else was using. What else? When you consider the size of the Great Lakes, with no visual offshore structures of any kind to guide you to fish, and know how lonely it can be out there at times, it helps to believe in something. Whether it's your own brand of luck or a special lure, or possibly both, is immaterial.

3

Seasonal Movements

The world of the fishes is a new world to us. No novel has so much interest, no fairy tale such charm, no work of imagination so strange a diversity as the simple story of their journeys.
—Louis Roule, Fishes, Their Journeys and Migrations

An ancient unknown warrior-philosopher once said that knowledge is the secret of overcoming all challenges. He had a point. There's certainly no question the more you know about a fish—its genetic background; life cycle; environment; responses to various motivating forces; where, when, and why it moves; where and when it spawns; what it feeds on— the better are your chances of finding a member of that species, and many more like it, dancing skyward off a fishing rod. So before we start fishing maybe we'd better take a quick look at the nature of the creatures we hope to catch.

As an angler I would define the most important senses of a fish as: hunger, sexual urges, sight (including reaction to light), long-distance sensory tracking ability (how well can it detect water disturbances created by unseen schools of passing forage fish?), sensitivity to water temperature, smell, hearing, and taste. Eight in all. Some, of course, are obviously more important than others. But only by knowing the interrelationships of the various senses and how they affect fish behavior can any angler hope to unravel the mysteries of Great Lakes fish movements, or make any real sense out of what knowledge we do have. Not that major puzzles no longer exist. They do, although anglers and scientists, sometimes working together on cooperative research programs, are certainly more capable of predicting where salmon or trout might be found at any time of year than they were five years ago, or even five months ago.

One reason for our increased knowledge is that there are now so many more anglers searching the lakes for fish. Another is the increasingly sophisticated fish-tracking sonar units that reveal new facts to anglers every year. Other tracking methods include clipping various fins or attaching tags prior to stocking fish to determine point of origin. This technique goes back to 1902 when C. Rutter, employed by the U.S. Fish Commission, marked 150 salmon in the Sacramento River of California with a cattle branding iron. Only three of the mutilated salmon were ever seen again. They were all caught in the lower river before they reached

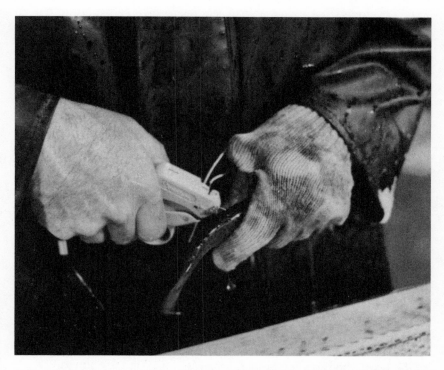

A New York fishery technician micro-tags young salmon at the state's Salmon River hatchery as part of a program to determine survival of stocked fish. (*Photo by John Georg, New York State Department of Environmental Conservation*)

the sea. Fish tags were first used six years later when Charles Wilson Green marked fifty-nine Columbia River salmon with metal buttons normally attached at that time only to the ears of sheep. Since then, hundreds of thousands, if not millions, of salmon have been tagged and numerically charted to list their comings and goings. The newest tagging technique involves the use of "microtags," tiny coded pieces of wire implanted by machine into the snouts of anesthetized fingerlings. The machine makes distinctive scratches on the wire that indicate which state or federal agency tagged and stocked the fish, the experiment being done, and when and where the fish were stocked.

An even more high-tech fish tracking method is now being refined on Lake Ontario by Dr. Jim Haynes of the State University of New York (SUNY) at Brockport, and on Lake Erie by Dr. Jim Winter of SUNY Fredonia. These sea grant research programs are using waterproof miniaturized radio transmitters that are attached to the fish. The tracking units are either wired externally to the dorsal fin or surgically implanted by incision in the belly area. Unfortunately, telemetry (radio) units have still to be developed that are capable of sending receivable signals from deep water. Once salmon or trout move below forty feet, which often occurs in summer, they are lost to aircraft or boats trying to follow them with special Yagi directional antennas. Another part of the Lake Ontario study, rarely used in Great Lakes fishery research work, is employment of vertical gill nets. The sixteen-foot-wide nets, hung off floats at depths ranging from twenty-five to six hundred feet, determine precise depth and temperature preferences of salmon and trout in summer by comparing the depth at which fish are caught with daily water temperature profiles.

With the Great Lakes acting as an "ocean," fast-moving, far-ranging salmon, which retain inbred, ocean-wandering instincts, are sometimes hard to find during the summer months when they are far offshore. The smallest of the Great Lakes, Lake Ontario, holds 7,500 square miles of water for fish to roam around in. Lake Superior, the largest lake, has 31,820 square miles of water surface; Lake Huron, 23,010 square miles; Lake Michigan, 22,400 square miles; and Lake Erie, 9,930 square miles. Given that kind of space, just how far and fast salmon can move is demonstrated by one radio-equipped $4\frac{1}{2}$-pound coho originally caught in the lower Niagara River May 19, 1984. By late May it had moved seventy miles east past Rochester, New York. In early June the fish was off the Niagara River again. Radio contact was lost until the middle of July when it showed up for about a week near Toronto Island, on the opposite side of the lake. Then, on September 7, it was caught in the Salmon River at Pulaski, New York, near the far eastern end of the lake. Known minimum distance traveled (which likely could be more than doubled, if not tripled) was 305 miles.

Compounding the difficulty of locating wide-ranging fish in the Great Lakes is a general lack of bottom structure—shoals, dropoffs, rock- or brush-covered bottoms—commonly used by anglers on smaller lakes to zero in on fish. The total area of each of the Great Lakes is immense compared to shoreline area. Bottom zones near shore are scrubbed clean by wave action and near-shore currents. In spring and fall, however, when the fish are found close to shore, riverbank and pier fishermen are often as successful in taking limit catches as boat anglers.

In spring, the seemingly ever-hungry foraging salmon and trout follow spawning smelt and alewife into the warmer water off the beaches. In late summer, as spawning time approaches, mature salmon will be found off the mouths of tributary streams (usually the same streams in which they were stocked), often congregating near shore early in the morning, wandering off into deeper water during midday, and returning to the shallows in the evening. As the season progresses and spawning runs start, the river fishermen take over. In my neck of the woods, the heavy currents of the lower Niagara River produce huge hook-jawed salmon for bank anglers right into December most years.

Some Natural History

As most fishermen know, the two Pacific Coast salmon of particular interest to Great Lakes anglers, coho and chinook, die after spawning. Coho have a normal life span of three years. Chinook (known in the west as "springs") usually live four years. Of the two fish, coho have the simplest, most consistent life history, spending one year in the nursery stream plus two years in "big water" prior to returning to their native rivers as mature spawners. The late Roderick Haig-Brown, a world-renowned West Coast writer, once described coho as a "swift, bold and silver fish, a surface lover and a magnificent jumper. In the river he turns scarlet and grows a hooked jaw, but seems to hold vigor and shapeliness longer than the other salmons."

The spawning movement of ocean-based coho takes place anytime between August and the following March. On the Great Lakes, the timing of the run largely depends on when the parent salmon were taken by fishery workers as a source of eggs and milt. Coho netted for spawn in, say, November, will normally attempt to produce offspring in November. Thanks to work done by Skamania River hatchery workers in the state of Washington, where genetic tinkering (using only the eggs of early-running fish) has produced steelhead that stage off spawning streams in summer, Great Lakes fishery managers are now paying suitable attention to planting fish that are genetically programmed to start the initial spawning act at different times of the year. The Skamania strain was first introduced into the Great Lakes with spectacular success in the late 1970s by Indiana, followed by Wisconsin, Michigan, and Illinois in 1984. New York's first stocking is slated for 1986. The result, of course, is greater angler success through increased access to the fish in shallow water close to shore.

But whatever time of year coho enter their parental stream or hatchery release point, they eventually will pair off in an area of their choice and, sweeping out a depression in bottom sand or gravel, deposit and cover anywhere from three thousand to four thousand eggs. Some of these amazingly adaptable Great Lakes salmon are spawning successfully despite the lack of iodine and other trace elements found in Pacific coastal waters, which once were thought necessary for reproduction. However, not enough young survive to maintain the fishery by natural reproduction. That the day will ever come when costly Pacific salmon hatchery facilities are no longer needed in the Great Lakes is highly doubtful.

The spring or chinook salmon, largest of the salmons, has a more complicated life history. As its West Coast name indicates, Pacific chinook spawning runs occur in springtime in some rivers, well ahead of all the other salmons. But, again, because of genetic differences that occur in biologically isolated watersheds, other runs can be found throughout the summer and early fall.

The majority of young chinook salmon leave their home river very soon after a three- to four-month hatching period returning as sexually mature four-year-old twenty- to twenty-five-pound fish. Fry that spend a year in the river (an estimated 20 percent) return as forty-pound five-year-old fish, although three-year-old and six-year-old fish are not uncommon. In all cases, and this is true of other species as well, the colder the water the longer the life span. In the Yukon River, females of the spawning run are usually six or seven years old, the males five or six. In Alaska, the Kenai River produces monstrous one hundred-pound eight-year-old fish. One specimen, taken in a trap net off Point Colpays in southeastern Akaska, weighed 126 pounds. The heaviest chinook taken on fishing tackle was a ninety-three-pounder caught in Kelp Bay, Alaska in 1977. The world's record coho, thirty-one pounds, was caught in the Skeena River in British Columbia in 1947.

Atlantic salmon (also successfully stocked in the Great Lakes by Michigan and New York state fishery departments) are, like Pacific salmon, anadromous, with one big difference: a small percentage of Atlantic salmon survive the physiological stresses of reproduction to spawn two or three times before dying. Like their Pacific cousins, Atlantics are born in fresh water. The young will spend about two years in the streams as troutlike parr, then move to the ocean as silver-colored smolts where they spend another two years before returning to spawn as four-year-old fish. Those that survive the spawning period either return to the sea before freeze-up or remain in the deeper pools of the river throughout the winter, heading back to sea the following spring as "black" or "spent" salmon. As of this writing, the largest Atlantic salmon caught in the Great Lakes, a Lake Michigan product, weighed thirty-two pounds, ten ounces.

All other species of interest, excluding rainbow trout, are fall spawning fish. Brookies, which reach the geriatric stage at five years, will grow up to fourteen pounds in big water; rainbows, living about seven years, have topped twenty-six pounds in Lake Michigan. Brown trout, capable of living ten years, have been boated up to thirty-two pounds. The heaviest lake trout to come out of the Great Lakes weighed forty-seven pounds. The average life span of a lake trout that avoids having its life juices sucked out by lamprey is approximately fifteen years.

With spring the beginning of the fishing year, we start in the shallows, follow the fish into deeper water as the lakes warm up and then, in August, start working back into the shallows as the fish begin their move-

Great Lakes anglers find exciting fall fishing action by concentrating their efforts on home streams of mature, king-size salmon. (*Photo courtesy of Ontario Federation of Anglers and Hunters*)

ments to the spawning grounds. The fish normally "stage" or congregate for several weeks near the mouths of the rivers in which they were stocked, providing the best angling action of the entire year. Occasionally, the fish fail to stage. In 1984, for example, the fish were seemingly widely scattered in deep water one day and in the rivers the next. This situation occurred (to the great dismay of charterboat skippers) in both Lake Ontario and Lake Michigan. Why? No one knows. Fishery scientists are hoping such abnormal fish behavior was only a quirky combination of identical offshore lake and river water temperatures and low river flows and is not likely to be repeated.

Importance of Water Temperature

A major factor influencing fish movement in the Great Lakes is water temperature. Each lake has its own seasonal temperature cycle. Lake Erie, being the shallowest, most southern of the Great Lakes, is the warmest. Lake Superior, the biggest, deepest, and most northern, is the coldest. Lakes Michigan, Huron, and Ontario are in the middle. The importance of water temperature in dictating general fish movement is the same on any of the lakes, only the timing may vary.

One reason temperature is so important is that fish, as cold-blooded animals, take on the temperature of the water around them. As a result, temperature—and the different physical densities or structure of water caused by different water temperatures—is not only a big factor controlling fish location at various times of the year but is also a key "trigger" affecting everything from how often fish will eat to when they spawn.

Each species has what is known as a "comfort zone," a water temperature range in which (laboratory experiments have shown) fish are most comfortable. But fish don't swim around, acting like a human dipping a foot into bathtub water, until they find a temperature that "feels good." Preferred temperature really means the temperature of water in which fish can most efficiently, most easily absorb oxygen. In the case of chinook salmon, this preferred, or most breathable, temperature belt ranges from fifty to sixty degrees Fahrenheit. Coho are happiest and most active in approximately the same water temperatures. Free-roaming rainbow trout and bottom-oriented brown trout will thrive in warmer fifty-five- to sixty-five-degree water. Lake trout, most bottom-oriented of all Great Lakes sport fish, like it much colder, and are often found in forty- to fifty-degree water.

To fully understand the relationship between water temperature and fish behavior, we have to delve into physics for a moment and consider the effects of temperature on water itself. The most vital point is that water attains maximum density at thirty-nine degrees Fahrenheit. Cold water sinks; warmer, lighter water floats near the surface. When water does turn into ice, it expands and, becoming lighter, floats. This is why large northern lakes don't freeze solid from top to bottom in winter. Equally interesting is that when spring rains and sunshine warm up winter surface water, the differences in density eventually create what is called "stratification" or three distinct layers of water: the hypolimnion, a cold layer near bottom often lacking in oxygen; the epilimnion, an oxygen-rich, warm-water layer up top; and the thermocline, a comparatively narrow belt of water which acts as a divider between the hypolimnion and the epilimnion. These summer stratification layers normally take shape by late June and are gone by October when the lakes start "turning over." At this time, cooler surface water starts sinking because of increased density and, aided by fall winds, mixes with the water below.

As with any transition between hot and cold, the summer thermocline holds a wide range of temperatures between the extremes above and below it. Put a temperature sensor down into a lake in July and, taking a reading every few feet, you might find sixty-five-degree water from the surface down to the forty-foot level. At this point the thermocline might start, the temperature rapidly dropping from sixty-five degrees to forty-five degrees in the next ten feet. Below that, from fifty feet to bottom, might be forty-five- to forty-degree water. Dr. Haynes' daily records on Lake Ontario show thermocline depths ranging all the way from ten to ninety-eight feet, with temperatures in the transition zone ranging, on average, from sixty-five degrees down to forty-six degrees. The average width of the thermocline itself was thirteen feet. I've charted thermoclines as narrow as three feet and as wide as twenty feet.

It's important to remember that the depth of the thermocline can vary from day to day or from one spot to another on the lake, usually because of underwater currents related to wind conditions. On an average day without continual checks, I'd guess the lures of most anglers trying to fish the thermocline are either above it or below it about 50 percent of the time. What often happens is that a steady north wind, for example, pushes warmer surface water toward the south shore. The resultant circulatory action causes warm surface waters on the windward side to be replaced by colder, deeper water, raising the thermocline on that side of the lake, while on the south shore the piling up of warmer water naturally pushes the thermocline deeper. I can recall many periods of tough fishing in strong northerly winds when I was using downriggers eighty feet down or more off the south shore of Lake Ontario, and fighting four- to five-foot waves, while northside anglers were enjoying flat water and excellent summer thermocline catches at the twenty-foot level (you can reach fish that deep with weighted flatlines). Was I upset? Not really. It all evens out in time. A strong south wind reverses the situation.

Complex, massive underwater movements involve much more than easily detected thermocline ups and downs, however. What I am discussing here is, I believe, the major key to summer offshore salmon movements and, without doubt, the biggest angling puzzle still to be solved on the Great Lakes. Too many anglers tend to consider a lake, excluding its surface, as static. We erroneously consider it a huge, hidden body of still water, almost a vacuum, in which fish wander about by chance. In reality, the unseen portion of any open lake is a tumbling, rolling, ever-changing series of conflicting water movements. Kinetic energy established by surface waves piling up on a shore creates an equal underwater force, the replaced water being pushed down and away from shore. Let the same wind blow for two or three days at a time and a complex series of cross-lake currents are set up. This unseen undersurface movement of water is sometimes deflected up and over colder layers of even deeper water. Sometimes it is visibly shoved to surface far offshore, creating an upwelling or "thermal break." Whatever form these subsurface "rivers" take, they provide natural travel routes I simplistically tend

Great Lakes research vessels such as the *R/V Aquarius*, operated by the University of Wisconsin Sea Grant Institute, are discovering more about salmon and trout movements every year. (*Photo courtesy of University of Wisconsin Sea Grant Institute*)

to think of as "fish highways." Wherever the highways are blocked by higher walls of heavier, colder water, fish pile up along the edge of the wall much like automobiles piled up bumper-to-bumper in a road construction zone.

One of the most spectacular examples of such dynamic lake thermal changes—and one of the best charted thanks to Dr. Mike Voiland of Brockport, a New York sea grant recreation specialist—occurred in August 1983. On August 9, there was normal stratification forty feet down, a north wind, and lake surface temperatures of seventy-two to seventy-five degrees. The wind switched to the east on August 10, and turned into a three-day blow, pushing warm surface water to the west end of the lake and pulling cold water in behind it. At Rochester, where Dr. Voiland obtained temperature data from area water treatment plants, the surface temperature dropped from seventy-three to fifty-four degrees overnight. The following day, August 12, the temperature dropped another ten degrees, to forty-four, reaching a low of forty-two degrees on August 13. (The change was so abrupt many warm-water species such as sheephead and smallmouth bass died from thermal shock.) Most New York anglers, unable to find water warmer than forty-five degrees even as far as five miles offshore, were "skunked" for three days. More adventurous souls fishing the center of the lake twelve to fifteen miles from shore finally discovered a gigantic, swirling surface thermal break of more than fifteen degrees, a big, easily spotted "river" in the middle of the lake where limit catches of steelhead and coho salmon were taken until the lake, aided by winds switching to the west, returned to normal on August 20.

The effects of a thermal break are even better seen close to shore in spring. As solar radiation and stream runoff warm up shoreline water, a predictable, comparatively stable, easily measured band of vertically stratified water builds up against the colder, heavier thirty-nine-degree water found immediately offshore. Continued warming of the shoreline creates additional temperature layers or "stacks" being added to the thermal wall, the growing bulk of the lighter, increasingly warmer inshore water slowly pushing the cold winter water away from shore. If surface water temperatures are measured by a boater slowly moving offshore, at some point over a distance of five hundred feet or so (depending on weather), it's usually an easy matter to find the distinctive break where warm water meets cold. A typical temperature change would be from forty-eight to thirty-nine degrees. As spring progresses and the wall moves further offshore, the surface temperature change might be from fifty-four to forty-five degrees.

More important to anglers, as Dr. Haynes of SUNY Brockport first

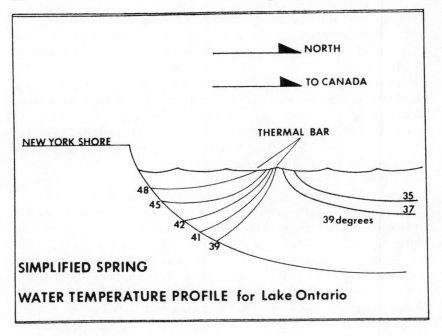

confirmed in 1982 during his early Lake Ontario rainbow trout studies, is that the thermal bar and other upward curving temperature gradients act as a barrier that seem to contain or fence rainbow nearshore. Only until nearshore surface temperatures approach fifty degrees, and the thermal bar is pushed farther offshore (5 to 20 miles), do the rainbow break free and spill out in the open lake.

The role of the thermal bar has since been modified by Dr. Voiland. He now believes, as a result of work done in 1985, that a temperature structure even more attractive to fish is a previously unrecognized "spring thermocline," a belt of forty-two- to forty-six-degree water located each spring at various distances between the thermal bar and shore. "We kept being told by anglers that water in this temperature range produced most of the fish but because of the thermocline often being so close to the thermal bar we had overlooked it," Dr. Voiland said. This spring thermocline (the very first rudimentary portion of what will become the summer thermocline) flattens out as it moves offshore and slowly submerges (as does the thermal bar underneath it) eventually to take its more familiar horizontal form, normally providing six to seven weeks of excellent fishing, from May well into June most years. The closer the forty-two- to forty-six-degree belt of water is to the thermal bar, the better the fishing.

At other times, the two areas of water can be separated as widely as a half-mile.

The outer thermal barrier is visually distinguishable at times, depending on the phosphorus content of nearby municipal sewage discharges or agricultural pollutant runoffs. The resultant increase in algae growth can, in places, create a noticeable color difference along the edge of the thermal wall; the warmer, chlorophyll-rich, onshore water becomes murky green compared to the clear blue of the lake's core. Any river dumping warmer muddy water into the lakes creates an equally distinctive color line to follow. Most of us just call it a "mud line." But there's also a thermal break there and such places do hold fish.

On Lake Erie, where Dr. Jim Winter of the Environmental Resources Center of the State University of New York in Fredonia has been conducting salmonid telemetry studies, springtime radio tracking shows steelhead and salmon close to shore where they are easily accessible to pier fishermen or anglers using conventional flatline trolling methods. Offshore movement occurs when the water temperatures reach fifty-eight to sixty-four degrees, usually in late May. During June and early July, Dr. Winter found salmonids widely distributed from forty feet below surface to bottom, the salmon predominantly choosing the forty- to fifty-foot stratum while lake trout were suspended between sixty to seventy feet. From late July to early September, both salmon and lake trout were found together along with concentrations of forage fish at seventy- to eighty-foot depths in water temperatures of fifty to fifty-two degrees. This area of fish concentration consistently corresponded to the thermocline. In late summer and fall, near-shore netting indicated all salmonids, with the exception of lake trout, began reappearing in shallow waters when the near-shore lake temperature fell below sixty-eight degrees.

Dr. Haynes' work on Lake Ontario—which concentrated primarily on brown trout—showed a similar pattern: brown trout roaming close to shore in spring until water temperatures exceed sixty-five degrees in June or July. Summer dispersal of browns is normally confined to within three miles of shore in less than one hundred feet of water, the fish preferring to be as close to shore as possible given suitable water temperatures (fifty-five degrees). There was also a marked association with both the thermocline and the bottom. More than 75 percent of all brown trout netted in a two-year period were in or within ten feet of the thermocline. About 30 percent of the trout were netted within ten feet of bottom. Of those fish, 80 percent were caught where the thermocline intersected the bottom.

Summer netting of Lake Ontario lake trout showed clearly defined temperature preferences between forty-three and fifty-five degrees, the

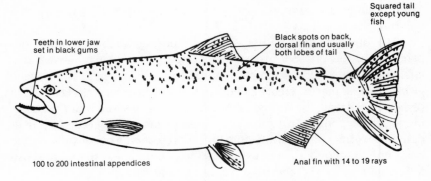

Squared tail
except young
fish

Teeth in lower jaw
set in black gums

Black spots on back,
dorsal fin and usually
both lobes of tail

100 to 200 intestinal appendices

Anal fin with 14 to 19 rays

Chinook salmon (*Oncorhynchus tschawytscha*).
(Note: Identification drawings courtesy of Illinois Department of Conservation)

majority of the fish being netted in less than one hundred feet of water. Like brown trout, many lake trout occupy the thermocline zone, but 35 percent were netted within ten feet of bottom, indicating much stronger bottom orientation than brown trout. Most lake trout were also netted in less than one hundred feet of water suggesting again, like brown trout, they have a built-in bond with shoreline structure.

Incomplete summer salmon/steelhead studies indicate chinook prefer temperatures from fifty-seven to sixty-three degrees, which puts them in much warmer water than our angling results show to be the preferred range. The explanation, I think, is that Dr. Haynes' nets were left in the water overnight, and pulled in each morning. As a result, salmon moving upward with diminishing light, following a normal daily cycle of plankton and forage fish movements, were taken at temperature levels not usually

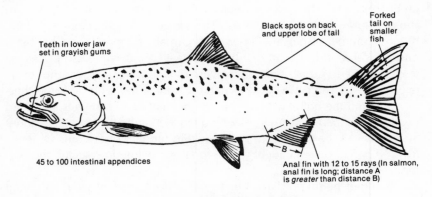

Forked
tail on
smaller
fish

Black spots on back
and upper lobe of tail

Teeth in lower jaw
set in grayish gums

45 to 100 intestinal appendices

Anal fin with 12 to 15 rays (In salmon,
anal fin is long; distance A
is *greater* than distance B)

Coho salmon (*Oncorhynchus kisutch*).

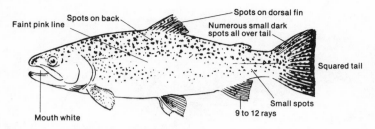

Spots on dorsal fin
Faint pink line
Spots on back
Numerous small dark spots all over tail
Squared tail
Mouth white
9 to 12 rays
Small spots

Rainbow (steelhead) trout (*Salmon gairdneri*).

occupied in daylight angling hours. At best, the findings support a time-tested angling theory, also supported by Dr. Winter on Lake Erie, that the location of bait fish can sometimes be a more important factor than water temperature in determining fish depth selection. But because the thermocline or middle layer provides fish with the water temperature we know they generally prefer, knowing the depth of the thermocline, and the depth you should be running lures, is an obvious advantage to any angler. Not that fishing the thermocline guarantees summer angling success day after day. But lacking local angling knowledge to the contrary—or sonar showing fish in other locations—it is certainly the first place to start.

Influence of Underwater Currents

Another little-known lake current—moving laterally up to ten miles a day—is found along all the Great Lakes shorelines. Called a "jet effect" or "shoreline current," this invisible coastal river, running up to three miles across and more than one hundred feet deep at times, is another

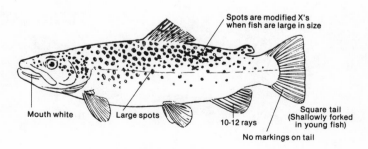

Spots are modified X's when fish are large in size
Mouth white
Large spots
10-12 rays
No markings on tail
Square tail (Shallowly forked in young fish)

Brown trout (*Salmo trutta*).

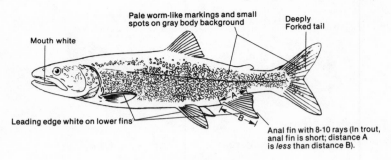

Pale worm-like markings and small
spots on gray body background

Deeply
Forked tail

Mouth white

Leading edge white on lower fins

Anal fin with 8-10 rays (In trout,
anal fin is short; distance A
is *less* than distance B).

Lake trout (*Salvelinus namaychush*).

potentially important factor controlling fish movements and, until now, has never been discussed in an angling context.

Environment Canada scientists T. J. Simons and David Lean of the Canada Centre for Inland Waters in Burlington, on the north shore of Lake Ontario, have done the bulk of what little research has been accomplished in this new field of study. Their findings, largely gained while trying to determine whether current-carried lake pollutants pose a threat to the quality of shoreline municipal drinking water, include the discovery that Lake Ontario's shoreline current tends to flow along the north shore from east to west from spring until fall. In winter it reverses direction. The prevailing westerly summer flow is caused by a combination of wind, sun, and the "Coriolis" effects of the earth's rotation, which at 24,000 miles an hour literally spins water to the right, in our part of the world. Below the equator, the spin is to the left. The easterly winter flow is attributed mainly to prevailing northwest winds. Along the south shore the "river" always flows from west to east, driven by the earth's spin, prevailing winds, and the massive outflow from the Niagara River.

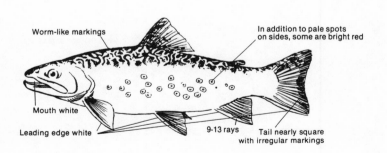

Worm-like markings

In addition to pale spots
on sides, some are bright red

Mouth white

Leading edge white

9-13 rays

Tail nearly square
with irregular markings

Brook trout (*Salvelinus fontinalis*).

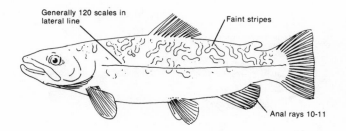

Tiger trout (brown trout × brook trout).

Generally 120 scales in lateral line

Faint stripes

Anal rays 10-11

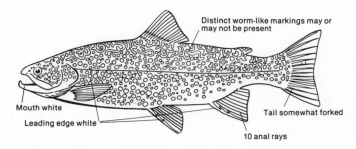

Splake (lake trout × brook trout hybrid).

Distinct worm-like markings may or may not be present

Mouth white

Leading edge white

Tail somewhat forked

10 anal rays

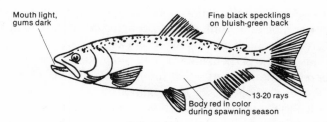

Kokanee salmon (*Oncorhynchus nerka kennerlyi*).

Mouth light, gums dark

Fine black specklings on bluish-green back

13-20 rays

Body red in color during spawning season

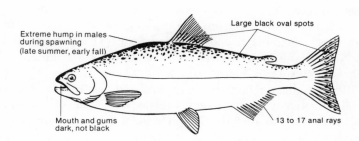

Pink or humpbacked salmon (*Oncorhynchus gorbuscha*).

Large black oval spots

Extreme hump in males during spawning (late summer, early fall)

Mouth and gums dark, not black

13 to 17 anal rays

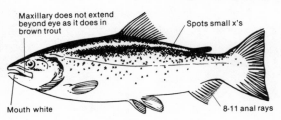

Maxillary does not extend
beyond eye as it does in
brown trout

Spots small x's

Mouth white

8-11 anal rays

Atlantic salmon (*Salmo salar*).

Take a look at any chart of western Lake Ontario and it's fairly easy to visualize a giant, slow-moving whirlpool, the water moving west along the north shore, then east along the south shore to the Niagara River where it is propelled out to midlake or beyond to resume its circular movement. My angling knowledge of the same area, based on peak catches in different parts of the lake at different times of the year, indicates many salmon move the same way: starting in spring on the shallow, quick-warming flats at the far southwestern end of the lake; gradually moving east toward the Niagara River; moving offshore with the river's currents; showing up in midsummer in the Cobourg–Port Hope area on the other side of the lake almost opposite the Niagara River; then slowly moving west along the north shore to congregate off the Credit River and Bronte Creek areas where most were stocked.

At the risk of perpetuating a better-forgotten dream of almost all Great Lakes salmon anglers—that somewhere out there on the lakes are huge summer schools of big king salmon (the hard truth is that such offshore schooling doesn't occur)—we can find similar seasonal patterns in all the other lakes. Lake Erie, for example, like Lake Ontario, has two distinct fisheries. The western or shallow-end fish move out of their Lake St. Clair–western Lake Erie wintering areas in spring to circulate as far east as the Long Point area of Ontario, reaching there by mid-July, and then swinging south and west again along the American shore. Fish movements in the much deeper, eastern portion of the lake are still almost a total mystery, as is fish movement (excluding localized association of lake trout with specific bottom structure) in Lake Superior.

The lakes that run north to south, Michigan and Huron, tend to have general fish movements more closely related to the time of year and water temperature: the fish are found in spring in the warmer, shallower southern ends of the lakes and then move north in predictable fashion with the climbing sun. In Lake Michigan, for example, fishing action starts most years in the Chicago–Michigan City areas in early May. By June, salmon will be found off St. Joseph. By July, the fish, still heading north, are normally concentrated off Muskegon. August action is hottest off Ludington and Manistee. September fish not congregated off spawning streams are found off the Manitou Islands and Charlevoix at the far northern end of the lake.

Although predicting salmon movements is on a par with picking horse-race winners, an even simpler way of determining where to fish on any of the lakes at any specific time is simply to obtain readily available lists of fishing derbies from the various state or Ontario tourism agencies. Municipal or regional derbies are invariably held during peak fishing periods, the dates being based on best local angling results of past years. Other easy sources of information include state or regional telephone hotlines, local newspaper outdoor columnists, angling clubs, and marinas and fishing tackle outlets.

Wave action, or lack of it, is also extremely important as a controlling factor in shallow water fish movement. Fish, not having eyelids, shun light (especially chinook and lake trout). On a flat day, when the surface is calm and the sun is high overhead, look for fish in deeper water. The higher the sun, the deeper the chinook will be found, often moving down into water much colder than temperature preference charts tell you they'll be found. If you're restricted to inshore fishing, this means getting up early in the morning. The larger fish will usually move close to shore only during the night, leaving shortly after the sun is high enough in the sky to penetrate the surface any distance. Big chinook can also be driven into deeper water by heavy boat traffic. This is another reason for being an early bird, especially off river harbor entrances. Most chinook specialists are usually on the water before daybreak.

4

Onshore Tackle Needs

*There are two distinct forms of angling on the Great Lakes,
onshore fishing and offshore fishing.*
                                              —Gerry Wolfram

A novice Great Lakes salmon angler, if he's lucky enough or spends
enough time at the game, will sooner or later hook a fish strong enough,
and fast enough, to empty his reel of line. Not that this is a tragic experience. In fact, a really strange thing happens once you hear your first
big, explosive POP signaling a fish has broken off on a bare reel. Once
your nerves settle down and your hands stop shaking, you can't wait to
go out and do it again. It's fun. It's exciting.

But be warned that these fish are the biggest, crankiest, toughest,
fastest-moving fish you are ever likely to encounter. A chinook salmon
over thirty pounds can strip, break, or seize ordinary freshwater tackle
so fast you'll wonder whether you might be better off fishing for perch.
At least with other normal freshwater fare you can crank fish in almost
at will. With big salmon, the situation is reversed. A trophy salmon, still
full of life, will take line away from you at will.

On the other hand, one of the most pleasant aspects of Great Lakes
angling is that you can use almost any form of tackle successfully at one

time or another. There's no need to be extra nice to the loan officer of your local bank, or to remortgage your house to get involved. If you're content to enjoy the spring and fall fishery when salmon are reachable from shore or accessible by trolling from a small boat, you can just dust off the old bass or walleye fishing outfit hanging in the basement and go find yourself a river breakwall or lakeshore pier. Anything goes—until the excitement of hooking big, heavy fish, and the unavoidable loss of tackle, prompts you to buy more suitable equipment.

Most small-boat anglers do amazingly well with standard freshwater gear. I would guess, out of the thousands of fish caught each year in western Lake Ontario alone, that 80 percent or better are boated by anglers using standard six- or eight-pound-test general purpose gear. One reason they do so well is the tremendous advantage shallow-water trollers have over pier or beach anglers. If you hook a heavier-than-average fish while trolling, you can easily accelerate or turn the boat to follow the fish—a move that cuts to almost zero any chances of feeling empty-reel blues on light bass tackle. Based on my observations, if a small-boat angler loses a trophy fish, chances are he'll do it at the boat while trying to net the fish.

What a shore angler needs above all else is a rig that will cast extra-long distances off a beach or pier and, at the same time, be hefty enough to handle the "screamers"—the big hard-running fish that make a fishing reel yell in mechanical protest as the salmon heads for the other end of the lake. You also want tackle sporty enough for shallow-water trolling cottage-country style (known in salmon-fishing circles as "flatlining"), where you simply crank up your "Ol' Dependable" 3.5 horsepower outboard motor and let out as much line as you dare behind a twelve- or fourteen-foot cartop boat, or whatever craft you own that can be used safely near shore. The same rod should also be usable fishing offshore with downriggers.

The most complete answer to the average shoreline angler's tackle needs is fairly simple and comes in one comparatively inexpensive package. Buy what is known in the outdoor retail trade as a light saltwater surf-casting rod with a matching open-face spinning reel. The double-handed rod will help you cast a salmon spoon a country mile (or so it will seem in comparison with your old freshwater rig). The larger reel, with its bigger spool (and thus more line coming off per loop), will also enhance casting. More important, the bigger reel holds more line, at least two hundred yards of 10- or 12-pound-test line, to control big-running fish, is built stronger to take the pounding salmon will give it and, as part of that built-in strength, should have a smoother, more dependable line-braking system.

I should caution that this recommendation is based, like all angling opinions anywhere, on highly personal prejudices of the worst sort. For starters, an inordinate fondness for ocean fishing over the years has resulted in an accumulation of more saltwater tackle in my house than any reasonable angler could ever hope to justify, especially when the nearest salt water is fifteen hundred miles away. Salmon introduction in the Great Lakes changed all that. All my guilt complexes are gone. My collection of saltwater gear is now economically justifiable if only because I can use the equipment on a regular basis. Not that the urge to feel Cape Hatteras beach underfoot while casting for shore-water blues, or to feel Pacific spray on my face while night fishing for totuava (giant croakers) off Baja doesn't rear its head occasionally. But it's controllable. Now I can find a local beach, ten minutes away, and chuck a heavy lure off a two-handed surf rod with a chance of catching big fish any time I wish. What this has saved me in costly airline tickets to distant surf is difficult to estimate, but it's been a bundle.

Any discussion here of shoreline casting tackle is always with the understanding that what suits me probably won't suit you. We all move to slightly different currents. Your strength, size, muscle coordination, angling background, casting style, preformed opinions or prejudices, are all factors in tackle choice. Equipment selection is a very personal matter, or should be. And as you become more experienced as an angler, tackle that suits you this year likely won't be considered adequate next year, or the year after. So without knowing you fairly well, please don't expect anyone to reel off specific brand names and model numbers of rods and say, "Get this, or get that, you can't go wrong." You can go wrong. We've all gone wrong. Show me an angler who hasn't made a mistake buying tackle and I'll show you a one-rod fisherman who spends more time on a golf course or building furniture in his basement than he does on water. And why deprive yourself of the fun of shopping around, asking questions, and trying out every rod and reel combination you can lay your hands on?

Of all the saltwater rods I own (never mind how many, even I am still embarrassed by the number), the one I most use is a $9\frac{1}{2}$ foot, long-handled fiberglass rod with a lighter-than-normal tip action that I bought years ago in North Carolina. My heavier, stiffer, longer rods will, of course, throw a longer cast, but because popular Great Lakes lures aren't as heavy as saltwater jigs or plugs (five-eighths of an ounce versus up to three ounces), it all balances out quite nicely. The lighter rod has a better, sportier feel while casting lighter lures and playing fish, and because of the oversized (at least by freshwater standards) reel, it will throw a lure a long way.

Any mention of lure weight raises another point about buying tackle,

Lures used by the author when wading Great Lakes beaches include (*from top to bottom*): Luhr Jensen Krocodile, Topsey, Pixee, Williams Wabler, Abu Toby, and Hopkins Shorty.

a point that is never stressed enough, if discussed at all. Novices invariably make tackle purchases in totally "bass-ackward" fashion. They buy the rod, followed by the reel, then the line, and then, almost as an afterthought, depending on how much money they have left, the lures. But the process should be completely reversed. Your starting point should really be the lure, specifically its weight. What are other local anglers using to catch fish? The heft of the lure decides line strength. A five-eighths-ounce lure requires a 10- or 12-pound-test line. A half-ounce plug suggests 8-pound-test line. If you think you'll be tossing quarter-ounce lures, to cast them well you'll need 6- or 4-pound-test line.

Only at this point can anyone make a reasonable judgment on the action of the rod and the size of the reel that they need. Any tackle salesman worthy of the name, on discovering a customer is a novice angler (and he'll spot lack of experience as soon as a novice picks up a rod), should gently inquire what you plan to fish for and where. Knowing this, he can then recommend the right tackle. All of which, incidentally, is a very good reason to shop at only the most prestigious tackle outlets. Granted, such stores inevitably charge more. They have to in order to keep knowledgeable staff. But those salesmen can, in the end, save you money despite higher initial costs.

Two things I would absolutely insist on when choosing an all-purpose rod good for both shallow and deep-water fishing are: (1) that it have a double-locking, two-ring reel seat and, (2) that it have a carbaloy tip guide. Any firm that produces rods with only one reel-locking ring is sending out a very loud message. It is saying, as I hear it anyway, that it is no longer controlled by anglers turned businessmen but by cost-cutting accountants. Pet peeve? Sure. But until you have a reel drop off in the sand, making it totally useless until dismantled and cleaned, or, worse, have one come free of a rod while fighting a fish, you can't possibly appreciate the necessity of the all-important second locking ring. If your rods do have single reel-locking rings, lock the ring in position with a wrapping of tape or tiny drop of epoxy before challenging big salmon. Ultra-hard carbaloy is equally necessary on the rod tip, where the bulk of line pressure comes into play on each cast, to prevent the line from eventually wearing a rut into softer line guide rings.

Reels? Buy the very best you can afford. For working a beach you'll want a unit capable of holding at least 250 yards of 10- or 12-pound-test line without overcrowding the spool or allowing the loaded line closer than one-sixteenth of an inch to the rim of the spool flange. You also want a fairly fast reel retrieve ratio. A minimum would be 3:1, which means the reel is geared so that rotating the handle one complete revolution revolves the reel's spool three times, an obvious benefit when trying to recover line against a running fish.

Again, my prejudices loudly proclaim the best, toughest reels tend to have a saltwater background, simply because saltwater angling conditions, and the bigger sea fish, are tougher on equipment than freshwater conditions. A larger, heavier reel should also have a bigger and smoother drag system built into it. Lightweight drags, the spool-braking machinery incorporated into most modern spinning reels (usually a friction washer held under adjustable tension) tend to fade out, lock up, or, more commonly, sporadically grab harder than they should and, between grabs, let go almost completely. Line is rarely released for any distance under consistent pressure. It is sometimes pulled out by fish at a level far above the preset drag tension. At other times, it can be taken out well under the desired tension level.

As the problem here is friction and heat build-up from two moving surfaces coming together (which can even cause car brakes to fail), the smoothest reel drag systems, like the best car brakes, are obviously those that take the longest to heat up and, once heated, are quickest to dissipate the heat. Choice of washer material (at one time anything from leather to brass but now mainly composite materials of various sorts) is one key to the problem. Other partial solutions include periodic cleaning by the angler or, at the manufacturing end, increasing surface contact by using larger than normal washers or by using a series of washers. The simplest way to determine whether you have a problem is to watch the rod tip. If it is bucking up and down against a running fish, you know the drag is either defective, needs degreasing, or is improperly set. When the drag is working well, the rod tip will simply bend toward the direction of the pull and stay almost stationary as additional line rolls off.

Basic treatment for an uneven drag starts with a thorough cleaning to get rid of grit or dirt that has likely accumulated in the reel. A common problem stems from accumulation of grease applied too heavily to adjacent reel gears. Old leather washers needed oil periodically to keep the leather from drying out, but slippery grease or oil on the newer materials makes it impossible to maintain tension of any kind. If cleaning doesn't work or the drag gives out again on the next big fish, give the reel away to a bass fisherman, or junk it.

Assuming you don't have the "educated" human thumb needed to brake a revolving spool (bait-casting) reel expertly, a spinning reel is an absolute must on a beach. Just start out with medium strength line and set reel tension well below the line's breaking point. Light-line spinning skills and the special gear needed to use lighter lines may come later if your interests take you in that direction.

The ability to cast a lure the proverbial country mile is more than just satisfying a competitive urge to outcast everyone else on a beach. It also often means extra fish. Longer casts will result in more fish caught simply because you are covering more water, including offshore mud lines out of reach of standard freshwater casting gear. A little-known area off most beaches that also consistently holds fish is the first ridge of submerged bottom sand that usually develops because of wave action about eighty to one hundred yards offshore, accessible from a beach only with surf-casting equipment. Brown trout and occasionally steelhead and salmon are not only attracted to this underwater structure, usually the only bit of structure around, but will often follow the ridge long distances as they roam the shoreline in spring and fall.

So now you have a starting point in any practical discussion of casting distance and tackle needs. How far is far? Knowing about the ridge, you'll want to be able to cast a lure at least one hundred yards, which isn't a difficult chore with a one-ounce lure. A two- to three-ounce lure tossed the right way should travel close to 150 yards, sometimes more, depending on wind direction and how hard it's blowing. A four- to six-ounce weight can be cast past the 150 yard mark. Surf distance-tournament casters using special gear can throw weights 250 yards.

Given a standard eleven- or twelve-foot surf rod with a stiff butt, powerful medium-action midsection, and a flexible tip, plus the lightest line your rod can handle doesn't mean you'll be able to outcast everyone on the beach the first time out, however. It'll take time, and experimental work, to get the feel of any tackle and to learn how to stretch the most distance out of it.

Once you do start pushing for extra distance, either by using heavier lures or by putting extra muscle power into casts, you'll need a shock leader to cushion the extra strain on your casting line. That or you'll be popping lures off. As the name suggests, a shock leader is just a few feet of heavy nylon tied to the end of the casting line to absorb the initial shock of the cast. The rule-of-thumb formula used to calculate necessary leader strength is to multiply sinker or lure weight by ten and call the result pounds. A two-ounce casting weight, for example, requires a 20-pound-test shock leader, a three-ounce weight needs 30-pound-test, four ounces 40 pounds, and so on. Leader length is normally rod length plus six to eight turns on the reel spool when the sinker or lure is suspended in casting position off the rod tip. You'll find this length of extra-strong line is also handy in the final throes of beaching a fish; the heavier line sometimes prevents the loss of a big fish making an all-out, last-minute effort to escape. Don't buy extrastiff, cheap leader material. The more pliable the leader material, the better it will cast. As with all leaders, the monofilament must also be checked for wear periodically and replaced as needed.

Over the course of a surf-casting year you'll find, once you try bait fishing, that sinkers, although comparatively cheap, are vital pieces of equipment. A sinker has two main jobs: to carry the centrifugal force of the cast through the air efficiently, taking the bait along with it, and to provide stabilization of the bait once the cast is completed. Sound simple? It is. But the sinker still has to be carefully matched to both gear and angling conditions. Offshore wave action or currents, size of bait, casting distance, and water depth must all be considered.

Another rarely considered but important factor in bait-fishing is choosing a sinker that allows you to make the slowest possible cast. The faster and harder a rod is flexed to achieve casting distance, the better the chances bait will be ripped free of the hook by momentum. So given the choice of, say, using a two-ounce sinker under high speed conditions and tossing bait off, or using a four-ounce sinker, which only needs to travel at half the speed to carry the same distance, you'll naturally make the switch to a four-ounce sinker. Generally, two- or three-ounce weights are suitable only up to seventy or eighty yards fishing distance. Standard weights for long-range use are five or six ounces of lead. The best sinker design for all-round Great Lakes use is a sharp-edged pyramid which holds best in sand and mud. The rounder contours of dipsey or bank sinkers work better around rocks where pyramids often hang up.

Every angler seems to have his own way of rigging terminal tackle. The best surf technique I've discovered over the years, a saltwater trick passed on by an old-timer who, luckily, got tired of watching me lose terminal gear one day off a pier, is not only easily rigged but, unlike many systems, allows the fish to take bait without feeling the weight of the sinker. Simply feed your line through the eye of a big brass swivel. Once through, tie the line to one end of a barrel swivel. Link a short terminal leader, or tippet and hook, to the other end. At this point, snap the sinker onto the original sliding swivel in front of the leader. You'll find the weight rides nicely down the line on the cast but is prevented from reaching the baited hook by the smaller leader swivel. Once the sinker is on bottom, the unweighted line slides very easily through the eye of the snap if a fish decides to carry the bait off. You can achieve similar results by using a hollow centered egg sinker, and inserting the line through the sinker. A swivel or split shot prevents the "egg" from sliding down to the hook.

When to set the hook? That's always a good question. Do you let the fish run with the bait, taking the chance it won't spit the bait out before you can hook it, or do you strike the fish as soon as the bait is taken? The answer can depend on many factors: size of hook, size and softness (or hardness) of bait, water turbulence, species of fish, its size and aggressiveness, and so on. But, as always, the only definite answer must come from experience. If you lose a fish on a slow strike, set the hook faster next time. Most fish-hooking problems stem from the use of oversized hooks, or hooks with shanks that are too long. Try a smaller size.

Casting techniques vary from angler to angler. Novices on the Great Lakes invariably start by using the same backward-forward rod flip technique employed with freshwater gear. A much better method, usually employed by veterans to cast heavier lures on longer soft-action rods, is an overhand cast that starts with the lure or bait close to the beach behind the angler. The rod butt is facing the direction of the cast. The angler, standing sideways to the water, one hand clutching the lower portion of the handle, the other controlling the reel, pushes down with one arm on the handle while the other brings the rod tip up and forward to make the cast. Advantages of the technique, even with today's rods, include ease in controlling the momentum of the lure. The difference between a gentle lob cast and a hard, driving throw is only in the speed and power of the rod's forward movement.

For extra casting distance, most expert "surfers" are now using a tournament-casting technique called the "pendulum swing," in which the caster puts the full power of his body into the cast. It takes precise timing, but the distance you can chuck a lure is astonishing. You start by standing sideways to the direction of the cast, as with the previous technique, but twist your upper body somewhat like a coiled spring toward the rear. Extend ten feet or more of shock leader plus terminal gear from the tip of the rod, which you hold in a near-vertical position. Start the pendulum action by slowly moving the rod back and forth so the sinker and terminal gear are swinging pendulum fashion. Gradually increase the swing by rod movement until rod and terminal gear are almost in a straight line. At the precise moment when a rear swing of the pendulum puts the line straight out from the rod, transfer all of your weight to the left foot (if you're right-handed), and as you uncoil your body toward the direction of the cast, you have the combined extra power of body weight, legs, waist, and shoulders added to normal arm casting movements. The results are unbelievable, especially if you run into an expert tossing eight ounces of lead off a massive fifteen-foot rod. The built-up power of this cast can yank a light eye ring right out of a freshwater lure, straighten split rings, and tear apart lightweight freshwater swivel snaps.

Other gear required by a happy beach fisherman are chest waders and a small knapsack in which to carry a thermos of coffee and sandwiches, if you're going to be out that long. You'll also need a few boxed lures (each part of the various lakes has local favorites—just ask), a sand spike to hold the rod while bait fishing, a variety of hooks and weights, a few smelt or roe bags for bait, line cutters or a knife, and maybe a rain slicker. An old but clean potato sack is also handy to store newly caught fish in while on the beach. The dampened bag will keep the fish reasonably cool on a hot day and, on the way home, protect the interior of the car from an inevitable fallout of shiny salmon scales and various forms of fish goo.

Shoreline boat anglers and pier fishermen need landing nets, the longer the handle and the bigger the net hoop the better. On most piers, unless low to the water, the best way to land a trophy-size fish is to walk the played-out fish to the shallows and beach it just like you would land a fish while angling in surf. On a long crowded pier where beaching a fish would mean risking the wrath of fifty other fishermen between you and shore, there are usually two or three anglers nearby eager to lend a hand with special home-built nets. The ultra-long net handles necessary for use on high piers are usually made out of five-foot, hollow sections of one-inch threaded metal pipe. The only commercially available nets I know of with handles long enough for high-pier fishing are made in England. Hardy Brothers, a well-known fly rod manufacturer, sells nets with sturdy ten-foot handles that are used by European anglers fishing from high canal banks.

5

Offshore Transitions

While shallow-water anglers can enjoy Great Lakes angling each spring and fall at little or no cost, offshore anglers will find the deeper they fish, the farther from shore they go, the more expensive the sport becomes.

—Gerry Wolfram

It's always fascinating to watch an onshore small-boat angler turn into the captain of a big, gadget-laden offshore fishing boat. The chrysalis usually forms without the angler realizing a major personal transformation is under way, which is a normal situation, I suppose. Does a coral algal cell know it will become a vast reef? Does a caterpillar know it will become a butterfly? Even if the angler did know, who wants to admit to being in any kind of pupal development stage anyway? But it all starts very innocently. It is a process so gradual few anglers are able even to recall its beginning, to look back in wonder after the metamorphosis is over and, pinpointing one moment in time say, "There, it was right there that it started." Yet the true beginning, the first purchase of auxiliary gear, is as predictable as the beat of rolling surf.

Sooner or later, it seems, extra equipment starts popping up on small twelve- or fourteen-foot boats like rings of nautical mushrooms, the accessories threatening in time to swallow the anglers whole as their tiny boats sink lower and lower in the water under their weight. Whether the process takes six months or six years makes little difference. In the end, the angler discovers (usually his wife tells him) he has ten times as many dollars sunk into so-called extra gear as he has in his little boat and motor. He has no doubt ventured offshore many times and is thoroughly weary of getting wet, possibly scared, every time he is chased off the lake by dangerously high winds and waves. At this point, he has no choice but to buy the bigger twenty-one- or twenty-four-foot boat he needs to go where he really wants to go anyway: out in the briny blue where the big fish of summer roam. Thus most offshore anglers are born.

The first step toward becoming an offshore angler can be as innocent as buying a new rod, maybe a few lures—nothing of any importance, or so it seems, even though the purchases are likely triggering a sequence of events that will completely change the angler's life. A few new lures naturally lead to the purchase of more lures. If other anglers are suddenly taking salmon on blue-spotted Yellowfins, you of course have to have one of the same. I've seen such word-of-mouth advertising catapult many lures out of obscurity into short-lived local angling fame. The resultant buying rush on area sporting goods stores for the top lure of the week has sometimes cleaned puzzled shopkeepers out of a normal year's supply

The size of an offshore angler's boat is normally related to volume and variety of auxiliary fishing gear. Here we have a classic example of anglers who, by now, are no doubt fishing out of a much larger boat. (*Photo courtesy of Outboard Marine Corp.*)

of stock in a matter of hours. Next week, the "hot" lure will be something completely different, of course, but it's all part of the game and, compared to everything else, lures aren't really that expensive anyway. Next thing you know, however, the tackle box is overcrowded. So we innocently say: "Well, the old box has been around a long time. It doesn't really owe me anything. I'll get a bigger one."

The biggest step is the purchase of the first downrigger. These units, little more than a manually or electrically operated spool holding two hundred feet of 120-pound-test steel aircraft cable, lower 8- or 12-pound weights, called cannonballs, measured distances into the depths. Crimped into the system, linking the cable to the ball, is a release, which holds fishing line under preset tension until pulled free by an irate salmon. The name cannonball, incidentally, in case you're an angling history buff, goes back to early West Coast sport salmon anglers who attached needed weight on light breakaway secondary lines in order to fish deep water. As the weight was broken off and lost with every fish, they naturally used

Fishing tackle used by the author include (*from left to right*): light line downrigger rod and reel, heavy-duty trolling outfit, a mooching rod with single-action reel, a heavy-line downrigger rod and reel, and a light saltwater surfcasting rod and reel.

the cheapest chunk of lead they could find—in their case old surplus military cannonballs.

Using a downrigger is very easy. A lure is let out behind the boat any distance the angler thinks is necessary to catch fish, and is then set in the release and lowered behind the ball to any desired depth. When a fish strikes, it pulls the line free of the downrigger and the angler can then fight the fish in a sporting manner, free of any weight.

Fortunately, choosing a downrigger, like picking most tackle today, has few real challenges. If the manufacturer's name is familiar, the odds are good you will be satisfied with the product. Market competition is so intense, anyone making an inferior unit isn't likely to be in business very long. Unless, of course, the tackle (usually rods and reels) is being built only for "El Cheapo" garbage markets. Talk to other anglers. Hang around a marina for a day or two and when a fully rigged boat comes in, wander over and chat with the owner. (Remember, though, that charterboat choices are often based only on which company offered that particular skipper the biggest price discount. The companies presume, quite accurately, I think, a highly visible array of their tackle on a charterboat helps sell equipment.) I'd be very surprised, however, to find any angler, professional or amateur, truly unhappy over the choice of any well-known brand-name downriggers. The only regrets you might hear would come from owners of manually operated downriggers who occasionally kick themselves (after a hard day of cranking) for not having bought electrical units.

Line releases vary only in how the line is freed. My first downrigger used a clevis or "hairpin" which clipped onto a downrigger cable anchor made in the form of a grooved metal dowel. The three grooves were machined to different depths; the deeper the groove the easier the clevis could be pulled free by a fish. A similar unit I still use occasionally has a small plastic ring, called a "donut," through which the line is inserted, then twisted to hold it in position when the donut is inserted into one of four different sized notches of a plastic rudder that is attached to the downrigger cable. Again, the size of the notch determines the amount of pressure needed to free the line. Still another form of release, probably most popular of all, incorporates an adjustable threaded tension system. The unit, shaped like a streamlined lipstick tube, has a tension adjusting base at one end. At the other, the line is wrapped between the body of the release and its adjustable head. When pressure is put on the line by a fish, the line-holding portion of the release slips forward to free the coiled line behind it.

Available to simplify the use of two rods on one downrigger are a wide variety of releases that can be clipped on the downrigger cable

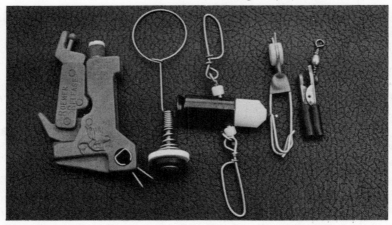

Types of Great Lakes fishing line releases include (*from left to right*): the Roemer, which can be attached anywhere on a downrigger cable; a slider release, used mainly with planing boards; a Walker downrigger release; a "donut"-style release, used by the author on early planing boards; and an "alligator" clip release, used with fishing kites.

wherever desired. Other, more permanently attached units have the cable inserted through them so they can slide up and down. My "slider releases" are held in tackle-rigging position prior to use by horseshoe-shaped plastic clevises wired to downrigger arms. When the bottom cannonball release has fishing line clipped into it and I'm ready to sink the first lure, the ball is lowered five or six feet to get everything out of the way. The slider release, still being held in accessible position on the cable, is then rigged and as the cannonball is dropped farther into the water, a metal "collar" clamped around the cable ten feet above the lower release knocks the slider free of its holder. Rod tension continues to hold the release up against the collar until a fish hits. At that point, with nothing holding it, the release slides down the cable out of the way, stopping at the arm that connects the cable to the cannonball release beneath it.

Running two lures (or more) off one line—a process called "stacking"—is equally simple. One way is to use a fishing alligator clip (a miniature version of the jawed clips used on battery cables), which has a snap and swivel on its other end. A five- or six-foot secondary line and lure are connected to the snap, which also encloses the main line, and the clip is then clamped onto the cable. When a fish hits, the clamp pulls free of the cable, the secondary line and lure are pulled down the main line via the snap to the lower release, which triggers it and, presto, you're free of the cannonball. From there, the fish will continue sliding the secondary line down to the main or lower lure, which is why (to answer a question you're going to ask sooner or later) you can't run a stacked lure on line much longer than the length of your rod. With two lures out and the fish on the trailing lure, the first lure would stop you from bringing any fish on a longer line close enough to the boat to be easily netted.

Another way of doing the same thing is to loop hitch a No. 16 rubber band where you want it on the cable. A No. 7 or larger snap is tied to the second line and trailing lure. Both the main line and the looped elastic band are enclosed in the end snap. When a fish hits, the elastic band holding the lure in position breaks, resulting in the same situation as with the alligator clamp. Using the break-away rubber band or clamp system means you don't have to stop to remove a release when lifting a cannonball after a strike. The remnants of the soft rubber band can roll right onto the downrigger winch without damage. If you're using an alligator clip, it, of course, has pulled free and is with the fish. Plastic or metal clip-on releases allowing use of extra lines must be removed from the cable before the cannonball can be brought all the way up.

A distinct advantage of using a rubber band is that an elastic release eliminates the "shaker" problem. Small fish not big enough to trigger a standard release (all they can do is shake it) are often hooked without the angler knowing it. So we drag these tiny immature fish around behind us, not discovering them until we raise tackle to switch lures. With a rubber band, which even a "shaker" can stretch, the fish signal their presence by moving the rod tip up and down as they pull against the elastic. Almost any type of rubber band is usable. The breaking point of heavier bands can be weakened by leaving them in the sun for a few days or by just snipping a notch of rubber out of an edge with your line cutters.

Basic elements to look for in any downrigger start with solid, non-corrosive construction. Between heavy cannonballs and bouncing waves, downriggers can take a real beating at times. Materials in use today vary from stainless steel to space-age, almost indestructible, plastics. In addition, I'd want a choice of strong pivot bases of whatever height I needed for simple mounting on any boat. Don't forget to check to see how firmly the downrigger can be bolted to the base plate (which is permanently attached to the boat). The more bolts the better. At least one downrigger every year is lost overboard in our part of Lake Ontario, usually because of angler carelessness. You do have to retighten the bolts occasionally.

Also at the top of any downrigger shopping list would be an automatic shutoff or circuit breaker to avoid electric-motor burnout if you should forget to turn a unit off after hitting the "up" button. It can happen very easily—all you need is a double hit. You have two big salmon running two different ways, you're trying to clear tackle, run a boat, net fish, and

The first computerized downrigger, Cannon's Digi-Troll, has a built-in memory to lower a cannonball to a pre-set depth. It also has a cycle operation, which oscillates the ball and attached fishing lures up and down for a distance of five feet on each cycle. (*Photo courtesy of Cannon/S&K Products, Inc.*)

keep track of anglers going crazy with excitement, all at the same time, and under those conditions who's always going to remember a downrigger is running?

Look for built-in or bolt-on rod holders, a cable footage counter, and a built-in friction clutch to avoid cable breakage or downrigger damage if a ball hangs up on bottom. You should have a choice of downrigger arm lengths. Longer-arm models are called sideriggers for mounting over the sides of a boat. The extra length of a three- or four-foot arm keeps tackle from tangling with gear hung off the regular downriggers with two-foot arms, which are usually mounted on the stern corners of a boat. The cable-guide pulley at the tip of a downrigger arm is important. It should be big, the bigger the better, deeply grooved to prevent the cable from slipping out, and built to swivel from side to side to reduce cable wear. The cable itself should be made of woven or twisted stainless steel. Solid wire cables kink and break too easily.

Oddly enough, the most heated discussions about downriggers usually center on cannonballs, not the downriggers themselves. Fishermen can argue for hours, it seems, over which shape of ball tracks straightest in the water. Three of the most common cannonball designs are round balls with fins; fish-shaped balls, with the tail of the fish acting as a fin; and streamlined torpedo designs with fins. Some anglers complain the torpedo or fish shapes tend to wander around and sometimes foul up tackle. Others claim a fish-shaped ball acts as a decoy and that they catch more fish with them.

What I have yet to hear on a dock (and any physicist will tell you this if asked) is that a plain round ball, although not as pretty, is by far the most efficient shape for creating maximum weight. By having the smallest possible surface area, it creates the least drag in water. This means that, although streamlined cannonballs may look nicer and cost more money, increased friction caused by their larger surface area results in less depth per pound. A plain ball with a fin not only sinks better but holds better in the water.

In actual practice (so much for theory), I run balls and torpedoes indiscriminately. Any loss of depth with the torpedoes is more than compensated, in my mind at least, by underwater oscillations, which potentially add extra movement and thus fish-drawing attraction to trailing lures. As long as the cannonball is heavily coated with plastic to prevent the ball from chewing up the boat and has a strong cable attachment ring, I really don't care what it looks like. Although if I were a Lake Michigan or Lake Superior lake trout specialist sacrificing cannonballs on sharp rocks occasionally to take bottom-hugging fish, the lesser cost of the round balls would no doubt change my thinking.

Another standard piece of equipment for any Great Lakes offshore angler is a diving planer (a poor man's downrigger), which permits controlled depth fishing down to one hundred feet or more. These keel-weighted plastic units, sold under such trade names as Pink Lady or Dolphin Diver, trail lures on separate leaders three to five feet behind them. You simply snap one onto a fishing line so it is tilted forward in diving position on entering the water. The depth it will dive depends on the size of the planer, the force of water against its face, and the amount of line let out. It's an easy way of running additional deep-running lures at fairly precise depths well behind downrigger lures. When a fish hits, the impact knocks it out of diving position and, having lost its tilt, it will plane to the surface. My smallest planer, on 20-pound-test line, will hold a lure fifty feet in back of the boat at a depth of thirty-three feet; seventy-five feet of line will put a lure down forty-eight feet; one hundred feet of line, sixty-two feet down, and so on. My biggest unit, a Size 2 Pink Lady, will run a lure on 20-pound-test line 35 feet deep when the planer is 50 feet behind the boat; 66 feet deep with 100 feet of line out; 93 feet down on 150 feet of line; and 116 feet down on 200 feet of line. A close cousin of the diving planer is a floating sideplaner (to be discussed in chapter 7), which uses the same basic principles to carry shallow-running lures well off to the side of a boat.

Oddly enough, one of the most important pieces of offshore fishing equipment I own, a compass, is rarely considered an angling accessory. A compass is usually associated with boating safety but, lacking specialized navigational equipment, a compass can accurately return you to a midlake angling hotspot, if you develop the knack of using it in conjunction with sonar and your boat's tachometer or speedometer. Not that we're going to get involved in a lengthy discourse on offshore navigation here. There have been dozens of technical (a polite word for "confusing") books written about that subject alone. Despite the experts, "dead reckoning" your position on a lake, and being able to get back to approximately the same spot next day, isn't that complicated. After a while, you'll find you're doing most of the work subconsciously, keeping mental track of various directions taken, running speeds, and times between course changes. If you can continually visualize your changing position, you can go anywhere you wish on a lake (or an ocean for that matter) with a fair amount of confidence.

However you use a compass, even if it's only to point out the direction of north on a day when the sun isn't visible, it's important to buy a good one. Instead of the familiar needle compass of Boy Scout days, get a mariner's compass, which usually has an easily read magnetized card that breaks all 360 degrees of the directional circle down: 000 at north, 090 for east, 180 for south, and 270 for west, plus points in between. On a normal "wet" compass, which means the card is floating on an alcohol mix or petroleum-base liquid to dampen oscillations, the card should hold its position on magnetic north during any kind of turn. The steadier the card, the better the compass. In fact this is a good buying test: Pick the compass up and turn it quickly. The card shouldn't rotate. If it does shift or hang off line, try another compass. Tied in with use of the card is the "lubber" line on the face of the compass, which, assuming it's on line with the keel of the boat, provides an easy readout against the card behind it to tell you the direction you're going. (Now you know where the word "landlubber" comes from; it's anyone who is happiest on water only when the lubber line is taking him back to land.)

Insist that the compass have adjustable secondary magnets in its base to allow easy correction of any minor magnetic deviations caused by other equipment on board the boat. Problems usually occur when electronic gadgets such as tachs, radios, or sonar are too close to the compass.

As electrical currents powering such accessories can produce compass-disrupting magnetic fields, you can correct most of these deviation problems by just twisting the single-current wires leading to the tachs or whatever around each other, cancelling out any magnetic fields they produce. Don't keep binoculars or any other metallic objects near a compass. Also, be sure the compass face is illuminated for night use.

Once the first downrigger appears on a small boat, other developments follow fairly quickly. The angler involved has unknowingly "crested." From here on, he is riding the down side of a fast-moving wave of tackle acquisitions. With one or more downriggers, he obviously must have downrigger rods, built long (9½ feet) with extra-long handles to sit securely in downrigger holders, and possessing a softer action to absorb the stress of being clamped in a tight semicircle over a downrigger day after day. With the downrigger rods also come the heavy-duty bait-casting reels. My downrigger reels, bigger and heavier than most because of charterboat work, hold 275 yards of 20-pound-test monofilament. Other features include a 3:1 gear ratio, a star-drag braking system, and a freespool lever rather than a button-style release. These reels also have rugged saltwater-style rod attachment systems. Two bolts and wing nuts attach a clamp, curved to fit the underside of the rod, to the base plate of the reel, locking it on just in case the rod's double reel-seat rings ever come loose on a trophy fish.

Any self-respecting offshore angler must also have such items as a thermometer to measure surface water temperature and, eventually, a self-contained battery-powered temperature probe with a cable footage counter on it—much like the footage counter of a downrigger—that can be lowered into the lake to register water temperatures at various depths. Fancy temperature units have the sensor attached above the cannonball, giving a quick readout of water temperature at cannonball level at the flick of a switch. Another unit measures not only water temperature but trolling speed. Still another, if you were to buy all available computer monitor options, measures surface temperature, temperature at the depth of the cannonball, trolling speed at downrigger depth, trolling speed of the boat, and pH (acid-alkaline) content of the water at both surface and cannonball. There is no end to the gizmos waiting to be purchased by an eager angler.

A popular, inexpensive trolling speed indicator measures boat speed by the amount of drag against a small bell-shaped weight lowered into the water on the end of a light cable. Up top, the monitoring unit is clamped or mounted in a convenient spot on a side of the boat. On its face is a movable arm, centered in a slot, which gives a color-coded reading of speed based on the amount of water pressure against the sunken weight. It works on an extremely simple lever system. The greater the

A water temperature sensor that measures temperatures at different depths, including the important thermocline, is a vital offshore Great Lakes fishing accessory. (*Photo by Gwynne Wolfram*)

rearward tilt of the weight in the water, the higher the speed reading. If you catch the first fish of the day while the indicator is in, say, the red zone, by doing what you have to do with the throttle to keep the arm in that color zone you can maintain the same speed to catch other fish, no matter how badly wind or waves might affect boat movement any time you change course. Some offshore anglers can also measure boat speed with surprising accuracy by the passing flecks of surface foam or bubbles coming off downrigger cables beside the boat.

If you've purchased electrically operated downriggers (you will, sooner or later, once you start fishing deeper water), you've also bought a heavy-duty twelve-volt marine battery as a source of power. And with "hydro" in the boat it now makes a lot of sense to pick up a CB radio, plus antenna, to find out what other anglers are doing. When fishing turns slow, why waste time trolling when, thanks to radio, you can find out other fishermen are taking limit catches a few short miles away? It makes sense.

If you're a veteran highway CB operator accustomed to the special

VHF and CB radios play an important role in helping Great Lakes anglers stay on top of fish. Sharing of information and angling results has simplified the task of finding and catching offshore salmon. (*Photo by Gwynne Wolfram*)

language of passing truckers, it's an easy switch to marine CB. The only real difference is that lake talk of course is about fish—where they are found, what they are caught on—rather than about where Smokey is taking pictures and other vital bits of high speed road information. It's all good fun. If you're a novice, just switch on Channel 13 and get ready for a lot of friendly banter. You'll find that although Channel 13, like Channel 9 on the road, is supposed to be a "working" channel and used only to make brief contact prior to switching elsewhere to chat, few users make such distinctions today. So you shouldn't hesitate to interrupt someone's idle chatter with a "breaker" call. If you don't, you'll likely never use your radio.

Start out by asking for a radio check on your first call. Someone will usually reply (a "comeback") to tell you how well your transmission is being received. Marine CB users use the "10 code" (10-20 asks What is your location?; 10-4 means Message received), plus a lot of colorful lingo that, like truckers' jargon, can puzzle CB novices. You'll hear things like "sweeping the walk" (fishing close to shore) or "dredging bottom" (fishing a cannonball right on bottom), but things will become clear after a while. And you can even pick up bits of worthwhile angling information occasionally. In fact, you can learn a lot just from the volume of chatter. A basic rule of the Great Lakes is: The better the fishing the more noise on CB. When the CB is deafening you with its silence, you know no one is catching fish.

A CB radio normally has a maximum range of only five miles, so if you want to talk to the "big boys," you'll need a VHF (Very High Frequency) unit that will let you chat with another boater up to twenty miles away, depending on the height of your antenna. You also have contact via VHF with the Coast Guard, weather information stations, harbor masters, yacht clubs and, if you forgot to call in sick at the office, marine telephone operators who will relay calls anywhere. If that isn't enough, you can link VHF into an automatic direction finder (ADF) that, by triangulating other transmission sources such as weather stations and coast guard stations, will pinpoint your location on the lake. Even more fun, if your bank account can stand the jolt, is a single side band VHF unit that literally will put you in contact with outer space, its transmissions penetrating the earth's atmosphere and bouncing back to earth off the ionosphere, one hundred miles up. VHF costs depend on the number of channels and program features desired. In addition, as required by United States law, each radio has an automatic switch to cut power to one watt for close-in use in harbors.

If you really want to impress your fellow anglers you can buy a computerized navigational aid called the Loran C (Long Range Aid to Navigation, phase C), which, by measuring intervals between pulsating directional signals from coast guard broadcast radio beams, can compute boat speed and time of arrival, pinpoint your location within a matter of measured feet, take you to a specific spot in the middle of the lake, or give you a compass reading that will take you straight home in the heaviest of fogs. In fact, the first time I saw a Loran unit in use was about fourteen years ago while fishing the edge of the Gulf Stream forty miles off the South Carolina coast on a day when heavy fog rolled in. Other boaters, knowing our boat was the only one out there equipped with Loran, huddled nearby until our skipper did five minutes' chart work, programming everything into the receiver, and after getting his Loran coordinates, hit home port dead on with all the other boats trailing behind us like a family of ducklings. It was very impressive.

Hook a Loran C into an auto-pilot system that steers your boat on the Loran-set course and you can just sit back and enjoy the ride. But don't rely on it too much. It can be overdone. I know someone who, using Loran to get back to his marina, forgot to write in navigational data needed to detour around a man-made spit near the marina entrance. It was late at night and very dark. Crunch!

Another obvious angling need is sonar. (In fact this subject is so important to offshore anglers it's being treated separately in chapter 6.) As most know, these angling aids were derived from wartime SONAR units designed to detect enemy submarines by bouncing sound waves off the sea bottom. They not only measure depths for you—basic knowledge any downrigger angler must have to avoid losing all his expensive cannonballs—but also detect any solids such as fish suspended between bottom and the sonar transducer attached to the hull of the boat.

6

Blips or Bloops?

*More power means different things in different circumstances,
but with sonar it means better, all-round performance.*
—Lowrance Product Catalog

Magic box, underwater eye, sonar—call it what you will—sonar has had
more impact on deep-water angling than any other technological advance
in many, many years.

The only comparison might be the creation of silk fishing lines around
1840, allowing anglers for the first time to present a lure a greater distance
away than the length of a rod, a giant step which immediately opened
the door to basic rod and reel improvements still being enjoyed today.

Portable sonar, first sold by the Lowrance Company to anglers in
1957, has not prompted any basic changes in tackle. Its greatest, most
lasting impact has been on our mental approaches to angling. On typical
inland lakes, separate bits and pieces of local knowledge, such as the
gradual discovery of various weed beds and shoals, were suddenly transformed into an accurate visual display. Former underwater mysteries such
as basic bottom topography and seasonal fish movements became suddenly, almost magically, obvious to anyone reading the blips of the early

"green boxes" or, with today's equipment, studying paper chart printouts or video screen images. The transition was like sudden X-ray vision that allowed us to see and explore underwater worlds never seen before. For the first time, thanks to sonar and the temperature probes and oxygen measuring devices that quickly followed, anglers could gain an understanding of a body of water in its entirety, not just as stored liquid, but as a living, ever-changing ecosystem of many components, each part influencing the others.

There's little question a methodical, knowledgeable angler equipped with lightweight transistorized sonar can learn more hard facts about a small lake in a single day than most local anglers without sonar acquire in a lifetime. On big water, such as the Great Lakes, the underwater eye of sonar is even more indispensable, especially when fish are roaming freely far offshore in deep water. With no well-defined bottom structure in most of Lake Ontario to attract and hold fish or act as a rudimentary navigational guide, what offshore angler involved in such a large-scale game of "hide and seek" with salmon would give up his "eyes?" It's hard to imagine having to fish blindly again, never knowing whether fish are ignoring lures or not. Our effectiveness as anglers, and our enjoyment of offshore fishing, would certainly be reduced in a hurry. Without sonar, who'd even bother fishing deep water?

An increasingly competitive marketplace has resulted in many sonar manufacturers offering a confusing variety of ballyhooed refinements, all designed to convince us one machine is better than another. You now have the choice of flasher units, curved-line graph units, straight-line units, and video units, plus sonar with clean-line, grey-line, or white-line capabilities. If that isn't enough to send you back to dunking worms, sonar depth-reading adjustments run all the way from a simple one-scale capability to a computerized 32 million scale system on the new Lowrance X-16 graph, capable, with special transducers, of zooming in and magnifying one foot segments of water up to a depth of eight thousand feet.

I've used only four different units: a flasher and two straight-line chart sonar units, all made by the same manufacturer, and, occasionally, a black-and-white video sonar unit, which receives images much like a TV set except that fish normally marked as black on white chart paper are white against the black background of a screen. Not having used any of the others, or having had a chance to compare similar machines of different makes, I wouldn't even attempt to rate any of them. It would be a full time job just to keep up with technological changes. One manufacturer, Humminbird, is now bringing out a video unit that displays images in eight different colors! But, in the end, I suspect you pretty much

One of three basic types of sonar units used by Great Lakes anglers is the flasher unit, a sophisticated version of the original unit introduced in 1957. (*Photo courtesy of Lowrance Electronics, Inc.*)

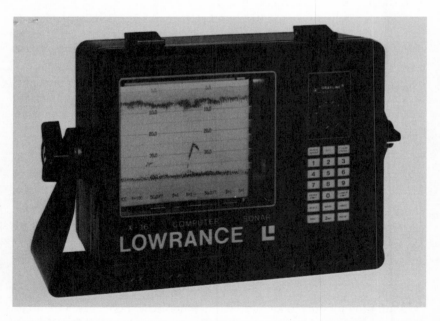

A paper graph sonar unit provides the greatest amount of easily read underwater details. (*Photo courtesy of Lowrance Electronics, Inc.*)

The video display sonar unit registers images on a TV-type screen. (*Photo courtesy of Lowrance Electronics, Inc.*)

get what you pay for. All of the various sonar units no doubt work comparatively well. The only real challenge is matching your angling needs and wallet to the capabilities and cost of whatever machine you're thinking of buying.

A basic understanding of how sonar works, how to read what sonar tells you, and how to know when the units are not being completely truthful should at least put you in a position where you won't wind up buying (at least I hope you won't) a Ferrari to deliver milk or, at the other extreme, a bulky van when what you really want is a high-speed Grand Prix machine.

Sonar, which comes from the words "sounding," "navigation," and "ranging," is a two-part electronic wonder, a sealed crystal or transducer that transmits and receives a high-pitched sound signal zapped back and forth off bottom at a speed of about 4,800 feet a second, and a "head" or recorder that displays what the transducer catches in the bounceback. It's often compared to shining a flashlight into a dark room. The tricky part is that sonar is calibrated to measure the time it takes the signal to bounce off bottom in order to tell you how much water you have under your hull. As the signal will mark anything, say at 20 feet, at something like .0084 seconds, we're dealing with space-age speed. By comparison, old-fashioned lightning is really a slowpoke. Equally interesting from an angling viewpoint is that any solid matter between the transducer and bottom, such as a hungry fish, is also registered and marked on the recording unit, either as a blip on a flasher, or a "hook" on paper or video.

Comparatively inexpensive flasher units use a small neon bulb that rotates on an arm behind the depth-measuring scaled face of the head, the flashing bulb creating bars of light that, by their thickness or groupings, indicate depth, bottom composition, and the presence and relative size of fish. The bulb flashes each time a sound impulse is emitted, marking zero or surface. Frequency of the flashes is forty per second on a 60-foot scale, and twenty per second on a 120-foot scale. The bulb flashes again on each bounceback, producing another belt of flickering lines opposite a number on the scale indicating depth of bottom. Anything in between, such as fish, causes yet another blip of red lines between the bottom blips and the surface reading.

Fish (unlike bottom which can give you a repeat echo) usually give only one, primary echo. They're marked once and are gone. Unfortunately, even though many flasher units now have audible alarms that beep or buzz whenever fish are marked, you still have to spend all your time watching the flasher dial to spot fish. Turn your head away and, even with a beeper, the fish marks are often gone before you see them. As a basic depth finder for locating, say, an underwater reef on a lake, they're great. But for fish finders, you'll soon yearn for something more.

Much better by far are straight-line graph units, which create a picture on paper of both bottom and fish. Instead of using a bulb, a graph unit uses a stylus or pen, which, as each impulse is received, shoots an electrical arc through carbon-impregnated graph paper to make a small black dot. As both the roll-fed paper and the stylus are moving at precisely coordinated speeds, the dots blend together into a line drawing of bottom. As with other systems, any fish that pass through the cone of the transducer are also recorded. Less expensive curved-line or circular graphs differ only by having the stylus powered by rotary drive rather than belt drive. As a result, the printout is curved slightly. Some are coupled with a flasher unit so you can save paper when all you require is a bottom reading.

All this is straightforward so far. The real differences between the various makes of sonar are in the dimensions of the signal, called a cone, and related power output. Much like the beam of a flashlight, the radius of the cone expands as it travels. The wider the cone, the bigger the underwater "picture." The size of the cone also depends on the operating frequency of the transmitting transducer. The real key to cone angle is the transducer, not the sonar unit itself. In fact, some units interface with a number of transducers with different cone widths, allowing manufacturers to match a specific cone with a unit designed to be sold to anglers with special needs. Such units also allow an angler to use more than one transducer, allowing a switch, via an accessory selector box, from a narrow cone to a wide cone transducer, the choice depending on the depth of water being fished.

Back in the old days (if you can call the 1970s that), wider cones were shrugged off by many Great Lakes anglers as being good only for Florida shallow-water bass fishermen. We all believed, rightly or wrongly, and some anglers still believe, that the wider the cone, or the bigger the underwater window, the more power was needed. We thought the wider cones put out a weaker signal, affecting the unit's ability to detect fish or read bottom. Manufacturers have now overcome the problem by matching signal rates (being sound vibrations, they're measured in kilohertz) to specific transducers for specific jobs. By matching a high operating frequency of 192 kilohertz, say, with a narrow, eight-degree or medium twenty-degree beam width, you wind up with the best resolution at depths of up to about five hundred feet. Low operating frequencies of 50 kilohertz (the average human can only hear up to 15 kilohertz) with a medium sixteen-degree or wide beam forty-five-degree transducer may lose a bit in definition but cover wider areas of water (at least the forty-five-degree unit does) at much greater depths.

In actual angling situations the high-frequency units do a much better job in separating fish from bottom, or even fish schooled tightly together. Another plus is their ability to record even at high boat speeds. Although I know a lot of Great Lakes anglers who figure a low-frequency forty-five-degree transducer is worth its cost just from the enjoyment they get seeing all their downrigger cannonballs and trailing tackle on screen. The greatest delight of all is watching a fish streak toward a lure, and excitedly announcing a strike just as a downrigger rod pops.

The earliest sonar units had an eight-degree cone that marked bottom (three hundred feet down on four tiny watts of power) like it was etched in stone. To get the same clarity with a sixteen-degree angle cone using the same frequency you needed eight watts, which, at one time, was maximum output. Now, manufacturers trying to stay ahead of each other are producing units of up to two hundred watts RMS (or one thousand six hundred watts peak-to-peak), good for midoceanic depths with a sixteen-degree cone. Competition between manufacturers has unfortunately resulted in what might politely be called deceptive advertising. Most sonar makers use a specific formula (-3 decibels of sound) to measure transducer cone angles. One highly advertised sonar unit is measured another way (using a -10 decibel formula) in order to claim sixteen- and thirty-two-degree cone angles when, in truth, the angle of the transducer cones are no wider than competitors' eight- and twenty-degree cone transducers.

One major manufacturer, explaining the relationship of power to sonar performance in its catalog, compares the situation to having the choice of two radio stations on your car radio. "Suppose one (radio station) is a 10,000-watt station and the other broadcasts with 100,000 watts of power. . . . As you get further and further away from the [weaker] station, it sounds weaker. You turn up the radio volume. You're not increasing the power because transmitter power is constant . . . it doesn't change. It's 10,000 watts and no more. As you turn up your radio, you're increasing the receiver sensitivity. Pretty soon you'll start hearing a lot of interference and the signal gets even weaker. Then more static and noise and finally the station is gone." With the more powerful 100,000-watt station, which comes in loud and clear, not having to turn up receiver sensitivity means you're not amplifying unwanted noise. In the case of sonar, greater power means better detecting abilities, cleaner signals, and the ability to register fish as separate marks from bottom.

Another manufacturer has devised an interesting rule-of-thumb formula for assessing a sonar unit's ability to detect fish. A sonar, the company says, will most clearly mark a one-pound fish at one-third the depth it will clearly show a mud bottom—which leads us directly into another problem area: because we're dealing with a bouncing signal, a soft bottom muffles the bounce. You now have two guesses which type of bottom is used to test sonar units prior to manufacturer advertising of maximum operating depth. If you guessed hard, you guessed right. A finder rated at five hundred feet for a hard sand or gravel bottom will, according to one firm, usually give a comparable signal off mud at only about half that distance, or 250 feet. If my basic math is correct, this means a one-pound fish will be well marked only down to about eighty-three feet. So if you want to pick up fish that are hugging a soft bottom, or break up screen-cluttering schools of bait fish, you need high wattage.

The first few months I used my paper graph unit, without even bothering to read the instruction manual, I knew I was getting a clean, black bottom line and lots of fish marks, as promised by the manufacturer. But after seeing chart paper from other sonar units showing fish twice the size of any I ever found, I started wondering why my fish were never as big (on paper) as those marked by other anglers. Proud fishermen pass sonar paper with big fish marks around like golfers with good score cards. At one point, I was even starting to think I somehow didn't have the knack of finding really big fish. What I didn't know at the time, of course, was those huge fish marks proudly displayed by other anglers were the result of transducers with much wider cone angles. The wider the cone, the longer the fish is inside it reflecting sonar impulses. The longer the read-back, or the greater number of return impulses received, the larger the image. It seems very simple now, but for a few weeks it just about drove me nuts even though I knew I was bringing in fish as large as anyone else's.

To illustrate what happens, let's say that a boat moving at a normal trolling speed of 3½ miles per hour is traveling a little better than 90 feet a minute, or about 1½ feet per second. A sixteen-degree transducer will create a sound cone about seven feet wide at a depth of twenty-five feet. Passing over a fish at that depth means the fish is being registered on sonar for 4½ seconds. Put that same fish under a transducer with a forty-five-degree cone, which gives you a beam of about twenty-one feet across at twenty-five feet down, and the marks of the fish are being received for about fourteen seconds, more than three times as long and, on paper at least, proportionately larger.

Fish marks will also be compressed by a slow paper-speed setting, especially when the boat's only moving at trolling speed. To get the sharpest printout the basic rule of thumb is to set paper speed opposite to the speed of the boat; fast when trolling, slow when offshore cruising at higher speeds in search of fish. I normally run my unit at a much lower paper speed than recommended, however. It's an easy way to economize. The "prettier" the picture the more you pay by literally burning up expensive paper.

The importance of reading instructional manuals was brought home to me in an embarrassing fashion when I took a new flasher sonar unit, a type I had never used before, into the Arctic a few years ago. Glen Warner, who operates a camp on Bathurst Inlet, on the edge of the Beaufort Sea in Canada's Northwest Territories, thought sonar might be a useful fishing tool for the Inuit band there in locating offshore fish. I lugged the machine north, with a stopover at Great Bear Lake to fish for lake trout, and on arrival at Bathurst became so engrossed in photographing musk ox and caribou that I didn't get together with any of the Inuit to show them how the machine worked until it was almost time to go home. By then, the Inuit who was to be the sonar expert had spent about five days poring over the sonar manual. As it turned out, when we did get out in the estuary to test it, he quickly proved he knew far more about fine tuning that particular machine than I did.

Having been chartered numerous times by unhappy anglers with fully equipped offshore boats who hired my boat to find out why they weren't catching fish, I've concluded the most serious misconception about sonar is the ingrained belief that sonar never lies. In reality, it often tells real whoppers, again because of the cone effect. If you don't know about it, and you're not putting your lures at the same depth as the fish, it can really knock your success ratio down. Yet how many anglers realize both fish and downrigger cannonballs are often not at the depth their sonar claims they are? Who would believe that a trophy fish, which you know you are dragging a lure in front of according to sonar, is so far away from the lure it might not even have seen it?

Let's suppose you are fishing for lake trout that your sonar shows are hugging bottom below the thermocline at ninety feet. You confidently rig your tackle, snap lines into downrigger releases, and lower cannonballs until the downrigger footage counters indicate eighty-eight feet. You're right where you want to be. Or so you think. Yet water drag against downrigger cables and cannonballs could have swung everything out a good ten to twenty degrees astern of the boat, the angle depending on trolling speed. The cannonballs are eighty-eight feet away from the boat's transducer all right, and they're being marked as such, but they could also be ten feet or more above bottom, well above the fish you're hoping to catch.

I once inveigled one of our kids, Daniel, a working mathematician, to try to figure out angle projections of cannonballs at different depths, but there are just too many unknown variables for anyone to come up with any precise, usable facts. About all you can do to ensure lures are running close to the depth shown on sonar is to take a lake bed reading while running at trolling speed, then lower a cannonball until you feel it bump bottom. If any errors exist, it is a simple matter to compensate for them once you know what they are.

Any tilting of the transducer will create false readings. Some anglers who cruise at high speed to find offshore fish will angle the transducer toward the bow of the boat. Others, using narrow cone transducers, will tilt the transducer slightly to the stern in order to keep downrigger cannonballs within coverage range of their sonar. Since recorders register depth from the center of the cone angle, the results in these cases can show bottom or fish deeper than they really are. The wider the cone angle or the deeper the water, the greater the possible error.

Remember how sonar recorders work: any fish entering the edge of the cone is farther away than it is when directly under the transducer. This is why, if the boat passes over a nonmoving fish, its mark on sonar paper is either an upside down "U" or inverted "V" shape depending on its depth. As the distance between the fish and the transducer is decreased, the reduction in distance is graphed by a rising mark. As the fish passes through the cone again, the increasing distance is recorded by a dropping mark. The shallower the fish, and the faster it passes through the cone, the more abrupt the mark. This situation will result in a sharply pointed V hook. Deeper fish, staying in the cone longer, mean the change in distance will be marked more gradually, giving you a softer, more rounded mark that often resembles a downward curved banana. Swimming fish can create other marks, ranging from dotted streaks to all angles of hooks. Put those same moving fish near the edge of the cone, and the size and shape of the mark is affected in even more unpredictable fashion.

The varying relationship of fish to the center of the cone makes it impossible for anyone to identify fish species or even tell the size of the fish by different-shaped or different-sized marks on sonar. I know people who claim they can do it. At least they never hesitate to tell their eager-to-believe anglers exactly what fish are looking at their lures. But I always manage to keep my mouth shut at such times. They obviously think they know. And without catching the fish, or not having an observer on a towed underwater sled to identify the fish, who's to say they are wrong?

You can make a good guess about what you're seeing from the relationship of the graph marks to the thermocline or bottom—the time of year, the way fish are schooled or whether they are alone. Midsummer marks near bottom, well below the thermocline, could very well be lake trout; a single fish near bottom in warmer water could be a brown trout. Big chinook may be suspended slightly below the thermocline; coho might be in the top half of the thermocline or above it. Rainbow trout could be suspended at even shallower depths. Alewife tend to cluster near the thermocline. Smelt often school in colder water below it. But none of this has any real relation to so-called identifiable fish marks on sonar. Anyone who says otherwise is either fooling himself or trying to fool you.

The biggest, simplest "secret" of successful sonar operation is to have the unit properly installed to start with. Whether you are using an internal- or external-mounted transducer, there are always places on the boat where the unit works good, better, or best. If you must have an internal mounting (necessary with most inboards), your first problem will be that your unit is going to lose a lot of its signal—up to half—by transmitting through a hull. One alternative, with a multilayered or sandwich-type hull, is to cut out all the interior layers until you're down to the exterior coat of fiberglass. Another alternative is a through-hull transducer, which means drilling a big hole. Whatever you do, it's a trial-and-error job in which the manufacturer's instructions must be followed as closely as possible. It also pays to talk to anyone using similar equipment to discover what has worked, or what hasn't worked, for him. For example, an installation technique that works on a fiberglass boat may be far from satisfactory on a metal boat, or vice versa. Exterior mounts on outboards are usually located on the stern transom, flush with the hull.

The vast majority of sonar user complaints invariably go back to the angler not having done his homework. The instructional manual wasn't read thoroughly enough. The underwater transducer was placed in an area full of air bubbles from prop wash. The sensitivity dial was set too high, causing double or triple echoes—turn it up high enough and the result could be one big black blob. I usually adjust the sensitivity dial by turning it up until a second bottom echo just starts to show, then reverse the dial a smidgen until the duplication disappears. My normal setting is around the three-quarter mark. In extra deep water or over a mud bottom, both situations absorbing a lot of signal, you'll need a higher setting.

Another common error is not to connect sonar power cables directly to the battery. If you don't do this, your unit can pick up all kinds of electrical interference that will play hob with sonar images, although chances are good your unit will have a suppression control dial that will eliminate most of the problems associated with outside electrical interference.

Suppression control is undoubtedly the least understood, most misused item on any sonar unit. Most anglers think if it's there, it has to be used. In reality, you should use suppression as little as possible. Suppression control works by lengthening the duration of the sound pulse. The fewer or shorter the gaps between signals the less chance unwanted interference signals have of creeping in. (You can compare it to a gabby relative who won't let anyone else get a word in.) But the longer signal also means much poorer definition. Two fish close together, reflecting one long signal rather than a series of sharp, short impulses, will appear as only one fish. Fish close to bottom won't even be seen at all. So to quote a favorite mechanic, "if it ain't broke, why fix it?" If your sonar's image isn't marked with nonsensical lines, leave the suppression dial in the "off" position.

I've even had anglers ask me, two of them known users of sonar for years, how often they should change the stylus—even though a new stylus came with every roll of chart paper they purchased. Using a burned-out stylus will give you bad pictures every time. Another surprisingly common cause of poor sonar reception is not cleaning water scum off the face of the transducer with detergent on a regular basis. Other basics include blowing out the carbon dust that builds up inside the recorder every time you install a new roll of paper. Carbon dust will also accumulate on the inside of the plexiglass screen and should be cleaned as needed with a soft, moist tissue. Don't use alcohol as a moistening cleanser as it will remove paint. A rough cloth is liable to scratch the plexiglass.

The biggest secret, next to reading the manual until you've almost memorized it (and there are no shortcuts here), is to be able to read the first roll of paper going through your machine the same way you would read your fiftieth or one hundredth roll. Nothing matches the valuable experience that comes from having used dozens of rolls of chart paper. The more time you spend watching sonar, the more its wiggly images will tell you.

Another sonar feature I would insist on having is grey-line or white-line capability. Different manufacturers call it different names but the more sophisticated circuitry of a grey-line unit is indispensable in telling apart bottom-hugging fish from logs or rocks. The unit is capable of marking the fish as separate entities rather than just showing them as bumps on bottom. The grey-line feature also makes it easier to define bottom composition. The harder the bottom, the wider the grey section of the graph bottom printout.

So what's left? The only thing I can think of (and it's time we went fishing) is that often-asked but rarely answered question: How much is your sonar actually seeing down there? How wide is the cone? Next to How's the fishing? this is the most common question asked on my boat. Just for the record—and I'm willing to bet there isn't one guy out of a hundred who knows the diameter of his transducer cone at various depths (I know I waffled on the question for a long time until embarrassment prompted necessary research)—a forty-five-degree cone measures 8 feet across in 10 feet of water, 41 feet across at 50 feet, and 83 feet across at 100 feet. A twenty-degree cone shows $3\frac{1}{2}$ feet at 10 feet, just over 17 feet at 50 and about 35 feet at 100. An eight-degree cone has a diameter of only $1\frac{1}{2}$ feet at 10 feet, about seven feet in 50 feet of water, and about 14 feet at 100.

To make it even simpler, if you have a forty-five-degree cone, its diameter is 80 percent of depth (actually it's 83 percent, but why complicate our mathematics for a few inches?). The diameter of a twenty-degree cone is 35 percent of depth, or simply divide by three and you'll be close enough. The diameter of an eight-degree cone is 14 percent of depth, or divide by seven.

7

Shallow Water Fishing Techniques

Some fishing is better than others, but there is no such thing as bad fishing.
—*Francis Francis,* A Book of Angling

Most days, when the fish are close to shore, fishing the Great Lakes can be easy. Not that angling isn't full of complex variables. Many mysteries do exist. But boiled down to basics, ignoring minor day-to-day differences, which could be happily (and fruitlessly) discussed in endless hair-splitting fashion from now until doomsday, I'm convinced the subject could be easily programmed into a computer, using such factors as location, time of year, known seasonal fish movements, and basic angling techniques. For the cost of computer entry (I have yet to figure out how much I'll charge for this imaginary service) you will receive a personalized instructional printout guaranteed to produce fish nine days out of ten. (The tenth-day escape clause is deliberately included to avoid lawsuits, violence, and other equally unpleasant situations.)

Simplicity doesn't mean that fishing the Great Lakes is boring. Quite the contrary. Let an angler, after a day or two of superlative fishing, think he (or she) has finally achieved total mastery of the lake and, Whammo!

next time out he is back where he started. The fish have moved, water conditions have changed, new lures need to be used (or more often old lures need to be trolled at a different speed), whatever, every day is different. Or should be. Show me an angler who fishes the same way trip after trip and I'll show you someone who comes home fishless more often than not.

On the other hand, looking back at the early days and comparing the equipment and knowledge we have now to what was available then, I think we've never had it so easy. I know my earliest exploratory salmon fishing attempts on Lake Ontario in 1970 involved the use of traditional lake trout equipment. But realizing the futility of wire lining a series of spinners sometimes called "cowbells" and a Williams Wabler around a vast, seemingly empty lake, I quickly switched to an equally old-fashioned Seth Green rig (the equivalent of today's downriggers), which allowed me to stagger as many lures as I dared use at every imaginable depth.

A Seth Green, by the way, is an old landlocked-salmon fishing rig still used by deep-water anglers in Maine, Vermont, and parts of New York. It's little more than a heavily weighted level fly line with loops tied into the line about ten feet apart, from which you can run different lures on ten- to thirty-foot staggered lengths of monofilament. If a fish hits a bottom lure, the rig is hand lined up, and each of the top lines is unsnapped as it surfaces, until the fish is reached. With two anglers, one doing nothing but clearing lines, the system worked (and still works) quite well. Fishing alone, unless the fish is a small one, you'll usually end up with a horrendous mess of snarled lines and lures.

I remember being completely alone on the lake most of the time, knowing nothing about salmon movements, and lacking a temperature probe, sonar, downriggers, CB radio (not that there was anyone to talk to) and all the other basic equipment we take for granted today. Frustrated? You better believe it. My first fish, a small Lake Ontario coho caught off Jordan Harbor in the spring of 1971, culminated a year of futile experimentation. But it's been getting simpler ever since. More salmon, about 40 million a year, are being stocked in the lakes. More anglers (thousands of them) are out on the lakes looking for fish and learning from their experiences. More specialized angling accessories are available.

I suppose the biggest change over the years, in terms of producing fish at least, has to be the easy availability of today's local fishing knowledge. Once out on the lake, if you're still in doubt, just follow the crowd. Duplicate what everyone else is doing and you can't go too far wrong. You rarely learn much about fishing this way, but you should find some action.

Experimentation Can Pay Off

Going it alone, ignoring the crowd, has its own special rewards. Sometimes the self-taught lessons are meaningful, sometimes not. But if you like to experiment with different angling techniques—and one of the basic starting points of any worthwhile research is to question even the most simple, widely accepted assumptions—you will find few, if any, standard angling practices can't be proven wrong, at least under certain conditions or with certain species.

For example, anything you have heard or read in the past about early-season Great Lakes fishing undoubtedly stressed the importance of trolling very slowly. We have been told time and time again by angling experts of all sorts, and even scientists, that frigid water always means fish won't react, or move as quickly, as they do in warmer water later in the year. The name of the game for early season fish is to slow your boat down to a crawl. It's unquestioned angling gospel. I even believed it for a long time, primarily because I was taking fish and there was a fair amount of scientific evidence to support the practice. One laboratory test I recall showed the normal heartbeat of brown trout in fifty-four-degree Fahrenheit water at eighty-one strokes a minute. In thirty-four-degree water, a brown trout's heartbeat drops to thirty-two pulses a minute. A similar metabolic slowdown exists with other species. So who would question whether fish are sluggish in cold water, especially when we've traditionally fished at a slow pace and, on most spring days, have boated a reasonable number of fish?

Two basic angling concepts I have slowly accepted as truisms over the years are: (1) if a technique or trolling speed doesn't work as well as you think it should, try another (a theme that will be repeated with variations throughout the book), and (2) the number of hesitant, unde-cided fish that might have been caught on a slow-moving lure is usually less than the number of more aggressive fish caught by covering more water at faster speeds. In other words, the number of fish in my boat at the end of any day is directly related to the number of fish that see my lures. Very basic, you say? I hope so. But much of it is based on thinking that is totally contrary to the thinking, and the springtime angling tech-niques, of most anglers today. I've not only caught springtime salmon and steelhead at speeds of up to about 5 miles an hour, which is twice as fast as most other boats are going, but I've also done it on comparatively short lines off downriggers, which completely shatters another longtime, popular spring angling theory.

Many anglers, including myself, find it difficult to discard a lot of the hard-won angling lessons learned from years of fishing with different techniques in different waters for the same species (prior to the development of today's Great Lakes fishery). As a fly fisherman, for example, I had difficulty thinking of brown trout or Atlantic salmon as behaving much differently than the fish I first came to know in rivers and streams. The deliberate rise of a big Atlantic salmon to a surface fly is so painstakingly slow that one of the first lessons to be learned is not to yank the fly away. Yet some of us now wonder, as a result of exotic, no doubt scientifically questionable midsummer Great Lakes angling experiences, whether we can ever truly troll too quickly.

Similarly, a brown trout that will examine a fly drifting down a section of stream—almost as though it was checking out each of the fly's various features, comparing it with the shape and color of a real fly before making up its mind whether the fly is edible—is a far different creature in any of the Great Lakes, if only because of a much different environment. Of all the fish trying to adapt to a Great Lakes environment, I think newly stocked brown trout must be forced to make the greatest adjustment of all the introduced species. Attempting to maintain genetically ingrained, stream-based territorial behavior, which brown trout do, must be physically demanding and frustratingly unrewarding.

What actually triggers a fish into striking a lure is not known and I hope will never be known, not as long as there's a recognized difference between sport and meat fishing. But it's a fascinating subject often discussed long into the night. Some simplistic souls say a feeding fish is likely only a hungry fish. (Which also prompts the contrary thought that choice of lures is often unimportant; a truly hungry fish will hit anything in front of it.) What percentage of fish we mark on sonar are active feeders or simply hungry—remembering cold water not only slows down heartbeats but digestive systems—is equally unknown. If we somehow knew the percentage of fish that ignored our lures compared to those that strike, I suspect we would be forever humble. Ten to one? Twenty to one? Fifty to one? Even worse is to consider the equally high number of fish that likely come to a lure but turn away at the last moment. All are good reasons to cover extra water in a hurry to find fish hungry enough to ignore the artificial aspects of our offerings.

Wildlife behavioral studies of all kinds indicate predators first concentrate on prey acting differently from the rest of the herd or school. Abnormality suggests weakness. Do we assume that the undeniably different look of a fishing lure from living bait fish is a key to the success we do enjoy? (Which is cause enough right there for lure manufacturers seeking accurate imitation to start pounding walls in frustration.) A fast-moving lure may suggest undue fear. Big trout or salmon, like schoolyard bullies, might prefer picking on obvious cowards. Or they just might like the challenge of the chase. But I also like to think that human knowledge in choice of lures and methods of presentation—the way we stage the illusion—makes a difference in the number of fish caught at the end of a day. Eliminate the element of outwitting fish and most of the fun of fishing disappears.

For example, the illusion of speed, the presentation of a lure that, possibly, says to a fish, "Grab me quick, fellow, you don't have time to dawdle. It's now or never because I'm going to be long gone," can be created without trolling at high speed. Frantic, fast-swimming action can be simulated by deliberately using big-lipped lures such as Tadpollys, Flatfish, or Kwikfish that have more built-in waggles than most lures. The illusion of helplessness can be aided by using slightly smaller-sized lures. One of the biggest mistakes made by slow-trolling shallow-water anglers is to use lures designed to wiggle most seductively at a fast trolling speed. At whatever speed I'm trolling, I want lures out there most of the time that look as though they are almost jumping out of their skin in fear of being eaten.

Spring Shore Fishing

Given good weather, shallow-water angling in spring is undoubtedly the easiest, most enjoyable form of all Great Lakes angling, although every spring also holds dark, windy days of blowing snow and cold rain. At such times it is difficult to stay comfortable in a boat even while wearing a wool toque, snowmobile suit, and felt-lined boots. I usually carry extra snowmobile suits for clients who aren't dressed warmly enough. But the cold is easily forgotten on days when noses and foreheads are turned red by the sun, and a gentle southern breeze coaxes anglers to shuck coats, if not shirts. Spring provides exciting, mixed-bag, light-tackle fishing at its best. It is almost a holiday time for both fish and fishermen, a celebration of the start of a new cycle. Silvery coho, rainbow, brown, and lake trout, newly released from cold winter exile, are energetically prowling the warmer, highly oxygenated shallows and are easily caught on most types of tackle.

The disappearance of winter shoreline ice is always the first sign of the start of a new angling season. The sun-washed brown sand of an empty wave-lapped beach eventually beckons you each spring to walk its length, surf-casting rod in hand, in search of passing trout or salmon. The odds are against you that early in the year, at least I have yet to find fish then with any consistency—not in the middle of March—but the chance exists and, given a day of bright sunshine, what better way of spending a few hours outdoors? Come April, when shoreline water lapping the beach hits the forty-degree mark, your chances of success suddenly improve.

Fish or no fish, I enjoy such outings, if only because of the time of year. It's too early for boat fishing. Docks are not yet in place at the marina. And the boat is too large to keep in the driveway like a cartopper to be easily dumped into the lake on a whim and brought home again. So the next best thing is to walk a beach or harbor pier and let a lake breeze, with its fickle promises of better weather, blow the last traces of winter out of your head.

As often happens, and this is true of any form of angling I think, the best-remembered incidents involve totally unexpected fish. Although casting off shoreline, whether you're seeking salmon off a Michigan beach or browns off a Chicago pier, tends to provide the biggest surprises. A typical example occurred one early spring while I was visiting a friend, Vern Woods, who, at the time, had just purchased an apple farm on the north shore of Lake Ontario near Brighton, Ontario. I followed a tiny stream on his property down to the lake on an exploratory early-morning walk, carrying light spinning tackle, thinking of nothing more than the possibility of brook trout. The meandering spring-fed creek with its grassy, undercut

Shallow-water springtime fishing often provides maximum action for anglers such as this Wisconsin group. Spring is a time for light tackle and small lures. (*Photo courtesy of Wisconsin Division of Tourism*)

banks could be stepped over at almost any point except at its mouth where its flow had been backed up by a sand bar created by the lake. Two large aspen, the base of their roots bared by high waves of past storms, formed an umbrella over the lakeside pool. I worked a tiny spinner along its edges. Then, for lack of anything better to do, I impulsively chucked the lure out in the lake. A silvery, high-jumping steelhead took the spinner on the first cast, the fish dancing its way out of the shallow water four or five times in a spectacular display of acrobatics before it was beached. Two tail-walking twins of the first brightly colored six-pound fish quickly followed. But when I returned with Vern in the evening, the schooled fish had moved on in search of a more suitable spawning stream.

Similar fishing is available to anyone willing to spend a few hours trolling near shore, casting off beaches, or fishing bobbers with live or dead smelt off lakeside piers. Beach or pier fishermen should also not ignore the fish-catching powers of bagged spawn. Normal technique is to use a small marshmallow or piece of styrofoam to float the spawn just off bottom. Styrofoam can also be used to keep dead smelt or minnows floating effectively off bottom. Slit a section of belly, insert a narrow strip of styrofoam from a picnic cup, the amount depending on the size of the bait, and sew up the incision with a needle and light monofilament. When you're fishing bottom, use big pyramid sinkers or hollow-centered barrel sinkers so fish can pull line out when taking bait without feeling any real weight. The most basic pier fishing technique of all is to float a gob of worms five or six feet under a big plastic bobber.

A little trick that a bait-fishing acquaintance using a rod holder on a beach learned the hard way, is to never, but never, close the bail of an open-faced spinning reel while the rod is unattended in a holder or left lying on a pier. He still shudders at the horror of helplessly watching a heavy fish pull his tackle out of its holder and drag it across a narrow strip of lakeshore gravel before rod and reel disappeared into the lake. One way of holding line, when the bail of a spinning reel is left open so that fish may swim away freely before striking, is to tape a small bobby pin to the foregrip of the rod as a line clip, the line pulling free when a fish swims off with the bait. Equally simple I think, as long as you have an excellent memory, is to defy fate by closing the bail but turning the reel drag system right off. If you know what the normal line tension setting is, it's an easy matter to reset drag as you pick the rod up to strike the fish. Most reels use a symbol system of some sort or a numbered scale as a line-tension setting guide. The only danger, of course, is forgetting to put the reel into the equivalent of freespool when you start fishing.

Sitting and waiting for fish to come to you is never as much fun as going to the fish, however. Maybe I've done too much river fishing where walking banks, trying different pools, seeing where a raccoon had been feeding on mussels, or being squawked at by a kingfisher for trespassing was all very much a part of the fish-catching game. Or maybe I just don't like sitting too long. If bait fishing off an often-crowded downtown city pier provides the only action, fine; it's that or nothing. But exploring a lake shoreline while wearing an old pair of chest waders gives a totality to an outing, sometimes even a sense of adventure, especially when clambering over slippery, moss-covered boulders.

Come to think of it, spring shoreline fishing in waders is very close to big-river angling in a broad environmental sense. If you ignore the cold, huge expanse of lake beyond the shoreline strip of warmer water, or try to think of it as a bank, you have a confined river-fishing situation of sorts. All that's lacking are food-carrying currents and rapids to dig out holding pools. The fish are cruising up and down the shore, many well within casting reach, and if an angling problem exists it is largely one of being in the right place at the right time. If you're lucky enough, the best,

Early-season shoreline fishing gives wading anglers a chance to take lunker-sized brown trout in many parts of the Great Lakes.

most exciting place is where the water in front of you is suddenly ripped wide open by swirling, leaping bait fish desperately trying to escape feeding trout. I've had this happen twice so far. On both occasions, a small spoon cast into the middle of the surface disturbance took brown trout, a 4-pounder and a 6½-pounder. Because I make it a practice to always have a prerigged casting rod handy on my boat, I've also taken coho and steelhead in similar fashion while trolling. But normal shore fishing is a matter of searching the water with a fanlike series of casts, then moving down the shore to repeat the procedure. Lures that have worked well for me are Little Cleos, Tobies (both silver and blue), silver and chartreuse Krocodiles, and silver and orange No. 3 Mepps spinners.

The only real drawback to wading a lake shoreline is that brown trout, the primary target, being the wary, contrary fish they are, don't agree with us on the best time to fish. We obviously want to play at different times. In spring (and fall), the nicest time to go out is naturally during the warmest part of the day, from 11:00 A.M. to 3:00 P.M., when the sun is highest in the sky. Browns, on the other hand, not liking bright light, prefer the dull days and, in sunny weather, are found in the shallows in the early morning and evening hours. If we like a calm day, browns like wind, the resultant ripple or waves reducing light. The best days of all to catch big browns are those which combine wind with clouds and rain; the heavier the rain, the better it seems to the trout. On such days not only is fishing good, but you're almost guaranteed to have the beach to yourself. Any anglers you encounter are usually masochistic moon-lighting duck hunters keeping themselves trained to enjoy (so they always claim) the nasty weather of the hunting season to come.

Despite occasional beach excursions in March, our spring season really starts in April. This is the best time to unlimber the long surf-casting rods or hose down the aluminum cartop boat that has spent the winter behind the garage. Because of the fish seeking warm water anywhere they can find it, the good fishing spots in early April are off the mouths of streams or power plant thermal discharge outlets (which normally provide angling action even in the middle of winter). By late April, when-ever the water warms up to about forty-five degrees, the smelt runs start, which is when you want to start concentrating your fishing efforts off the streams or beaches where smelt spawn each year. At this time, a vertical thermal wall should start forming offshore. You will remember this belt of rapid water temperature change tends to act as a barrier, holding fish between it and the shore. Most years this thermal break is found very easily. Occasionally, because of unusual wind and water conditions, the wall may not form, as happened in my part of the lake in 1983, for example. The reason for the thermal bar not showing that year was that an extra-mild winter didn't cool the lake as much as normal. As a result, the spring lake temperature was the highest recorded in many years.

The difference created by a severe or mild winter is best seen in infrared satellite photos of the lake. In mid-May of 1982, following a more normal winter, the main body of Lake Ontario was 35.6 degrees while shoreline temperatures were as high as 50 degrees. A textbook perfect thermal bar existed around the entire lake. In mid-May of 1983, however, infrared photos showed the vast majority of the lake had temperatures ranging from forty-three to fifty degrees. There were only three tiny areas off western New York, Oswego and Oak Orchard, where water registered as cold as forty-one degrees. The 1983 photo also showed a number of thermal breaks, narrow bands of rapid temperature change from about forty-eight degrees to forty-three degrees, where anglers predictably took limit catches.

The differences in lake temperature in 1984 and 1985 were equally inconsistent. A colder than normal winter resulted in Lake Ontario being much colder in the spring of 1985. A Canadian government infrared satellite scan taken April 12, 1985, for example, showed that almost all of the lake's surface measured in the low thirties, the warmest water (thirty-six degrees) found near shore off Wayne County and along the eastern Oswego—southern Jefferson County shore of New York. In 1984, however, on April 9, satellite imagery showed not only much warmer water but another classic thermal bar, a distinct narrow band of water one to two miles wide, hugging the entire south shore of the lake in which surface temperature exceeded thirty-nine degrees. As expected, 1985's colder water, when it did warm up a bit, produced almost three extra weeks of excellent spring fishing, a little bonus to help make up for the bone-chilling winter that caused the situation.

Spring Boat Fishing

When flatlining or trolling a lure behind a boat, few anglers do more than add a small clamp-on sinker a foot or so in front of the lure, if it's a floating plug, so the artificial is running three to five feet below the surface. Another important point is to run your lures as far behind the boat as possible. I usually have at least one hundred yards of line out. As few people can judge distance well, a good rule is to let out what you think is enough line and then let out half as much again. Just remember that fish are aware of their extreme vulnerability to predation in shallow water and can be frightened off by even the tiniest boats passing directly overhead. On larger craft, most of our fish are taken off sideplaners being trolled sixty or seventy feet off to the side, away from the bulk of the boat's hull. I also use a set of fifteen-foot outrigger poles to get lures out and away from the hull. Both the sideplaners and the outriggers use adjustable line releases similar to those used on downriggers so the rod line is pulled free by the force of any striking fish.

How far from the boat to run a planing board depends on such factors as the height of the towline attachment point on the boat, boat speed, wave height, and board size. The larger the board, the higher it rides to help keep the 50-pound-test monofilament towline out of the water. Run the boat end of the line through the tip of a vertical outrigger pole 18 feet or so up in the air, and you can easily put the board out 150 feet or more before the towline snubs in the water. My normal practice of running the control line off an old lake trout trolling rod and reel, the rig just stuck in a convenient rod holder, cuts the distance almost in half.

Distance also depends, of course, on how thickly, and how close, other boats are clustered around you. The bigger planing boards, being more easily seen, are a definite advantage in a crowd. Mine have small, bright red flags mounted on flexible wire arms to make them even more visible. At one time, when boards were a rarity on Lake Ontario and few anglers—except those with Lake Michigan fishing experience—knew what they were, I was continually hauling my boards out of the way of on-coming boats. Now, I think most anglers look for boards almost auto-matically and, if they see them, at least try to give you needed room. Ten years or so ago, when I first started using planers, most Lake Ontario anglers were completely mystified by them, pointing the boards out to their companions as they passed. One small-boat skipper, after I had trolled a tiny Yellowbird planer alongside his boat, obviously concluded a big fish had to be pulling this unknown object through the water. He was preparing to net it until I informed him, possibly louder than nec-essary, that it belonged to me.

Given uncrowded water and anglers with a yen to catch big, deep-bellied brown trout, it's always interesting early in the year to run a board within a few feet of shore, trolling a floating minnow imitation Rapala or similar lure way behind the board in five or six feet of water. I run much less line off a board than I do off the boat, about seventy-five feet or so, depending on the lure. A diving plug liable to hang up on bottom is rigged even closer, fifty feet or less. One favorite area, well known for chewing up propellers of unwary boaters, holds big rocks that were dumped over a steep bank to control lakeshore erosion. They now shelter big browns in early spring and, once in a while, lake trout. Such cover is always worth seeking out.

When you fish spring-warmed water at all depths close to shore, fish are truly where you find them. They may be cruising in the shallowest of shallows, suspended midway in ten to fifty feet of water, or hugging bottom at any depth, depending not just on species as much as time of day, height of sun, calmness of water, and boat traffic. I tend to think of chinook as being most sensitive to light and water surface disturbance by anglers, the bigger kings scattering offshore early in the morning and not to return to shoreline waters until dark. Bottom-oriented lake trout are equally sensitive to light, of course, though low on the intelligence scale—with these fish, who knows? Coho salmon and rainbows are usually midway fish, halfway out between the classic brown trout water just off shore, and the fifty-feet-and-up depths where spring chinook are often found in daytime. Brown trout, lacking shoreline cover, will either move into deeper water when bothered sufficiently by boats or move along the shoreline until broken bottom cover is found.

One puzzling aspect of fishing shallows for brown trout is that although these prized fish are noted by stream fishermen as active night feeders and are consistently caught by anglers casting off shore at night on the other lakes, especially Lake Michigan and Lake Huron, my night fishing attempts for browns on Lake Ontario have so far been a total flop. I've used the same techniques and lures, Krocodile spoons, Little Jewels, Williams Wablers, and others employed by anglers elsewhere, even going so far as to try a popular Lake Huron pier-fishing trick of adding phosphorescent glow tape to the spoons and "recharging" the tape every half-hour or so with the light from a camera flash strobe.

One explanation is the reduced clarity of Lake Ontario water. While the upper lakes certainly have much cleaner water than Lake Ontario, it is still hard to believe slightly reduced visibility can be that much of a factor. I've taken daytime browns out of even murkier runoff water than the lakeshore water I fished at night. On the other hand, I can't believe there is any genetic difference between Lake Huron brown trout and Lake Ontario browns. The thought that local brown trout have somehow lost any urge to feed at night is difficult to accept. The only conclusion that makes any sense is that I've simply been fishing the wrong places. Somewhere along our lakeshore must be a preferred nighttime habitat of these fish, even though I've drifted a lot of it, casting out of a small boat while the rest of the world slept. But it does make an interesting puzzle, which, as far as I know, has yet to be solved.

The highly visible breaks in the color of surface water created by river runoff each spring and the mud lines often found off beaches are another form of easily found thermal breaks that, in my experience, can be counted on to produce fish year after year for anyone trolling lures along their edges. The mud line of a typical river can be followed by anyone out into the lake, the distance depending on the strength of river currents. The further out you go, the weaker the flow of the river obviously

A typical catch of springtime salmon caught by fishing a Great Lakes mudline off the mouth of a river.

becomes until conflicting lake currents and wind alter the direction of the mud line, usually forcing it to move parallel to the shore until it gradually disappears.

My best mud line catches start at the point where lake currents and river currents are equally matched, just where the mud line starts to curve in snakelike fashion down the lake. Follow what's left of the line until it completely dissipates, then turn the boat around and fish it back, weaving your boat in and out of the line. This often produces good catches of coho and, occasionally, rainbows and lake trout. Because you're in much deeper water than most boats, you also have an excellent chance (and may be the only boat to do so) to take solitary trophy-sized chinook, which tend to shun the shallows (and the crowds of anglers found there) in daylight hours. Because most anglers are content to troll shoreline shallows, another bonus is you won't be as crowded by other boats, an important point when trolling shallow-running lures on long lines. In fact, I've enjoyed highly successful offshore mud line fishing all by myself on days when a traffic cop was needed to direct boat movements closer to shore.

A little-known aspect of mud line fishing is that discolored runoff water is a strong fish attractant for a totally different reason than its warmer temperature. It's obvious that most, if not all, anglers think of mud only as mud, and think of soil sediments on the surface as a solid top-to-bottom block of nonbreathable, fish-repelling irritants. As a result, few mud line—edge fishermen deliberately venture far into sections of lake muddied by stream runoff. Actually, the discolored water quickly becomes layered on entering a cold lake. The result is not only a horizontal thermal break of a totally different sort, but discolored runoff also creates attractive shade, filtering out uncomfortable light for trout and salmon on a bright, sunny day.

The farther out you troll from the mouth of any spring-swollen river, the thinner the top mud layer becomes, as the warmer river water is deflected upward by the heavier, colder water of the lake. It might help to think of river currents entering a lake being shaped much like a horizontal floating wedge with the thick end at the mouth of the river. As river water and the sediments it carries begin to dissipate, with the heaviest fallout of silt particles occurring closer to the mouth of the river, the surface layer of discolored water becomes even thinner, gradually tapering upward until lake wave action washes it out completely.

The point to remember is that although surface water may still be discolored, comparatively clean water underneath can hold a surprising number of fish in the middle of the day, but you have to deliberately run lures off cannonballs below the muddied top layer. Flatlining in the surface muck, as most anglers who cross spring runoff areas do just to get to the other side, will rarely produce fish except at the outer edges or out on the lake where visible runoff is little more than surface film on the lake. Ironically, some of our best fish caught below heavily discolored surface water have been lake trout, the fish we most closely associate with pristine, sparkling-clean water. Of course, lake trout also like darkness normally found only in deep places. I suspect that this is the real reason for the lakers being under the mud in the first place.

Equally important I think, especially with a larger boat in comparatively shallow water, is to add even more distance from the fish-frightening bulk and noise of your hull to your lures by running a zigzag trolling course rather than a straight line, another reason I don't like being crowded by other boats. By trolling in a series of S-curve patterns, occasionally making a complete circle whenever large schools of bait fish are marked on sonar, and working the edges of the schools with every lure you can put near them, you'll be running lures more than 50 percent of the time through water your boat hasn't disturbed at all. You'll also be fishing a wider variety of water depth by running curved trolling patterns.

Just as interesting, and possibly of more importance than anything else, you are deliberately showing fish an ever-changing variety of speed and lure actions, the outside lures on the planing boards moving faster and wiggling harder than normal on a turn, the inside lures slowing down and sinking deeper in the water. The scene of course is reversed on the next turn in the opposite direction. If you hit a day when all of your strikes are occurring on inside lures halfway through a curve, the fish are obviously telling you you're trolling too fast or too shallow. You should also remember this same trolling lesson when fishing the middle of the lake in summer.

As most of Lake Ontario holds little bottom structure, and with fish wandering in will-o-the-wisp fashion in and out of the shallows, another dependable holding place for fish is any change in bottom contour, especially trenches dug out by spring river currents. Even currents from the lock at the Lake Ontario entrance to the Welland canal, which spills water every time an upbound boat enters the lake, have dug out a channel a good twenty feet deeper than surrounding lake bottom. Fish are consistently found holding either at its edges or part way down its underwater banks. Schools of bait fish on the adjacent flats are as easily found by hungry fish as they are with sonar. My only problem with this situation is that the fishing is located only a few hundred yards from the marina. As a result, I'm always reluctant to spend too much time there; anglers tend to feel shortchanged if they don't have a real boat ride somewhere. (As usual, fishing is always thought to be best far away.) The alternative, involving a more acceptable ten-mile run, is a classic spring fishing setup of another sort, where the Niagara River's swirling, cold spring currents form a temperature wall that stops fish wandering the lake shallows as effectively as an underwater cage. Because of the placement of an ice boom across the upper, Lake Erie end of the river to lessen disruption of hydro production in the winter months, the jammed-up ice continues to flow down the river, and keep it cold, long after ice has disappeared elsewhere.

The most satisfying shoreline fishing technique of all, given uncrowded water and a slight breeze that will slowly drift the boat parallel to the shore, is to cut the motors, position anglers around the boat with casting tackle (the favorite, most productive spot is always up on the bow), and let everyone fish the water in every direction. Shoreside casters should use floating plugs to avoid bottom hang-ups. Anglers on the deep-water side should use fast-sinking, long-distance casting spoons such as silver and blue Tobies, a Swedish lure I often use to imitate smelt.

Considering the catches and the sheer fun involved, especially early in the morning before other boats have disturbed the water, the only puzzling point about this technique is why I've never seen anyone else doing the same thing. Quietly covering a wide area of water with a variety of lures worked in almost every direction from a slowly moving boat gives you as much advantage at times over a troller as trolling has over a caster stuck on a beach. On a good day, when it's not unusual to have more than one fish hooked up at once, nothing beats it for getting anglers excited. I once had cool-headed bass-tournament veterans on board, newcomers to Great Lakes angling, who literally ran themselves off the boat one morning. The name of the game with ultralight casting gear, and the measure of a fish, is the number of times it takes you completely around the boat. A heavyweight brown can make a long run, forcing you to rush forward to keep the line free of the cabin structure and then, once on the bow, racing back to the stern to clear line when the fish takes off in the opposite direction.

Another angling variation still waiting to be tried on the Great Lakes is West Coast–style "mooching," a system long rated by knowledgeable British Columbia anglers as the most enjoyable, most productive form of near-shore angling for salmon. It's certainly one of the most leisurely forms of angling I've tried. All you're doing is bait fishing with a belly-cut slab of herring (smelt or alewife would do fine in fresh water), or a whole fish. The normal technique is to fish from an anchored boat in current or, if fishing still or nontidal water, from a small boat that's either rowed or allowed to drift in order to impart action to the lure. There's no question mooching would work extremely well in fresh water—it's just a matter of finding time to prove it. My mooching rods, used so far on the Great Lakes only for light-line salmon trolling, are ten-footers with extra-light tip actions rigged with oversized, single-action (fly rod) reels, although a normal downrigger rod or extra-long soft-action spinning rod would no doubt work as well.

The fishing method itself is simple. All that's needed is a sufficiently heavy keel sinker with swivels at both ends to get your bait down to the same level as feeding salmon. Hook size depends on bait size. Generally, two No. 10 or No. 8 trebles are tied about three inches apart on the end of a five to eight foot, 15- or 20-pound-test leader. Both hooks are placed in the bait, one up front, the other about halfway to the end. On a whole herring, a single barb of the first treble hook goes up through the lower jaw to keep the mouth closed. A single barb of the rear treble is inserted in the bait just behind the dorsal fin. Veteran moochers point out that rods should not be hand held but placed in holders, and they insist the extremely soft tips of the rods tell whether a fish is mouthing the bait faster than you can feel it. Always wait until the fish moves off with the swallowed bait, pulling the rod down, before striking. West Coast specialists using extra-long, 4- or 2-pound-test leaders, don't strike a running fish at all; they simply pick up the rod and gently brake the reel for a second or two with a finger, the braking action being enough to set hooks.

Still another spring fishing gambit I employ had its beginning seven or eight years ago as an attempt to reduce the possibility of tangling surface lines while making turns or weaving around other boats. Between sideplaners, outriggers, and rods dragging lines off the stern, a charterboat can sometimes take on the appearance of a spider web—you can have lines all over the place. One day, with a larger number of anglers than usual on board and wanting to use extra rods, I hooked up two lines to downriggers, dropping both lines five to ten feet down on cannonballs just to get them out of the way. After catching three-quarters of all our fish that day on the deeper-running lures, it took no special angling genius to realize something very good was happening out there behind the boat. And deep- versus shallow-line catch percentages since then have done nothing to change my mind. Whether the fish hitting the deeper-running lures would have come up for the shallower lures anyway is unknown, of course. Because I'm normally well offshore compared to most boats, the fish are likely at a deeper depth if only because they're in deeper water. But even fishing close to shore, in fifteen or twenty feet of water, sunken downrigger lines still take a high percentage of fish, so much so the "down" lines are now always the first to be set, the lures being let out the normal distance of three hundred feet or so before being snubbed into downrigger releases.

The use of downriggers allows an even wider variety of ways to present lures. The more anglers present, the greater the variety and, if we do our job right, the greater our chances of taking fish.

Fortunately, there is now a sufficient choice of line releases commercially available to allow unlimited use of all our auxiliary gear. One of the handiest for fishing near the surface is a "slider" release that not only allows you to run as many lines as you wish off a sideplaner, but makes it possible to reset sideplaner fishing lines at any position without having to waste time by bringing the trolling board into the boat and resetting it. These units simply snap onto the sideplaner tow line—the separate fishing lines being held by a spring-screw tension device until a fish pulls the line free—and can be slid out to any position between the boat and the sideplaner by freeing line from your fishing reel.

Thus it's possible (see sketch) for anglers to run a lure off a sideplaner sixty feet or more off the side of a boat. A second lure can be rigged off the sideplaner line halfway down between the board and the boat. A third lure can be flatlined off a corner of the stern in normal fashion. And a fourth lure can be dropped below the nearest flatline lure by using a downrigger off the other corner of the stern. You can achieve much the same result with the fourth lure by using a deeper-running artificial such as a heavy spoon or, as another alternative, adding an extra-large rubber-core sinker in front of the lure. Other lure combinations, and methods of presenting them, are limited only by your imagination.

Lure choice is usually related to the position of the rod and the depth of water being fished. For example, the inshore rod which is obviously fishing shallower water will be pulling a shallower-running lure. For starters, try a floating orange or red Rapala, which, at normal trolling speed, should be running anywhere from fifteen inches to three feet under the surface. Outrigger and stern lines in water ranging from ten to twenty feet can be rigged with lipped, water-digging lures such as a Flatfish X-5, Tadpolly, or Quick-Fish. Also used as a contrast lure on at least one of the other lines will be a light spoon such as a Flutterspoon, Andy Reeker, or Northport Nailer.

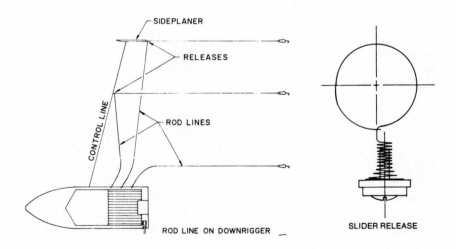

Modern trolling gear allows a wide range of multi-lure presentations. (*Illustration by Kurt Wolfram*)

Of course, while all this is happening, you're also checking sonar to mark concentrations of bait fish, and listening to the CB radio chatter of other anglers. If you have VHF radio, you're also in touch, if need be, with charterboat skippers. On weekends, however, when a calm lake and warm sun can bring out anglers in record numbers—I've often counted up to 150 boats in sight at one time on a nice spring day—I tend to separate myself from the pack, even if it means abandoning an area where I know I can catch fish. Put yourself in the middle of one hundred boats, with anglers ignoring trolling patterns, cutting across other anglers' lines, forcing you to troll in unwanted directions, and it's a circus-style event I'm happy to leave.

Also, I know individual fish in my section of the lake are not holding in one spot anyway. They are cruising a shoreline with little bottom structure, often traveling two to three miles a day, and the traditional hotspots of spring, as measured by boat numbers, are surprisingly often no better or worse than less heavily fished shoreline areas elsewhere. A lone boat consistently taking fish is soon surrounded by other hawk-eyed anglers, so it is fairly common, if you like the tackle-handling maneuverability found only in open water, to pull anchor and fish another part of the lake three or four times a day, including former "hotspots" magically emptied of boats by reports of better catches of bigger fish down the shore.

In daylight hours, on a normal outing we'll start the day by running a planing board in five to ten feet of water close to shore, plus as many flatlines as possible behind the boat. As the sun rises, we will work progressively deeper water, ten to twenty feet, switching to deeper sinking lures as we go out, including use of downriggers. By noon, when the sun is near its peak, we'll often be fishing forty to sixty feet of water, depending on the location of the offshore thermal bar, with lures staggered all the way from near surface to bottom, unless the fish tell us by hitting lures only at one depth we should concentrate our efforts in that particular zone. And even then, given enough rods, we'll always have a couple of "outlaw" lures out there, one high, one low, for the unpredictable fish. Lures scattered in such fashion also provide an easy check in case the fish suddenly move to another depth, either because of bait fish movement, weather changes, or simply because of an unexplainable herdlike instinct to go elsewhere. If our fish box is suitably full from the weight of our catch, then, depending on angler wishes, we will go out even deeper in search of widely scattered, trophy-sized chinook for an hour or two before returning to shallower water and the almost guaranteed action to be found there.

To add even more spice to the game, unless you are deliberately

Typical body baits used in spring and fall when salmon are close to shore (*from top to bottom*): Rapala, a minnow imitator, Thinfin, Tadpolly, Flatfish, and Tiny Tad.

seeking spring chinook in the twenty-pound-and-up class, you will be missing much of the fun of spring fishing by not using the lightest tackle you own. The majority of fish we catch in the shallows are 2- to 3½-pound cohos, with an occasional lake trout or rainbow running up to the 10-pound mark. As an extra incentive to fish light, the heaviest spring shoreline fish of all—big football-shaped brown trout that can tilt the scales up to fifteen pounds or better—not only call for light lines but, in many cases, demand it. These wily transplants still retain the instincts of their trout stream ancestors. If there's a secret to successful springtime brown trout fishing, it's use of lightweight, 4- or 6-pound-test monofilament.

One of the biggest advantages of shallow-water fishing as compared to deepwater angling, which we'll get into later, is the ability to change lures without having to dredge cannonballs up from deep water and reset lines, a time-consuming chore at best. The quick simplicity of just reeling a flatlined lure into the boat means anglers should be more willing to experiment with different lure colors, actions, and running depths, all of which add not only extra interest to any outing but, once the prime locations and lure preferences of the fish are established, usually mean more fish in the boat at the end of the day.

Favored shallow-water colors range from smelt-imitation silvers, silver/blues, and silver/greens, to the reds and oranges favored by most anglers, the latter colors being extremely effective down to about twenty feet. In deeper water I prefer the silver/blue, silver/black combinations, plus solid yellow, green, blue, and black colors.

Always dependable fast-trolling plugs include Rapalas, Rebels, Thin-Fins, and J-Plugs. Lures that work well at slower speeds are Tadpollys, Flatfish, Canadian Wigglers, and AC Shiners. Spoons include almost any herring imitation flutterspoon plus such well known Great Lakes lures as Alpena Diamonds, Westport Wobblers, Locos, and Rattlesnakes.

8

Going Light

Viator: This is a very little hook.
Piscator: That may serve to inform you, that it is for a very little
  Flie . . . .
  —Charles Cotton, The Compleat Angler Part II

Why anglers using light lines consistently catch more fish than anglers hauling heavier lines is still open to debate. Although most of us no doubt grew up in the belief that light lines trick fish into hitting a lure because smaller diameter lines are harder to see (making lures look more like free-swimming minnows), I still can't help but wonder whether we're not crediting success to the wrong thing.

Lures undoubtedly have a better, more natural free-swimming action on lighter lines, but this could also happen because finer, less water-resistant lines are less restrictive and, because of their lightness, give lures greater freedom to wiggle. Line visibility itself may have nothing to do with it. Even the lightest of lines must be visible to fish at close range. Whatever happens obviously works, which is all that matters to a practical fisherman. Another rarely recognized advantage of light lines is the ability of smaller diameter lines to carry trolled lures much deeper in the water than similar lengths of heavier lines, the tinier lines knifing through water more easily.

The biggest disadvantage of using a light line, of course, is that it takes less tension to break it, which puts pressure on an angler to properly play a fish. To improve our odds, many of us have partially compensated by switching to longer, more flexible West Coast mooching rods, fly rods, or noodle rods. In fact, one of the most interesting developments in the Great Lakes angling scene in recent years is the growing switch to such tackle. Twelve- or thirteen-foot-long noodle rods (the name comes from comparisons of their soft, floppy rod action to the proverbial "wet noodle"), once only used by fall river anglers to drift dime-sized bags of roe, are now appearing not only on boats but also on beaches and piers, replacing traditional, heavier equipment in order to more safely cast 4- or 6-pound-test monofilament into the surf. Some Niagara winter steelhead "noodlers" even use line as light as 2-pound-test. But without a boat to follow a running fish, they lose more trout than they catch in the heavy currents of the lower Niagara River. The few fish they do beach, however, usually trout that foolishly decide to stay in the pool in which they were hooked rather than run, have an extremely high trophy value.

But no matter how you fish, a switch to lighter tackle makes angling a vastly different sport for even the most experienced angler. In fact, the more experience you have as an angler, the greater its appeal should be. If you're a veteran, some of the original sparkle of fishing has no doubt disappeared. If that's the case, a switch to lightweight equipment is guaranteed to bring all the old fun back. If angling isn't as exciting as it used to be, if you feel there are no mountains left to conquer, no new techniques to master, you're a perfect candidate for light-tackle use. Lighter lines on longer, softer rods make little fish into big fish, and big fish into monsters. You double your angling fun by doubling the challenge.

As with most sophisticated forms of angling, the key starting point is awareness of the importance of matched tackle. Unless rod, reel, line, and lure are balanced, you'll be faced with major problems even before you start. Light line on a rod that is too stiff can mean breakage on the first cast or first fish. Try casting an overweight lure on extra-light line from a beach and you'll probably watch the lure sail high in the air toward a distant horizon all by itself. The reel must be the best available with the smoothest, most faultless drag you can find. The slightest hesitation or grab in the reel's line tension system against a hard-running fish can mean angling disaster.

Another light-tackle problem not solved easily is the surprising amount of line stretch caused by extra-long lengths of line used while trolling flatlines in shallow water. As most monofilament is capable of stretching 20 percent or better before breaking (which is a great safety factor when playing a fish well away from a boat, and the reason so many fish are broken off on short lines close to the net), you have to move more than ten feet of line on the strike to wallop a fish two hundred feet away. That's assuming you have a straight line with no belly in it, which never happens. Compounding the problem is that once nylon lines get wet, the lines stretch even more. Some stiff nylon lines now on the market have a stretch factor of more than 40 percent!

So, on a bad day, when fish aren't taking lures well, and considering the impossibility of sinking steel into a fish by hauling a rod back on a long line, about all you can do to reduce line elasticity is to increase boat speed to reduce line slack, or troll the lure closer to the boat. Another way of improving catches under such conditions is either to switch to a smaller lure that fish will literally inhale, or to find a similar size lure with a better hooking design. Luckily, most fish hook themselves.

I can remember one spring day when the coho salmon were really playing tricks. My anglers had lost six fish in a row. The salmon were hitting, knocking off downrigger releases, the anglers were grabbing the rods while they were still bent against the fish (or so I thought), striking, and then nothing. The fish were gone. As always, they'd look at me each time and ask "What happened?" (which is where a charterboater really starts earning his pay). Fishing without Gwynne that day, I volunteered one of the anglers to take over the wheel. Then I waited at the stern, close to the rods, to handle the next strike. It eventually happened. Wham! Zap! Nothing! Another fish gone. But the feel of the action or, more accurately, the lack of any feel, gave me the clue I needed. On the next fish, I reeled in hard until I felt the fish and then hit it. The coho were coming in from behind the lure, mouthing it, and then, instead of veering away, swimming straight at the boat, forming such a huge belly in the line that any force of the strike was lost long before it reached the lure. After that, once instructed to "reel like hell" and not strike before feeling the throb of fish, my suddenly happy anglers started boating salmon.

A similar, even more frustrating hookup problem I'll never forget occurred a year or two later when one of the guests turned out to be an absolute novice, someone I always enjoy having come on board. No one grins wider, or has a better time, than a new angler going home with fish bigger than anything he ever dreamed of catching. Normal routine in such cases is to give a little spiel while setting tackle, explaining how everything works, what the angler can expect, how the weight of a big fish can make it physically difficult to get a rod out of a downrigger holder—you really have to hang on tight and muscle it out—plus a quick demonstration, after actually removing a rod from a holder, on how to hook and play a fish. Because the client was a novice, other members of the group typically insisted he catch the first fish. "Nothing to it, buddy," they all said with ear-to-ear grins. "It's a piece of cake." He, of course, facing a brand new experience, was trying hard to hide his nervousness. He obediently stayed by the rods, attempting to watch everything at once, and when the first rod popped free of a downrigger he was on it fast (more experienced, blasé anglers should only be as quick) and slammed the rod back over his head in overeager newcomer fashion to set the hook. The rod went limp. No fish. "You win some, you lose some," he was told. The same thing happened three more times. From my position at the wheel I couldn't see that he was doing anything wrong. Concerned, I went back to stand beside beside him, just to watch. It took two more lost fish before I caught on to what was happening. In his excitement, he was forgetting, or maybe I hadn't stressed the point strongly enough, that he had to clamp a thumb down on the line spool prior to striking. With the light reel drag setting I use, the line was just pouring off the reel every time he tried to hook fish.

These are the things that make a skipper's job interesting. The angler learned something. I learned something. My instructional spiel has since been expanded in that specific area. (In fact, come to think of it, it seems to be expanding every year in many directions.) But the most important thing was that he went home with two coho after, as he described it, "one of the best days of my life."

Next to having cooperative fish swallowing lures whole rather than daintily nibbling at them, the best thing a light-tackle, long-line troller can have working for him (or her) is sharper hooks. With softer rods in use, making it even more difficult to drive hook points into fish, plus the big trend away from small-diameter treble hooks to larger, single, salt-water Siwashes, sharp "sticky" points are becoming even more important. The larger the diameter of the hook, the more difficult it is to embed it into a fish, even though it's popular to say today that single hooks "grab" better.

The energy-penetration ratio differences between the comparatively tiny, sharp hook points of the old treble hooks and the bulkier points of today's popular larger-diameter Siwash hooks are so obvious it's difficult to know how this angling belief could originate, no matter how sharp the larger hook point might be. But aside from that observation (I don't dare call it a point), it's hard to think of anything an angler can better do with his time, if he likes catching fish, than spend the few moments necessary to check and sharpen the hooks of his lures. This is all very basic, I know. I also know it's one of those ho-hum subjects we all sagely nod our heads in agreement with, yet rarely follow through on, even though most experienced light-line anglers will all agree that sharper hooks could cut fish losses by a conservative estimate of 30 percent.

One revealing study of fish hooking problems was conducted a few years ago by researchers employed by the Berkley/Trilene line manufacturing firm in Spirit Lake, Iowa. The Trilene underwater hook set study first determined the pressure in pounds of an average strike at the hook end. Tests showed experienced anglers rarely exerted more than two pounds of pressure: typical weekend fishermen had an average strike force of between three-quarters of a pound and one pound. As the measurements were made in a swimming pool, a light-tackle long-line Great Lakes troller can no doubt figure on no more than a half-pound hooking force, if that, at the best of times. The "fishing scientists" then measured the force needed to embed a hook into the mouths of various game fish. They found bony-jawed fish such as muskellunge and pike required a minimum hooking force of three pounds, often more. Soft-jawed fish such as trout only required about two pounds of force. However, by using only well-honed fish hooks, it was found the force required to hook any fish could be reduced almost 50 percent.

Whatever we do, the fact still remains that the greatest weakness of all small-diameter line is its reduced breaking point. Any discussion on the care and feeding of 2- to 6-pound-test line must center on the fact that the more fragile the line, the more easily it is damaged, and weakened even more, by angling use.

One of the simplest ways to help maintain the strength of any line is to take more care when knotting the line to lures or swivels. Next to an angler being too heavy-handed, I suspect line-weakening nicks or abrasion created by a hastily tied knot is one of the greatest single reasons for breakage. Oddly enough, most of the damage is done when many anglers least expect it. It's not the actual knot tying that can do you in, unless, of course, the knot is tied improperly. The real damage occurs during the final tightening or snubbing of the knot against the line ring of the lure or swivel. The resultant abrasive friction as the knot is slid forward, plus the nicks created by monofilament grabbing and cutting into itself on tightening, can and does break down the protective hard surface of the line. Solution? Because heat is involved you do what you'd instinctively do with most fires—put water on it. Thoroughly wet the preformed knot, and the line in front of it, in your mouth prior to snubbing or tightening the knot.

Preventing line damage while tightening knots is so important, some of the best world-record light-line tournament anglers I know go one step further. They carry a tiny gob of hard wax with them, coating the end of the line with the slippery wax prior to tying the knot, and adding saliva on top of the wax before the final tightening.

Whether avoidable line breakage occurs on the first fish, the second, or the tenth isn't as important as remembering that any line is weakened by a knot. Any vulnerable spot quickly becomes weaker, wearing away at itself under stress, and unless a knot is retied often it will sooner or later give way, even though the angler is successfully maintaining pressure against fish well below the line's original breaking strength. Anyone using ultrafine 2- or 4-pound-test line should reknot his lure, using plenty of spit, after every fish. I've also forced myself over the years to leave a bit of the tag end when trimming a finished knot; like most boatmen, I no doubt place too much importance on neatness, and having a bit of line extruding from a knot never looks right in my eyes. But the tag does provide insurance against line slippage.

Another potential source of trouble for a light-tackle fan is rod guide rings, which should be checked with a magnifying glass occasionally for microscopic line-damaging nicks. Faulty rod guides are without question one of the most common causes of line failure. An even simpler way of checking line contact points for smoothness is to brush a cotton swab or strip of nylon stocking through the guides. Any rough spots will grab the cotton or nylon. If you're trolling for any length of time, just the continual back and forth rubbing of the same section of line against a perfectly smooth guide will create line wear. The positioning of guides on many rods can cause line to rub against the rod itself when the rod is arced over in trolling position or clamped into a downrigger. The heavier the lure being trolled, the more erratic its action, the greater the potential for abrasive wear. Other trouble spots can be worn line rollers on open-face spinning reels or similarly worn shrouds on closed-faced reels.

A new development in custom-rod building circles to help alleviate rod-rubbing problems for anglers who longline with 2- or 4-pound-test lines on noodle rods is called the "Roberts Wrap." The first guide is placed eighteen to twenty inches, in normal rod position, in front of a level-wind reel. The line then passes through a second guide positioned at a ninety-degree angle, and about $4\frac{1}{2}$ inches above the first guide. From there, the line carries through to a third guide rotated an additional ninety degrees, putting the line on the underside of the rod. Remaining guides are lined up with the underside guide for the rest of the length of the rod. The result, when the rod is in trolling position, is absolutely no contact at all between the ultralight line and the heavily curved upper portion of the rod. It works so well that one rod manufacturer, Woodstream, is now producing such rods commercially.

I'm normally reluctant to rig any ultralight gear for unknown charter customers. Quite frankly, I wouldn't want to be stuck with the cost of potential tackle loss. On the other hand, I also know that if clients are serious light-line anglers, or willing to spend time on my boat optimistically searching for a world record line-class fish, they'll want to use their own familiar tackle anyway. But unlike a lot of big-game saltwater charterboat skippers who cringe when they see an angler heading toward their boat carrying ultralight 30-pound-test rigs, or even 80-pound-test

An extended double-handed grip on a fly rod makes it physically easier to battle a hard-running salmon into the boat.

tackle—normal line strength used on the bigger saltwater fish is 130 pounds—I truly enjoy the light-line game. In defense of saltwater charterboaters, it should be added that they usually have a lot of money at stake in the larger fish. A lost trophy means that much less meat to sell at the end of the day, not to mention a percentage of taxidermy fees if the angler wants a boated fish mounted.

When Gwynne and I are messing around on our own with ultrafine gear, or when we have light-line anglers on board as guests, we have a couple of little tricks we use with downriggers that eliminate the normal wear and tear of lines when fishing deep water. As we naturally can't use heavy terminal gear such as flashers or dodgers on 2- or 4-pound-test lines, the heavy drag of a wobbling dodger alone being enough to wear down or break the lines, I'll attach a dodger directly to the cannonball when I feel an attractor is needed to draw fish, linking it to the cable ring with heavy monofilament so the dodger is flopping around maybe three feet behind the ball. The tiny light-tackle lure is then run clean off the cable three feet above it on about four feet of line so the lure is holding a bit above and behind the dodger.

Another trick I use is designed to avoid any line wear from standard mechanical downrigger releases, which can badly grind ultralight line at times. Even the tiniest spoons can badly twist up a short section of line occasionally, causing excessive wear at the release. My answer, until I come up with something better, is the old soft rubber band trick explained in an earlier chapter. If I'm forced to run a much longer line off the ball in shallower water, and the fish insist on a potential line-twister, I'll give them what they want to try to eat by tying in a short section of 12- or 15-pound-test mono at the point in the line where it'll be snubbed into the release.

Another way of getting the most out of light line is treating it the same way you would camera film. Leaving line exposed to sunlight on a boat or back window of a car is one of the surest ways of reducing its strength. You should always keep spare line spools in a box or store them in shade. I keep my extra spools in the bottom storage area of an oversized tackle box, always remembering that if the box is left in hot sun long enough that excess heat will also cause line deterioration. Avoid car trunks or even closed-up boat cabins if you're not going to use the boat for any length of time.

Line twists or kinks can also mean trouble. Cut off and discard any twisted line.

9

Deep-Water Fishing

Why fish for small stuff when you can go out and catch big ones?

—Overheard on a dock

We've covered a fair amount of territory up to now, exploring areas of Great Lakes fishing that, I hope, were worth the price of admission. Now it's time to go for the big deep-water stuff, the exciting, motor-roaring, hull-thumping challenges that separate the kids from the boys.

On the Great Lakes, where Nature can swing a bold hand as rough as you'll feel anywhere, the real game is found far from shore where a boat is only an insignificant speck in an ocean of open space. The big silver king salmon, the red-painted rainbows, the wallhangers are all out there somewhere, but first there's the matter of finding and catching them.

With the lakes as large as they are, and the fish able to move great distances, the accent is usually on the "finding." And I'd better point out here, I'm primarily interested in free-roaming chinooks, rainbows and, to a lesser extent, coho. Once Atlantic salmon start showing up in more catchable numbers in western Lake Ontario, they'll no doubt be added to the list, probably right at the top. But at the moment we seek only the

In the early days of the fishery, fishing miles from shore in search of Great Lakes salmon was a lonely job. Now it is rare to have a big chunk of water to yourself. (*Photo courtesy of Wisconsin Division of Tourism*)

"big three," not having the right kind of bottom structure available—the deep rocky shoals—to hold lake trout in quantity at our end of the lake. However, lakers and brown trout can usually be caught on any of the lakes most days if you want to spend the time dragging small silver spoons closer to shore where the thermocline intersects with bottom.

The effects of shoreline geography on fish location are of major importance in many areas of the Great Lakes. One example I know best is Long Point on the north shore of Lake Erie. This twenty-mile-long sandspit that juts out into the lake, once famous as a graveyard of old sailing ships, is still noted for the strength of the potentially dangerous undertows close to its beaches. The strong underwater currents—made even stronger by the shallowness of the lake—pile up off the end of the point, mixing with warm currents moving parallel to shore and the still warmer water of Long Point Bay to create a huge boiling cauldron of warm and cold water that draws plankton, bait fish, and salmon in surprising numbers each July when fishing is slowest elsewhere. Adding to the sport of fishing this summer feeding ground of salmon is that the same turbulent water off the tip of the point also holds a unique variety of other fish species that hit trolled coho dodgers and flies fished behind deep-water cannonballs. Catches include walleye up to fourteen pounds; five-to six-pound smallmouth bass; and sheephead, many of which top the two-pound mark.

Any major watershed emptying into the Great Lakes must be given similar consideration by summer offshore anglers. All of Lake Ontario, for example, is influenced by the Niagara River. This turbulent, fast-moving river that pours 201,000 cubic feet of water a second into Lake Ontario from Lake Erie, is the source of 85 percent of Lake Ontario's total water volume. So it is easy to understand why differences between the temperature of the river water and the lake water—the river usually being colder than the lake shallows until late May or early June—can provide excellent near-shore angling every year. As the river warms, an angler following its currents far out into the colder water of the lake can usually find well-defined thermal breaks, and fish, all summer long. Combine such temperature variations with abrupt bottom contour changes often found off a river and it can mean fish no matter which of the Great Lakes you might be on. The more erratic the bottom change, the more fish will usually be held.

Another, more typical example of river currents creating fish-holding bottom structure is found off the mouth of our next largest river, Twenty Mile Creek, at the far western end of the lake. Even this comparatively mild stream has formed four twenty-foot ridges of bottom sand off its mouth in about sixty feet of water. Fish found in the hollows between the ridges in spring and early fall are absent only in the hot days of summer when warm water forces them farther offshore.

Similar influences in lakeshore topography are rarely considered, yet the shape of shoreline is a simple indicator of whether fish might be found offshore, how far, and of what species. The smaller the lake, of course, the easier it is to predict both the slope and type of bottom, and the area's potential value as fish habitat. There's no magic involved. It's an old presonar trick developed from years of fishing northern trout lakes. You gain a clear picture of any lake bottom by simply visualizing underwater extensions of the shorelines. Cliffs beget cliffs; rocks beget rocks; marshes beget shallow mud flats.

Some basic knowledge of geological history also helps to find fish (an offshore angler must develop many interests). Certainly some of the most abrupt changes to be found anywhere on the Great Lakes are ancient underwater geological formations. For example, an underwater escarpment face (once the edge of a lake) can be found off the Niagara River, and has a vertical, clifflike drop of more than one hundred feet. Trout can be found hovering at the edge of the dropoff or partway down its face all summer long. Any shore edged by high hills or cliffs likely holds equally interesting offshore bottom formations. Another similar dropoff in western Lake Ontario—and I only know of the two—is again an ancient edge of the lake which plummets one hundred feet down in eighty feet of water off the north shore. As expected, existing shoreline behind it, known as "the Bluffs," has an even greater drop.

The Great Lakes are also becoming more divided each year, different fish species congregating more and more in different parts of a lake at certain times of the year because of conditions best meeting their physical needs. This form of environmental isolation means offshore anglers must concentrate fishing efforts on either salmon or trout, depending on which species is known to be present in greatest numbers. For example, the south shore of Lake Ontario (and similar situations are found elsewhere on the other lakes) now holds the main summer offshore salmon fishery at its western end. The central portion of the lake has become famous for its huge brown trout, and the far eastern end of the lake, with its increasingly rockier bottom, is where lake trout are king.

Adding even more interest to the game are the environmental pockets, or tiny portions of such areas, that attract other, less numerous fish species. I know sections of my part of the lake, such as the big underwater cliff mentioned earlier near the Niagara River, hold many big lake trout, but the fishery has never really been touched because most anglers fish the water with salmon lures at fairly fast salmon trolling speeds, rather than slow down and use smaller lake trout lures. Granted, there are some salmon found there as well, but most of the fish are lake trout, and if you want action you go with numbers, even if it means rerigging all your tackle.

To be successful you really need to stay on top of the big salmon day after day, and even then it's easy to lose them. So you try other places on such days, hoping to find the new location of the fish. Sometimes information you need to put a few salmon in the boat comes visually, in the form of an easily seen "slick" or river-like thermal break altering the appearance of the lake's surface. Sometimes your sonar will tell you where a few fish might be found by marking clustered bait fish or, equally good, individual salmon. Sometimes you find fish just by unexplainable gut instinct or old-fashioned luck. There are times too, when having spent sixteen years on the water, five of them as a charterboater, and the accumulation of knowledge gained from spending that kind of time on a lake, can pay off. For example, an area that produced fish the same time last year under similar circumstances will likely hold fish again.

Also, consider the weather. An offshore charterboat skipper probably thinks about weather more than anything else. He becomes part meteorologist, part soothsayer. It doesn't matter where he is—at home, in the car, on the water—whenever he sees clouds building up, wherever a radio weather forecast is heard, he should always be visualizing how coming changes might affect the lake, especially changes in wind direction which can alter the flow of offshore undersurface currents and the location of the summer thermocline—the lake's only structures.

Also helpful, of course, are any bits and pieces of information that can be picked up from other anglers who are far out in the lake looking for fish. A call on CB radio channel 13, used by most boaters, may produce some angling tidbits. If you have a long-range VHF unit, a specific call to a known salmon angling expert out on the lake, or a charterboater, could also help. Dockside talk, spotting anglers with fish and talking to them, or, if there is a derby going on, calling derby organizers or a local weigh-in station will usually give the novice a general starting point. In summer, typical information is likely "thirty-five feet down in two hundred feet of water off Port Weller, hitting green . . ." So you simply crank up your boat, head out to where your sonar measures bottom two hundred feet down off Port Weller (or wherever), lower green lures to a measured thirty-five feet via downriggers, switch on your radio or radios for updated information and relax, secure in the belief, if not knowledge, that you'll find fish before the day is out.

How to Read Underwater Currents

With high hopes of finding fish, and with lures staggered at various levels, our next offshore angling concern should be finding out what we can of the underwater currents in our fishing area. If a deep, invisible current does exist, how fast is it flowing and in which direction? What is its effect on our lures? If a boat is moving at 3 miles per hour in the same direction as a 3-mile-per-hour current seventy-five feet deep, the lures being fished at that level could be hanging limp in the water. Trolling against the current and doubling lure speed could make lures spin wildly, twisting and weakening lines and producing no more fish than non-working lures hanging in limbo below the boat.

Few charterboat skippers, in my part of the country at least, have given this unknown bogeyman of Great Lakes trollers the consideration it demands. I know one skipper who sold an underwater current meter at less than cost, almost giving it away, because he simply didn't believe what it was telling him. Yet what better explanation for days when fish can be caught only by trolling in one direction? Or how about the days when tackle that has worked perfectly before suddenly starts tangling up for no obvious reason? The villain is normally an underwater crosscurrent sweeping lines together. To complicate the situation, there's often no similarity between sometimes visible top-water currents and subsurface currents. In deep water of one hundred feet or more, underwater currents are normally not only moving at a different speed but often in a different direction from water on the surface.

Catching fish while trolling in one direction is fairly common when fishing in a pack close to shore in spring or fall. At such times, with a crowd of anglers on the water, it's easier to move with the other boats, trolling parallel to the shore like everyone else. Yet this is one angling situation where you can almost be guaranteed there will be a mild "jet effect" current. This shore-hugging flow, discussed in chapter 3, always moves parallel to shore (in my part of Lake Ontario, west to east). How to fish it? Where I am, you troll at a slightly higher speed going east, and slow down going west. Even better, if you can find room in the pack, is to troll across the current, straight in and out, making your turn and heading back out into the lake again only when sonar indicates cannonballs will soon start banging bottom. A variation of this technique also allows anyone to use offshore currents to their advantage even when they don't know for certain they are there.

Unfortunately, there is no easy way of pinpointing such currents, or knowing at all times whether your lures are wiggling and waggling as they should, unless you have a sensor that calibrates speed of movement at cannonball level on your boat. Two such current-measuring units are available at this writing. Pro-Combinator, made by BC Electronics in Lynnwood, Washington, transmits water speed and temperature data up top via a special downrigger cable bought as part of the system. The Thermo-Troll 800 Computer, made by Fish Hawk Electronics in Crystal Lake, Illinois, operates much like sonar, the digital readout receiver getting cannonball depth information (plus surface data) through a hull-mounted transducer. Are they worth the high cost? Most charterboat skippers think so. And the sensors sometimes reveal many almost unbelievable angling situations. One example, reported by Wisconsin charterboater Larry Presnall in a recent issue of *In-Fisherman* magazine, involved catching lake trout while Presnall's boat was drifting backward over a sunken current moving fast enough near bottom to activate his lures. I have yet to discover such a strong (probably a 4 or 5 miles-per-hour) undersurface current. But I have no doubt they exist. I know 3-mile-an-hour currents are not unusual, which is the average trolling speed of most anglers.

But don't give up. Lacking a man-made current sensor, you can use fish as sensors. It's not as quick, granted. Yet given time, salmon reveal many things, transmitting all kinds of vital information either by slamming lures or ignoring them. In order for fish to tell you anything of value, however, you should always assume, when far offshore, that an under-water current of some sort does exist. Once that assumption is made, it is then easier for you to remember never to troll for any length of time in a straight line. Call it current insurance. Call it duplicating nature—bait fish never swim in a straight line either.

If you mark a school of bait fish on sonar, for example, you cover the water in a figure-eight pattern, working the area from four different directions, knowing two of those must be sideways to any suspected current flow. Chances are good in such crosscurrents that your lures will be working in even better fish-enticing fashion than usual. When you're running high lines on the edges of a thermal upwelling, where most of the current is obviously rising upward, run a zigzag course in and out of the slick, then reverse your field to cover the same water from the opposite direction. If a thermal break is visible in an east-west direction, you know any current causing it is moving either north to south or south to north. If you've kept track of weather and the direction of any recent blows, you can also predict the precise direction of the underwater flow by deduction.

Under the worst possible situations, your lures, trolled in a circle, are still working reasonably well half of the time. Which is a great im-provement over trolling a straight line and, if going with a current or trolling at the wrong speed, not having lures working at all. And it's worth repeating that salmon will tell you many important things if you take the effort to translate their actions. If the first fish is taken while you're running a north-south course, spend a little more time working water in that direction. If the second and third fish also come into the boat while on that same general course, or a reverse of that direction, how much clearer can any message be? If you're catching boatloads of fish no matter which direction you might be holding, then relax and enjoy your bonanza while it lasts. Under these conditions, you can at least give me a holler on VHF. If I'm not on the water I'll sure try and get out in a hurry. Such easy salmon days in summer are a rare gift.

With or without advance information, the beginning of any angling day should always start with a water temperature check. Run your boat out as far as you have to go on the lake for sonar to mark sixty or eighty feet of water, stop the boat, and, using a temperature probe, take a series of water temperature readings to locate the thermocline. If you can't find the thermocline, and water temperature is the same from surface to bot-tom, go out into even deeper water until you do find it. If there have been no drastic weather changes, chances are the thermocline will be at the same level as it was the day before, but chart it anyway, day after day without fail, logging the data in a notebook along with the date; air temperature; water surface temperature; whether the lake is calm, choppy, or wavy; wind direction and velocity; cloud cover; and anything else you feel might be of interest.

Additional log information, with any luck at all, should include number of fish caught, species, size, what they were caught on, and the depth at which they were caught. This type of information, collected over a season or two, not only makes extremely interesting winter reading but, as the seasons pass and the data bank grows, should also help create an increasingly clearer picture in your mind of the all-important relationships between water conditions and fish movement at different times of the year.

I can't stress the value of such information enough. My biggest regret is that I haven't kept a more thorough record of angling conditions and my successes and failures over the years. I like to think anything of any importance not on paper is bouncing around in my head, of course, but in computer terms that kind of information-retrieval system (knowing my head) is far from infallible. Little things forgotten, if combined with other bits of information might prove valuable some day. So a wise angler, if he hopes to acquire any meaningful knowledge of his own, develops the habit of logging the circumstances of his outings, no matter how trivial, day after day.

Once an offshore angler has located the thermocline and noted its thickness—let's assume his probe says the underwater belt of rapid temperature change starts at sixty-five feet and extends down to seventy-five feet—he now has a choice of staying approximately where he is on the lake and rigging tackle for lakers or brown trout, or heading out into even deeper water for big rainbows and salmon.

But before we get into that order of business, an extremely important point should be made here. The only difference, it seems to me, between consistently successful offshore anglers and pack fishermen who often pay the penalty of relying only on the "luck of the draw," is observation and attention to detail. There are thousands of things to see on a lake, many of them little things that only an experienced angler might look for or understand the possible meaning of. A concentration of sea gulls, for example, might be feasting on bait fish crippled by hungry salmon. A slight change in the ripple of the lake's surface or a line of debris on the water could mean thermal breaks, upwellings of cold water that hold fish. In addition, there are also many unseen angling factors to consider, like reaction (or lack of reaction) of salmon to action, color, and size of lures. Like any experienced woodsman, to draw a parallel, you train yourself to read "sign," to notice tiny details.

In a similar vein, take nothing for granted, including your temperature probe telling you the thermocline is located between sixty-five and seventy-five feet. It isn't. Not if you're using a hand-held temperature probe as most of us do. Details again. Let's explore the point. Unless it's a dead calm day, a rarity, your boat is no doubt drifting. You also undoubtedly have a belly in the sensor cable. The weight of any sensor I've used won't take the probe straight down, not with any boat movement. At sixty-five feet, depending on drift speed, the actual depth of the top of the thermocline could be anywhere from fifty to sixty feet. Important? This type of observation (the bellied line is visible if you're looking for it) can make the difference between a successful fishing day or a plain boat ride. With any kind of breeze on the lake either add extra weight to the temperature sensor by attaching heavy sinkers, or hook it to a downrigger cannonball.

Once the thermocline is found, one bit of information gleaned from my fishing records and proven time and time again to pay off with fish provides an amazingly simple starting point for any offshore salmon angler. Oddly enough, I have yet to hear this discovery mentioned anywhere nor have I ever seen any hint of it in print. There is certainly no scientific explanation for it (which bothers me most of all). But the hard fact remains that some salmon, particularly coho, can usually be found where the thermocline is exactly halfway between surface and bottom. If the thermocline ranges from 60 to 70 feet, I can find fish where the sonar tells me I have 120 to 140 feet of water under the boat. If the thermocline is 80 feet, I fish 160 feet of water.

I rarely spend a whole day fishing this one specific portion of the lake, although it's always where I first set tackle before working progressively deeper in search of trophy-sized chinooks. On half-day charters, or when we take friends out for a picnic-style lunch or dinner on the boat, it is much more convenient to fish this water only a few miles offshore than to make the normal all-day trolling trip, a twelve-mile jaunt each way, to fish summer chinook water at the two hundred- to three hundred-foot depth. As noted, this "half-way" water can usually be counted on to provide fish. If nothing else, assuming that the finding is only a quirky local summer situation, the discovery does point out once again the importance of keeping records, and that valuable gems of information can occasionally be siphoned out of them.

My fishing logs also reveal a rare and possibly important glimpse of offshore rainbow trout activity. Of all the fish in the Great Lakes, rainbows are the most mysterious, the fish we know least about and, as a result, the hardest to catch with any consistency. Where they move in the lakes, and when and why, is still unknown. This huge gap in Great Lakes knowledge stems, I believe, from years of looking for rainbows in the wrong places. Our error is that our thinking has been too salmon oriented. We've been comparing rainbows to the more familiar salmon activity. We've been fishing deep, near the thermocline level or below, while rainbows are cavorting, it turns out, at much shallower levels, including the surface itself at times. Just as taking a boy out of the country is easier than taking country habits out of the boy, the planting of rainbow trout in the Great Lakes has not eliminated their strong, genetically programmed surface orientation. In fact, stomach analyses of Lake Ontario rainbow show 50 percent of their diet is composed of insects, the bulk of which must be taken while the insects are floating on or near the surface! Whether the same situation exists on the other lakes, as I'm sure it does, can easily be proven by stomach analysis work elsewhere. But with an obscure four-year-old State University of New York trout diet study as a starting point (I must be the only angler to have read it), I am now involved in an extension of that work through increasingly successful use of shallow-water angling techniques—flatlines and planing boards— far offshore in the middle of summer. I'm concentrating my efforts on current upwellings, which, if you look closely enough (minor details again), often collect on their edges enough drowned, protein-rich insect life to keep any refugee from a trout stream happily gorged, no matter how big it grows.

Also part of this same angling experiment is an effort to correlate water oxygen levels and temperature with feeding activity in hopes of gaining a better understanding of the environmental "triggers" of both rainbow trout and salmon. Unfortunately, this total package, and the theory behind it, is still too tenuous, too incomplete, for publication now. If it works out, it could provide subject matter for another book. If it doesn't, I have only fallen (quietly I hope) on my face once again.

Personal catch figures and analyses of lures used has prompted another equally drastic change in tackle-rigging techniques used to catch big chinooks. At one time, I think everyone on Lake Ontario relied on large, hard-wobbling dodger and lure combinations to stir up king salmon in deep water. Most of us still do. Yet my experiences, confirmed by a few other Lake Ontario charterboat captains questioned on the subject, show an increasing percentage (85 percent last season) were caught on "clean" lures fished without wobbling plates in front of them. Of that 85 percent, almost 90 percent were taken on medium-size silver/blue, silver/green, or black spoons. What, if anything, triggered the change? We know chinook salmon will alter behavior patterns because of angling pressure. One example is their quick daytime abandonment of shallow water in spring when boat traffic becomes heavy. A lesser-known but even more interesting reaction to a buildup in angling pressure is found on the Pacific coast, where commercial trollers are reporting chinook as deep as six hundred feet, an unheard-of depth, presumably to avoid gill netters and seiners. Are Great Lakes chinooks being similarly turned off by big wobblers?

The importance of noting the reaction (or lack of reaction) of fish to different lure actions, mentioned earlier as only one of the many details that must be acted upon to catch fish, is worth expanding here. It might be a partial answer to our chinook puzzle. Fish do react differently on different days. If chinook salmon were human we might quite accurately describe them as "moody." Sometimes they'll readily strike a fast-moving, big-wobbling lure with a dodger in front of it to add even more action. Sometimes they'll demand a quieter, smaller, less erratic lure—which is what Lake Ontario chinook have been doing more and more. Why? No one knows. Other times, of course, chinook may ignore all lures completely.

An extra-large variety of lures can pay off when summer fish are in a finicky mood. What works today may not work tomorrow.

Different Species and Different Techniques

A good angler knows that the reactions of fish to different lures can vary greatly between species. Different fish have different personalities. Coho salmon, for example, are usually a much more excitable, aggressive fish than chinook, and seem always hungry, probably as a result of being a school fish. When you're in a pack, surrounded by competitive eaters, indecision of any sort may sometimes mean the loss of a meal. So I tie squids or flutterspoons closer than normal to dodgers and run the dodgers close (three to five feet) to cannonballs to provide absolute maximum lure action when coho are around. By contrast, chinook lures may be run fifty feet or more behind cannonballs at times. Salmon, however, when they're in a frenzied feeding mood will slam anything, even cannonballs occasionally.

The greatest contrast of all between species is found in the differences between lake trout and salmon. The almost totally opposite personalities of these two salmonids are enough to turn an angler schizophrenic. For example, although coho and chinook can sometimes be teased into hitting a lure, Great Lakes lake trout, with lots of easily obtained food close at hand, often won't budge until they are ready to feed, no matter what you do. You can fish lake trout water for hours without any action and then, wham! your boat will suddenly start looking like a fresh fish market, trout coming on board one after the other so fully gorged that tails of bait fish are often sticking out of their mouths.

Lake trout are less aggressive than salmon, refusing to swim very far or very fast for a lure, although once they become interested in a bait they will timidly follow it a surprising distance before mouthing it. Being trout, they are also very selective at times, as are browns and rainbows, about the color of a lure. So an angler must spend a lot of time switching lures until he finds one that works. This color choice can change during the day. You might start out doing well with green and then, after hitting a wall of no action, start catching trout again on blue lures.

Another major secret of catching lake trout consistently is to display lures that come closest to duplicating the action of live bait—lures that move up and down, moving slow one moment and darting away another. So you'll jiggle cannonballs up and down, sometimes deliberately hitting bottom to stir up clouds of silt. Boat speed is nudged with a tiny burst of power then throttled back to crawling speed again. It's interesting fishing.

One of the most important lessons I ever had on the importance of keeping lake trout lures moving erratically occurred about eight years ago when I had an angler come aboard clutching an old-fashioned wire-line lake trout trolling rig. Remember those short, heavy rods with the oversized reels that look like, in today's world, downrigger winches? This guy was a lake trout specialist from Year One. He had caught lake trout almost everywhere the big grey trout are found in North America, from the high Arctic of the Northwest Territories to Labrador. All he needed, he told me, was a bit of room off the stern. I let him have his fun, giving him the center of the boat to work in. "Are you sure you don't want to fish with downriggers?" I'd ask occasionally. "Nope. This is fine," he'd reply, methodically keeping that powerful rod moving back and forth like a clock pendulum. He did everything in classic style, slowly letting out wire until he bumped bottom and then reeling the lure in a foot or two. If any major depth changes showed up on sonar, I'd let him know so he could start adjusting the length of his line ahead of time. "It's a great day isn't it?" he'd say every so often, thoroughly enjoying himself. He did have a lot of fun as it turned out. His so-called obsolete wire-line rod outfished the rest of his four-man group (using downriggers) that day three to one. I'm still shaking my head. I have also not repeated the experiment.

The four primary concerns of offshore salmon anglers should be depth of lure, trolling speed, lure action, and lure size. Most anglers claim lure color is of top importance. They may be right. We've all heard fondly told tales of days when no salmon were taken until a specific color lure was used. To add even more impact to such stories, the only difference between the successful lure and those used earlier might possibly have been two black dots or some other miniscule color variation. But I suspect the real reason for such sudden success is something totally different. The lure action was improved either by changing course and boat speed, running with or against a breeze, for example, or more likely, by just putting the lure in the water at a time when previously sluggish salmon began feeling pangs of hunger.

Of all the various theories involving lure colors, I imagine the best known, most widely accepted truism is to start each fishing day with light-colored lures and to switch to progressively darker shades as the sun climbs higher in the sky. Certainly this belief is widely quoted. I must confess I find the actual practice of such a simplistic notion rarely succeeds in normal offshore angling situations. Even close to shore I can't recall ever fishing water so clear that a bright lure frightened fish away, which is what I suspect the recommendation of using dark-colored lures in midday must be all about. If you are fishing shallow and are moving further offshore to fish deeper in the water as the day progresses, then such advice makes sense, because dark-colored lures should be more visible to fish. Black or dark blues and greens should be well up on anyone's favorite offshore lure color list.

If a lure also holds a shimmering flash of silver to emulate light bouncing off the sides of a fleeing alewife or smelt, so much the better. Even in the depths, or as deep as most of us ever fish, some light still exists to be caught and reflected off the mirrorlike sides of forage fish as they dart and turn in the water. Big predator salmon and trout no doubt zero in on such things. The higher the sun and the calmer the water, the deeper light will penetrate. Predominantly silver lures with hints of blue or green take a surprising share of fish on the darkest of days. Dark colors or contrast lures with phosphorescent or glow-in-the-dark finishes are, however, basic fish catchers when the lake is blackened by rain or heavy cloud.

Knowing how often salmon must feed, I don't think they can ever be considered truly "picky" eaters. The skill of an angler—and the value of a tackle box bulging with lures—might only be in tempting a fish into eating when the fish is in a "will I or won't I" stage. Put the right kind of lure in front of it, make it attractive and easy enough to catch, and a salmon, even though freshly gorged with bait fish, might say, What the heck—one more won't hurt me. Thinking about it, it would be interesting to know what percentage of an offshore salmon's day is actually spent in eating. It's possible a salmon might spend at least a third of its time feeding, another third in a "tempt me if you can" stage, and the last third just resting. Who knows?

Luckily for us, considering the importance we place on fish size, Great Lakes salmon have yet to discover they no longer face the ordeal of long, difficult spawning runs up turbulent West Coast rivers. They're still genetically engineered to store up sufficient body energy to achieve such goals, packing on tremendous weight in a hurry, often gaining well over a pound a week in preparation for spawning. As a two-pound coho in April can develop into a mature fifteen-pounder by late August, these fish must eat often. It is estimated that salmon during this five-month feeding spree will eat their own weight in bait fish every week, primarily alewife and smelt, the two most plentiful forage fish in the Great Lakes. As the preferred temperature range of the more numerous alewife (fifty-three to fifty-five degrees) neatly coincides with temperature preferences of salmon, coho and chinook feed mainly on that one species (alewife outnumber smelt in Lake Ontario ten to one). Smelt and lake trout are similarly paired off, smelt liking the colder water (forty-eight to fifty-two degrees) preferred by lake trout near bottom.

This special relationship between these species has been shown in many studies. Typical data is found in an Ontario Ministry of Natural Resources research project that showed, after sampling 973 fish stomachs in late 1983 (using fish entered in that year's *Toronto Star's* Great Salmon Hunt), that almost 49 percent of all chinook had alewife in their stomachs, as did 29 percent of the coho, 33 percent of the rainbows, 31 percent of the browns, and 27 percent of the lake trout. Only 5.9 percent of the coho had eaten smelt, as had 13.5 percent of the chinook, 6.2 percent of the rainbows, 7.7 percent of the browns, and 23 percent of the lake trout. What percentage of fish had eaten both smelt and alewife is unknown.

We're also fortunate, I suppose, that salmon are not regimented eaters. At least there's no big underwater dinner bell gonging periodically to mark the start or end of a feeding period. Barring an abrupt, major environmental change of some sort, we can usually count on finding a few fish with a yen to gobble lures no matter what time of day we're on a lake. On the other hand, if there was the equivalent of a dinner bell out there, our sport would no doubt be greatly simplified.

Not being aware of the difference between passive fish and actively feeding fish is, I suspect, the reason most anglers waste many of their precious angling hours on the Great Lakes. As one example: The most obvious, time-consuming mistake made by many offshore anglers is to concentrate angling efforts at the depth where sonar is showing classic banana-shaped fish marks on graph paper. Sonar ads, most of which proudly show such images as proof of their effectiveness, may be playing a subliminal role here. Whatever, I know anglers will eagerly spend hours, often days, trolling lures only where the big marks are showing, not realizing such distinctive registrations by sonar can only be created by completely still, largely inactive fish.

If those same marks are located out of the preferred temperature range of salmon, the fish suspended in ultracold water below the thermocline, it's even worse news. They're not only passive, but probably sound asleep, or what passes for piscine slumber. From observation of salmon in rivers, it appears fish do need periods of rest and, like most humans, can be difficult to move when sleeping. Of course, if you wake them the right way, some might come out of the sheets snarling, hitting a lure as viciously as we might toss a jangling alarm clock across a room. In fact, some very good fish are taken this way. But the vast majority of these fish will literally turn away, ignoring every lure you show them.

Adding to the confusion of novice, sonar-oriented anglers, salmon that are most easily caught are rarely marked on sonar. Actively feeding fish are fast-moving fish, which, when they do show on sonar, are called "streakers" because of the thin, streaky lines registered on graph paper as they pass through the cone or eye of the sonar transducer. Although such graph marks, when they appear, usually show a diving fish, the salmon are more likely moving sideways. They are displayed on the graph as a downward-moving streak because sonar is technically capable only of measuring distance of an object from a boat, not depth (despite their common name of depthfinder).

The ability of sonar to misdirect anglers reaches its most illogical point when fishermen whose sonar shows widely separated bait fish and salmon will devote most of their attention, and tackle, to obviously inactive fish. These fishermen ignore not only the presence of bait fish but, even worse, forget one of the few undisputable Great Lakes angling truths: The most catchable fish are hungry fish, and any salmon with an urge to eat must go where the food is found.

This takes us, in circuitous fashion, back to matching lures to the metabolism level of the fish we seek. Given the previous situation—bait fish shown at sonar at one level (usually alewife above or in the upper portion of the thermocline), salmon down deep and, with luck, the occasional streaker marked on sonar halfway between the bait fish and the passive or semiactive suspended fish (a fairly common occurrence on Lake Ontario)—I've found it's possible to take active fish and semidormant fish at the same time, but only by matching lure presentation at different depths to the different activity levels of the fish.

Aggressive, moving fish appear to like aggressive, fast-moving lures. Don't worry about not seeing the feeders on sonar; most of my boated fish, probably close to 90 percent, are not registered on sonar prior to strikes. They seemingly come out of nowhere. If you're marking bait fish, you can count on a few hungry salmon being not too far away. Occasionally, sonar will mark salmon many anglers don't recognize as fish. If the bait fish haven't schooled up too densely, showing as a black glob on sonar, you may spot big salmon holding right at the base of the clustered school, their backs almost touching this living food counter. Such fish are obviously not feeding at that particular moment, judging from the lack of concern shown by the bait fish, but the salmon have undoubtedly just finished feeding and, because of their position, will no doubt feed again, putting them well up on any angler's list of catchable fish.

But it's the off days, the slow fishing days, that demand most of our attention. And at the risk of unwinding circles within circles, trolling speed should be considered a separate, yet very important factor in whether fish are striking lures or ignoring them. Speed of lure movement not only affects the action of a lure but can, by itself, make a difference in the number of fish boated each day. We have discussed the importance of boat speed in relation to increased coverage of water and exposure of lures to the greatest possible number of fish. A third factor is providing the lure speed that best sparks fish aggression on a particular day. It might be described as matching your offering to that day's environmentally created rhythm of fish activity. A fish that has just completed a heavy meal, for example, or is resting after a long-distance move from another part of the lake, may only strike a lure with a waltz beat, ignoring tango or hard rock rhythms.

Inactive or semiactive fish holding below the thermocline, if they strike at all, usually demand a mood-matching lure, in this case, something appearing to move slow and easy in a quiet, subdued manner. Which raises the obvious question: How do you present fast, big-wiggling lures to active fish at one depth, and smooth-moving dipsy-doodlers to sluggish salmon at another level? The answer is in knowing how different lures act at various trolling speeds and, once the big movers are sorted out in your mind from less active lures, you have only to match the different actions to the moods of the different fish.

An oversimplification, granted, but it's where we can start. This means experimentation, running various lures alongside the boat at various speeds, and categorizing each style of action. You'll find some lures work well at extremely wide speed ranges, and others perform best at midrange speeds. Still others demand slow trolling speeds. Ignoring for the moment that factory-built actions of most lures are easily altered to provide any action you want—fast, slow, or in between—the only remaining chore is to combine the slow wigglers and the hard wigglers that work well at the same trolling speed.

For example, the famous J-Plug has gained its reputation for two reasons: 1) J-Plugs catch lots of fish and 2) the reason they catch a lot of fish is that J-Plugs (and similar lures such as Tiger Plugs and Squid Plugs) have an extremely erratic darting action that works well at almost any trolling speed. The action can be made even more erratic by combining these plugs with dodgers. Quieter moving lures that work best in the same speed range, 3 to 5 miles-per-hour, include the equally famous Northport Nailer and Andy Reeker spoons, or their many imitators. There are, of course, any number of other equally good lure combinations capable of providing the harmonized mix of actions we seek.

Generally, at the risk of continued oversimplification, hard-swinging dodger and fly combinations or plug-style lures, called "body baits" (as compared to wafer-thin metal spoons) are best used for actively feeding fish. Slower moving metal wobblers work best when used to entice sluggish, deeper-holding fish into action. Other plugs capable of catching fish at high trolling speeds are Dandy-Glos, Rapalas, Rebels, and Thinfins, to name only a few. Spoons that get wet most often off the stern of our boat are Williams Wablers, Little Cleos, Alpena Diamonds, Westports, Locos, Acmes, and Millers.

Always remember that salmon activity levels or underwater rhythms cannot only change each day, but each hour at times, the three prime offshore feeding periods often occurring early in the morning, near mid-day, and again in the evening. Once the thermocline level is determined, and "halfway" coho salmon water fished where bottom is twice the depth of the thermocline, my normal angling practice is then to wander further offshore, with, I would hope, one or two coho in the box, in search of bigger and better chinook. Skinny spoons that work well at fast trolling speeds are used in order to explore as quickly as possible offshore water where kings were found the previous day or, if we weren't on the lake, where other reliable anglers had found the big salmon. As dodgers aren't usable at such speeds, at least one lure will have one or two small Colorado or Indiana spinners in front of it as an additional attractor.

Given any kind of luck, we'll mark bait fish or salmon on sonar, or find a visible surface slick indicating a difference in lake surface temperature. At that point, we'll slow the boat down to try different lures at various trolling speeds, watching sonar closely and hoping to find any kind of hard evidence of salmon or some indication of what mood they might be in that day. This last vital bit of information comes, of course, with the first strike of the day. Lure speed and action that attract one fish will likely draw others. Until that first important strike does occur, the changing of lures, rerigging of tackle, and varying of techniques, make time pass very quickly. If need be, on a really slow day, we may even raise all the rods and cruise at high speed even further off shore until we do find an upwelling. If I can find a five-degree break in surface temperature I'm fairly sure we'll put fish in the boat; give me a ten-degree break and I know I will.

One point I didn't realize about thermal breaks, always assuming until recently that any upwelling would be visible on the surface or easily measured by a temperature gauge, is that there are times when the break can be hidden by a thin layer of normal warm surface water. I've never encountered it, and have only heard of it happening once. However, Lake Ontario charterboater Roger Lowden, who works out of Hilton, New York, reported in the *Great Lakes Steelheader* magazine (May 1984) of finding and fishing a typical upwelling some three miles offshore in about 240 feet of water. He writes: "We were making good catches of rainbows, cohos, and lake trout and we could easily find the break [48–44] with a surface gauge. On the fourth day we couldn't find the break; everywhere we went the surface temperature read about 48 yet we continued to catch fish only over that 220 to 260 depth range . . . Finally it occurred to us to lower the temperature sensor and we quickly found the answer. When we put the sensor down about six feet we discovered that the break was there after all. Apparently the light offshore wind had blown a layer of 48 degree water about two feet thick over the top of the break and our surface gauge was only registering the warmer layer."

But we still need the first fish of the day (or somehow realize an angling dream of having a talking salmon to call on for advice) to judge which style of lure presentation is best. Even more intriguing is to try to

A twenty-four-pound chinook salmon is swung aboard the author's boat. Fish of this size are typical of the salmon found each summer by Great Lakes anglers.

guess why it is best. All we know is that some fish are momentarily deceived into believing a wiggling piece of molded plastic or stamped metal is edible. Others, no doubt a huge majority, aren't fooled. Not at that moment. Or not by that specific lure. That decision is only made as a fish makes it first or second approach to the lure (underwater films show salmon rarely make more than two passes at a lure), swimming alongside at extremely close range, almost brushing it with its lateral line, reading vibrations, making unknown, instinctive judgments, before turning away to disappear into the depths or, on its next pass, increasing speed in an intercepting attack movement and viciously engulfing the lure. The persistent belief that salmon stun a target by slamming it with their tails before striking is only another angling myth, incidentally. If true, many salmon would be tail hooked. Can you imagine the ensuing struggle to boat such fish! A foul-hooked offshore salmon would fight like a fish three times its size. But I have never heard of it happening.

As anglers on the Great Lakes, almost the only basic assumption we can make about a lure is that the more lifelike or natural it appears, the more fish it will catch. In addition, effectiveness can sometimes be increased by deliberately making a lure behave in an abnormal fashion, by making it act as though it were crippled, for example. With luck, some fish will say, Hey, here's an easy meal. But even that abnormality is still very much natural behavior. Predators of all kinds instinctively seek out and kill the misfits and sick first. Taking advantage of this age-old survival-of-the-fittest law, I consistently run a side-swimming crippled minnow lure, an "outlaw" that is positioned well above or well below the other lures. This lure, or lures, as I have two types, will either be a black-and-white Heddon Prowler with a big slash of red in the gill area, or an old, no longer manufactured white-and-green True Temper Crippled Shad. Both are bass lures. I have yet to see their counterparts in any other Great Lakes salmon tackle box. But over the years they have probably produced as many fish on an hourly-use ratio as any body lure I own.

Another basic assumption is that, if one lure can draw the attention of a fish, two or five or ten lures will attract attention that much more effectively. A classic example of multilure presentation is found in continued use of time-honored gang-trolls or "cowbells" by many lake trout anglers. These trolling rigs are simply a series of differently sized spinning blades used in front of a lure to simulate a school of minnows. A Great Lakes salmon dodger or flasher plays a similar role. With power of numbers in mind, I often deliberately position lures to simulate a small school of forage fish swimming fairly close together. The exception, as noted, is one crippled outlaw deliberately left out of the pack. The more rods on the boat, and the more lures I can use, the better the simulation.

Using Tackle for Maximum Catches

We try to achieve two basic goals when positioning downrigger gear in deep water. First, we want to stagger lures from below the thermocline to above it, where water temperature is most comfortable for the fish we're seeking. In the case of salmon, most of us fish water that registers fifty-one to fifty-four degrees on our temperature probes. Lake trout will be found close to bottom in about forty-seven-degree water, usually where the thermocline intersects with bottom. Big roaming rainbows like water in the middle fifties. Brown trout, also thermocline-bottom oriented, can survive quite well in sixty-degree water.

The second goal is to run lures not only where the fish we seek are most likely to be found, but to run them in such a way that the lures are more noticeable or attractive to food-seeking predators. This brings us head-on to one other Great Lakes tackle-rigging rule we'd better dump into our angling bucket right now: The fewer the rods on the boat, the more important it is to stack two, three, or four lures on each line, whatever number the law allows. (Ontario has a four-hook rule that lets me run up to four single-hooked lures off one line. A treble counts as a single hook. So if I'm using a body lure with three treble hooks I can only use a lure with one hook, treble or single, in conjunction with it. However it's done, the combined total on each line can't exceed four hooks.)

Normal routine with, say, eight rods is to run one lure five to ten feet below the thermocline, two lures near the base of the thermocline, two ranging in the middle, and two near or above the top of the thermocline. The eighth lure I'll run shallow, especially if I suspect rainbows might be feeding near the surface. If sonar is marking fish, of course, lure depth will be adjusted accordingly. But using shallow-running lures far offshore does pay off with fish occasionally. One of my favorite rigging methods is to flatline the lure off the stern, letting out enough line so the lure is riding just about where the wake of the boat washes out. The calmer the water, the greater the distance. If the gulls aren't trying to eat the lure (my record to date is three hooked gulls in one day), I like it running close enough to the surface so that in a small swell it breaks water periodically. If you've ever watched a crippled bait fish swimming on its side at the surface, trying to dive but not able to do it, you'll know exactly what we're trying to emulate. When the gulls are extra hungry, a rubber-core sinker is added in front of the lure to sink it out of sight.

With only three or four rods to work with, I'll use releases or the elastic bands mentioned in an earlier discussion to stack lures into a fairly tight, imitative pattern of schooled fish. Which, in these circumstances, certainly answers that old query How far back should I set lures behind the cannonballs? (See sketch.) If you're stacking, you have no choice but to run lures about the same distance off the main lines, your pattern being controlled by the restricted length of your secondary lines. In fact, ten to twelve feet is about maximum length if you hope to bring fish into a waiting net in normal fashion. When a stacked line is released by a fish, it slides down and releases the main line holding the lower lure. Because the secondary line can only slide as far as the bottom lure or dodger, you can see the problem if you have a fish flopping around at the end of a twenty-foot secondary line and you can't reel it any closer than ten feet to the boat because of the other lure. Another penalty of stacking lures will become apparent on boating your first fish. The more lures stacked on one line, the greater the mess to untangle when a fish is netted. But because secondary lures are normally lightweight, single-hook flutterspoons, the unsnarling job isn't that much of a problem. If

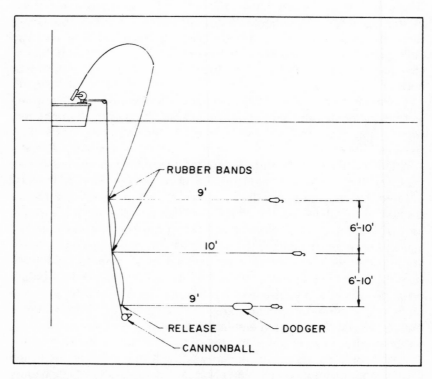

Stacking lures off one line or running more than one rod off a downrigger can simulate schooled baitfish to attract salmon. (*Illustration by Kurt Wolfram*)

you're using lures with treble hooks, however, you can figure on five or ten minutes of net-clearing work for every fish you net.

But stacking lures does provide an opportunity to make quick experiments with a wide variety of different types and colors of lures on slow fishing days when such experimentation is best done. Although the risk of fouling tackle on such short leads is minimal, it's also a basic offshore fishing rule to put the heavier, deepest-sinking lures, the dodger-fly combinations or diving body plugs, at the bottom of the stack. Being at the bottom they, of course, can be run any distance back of the ball. Flat-running flutterspoons go up top. Once the fish are found, if the first salmon boated snapped at a purple-spotted pink Wunderspoon, then a few more of the same will naturally go over the side. In actual fishing practice, I'll only stack lures until the first fish is boated. That kind of rigging is equivalent, or so I think of it, to waving a flag. And once the flag has been noticed, especially by big chinook, you'll find all those lures dangling off one line tend to create problems while fighting or netting fish. One of the extra lures will snag another line or get hung up at the worst possible time in netting. There's some kind of Murphy's Law at work here. The bigger the salmon, the more you want it in the boat, the greater the problem.

There's more than one way to run secondary lures, of course. I might stack an extra bait on a lazy day because of another, easier rigging technique (that and ever-present curiosity). There are no rubber bands or release clips of any kind involved in the process. Just snap the secondary line onto the rod line after the cannonball has been lowered into position. The flutterspoon or light spinner-streamer combination (this last used for rainbow trout) will slowly wiggle its way down, all by itself, to where your rod line has its maximum bend or "belly" between the rod and the cannonball, the bend created by the line being pulled through the water. This point will be halfway between the surface and the ball. If the cannonball is set at fifty feet, I know my secondary slider lure is working for me at twenty-five feet.

When you're only running a single lure off each rod, the next question (one I'm certainly often asked) is how far back should the dodger-fly combo or lure be behind the cannonball? My answer is always the same. It depends on what you hope to catch. (If you've already caught a fish you don't need to ask, you use the system that's working that day.) For coho, I'll generally shorten everything up close to the ball. Spookier chinooks usually demand a comparatively long lead, fifty to seventy-five feet or more within fifty feet of the surface. Chinooks at deeper depths seem to have a progressively greater sense of security the closer they are to bottom, so you can rig your leads shorter. If both coho and chinook are around, you obviously run both short and long leads off the balls. Give the fish a choice. Experiment. Keep trying different styles of rigging.

If you're in coho country, the biggest reason for running lures close to cannonballs is that the balls themselves appear to attract these fish. I've even gone so far as to attach strips of light-reflecting prism tape to the balls to make them even more visible. In fact, to digress a bit, if you're using fish-shaped cannonballs, which tend to wander around, amuse yourself some day by discarding your dodgers and attaching lures, via normal release clips, directly to the cannonballs. There are all kinds of interesting games you can play out there.

How far back behind a dodger should you tie a lure? The general rule is: The more built-in action the lure has, the longer the lead. You don't want a lure so close to the dodger that its natural wobbling action is completely destroyed. You just want to accent it by adding more side-to-side movement. Under normal conditions most wobbling spoons, for example, are tied in about twelve to eighteen inches behind the dodger. A fly or squid, not having any built-in action whatsoever (although you can now buy some with plastic lips) should be much closer, six to ten inches, even though most will be purchased with a much longer strand of heavy monofilament attached to them than you need.

How tightly line release tensions are set varies from boat to boat, depending on the past experiences of each skipper. Many anglers like a fairly heavy release setting, believing the tighter tension produces a higher percentage of firmly hooked fish. Most of us, belonging to the moderate school of thinking on the subject, use a midway setting if only because it seems the safest thing to do. If the tension is too light you can run into a problem when setting the rod, the line sometimes not being firmly held by the release when the rod is reel-cranked into a tight semicircle in the downrigger.

10

Tricks with Lures

Angling is the most difficult of all field sports. It requires all the manual dexterity that the others do, and brings more into play the qualities of the mind, observation and the reasoning faculties. In shooting and hunting, the dogs do the observation and the reasoning part of the business, and the sportsmen the mechanical; but the angler has not only to find out where his fish are but catch them . . . by an art of deception.
— *W. C. Stewart,* The Practical Angler

The biggest problem with tinkering with tackle is overcoming a major psychological barrier: New factory-built lures always look so pretty. In fact, if you hadn't admired a lure's artistic color, design or the way it looked in the store, chances are you wouldn't have bought it. So why change anything? Why alter obvious perfection?

One answer is that a comparatively simple alteration might result in catching a lot more fish. Not that tackle manufacturers don't work hard to make the best possible product. They do. And considering budgetary restrictions and the necessity of coping with the generalized demands of a huge geographic market, they are amazingly successful. The end product is a lure anyone can use to catch fish anywhere. The only snag is that concerns with local angling conditions or special needs of individual buyers are an unaffordable manufacturing luxury. This is where a tackle tinkerer can play a major role. Outside of having a lot of fun, he can also occasionally come up with a much better lure, if only because it is better suited to his personal angling style.

There are few anglers who haven't already altered some of their fishing tackle anyway. Anyone who has ever used a clamp-on sinker has tinkered with a lure. What perch or walleye fisherman hasn't improved catches on a slow day by adding a small worm to the trailing treble hook of a favorite spinner? I know a few stream trout wet fly anglers who, if frustrated badly enough, are not above adding a worm or, even better, a trout egg or two to their feathered offerings.

Similar basic time-tested lure modifications include adding a spinner or series of spinners in front of a lure. Carried to its extreme, you can wind up with the long, flashy "cowbell" or "Christmas tree" chain of spinners used by many Great Lakes lake trout anglers. In addition, those same anglers will often add a strip of freshly cut trout belly to the hook of the tail-end spoon as still another fish-enticing form of tackle modification. With salmon, however, one spinner immediately ahead of the lure is all that's necessary. Use too long a chain, and these more aggressive fish will often strike the spinners rather than the lure, obviously thinking they're slamming into a small cluster of forage fish.

One of the simplest changes I make to Great Lakes tackle involves replacing traditional freshwater treble hooks on most spoons with the stouter single Siwash hooks long used by West Coast salmon anglers. These single hooks, although more difficult to sink into fish, have less chance of pulling out and, with fewer hook points to snarl in mesh, make it much easier to remove a fish from a net. Another real bonus is the added ease and speed of releasing a fish when you have only a single hook to disengage from its mouth. The less you handle a fish the better its chances of survival. Most of the time, a played-out fish doesn't even need to be removed from the water. You don't have to touch it at all. You simply lean out over the boat with a pair of longnose pliers, work the fish within easy reach by grabbing the fishing line, then use the pliers to grasp the protruding shank of the hook as close to the hook point as possible—you can often slide the pliers partly inside the fish's mouth— and using the weight of the fish for leverage, take the hook out with a snaplike twisting pull. Over the years so many of us switched to single hooks that most Great Lakes lure manufacturers eventually paid attention to what we were doing. Many now rig their lures with heavier single hooks. Other lure makers give us a choice.

Another trick with tackle originated in what now seems like a long-ago, almost paleozoic bass-fishing era of innocent youth. (Does anyone even fish for bass today with big salmon so close to home?) Anyway, the trick goes back to guys like Jason Lucas, a top outdoor writer of the day, who argued very convincingly that bass, or any fish, looking upward at a shallow-running lure could see a black-bellied plug a heck of a lot better against surface light than a traditional white-bellied artificial. Reverse the situation. If a fish is topside looking down, a lure being retrieved over a dark lake bottom is more visible with white on top. Such color contrast made sense then and still makes sense today. Why copy the natural protective coloration of fish when we want to draw as much attention as possible to our lures? What tends to work best, I think, in the words of Englishman W. A. Adamson in his delightful book *The Enterprising Angler,* is a lure that is "an affront to the entire community of fish . . . an irregularity too flagrant to be tolerated."

Just don't try to tell a lure manufacturer he's been painting his lures the wrong way all these years. He won't like it. He knows, to give him his due, that if he did reverse normal color schemes, painting light on top, dark on bottom, his products would be shunned by most anglers as though they had some kind of infectious disease. So if you're going to start reversing colors, you're going to have to do it yourself.

I've never had enough nerve to go out and buy sufficient enamel paint and brushes to repaint all my lures. The results of my early experiments were too ugly. In fact, that is being polite. Those drip-dried plugs, although they caught fish, looked so bad I wouldn't even open my tackle box in public. Much better are my timid efforts of more recent years. I like to think of them as "artistic modifications." Rather than paint the whole underside of a lure black, for example, the use of two temporary strips of masking tape as painting guides can result in an equally effective, eye pleasing, sharp-edged bar of black running the length of the belly. This contrast color strip can be as broad or as narrow or as tapered as you wish. If you are a real artist with freehand drawing skills, another nice touch is to paint in a series of tapered "ribs" curving out of the black belly strip. And why stop there? If you have some bright red paint in the basement, try adding simulated gill plates on each side of the lure. Red is a real fish "turn-on" color.

The only rule to remember when repainting any lure is that light colors always go on first. If you try any of the fluorescent colors, you'll find a reflective undercoating of white paint is necessary to get the sheen you seek. To add professional-looking fish scales, in case you think they're necessary (and they'll certainly create extra pride in your finished effort), you'll need some spray-on paint (cans of auto enamel work well) and some tulle netting available at fabric stores. Simply tape or staple the material to a heavy cardboard or wooden frame (or use an embroidery hoop), hold the lure firmly against the netting, and apply a light coat of spray. The accent here is on "light." Odds are you'll overpaint. As the application is, admittedly, tricky at first, try a few practice runs on a piece of scrap wood or an old lure you've written off as junk. Another point

A variety of Great Lakes salmon lures "doctored" by the author include (*from top to bottom*): a belly-painted ThinFin, a tandem-hooked bucktail streamer and spinner, a Toby spoon with a plastic eye and scent strip, and a Williams Wabler with a strip of fluorescent tape added. The hollow ridge on the back of the wabler has also been tapped and filled with lint to hold fish-attracting scent. Scents in the background range from commercial mixtures to oil of anise, sardine oil, and WD-40.

to remember is that if you don't like the result, once you remove the netting you can always wipe everything clean with some turpentine before the paint dries. You can also use a strip of plastic window screening to add professional scale effects to any lure.

How about the eyes? Are they big enough? Are they colorful enough? This is important because predators zero in on eyes. You can either paint eyes larger to add prominence or, if you don't think your first effort looks that great, and it probably won't, you can simply cut out bigger and better eyes from light reflecting stick-on prism tape available in various bright colors. Even simpler, use a paper puncher. Tape works extremely well on thin flutter spoons. Best of all, especially on plugs with painted eyes or no eyes at all, are plastic glue-on eyes hobby shops carry in a variety of sizes for amateur dollmakers. Because the "pupil" is free moving and rattles when shaken, the plastic eyes add fish-attracting noise to a lure as well as extra reflective visual charm.

If you really like the rattle effect, lures are commercially available with a rattle built into the bodies. Or you can do the same thing yourself by drilling holes into your favorite hollow salmon plugs, inserting small split shots, and resealing the holes. Just don't go too heavy with the lead. Although two split shots will no doubt rattle twice as well as one, three or more might harm the action of the lure.

I use far more prism tape than paint these days. Painting can be a bit of a time-consuming trap anyway. Once you start messing around with aerosol sprays instead of painting by brush (and brushes always leave marks), the next step is cutting out cardboard lure templates so you can feather or blend body colors just like the pros. Then you'll find you need other gadgets such as masking stencils for spoons, paint spray collectors, and lure holders. And then, suddenly, you may be in the same situation as the fly tiers I know who find they're having so much fun they'd rather tie flies than fish. Whatever happens, you'll know you're in real trouble once you start whittling out your own lure bodies. At that point, the disease is incurable.

It's far easier and faster to change the color of a lure with tape and a pair of scissors. Plain spoons are quickly given a bright slash of extra color. Silver reflective tape adds minnow-like flash to the sides or top of any drab plug. Tape also saves money. Instead of buying sets of six or more different colored lures, one or two of the same lures, plus different colored cards of tape, give you the same variety of color mix at far less cost. If other anglers are reporting via radio that fish are taking "blue and silver," with tape you can easily offer the fish the colors they want even though you might not have a factory-painted blue-and-silver lure in your box.

Another interesting way to spend a few evenings is to start boiling up liquid fish scents, a simple way to test your marriage and neighborhood friendships; or, equally interesting, start modifying metal spoons or plastic lures so the scent doesn't immediately wash off in the water, something I've been fooling around with for years.

The historic attraction of fish to certain odors is, I think, well known. Like most eastern anglers, I was taught the vital necessity of touching lures only with clean, unstained hands (if you were handling an outboard motor you scrubbed off any grease or gas in almost surgical fashion before daring to touch a lure). So it was a major shock to me as a teenager to see West Coast commercial salmon trollers casually rig a spoon that had been carelessly left in oily bilge water in the bottom of their open boats and catch salmon with it, almost as soon as it was put in the water at times. To a visiting easterner, this was angling heresy of the worst sort. The sky should have opened up and zapped them with sea gull droppings if not lightning. "Hell, fish like the smell of oil," they'd all say when questioned.

Never having forgotten those experiences, and with the introduction of the same oil-loving Pacific salmon to the Great Lakes, it was a short, easy step for me on a quiet day to give a lure a quick coating of fishing reel oil surreptitiously. I also used WD-40, a highly scented lubricant available in spray cans that a lot of boaters use on everything from outrigger pulleys to sticky cabin-door locks. Because of ingrained eastern angling guilt complexes, we applied the oil when no one was looking— and I say "we," meaning a couple of charterboating friends in the same harbor also started using oil at the time—knowing that if clients ever saw us doing it they would immediately categorize us as being totally insane, and maybe demand to go straight back to shore. If questioned, and I never was, I had it figured I would simply reply the lubricant made the lure slip through the water easier and wait for the next reaction.

I don't think any of us used oil often enough as a fish attractor to prove anything, probably because we felt so foolish any time we tried it. Whatever the reason—lack of a fair trial, you name it—oil didn't produce any extra fish. Not in obvious numbers at least. But the age-old effectiveness of scent, whether originating from live bait or liquids such as commercially available oil of anise, kept bubbling up in my thoughts periodically. The biggest challenge, or so it seemed at the time, was figuring out how to modify lures so the scent was released slowly. The objective, of course, was to create behind each lure a long-lasting, inviting trail of fishy perfume that would drive all salmon in the lake crazy. So, for lack of a better idea, I started drilling holes in lures, tamping the cavities with lint from the family clothes dryer, and injecting various liquid scents into the cloth fibers with a hypodermic needle.

One commercial lure, my starting point, was almost ready-made for use of scent—Williams Wablers have a hollow ridge running along the top, which only needed to be tapped. Other early favorites were soft-wooded J9 and J11 Rapalas. The holes were angled into the balsa-wood body on each side of the lure, about where the gills would be on a natural fish. The only drawback, after I don't know how many nurses and doctors failed to supply hypodermic needles (they all said their hospitals threw hundreds of used needles out every day), was convincing a corner store druggist I wasn't some kind of junkie. "You want a hypodermic needle for WHAT?" he roared, letting everyone in the store think he was dealing with a weirdo addict. But I got the needles. He was still laughing when I left.

Once reflective tape came on the market, the ease of applying this stick-on material suggested a much simpler answer to the scent application problem. Why not glue a narrow strip of indoor-outdoor carpet, or any other material that would hold liquid scent, on the back of the lure? I did. And it worked. Still another refinement since then, used primarily with single-hooked spoons, is to clip a small triangle-shaped piece of cloth, preferably bright red in color, to the hook ring. Even simpler, as I later figured out (and why it took so long I'm not quite sure), is to just impale the cloth onto the hook so the material flutters behind the lure. You can do the same thing with strips of smelt skin cut much like pork rind. Home-brew scents I've used range from distilled smelt oil to boiled-down bologna juice. Ready-made scents include oil from cans of sardines, leftover juices from a lunch of freshly made sardine sandwiches, and store-bought hormonal fish scents, which manufacturers claim can be applied to lures without gluing or drilling.

Do the hormone-based scents work? Dr. Greg Bambenek, a Duluth, Minnesota psychiatrist marketing a liquid fish attractor (The Juice), says fish instinctively smell a lure while following it prior to striking. "If no natural fish odor comes from the lure or if there's a smell of plastic, wood, metal, or L-serine, they frequently won't bite," he says. Jerry Gibbs, fishing editor of *Outdoor Life* magazine, reported in June, 1984, that Lake Superior charterboat skippers testing Bambenek's pheromone-based product increased salmon, steelhead, and lake trout catches 25 to 30 percent. Two other believers in scent are Toronto anglers Gord Jackson and Peter Bauer, who credit coating their lures with anise oil for a two thousand dollar first-place finish in a special Lake Ontario two-man competition a couple of years ago. Anise oil is available in drug stores in spray or liquid form. Also available, and well worth trying, is cod liver oil, a once famous (but horrible tasting) wintertime tonic.

I think the recent discovery and use of specific scent molecules to trigger fish into feeding or striking a scented lure makes the use of scent an important Great Lakes angling tool. These new developments—and the potential of such hormonal substances in terms of arousing, attracting, and catching fish is only now being fully understood—are as different from traditional techniques as a space shuttle flight is from a horse-and-buggy ride. These newly discovered substances trigger reactions like mind-controlling drugs, the brain predictably responding to a specific odor just as Pavlov's dogs automatically drooled on hearing a feeding bell. Such reactions are not guesswork. They are measured by precise space-age lab tests, some involving the use of oscilloscopes to register electronically brain responses of anesthetized fish to specific scent molecules. Other experiments are carried out with free-swimming fish in tanks.

Pheromones taken from bait fish extracts can duplicate the communicatory scent used by forage fish to stay together in schools. Another pheromone copies the scent of fear given off by small fish under attack. Both smells, of course, are quite familiar to the trophy-sized fish sought by anglers, especially the sharp-nosed salmon. A third pheromone is based on the sex odor of the various fish species, making the attacking fish even more excited. Plant-based amino acids called kairomones reportedly reduce fear.

Chemists have also found a way to isolate and neutralize an amino acid called L-serine (mentioned earlier), an amazingly strong fish repellant found on all salmonid predators from sea lions to humans. Salmon can detect this acid in quantities as small as one part in eighty billion, or the equivalent of 0.02 of a drop in a 23,000-gallon swimming pool. As some of us exude more L-serine than others, the amount often varying from day to day, this discovery possibly explains that age-old mystery why one angler sometimes catches all the fish while a companion, fishing the same water, using the same technique, catches nothing.

As scientists gain an even better understanding of the olfactory senses of fish, even more potent scents can be expected in the future. The well-known Mann's Bait Company of Eufaula, Alabama, is the latest research-oriented firm to come up with a fish feeding stimulant. Their substance, called only FS-454, made its debut last year on Mann's Augertail Worm and Cajun Crawdad bass lures. A research team at the Duke University Marine Laboratory in Beaufort, North Carolina, headed by Dr. Joseph Bonaventura and Dr. Dan Rittschof, both experts in biochemistry and fresh and saltwater biology, say rigorous tests show they have a real winner. "If bass don't eat this product, they don't eat food," Dr. Rittschof was quoted as saying in a company press release. Their success will no doubt trigger additional research by the same company to find chemical attractors for other fish species, including salmon.

Where tackle manufacturers really get twitchy is when I start bending and twisting products around to change the actions of their lures or dodgers. Unfortunately, most of us tend to elevate factory-built lure action to the same high plateau as the need for squeaky-clean lures. In fact, one of the most widely accepted of all angling maxims, repeated season after season in most angling journals is, when trolling, always to check lure action against boat speed prior to use. So you wind up either adjusting boat speed (usually slowing down) to get the proper action of the lure, even though fish might strike only faster-moving lures that day. Or, equally ridiculous, you go the other way and restrict yourself to specific lures, all with a similar action, which happen to wiggle the right way with whatever trolling speed you might be using. One question: What do you do when fish want a big-wiggling slow-speed lure zapped past them at high speed? Or what if they demand a thinner high-speed lure fished slowly? The answer, on my boat, is to do what you have to do to the lip of a plug or the bend of a metal spoon to make it work at any speed you wish. It's your lure. You paid for it, you can do what you want with it.

You can't adjust some lures without performing major body surgery. The worst offender is the Flatfish style of lure. You either troll fairly slowly or you don't use them. But the majority of wobbling plugs can be adjusted to different boat speeds. In some cases, a tune-up might be needed because a lure came out of the factory the wrong way. Usually this just involves twisting the eye screw to straighten up an erratic swimmer. On lures with fixed eyes, such as Rapalas, you can minimize their action for high-speed trolling by bending the eye up, or increase the action for slow trolling by bending the eye down. Most spoons will fish well at almost any speed. The only metal lures that consistently need "improvements" are lightweight flutterspoons, which tend to be under set or too straight for the erratic wiggling action I prefer. Because flutterspoons are normally fished behind dodgers, I suspect manufacturers figure the dodgers whipping back and forth will supply the extra action some of us want. But others of us also fish flutterspoons "clean," at slow speed without dodgers, especially for early season brown trout in shallow water, and, along with the Flatfish, we want a wide-swinging, big-wiggling chunk of silver metal out there at such times.

Next to flutterspoons, I spend more time bending dodgers into different shapes than anything else. You can easily adjust these brightly painted metal plates by increasing or decreasing the angles of their fore and aft bends to give you whatever action you want out of them. Everyone will have their own idea of what is right or wrong in the wiggle department. So do some experimenting, bending metal, until the action of the dodger looks right to you.

One of the most important points about deepwater fishing with dodg-

ers—possibly one of the most important points to be made in this book—
is that you should always start a fishing day with at least two completely
different styles of dodgers working for you: one that's really sweeping
back and forth erratically, jumping the lure around behind it, and the
other set in more sedate fashion. Although salmon, unlike trout, aren't
truly selective in choice of lures, they can be very picky at times about
lure presentations. By giving them a choice, it takes only a few fish in
the box to determine what the preference of the day is, and to adjust
other tackle accordingly. To avoid spending a lot of time adjusting dodgers every day, the simplest approach once basic modifications are made
is to keep the big-action dodgers separate from the slow movers and use
them as you need them, preset. If you absolutely refuse to reshape dodgers
by hand, about the only alternative is to adjust the length of connecting
line between the dodgers and the lures. The shorter the distance, of
course, the more erratic the lure action.

There might be days when your favorite fly or squid-and-dodger
You can also play a lot of tackle tricks with the iridescent strips of
plastic used as skirts in lures such as the Luhr Jensen Twinkle Squid,
Sparkle Fly, or Michigan Squid. A half-dozen or so individual strips of
this glittering plastic glued on to the rear of any spoon adds extra lifelike
motion to a lure that fish like as well as anglers do on seeing its enticing
wiggle in the water. When attaching the strands, glue the material with
the open ends of the plastic toward the head of the lure so the strips
billow out around the hook.

A West Coast variation of this stunt, which can really pay off on the
Great Lakes in extra salmon and trout, is to take any lure such as a No.
4 J-Plug and glue a skirt from a Luhr Jensen Super Hoochytail on the end
of it. Just remove the leader and hooks from the Hoochytail body, cut
off about a quarter-inch of its head, and slide it up the tail of the lure as
far as it will go. Roll it back a bit, maybe a quarter of an inch, apply a
few drops of glue, then snug it forward over the glue and, presto, you've
just made your first unique fish catcher that some innovative, well-read
lure manufacturer is bound to produce commercially sooner or later.

There might be days when your favorite fly or squid-and-dodger
combination is producing short strikes, the fish mouthing the ends of the
skirt, and, being cantankerous to start with, hanging on just enough to
trigger cannonball releases. At that point, they just swim away, without
touching a hook. They might even be laughing as they leave, for all I
know. One solution is to tie in a trailer hook off the hook of the lure,
either a single or small treble, using only enough monofilament so the
trailer barely reaches the end of the skirt. After that you only need to wait
for a fish to make the mistake of nipping at another lure.

The same trailer tie-in technique also allows you to run two separate lures together. My best combination is an old Maine Green Ghost landlocked-salmon streamer pattern attached four to six inches behind the trailing hook of any spoon fished behind a dodger. The dodger adds zap to the spoon and the spoon, in turn, adds an erratic wiggle to the streamer. The fact that this obviously reversed, underwater scenario of a tiny fish chasing a larger fish (the spoon), which is chasing an even larger dodger, doesn't seem backward to salmon can only mean that the unpredictable fish we seek aren't as observant or as smart as we like to think they are. Or to put it another way, the illusory creation of life is more important than the sequential order of its appearance.

11

Big Fish Tactics

He who fishes without conviction seldom catches fish.
—Old Irish Angler

So you want to win a major Great Lakes salmon fishing tournament or set a new International Game Fish Association world line-class record? Great! The world needs more people willing to actively pursue a dream. Such a goal is certainly obtainable. We all know tournaments are won, and IGFA records are broken, by lucky anglers every year. In fact, as far as IGFA records are concerned, I can take you out on the lake tomorrow and guarantee a world-record catch. But I'm getting ahead of myself. All I want to say at the moment, considering the astronomical odds normally involved in such endeavors, is that you are going to need bushels of plain old-fashioned luck.

One of the few tournament anglers I know of who racks up trophy fish with any regularity is Tom Cassenti, an avid New York fisherman who currently holds the Great Lakes chinook record. Cassenti, a Lockport, New York fishing tackle dealer, has boated four outstanding kings since 1976, all caught on the same type and color of lure, a silver-and-blue-stripe Miller 06 spoon. Equally interesting, all the fish were taken out of

Smiles come easy when a forty-pound-plus salmon is held up for a camera. **This particular fish was the winning entry in a recent New York Lake Ontario derby, earning the happy angler a fully equipped offshore boat.** (*Photo courtesy of New York Division of Tourism*)

the same section of Lake Ontario, near Wilson, New York at the same time of year, September, while trolling the shallows for brown trout (a revealing aspect of Great Lakes trophy angling). His run of trophies began in 1976 with a 38.5-pounder, briefly recognized as a New York record. He beat that fish the following year with a 41.5-pounder, and in 1978 boated an even larger 44-pounder for an unprecedented three straight years of success. On September 18, 1980, still flatlining for big brown trout, and trailing his favorite lure about five feet down in twelve feet of water, he whacked into a giant chinook that officially weighed in at forty-seven pounds some twelve hours after being boated. The four-year-old male fish measured 54.5 inches long. Its girth measurement was thirty-one inches. Cassenti rightly claims his trophy would have topped the still-unattained fifty-pound mark if it had been weighed more quickly. Biologists estimate a fish out of water twelve hours loses about 6 percent of its original body weight.

Cassenti's angling success doesn't necessarily mean that if you want big chinook you should deliberately fish for something else, although the system obviously works and, based on the zany things I've seen happen on the lakes, probably makes as much sense as anything. Big fish can be found anywhere, anytime. But if you want a truly classic example of a tournament angler being hit over the head by Lady Luck more than once, consider the case of Jon Van Herwynen, a Burlington, Ontario florist who won a four-wheel-drive truck, and fully equipped boat and trailer, all worth forty-five thousand dollars in the 1981 Toronto Star derby with an eighteen-pound Lake Ontario coho. To make North America's richest tournament more interesting, every competitor who enters a fish has a chance with each fish entered to win a similar prize package in a derby draw. You guessed it. In 1982, out of about twenty thousand entries in a big drum, Van Herwynen won a second truck and boat in the derby draw. As yet, however, no one, including Van Herwynen, has caught the derby's specially tagged one-million-dollar fish, which is usually up for grabs each year.

There are a few simple rules to follow that will reduce the odds a little, however. At the top of the list, most basic of all, is to go where most big fish will be found at the time you are fishing. If you're an international big-game saltwater fanatic, that might mean a costly annual holiday in New Zealand rather than fishing the Bahamas. If you're a Great Lakes salmon angler, it only means keeping track of state or provincial stocking statistics. Where were most of the chinook stocked four years ago? Which home river gets the best return of adult fish? Double-check those findings against actual tournament results. You'll find the bulk of the winners come out of the same water year after year. So it takes no real genius to determine where you should be spending your valuable fishing time. Too basic? Too simple? You'd be amazed by the number of anglers who don't consider such things. Either that or they're operating on the theory that if you're going to be hit by lightning, it can happen anywhere.

With big king salmon capable of growing about a pound a week prior to making their fall spawning run, anyone planning on taking time off work to do some serious fishing should also obviously do his or her angling near the end of any fall tournament. If the contest runs into late fall, when the weather can be really horrible, your best chance of success will likely be in the rivers, not out on the lake. Example: Last year's winners of the Ontario Federation of Anglers and Hunters province-wide Big Fish Contest, a tournament I happen to know something about, were all river fish, including the top forty-four-pounder which came out of the Credit River. Also of interest, for figuring out where your best odds are found, was that ten of the top fifteen fish in the live-release section of the contest were taken out of the lower Niagara River. So assuming I wanted to take a real crack at winning that particular contest, I'd be spending most of my time in late fall on the Niagara. Similar information is no doubt easily obtained from any other tournament you might be interested in, no matter where you fish on the Great Lakes.

Still another factor in any deliberate pursuit of extra-big fish, if not the biggest factor of all, is mental attitude, even if it comes to no more than training yourself to make methodical, daily checks of equipment prior to leaving the dock. The sometimes weird and humorous psychological aspects of world class fishing or tournament angling will be discussed later. The point being stressed here is related only to that ancient, well-worn angling lament: The big one got away. Some big fish will always get away. Why not? Bigger fish are stronger, faster, and tougher than the lesser fish most of us are used to handling. Another factor is that the majority of lost trophies are also unexpected, almost accidental fish hooked only by luck on often inadequate tackle (we can't get away from luck). And if tackle does hold together, the trophy is lost at the boat at the last minute because of an undersized landing net or an overexcited angler, or because of any of a dozen or more catastrophes that can easily occur during the stress of such moments.

The worst lost-fish horror story I can think of, one I've tried to forget but can't, involves a retired gentleman whose daughter, a working gal, treats him to an outing on my boat every year as a birthday present. The first year we had weather problems and didn't fare too well, only boating a couple of small coho. The second year, for whatever reason, maybe it was just too much talk of big fish, the client made it clear he would like nothing better than to catch a truly big fish. A forty-pounder would do nicely, he suggested.

What left me with a permanent psychic scar is that I really did get him hooked into a forty-pound-class king salmon. The fish rolled on the surface several times, giving us a good look at it. Unbelievable. And then, as I was clearing the net, preparing to boat the fish, it was suddenly gone. As always, when a fish is lost, the angler looks at you in disbelief. "What happened?" he asked. "Damned if I know," I replied. "You certainly didn't do anything wrong." I took the rod from him, reeled the slack line in, and discovered a brand new heavy-duty snap had broken right off below the clasp. I cut off the remnant of the snap and presented it to him. "There's your forty-pounder," I said, trying to laugh it off. "The only good thing about it is it'll be a lot cheaper to mount that snap than the fish."

As far as I know he still has the snap, or what's left of it. That is a classic example of the idiotic, unpredictable, mind-boggling accidents that can happen to anyone. As it turned out, I checked the other snaps, bought at the same time, found defective metal in all of them, and wound up throwing them away. They came out of Korea via a major American tackle distributor. Now, as a result of that experience, I rarely use a snap, but take the time to retie lures directly to monofilament each time I change a lure. If a snap *is* used, I attach to the end of the line an American-made heavy-duty saltwater unit that no freshwater fish could ever possibly break.

To add salt to the wound, such incidents (and other equally silly things I'd just as soon forget) happen occasionally despite daily tackle checks. But imagine the situation, the lost fish, without such precautions. I shudder to even think about the number of "accidents" that must occur to anglers out on the lake day after day who don't regularly check equipment.

I have a very strict, methodical tackle-checking routine to follow, things to do every day before clients show up. And if customers show up early, as they often do, I'll politely suggest they go take a walk or enjoy the sunrise because what I'm doing, and the order of doing it so nothing is forgotten, is vital to a successful outing. As a professional angler, and this is true of any professional in any field, it seems silly—and unprofessional—to leave anything to chance. The best time to solve a problem is before it becomes a problem. And besides, charterboat skippers have enough to think about out on the lake without worrying about equipment failures.

On my boat, not counting such obvious things as plugging downriggers into electrical outlets to make sure they are working, I first lay out lures I figure I'll start the day with, carefully touching up hook points with a sharpener if they need it (and they usually do). This one trick alone, keeping hooks sharp, will have a magical effect in transforming "knock-offs"—fish that knock a lure out of a cannonball release and swim away—into extra fish in your boat. I then assemble rods and reels, carefully checking for line abrasion by hand lining thirty or forty feet of monofilament off each reel, and then reeling the line back onto the spool between a thumb and forefinger. With this technique you can feel any rough spots that might be missed by a visual examination. Regular abrasion checks are particularly important when you're using heavy, late-season dodger-lure combinations. Because I tend to set dodgers specific distances behind cannonballs, the weight of a dodger whipping back and forth will eventually wear down any line where it is snubbed into a cannonball release. Ignore such abrasion, and you'll wind up with another fish story about a big one that got away. Reel level-wind pawls get a drop of oil, reel seat clamps are checked for tightness and then, after the rods are set in the downrigger holders and ready to go, I double-check downrigger base-plate bolts for tightness and move forward and triple-check my fuel supply. Then, after pouring a coffee, I turn the VHF radio on for the latest local marine weather forecast.

In any fishing contest, read the contest rules in advance. I know one guy now running a charterboat who actually ate a major prize-winning fish after weighing it in, now knowing that the rules of that particular tournament stated the fish must be kept frozen and available for inspection by contest officials prior to prizes being awarded.

Quite often a big fish can be entered in more than one contest, each competition having slightly different entry requirements. That local club-tournament winner might also take a spot in a state-wide contest, or earn you a place in the annual International Game Fish Association record book. You should also know basic identification keys of the various fish. In smaller derbies sponsored by local fish and game clubs, volunteers staffing the weigh-in stations are usually club members with no special knowledge. A twenty-two-pound rainbow trout that would normally walk away with first prize in the rainbow division may be worth zilch if mistakenly logged in as a chinook salmon. Such things happen, unfortunately.

With three distinct salmon species intermingling with lake, brown, and rainbow trout in the Great Lakes, fish identification can be confusing at times, especially when coho are accidentally cross-fertilized with chinook, creating an oversized, mulish coho hybrid that leaves even professional ichthyologists shaking their heads. One such coho-chinook cross created a major problem at the Toronto Star derby a few years ago. As a result derby officials changed the rules so that winners are now judged solely on weight. The biggest fish wins, no matter what it is.

There is also a great deal of confusion at times in telling Atlantic salmon and brown trout apart. I remember another big fish identification problem in Michigan back in 1981 when a state-record Atlantic salmon weighing thirty-two pounds, ten ounces was first declared a brown trout. The controversy raged for about a month until Dr. Reeve Bailey, a noted taxonomist at the University of Michigan in Ann Arbor, declared the fish a true Atlantic salmon.

The brown trout–Atlantic salmon mix-up usually stems from anglers expecting browns to have heavily spotted gill plates and bodies. So do Atlantic salmon, however, although salmon are rarely marked as heavily as browns. The simplest way to tell the two apart is the shape of the tail. The caudal fin, or tail, of a brown trout is square; Atlantic salmon have a convex-shaped tail. If you still have doubts, try counting the rows of scales from the lateral line in the middle of the body to the center or top of the fish's back directly in front of the adipose fin (a small fin located on the back of the fish right in front of the tail). Atlantic salmon will have thirteen rows or less. Browns will have a minimum of fourteen rows of scales. You might also try just lifting the fish by its tail. If you can hold it easily, like gripping a knobby handle, it's an Atlantic. Chinook have the same type of tail. If the fish tends to slip out of your hand, it's a brown. After that, if you're still arguing the matter, clip and file Dr. Bailey's address. You'll need it.

Telling Pacific salmon apart is a little easier. I tend just to glance inside the mouth while removing the lure. If the gums are white or greyish, I call it a coho. If the interior of the mouth is completely black, congratulations, you've just caught a chinook. Another fast visual aid is to note how the tail is spotted. Coho are normally spotted only on the upper half of the caudal fin. A chinook's tail is spotted top and bottom. A slightly more scientific approach is to count the rays of the anal fin (located aft of the belly behind the anal vent). A coho has twelve to thirteen anal fin rays, a chinook fifteen to seventeen. This same anal fin, incidentally, also provides an easy way to tell salmon and rainbow trout apart. If the fin is longer than it is high, it's a salmon. If the fin juts out, obviously higher than its length, it's a rainbow. Also, the anal fin of a rainbow only has nine to twelve rays.

Where anglers really get confused, however, is in trying to meet the little-known requirements of the International Game Fish Association when

This thirty-pound chinook was caught in the swirling currents of the lower Niagara River. It's a big armful of fish, even for a father-son combination. Knowledge of local, regional, and state angling contests could mean even extra bonuses. (*Photo by Leonard LePage, The Standard, St. Catharines, Ontario*)

applying for their first world-record listing. Many anglers, after frustrating months of writing letters, scurrying around trying to find long-lost witnesses, and doing other things necessary to conform to IGFA rules, have simply thrown their hands up in disgust and abandoned (in some cases) legitimate claims to world records. It needn't happen. The happy secret is in knowing the rules in advance so applications are properly documented at the time they're being filled in. Problems arise only when you try to authenticate a claim months after you've caught the fish.

One basic point to remember is that the IGFA recognizes angling accomplishments two different ways: Line-Class records and All-Tackle records. The All-Tackle division, in which you're competing against everybody, recognizes the single largest fish on varying line classes, depending on species. For example, the heaviest line you can use on chinook salmon (as crazy as it might sound) is 130-pound-test, a carryover from big-game saltwater fishing. Lake trout can't be caught on line heavier than 80-pound-test. Maximum line strength for coho salmon, brown trout, and rainbow trout is 50-pound-test. The Line-Class group, in which you're competing only against fish caught on similar line strengths, is broken down into ten categories, 2-pound-test, 4-pound, 8-, 12-, 16-, 20-, 30-, 50-, 80-, and 130-pound-test.

That's not all. Before we get away from lines and explore related IGFA tackle restrictions, there are a few other things you should know. One is that you must send in a sample of your line with your application. If you used casting or spinning gear, the IGFA wants to see a minimum of fifty feet of line, plus leader if you used one. If you took the big fish on a fly rod, you must send in the fly, entire leader, and one inch of line, all still connected together as it was when you hooked the fish. And try to resist the temptation to jam the line sample into an envelope. Wrap it around a notched piece of stiff cardboard. If it can't be easily unwound, it won't be accepted.

The next point is that the line will not only be tested wet, to make sure the line test is what you say it is, but it will also be tested in metric designations. Not to worry, however. Both methods give you an edge, just in case the line manufacturer's test rating was a little on the low side. Some manufacturers rate their line a trifle under breaking strength; others list it as close to the rated poundage as they can make it. What's important, though, outside of buying the line strength you thought you bought, is that wet strength of a line is substantially more than dry strength. Ditto with metric differences. A 12-pound-test line, for example, is rated as six kilograms under the metric system. Six kilograms will break at about 13.22 pounds.

So who cares? You will—if your so-called 12-pound-test line doesn't break at the right poundage. If it doesn't, your catch will be automatically dumped into the next heaviest line category and, sometimes, thrown in with heavier fish. If the opposite situation occurs, however, and your line tests out lighter than labeled, your bid for a record is kept in the line-test division you've applied for. It's not put in the next lighter class. Which leaves us with an important question: How do you know whether line you buy has been properly rated and labeled? As a general rule, you don't. But if the line is carefully made to meet IGFA specifications—as are at least two major brands of American-made fishing lines—it will proudly say so on the label.

High on the problem list of becoming an IGFA world-record holder (after you have wrapped the fish in wet cloth to delay shrinkage) is finding a set of scales big enough to weigh your catch. Most store scales only register up to twenty pounds. A secondary problem is finding scales that have been government inspected for accuracy or certified for legal trade use within the past year. Once such scales are found, write down the serial number, name of manufacturer, the date the scales were last certified, and the name of the government employee who inspected it. There will be a brightly colored certification tag with the date and inspector's name stuck on the scale somewhere. Next, write down the name and address of the person doing the weighing, the time, place and date, and the agreed-upon weight of the fish. Finally, ask an independent bystander, not a fishing partner, to witness the weight and write down his or her name and address. As an added touch, to speed up IGFA acceptance of your documentation, take a photograph of the fish on the scales with the weight visible.

Other photos you'll need will be one of the whole fish lying on its side with a ruler or yard tape alongside it, and another showing the fish in an unobscured hanging position, preferably with nothing but sky behind it. IGFA also insists on a photo of the rod and reel used to make the catch, plus a photograph of yourself with the fish, this last to be used for IGFA publicity purposes. After that, it's all downhill, just like riding a wave into harbor. Get names and addresses of everyone you can who witnessed the catch, tuck the fish away in your basement freezer, and go out and buy some champagne. The fish has to be kept to be measured, of course. It's also needed in case IGFA questions whether it's a hybrid or not, which is a possibility on the Great Lakes. If the species is questioned, you'll have to find a qualified fishery biologist who'll confirm identity.

Just don't wait too long to contact the IGFA. Its address is: 3000 East Las Olas Boulevard, Fort Lauderdale, Florida 33316. The application form—which will show you how IGFA wants the fish measured—has to

IGFA World Record & Fishing Contest Application

FORM FOR RECORDING FRESHWATER & SALTWATER GAME FISH CATCHES

Read all IGFA angling rules and world record requirements before completing and signing this application. The angler's signature on the completed form must be witnessed by a notary. This application must be accompanied by line or tippet samples and photographs as specified in the World Record Requirements. Hybrids and other species which may pose a problem of identity should be examined by an ichthyologist or qualified fishery biologist.

I AM SUBMITTING THIS ENTRY FOR:

☐ An all-tackle world record.

☐ A world record in the following line class:

_____ lb/ _____ kg

☐ A fly rod world record in the following tippet class:

_____ lb/ _____ kg

☐ The annual IGFA Fishing Contest.

SPECIES

Common name: _____

Scientific name: _____

WEIGHT

lbs, oz: _____ kg: _____

LENGTH (See measurement diagrams)

inches: x to x _____ xx to xx _____

cm: x to x _____ xx to xx _____

GIRTH (See measurement diagrams)

inches: _____ cm: _____

DATE OF CATCH: _____

PLACE OF CATCH: _____

_____

METHOD OF CATCH (trolling, casting, fly fishing, etc.): _____

FIGHTING TIME: _____

ANGLER (Print name as you wish it to appear on your record or contest certificate:

_____

Permanent address
(Include country and address code):

_____

_____

_____

Angler's fishing club affiliation (if any):

_____

EQUIPMENT

Rod
Make: _____

Tip length (center of reel to end of tip): _____

Butt length (center of reel to lower end of butt):

_____

Reel
Make: _____ Size: _____

Line or tippet
Make: _____ Size: _____

SPECIES MEASUREMENTS
Measure as indicated below, taking lengths from X to X and XX to XX.
Take girth around the fish on line marked G or at largest dimension location.

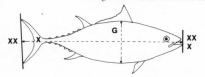 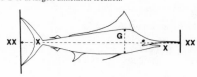

IGFA World Record & Fishing Contest Application (front).

Length of double line: _____

Make of backing: _____ Size: _____

Other equipment:

Type of gaff: _____ Length: _____

Length of trace or leader: _____

Number of hooks: _____

Name of lure, fly or bait: _____

BOAT (if used)

Name: _____

Make: _____ Length: _____

Captain's name: _____

Signature: _____

Address: _____

_____

Mate's name: _____

Signature: _____

Address: _____

_____

SCALES

Location: _____

Type: _____

Manufacturer: _____

Date last certified: _____

Person and/or agency that certified scales: _____

_____

Weighmaster: _____

Signature: _____

Address: _____

_____

WITNESSES

Witness to weighing (other than angler, captain or

weighmaster): _____

Address: _____

_____

Witnesses to catch (other than captain). List two names and addresses if possible. On fly rod records a witness is mandatory.

1. _____

_____

2. _____

_____

Number of persons witnessing catch: _____

VERIFICATION OF SPECIES IDENTITY
(See world record requirements.)

Signature of examining ichthyologist:

_____

Address: _____

_____

AFFIDAVIT

I, the undersigned, hereby take oath and attest that the fish described in this application was hooked, fought, and brought to gaff by me without assistance from anyone, except as specifically provided in the regulations; and that it was caught in accordance with IGFA angling rules; and that the line submitted with this application is the actual line used to catch the fish. I further declare that all the information in this application is true and correct to the best of my knowledge. I agree to be bound by any ruling of the IGFA relative to this application.

Signature of angler: _____

Sworn before me this _____ day of _____ 19 _____

Notary signature and seal:_____

When completely filled out and signed, mail this application with photos and line sample by quickest means to: INTERNATIONAL GAME FISH ASSOCIATION, 3000 East Las Olas Boulevard, Fort Lauderdale, Florida 33316 U.S.A.
(This application may be reproduced.)

IGFA World Record & Fishing Contest Application (back).

be notarized and returned within sixty days of the date of the catch if the fish was caught in the United States. Canadians who, I guess, move slower because of colder weather or a more inefficient postal system, have up to three months to complete the paperwork.

One thing you may wonder about when filling out an official IGFA application form is a series of seemingly innocuous questions about the rest of your tackle—tip length of rod, butt length of rod, size of reel backing, and other similar queries. If you don't know all the rules, these innocent questions could wipe out your hopes of a world record with one faulty stroke of a pen.

What the angling association really wants to know is whether you've met IGFA standards of sportsmanship. For example, the length of the rod has to be a minimum of six feet. Unless you're into surf casting, the rod butt can't exceed twenty-seven inches. (Believe it or not, there are some sad sack anglers out there who would crank prize-winning fish in on electric downriggers if the rules let them get away with it.) Another little-known rule, unknowingly broken by some Great Lakes charterboaters with little, if any, tournament experience, is that the maximum length of the net or gaff used to boat the fish can't exceed eight feet in overall length. (This limitation doesn't apply if you're fishing off a pier or bridge.) Still another regulation that has tripped up even experienced world-tournament anglers is the freshwater clause limiting the length of a saltwater-style double line or shock leader to a maximum of six feet. What many anglers apparently miss in reading the fine print is that the length of the leader also includes the lure and "other devices," meaning dodgers and everything else you may have strung out there.

The only IGFA regulation I really wonder about is the rule that says size or line-test of backing on a reel, if heavier than the fishing line, decides your line classification. In other words, if you're fishing with, say, one hundred yards of 12-pound-test monofilament and, like many freshwater casters, put twenty or thirty feet of heavier, bulkier line underneath it to fill the reel up and improve its casting abilities, any fish you catch would not be in the 12-pound line division but in the line-test division of your backing, which might be anything up to 50-pound-test or higher. There must be a reason for the rule. It's just that I can't figure how anyone could rig tackle to take unfair advantage of a fish with extra-heavy backing. A lot of thick line, I suppose, would create extra drag against a running fish if most of it was in the water. So does a fly line. But in both cases, one allowed, one not, with lightweight line up front it would still take angling skill to avoid breakage. Whatever the reason, the rule exists. Now that you know it's there, simply buy extra-large bulk-size spools of line and fill your reels with nothing but the one line.

Because of the maze of rules involved in world-class tournament angling—other regulations not mentioned range from allowable measurements of double-hook rigs to prohibition of wire lines or trolling with a fly rod—any angler with an interest in potential world records should become a member of IGFA for twenty dollars a year (twenty-five dollars in Canada), which is the simplest way of staying on top of rules and, equally important, knowing what you have to beat in the way of existing records that change from year to year. A few moments studying line-class records, for example, will quickly show which division of interest to you can be most easily broken or, if vacant, most easily claimed.

Just to show how easily IGFA records can be set at times, a Canadian outdoor writer, Bill Miller of Winnipeg, recently claimed something like six different freshwater fly rod records in one year simply by noting vacant classifications and fishing with tackle and fly rod tippet weights that met required IGFA specifications. Because the classes were wide open, anything he caught was a record fish. This is how I could brashly promise earlier to guarantee anyone an IGFA record fish. Not that I would do it. Nor would I think too highly of anyone who did. Yet the fact still remains that the 80-pound and 130-pound-test line classes are vacant in the freshwater chinook division as is, the last time I looked, the 50-pound line-class coho division. As a result, anything we caught would be (like Miller's fish) a recognized world record. But how you would handle the ridicule of knowledgeable sportsmen after fishing for ten-pound or even 40-pound chinook with 130-pound-test line, and then demanding world recognition for it, is another matter. If you still want to do it, please don't call me. Do it on someone else's boat. Miller's records were at least set in a sporting fashion. (Since writing this, I've been told a fourteen-pound chinook has been registered as an IGFA 130-pound line-test world record.)

One other necessary precaution, having mentioned the use of charterboats in trying for IGFA records: If you ever do hire a boat for such purposes, take your own tackle. For starters, it's not reasonable to expect any charterboater to rerig tackle to IGFA specifications, even if he knew how, just for one outing. You likely wouldn't be as familiar with his tackle as your own. Odds are certainly good his reel-drag systems wouldn't be properly set up, or maintained, for light-line use on big, hard-running fish. Normal charterboat equipment is, of necessity, on the heavy side. The name of the game, not counting avoiding breakage or loss of costly tackle, is to try to see that even the most inexperienced angler catches fish. Few charterboaters are interested in participating in time consuming thread-line angling challenges. Always make your angling hopes very clear to the skipper prior to paying any money, no matter where you are fishing or what type of fish you are seeking.

There are many obvious philosophical differences between fishing for a world record, which you normally do on your own, and tournament fishing where you and everyone else are in wide-open competition of sorts with each other. As far as that goes, competition of any kind, including the keeping of big-fish records, is anathema to a lot of anglers. The editor of a well-known fly-fishing magazine was strongly criticized by irate readers not too long ago for just advertising a small trout-fishing tournament. It was the first time such an ad had been accepted by that particular magazine, apparently. A lot of readers didn't want it to happen again. Tournament fishing, in their eyes, is seemingly on a par with dynamiting rivers. They are right in that a day or two on a trout stream, surrounded by the delightful sights and sounds of the river, is a total escape, or should be, from normal workday competition (may it always be that way). But so is a day on the Great Lakes, whether a tournament is on or not.

Tournament critics, from the way some of them talk, make it sound as though tournament anglers are involved in the equivalent of hand-to-hand combat out on the water. If they only knew the major role uncontrollable luck plays in big water tournament angling, however (and anyone who says otherwise is a charlatan of the worst sort), such criticism would likely be softened. Being aware of the importance of luck, I know I can never acquire any real feeling of competitiveness worthy of the name, or even worth criticizing. If a tournament is on, fine. If we take a super-big fish, great. Both my boat and I (I hope) are prepared for it. But I certainly don't spend nights dreaming up dirty tricks to gain an advantage over other anglers. On the other hand, the fact that someone wins a tournament doesn't mean they are a better fisherman. Lucky amateurs can beat pros any day of the week, and do it consistently, tournament after tournament.

Competitiveness is seemingly part of the human psyche. The vast majority of anglers I know like mild competition. Having a chance to take home a prize of some sort adds zest, a bit of extra harmless adventure to an outing. Come to think of it, I have seen some of those same trout-stream anglers who publicly deplore competitive angling in any form openly compete against each other during after-dinner fundraising auctions in a style that would shock a lot of tournament anglers. Don't ever play cutthroat poker with them, either. Sure, the trout club money goes to a good cause. But so does a lot of money raised by most fishing tournaments. Derby fish also provide fishery management workers with invaluable biological data ranging from the survival rates of stocked fish to success of past lamprey control work.

12

How to Fight a Heavyweight

I keep thinking I've seen every way there is to lose a fish but I keep finding out I'm wrong. There's always a new way.
—Charterboating Lament

Giant fish can do strange things to anglers who are accustomed to fish they can hold in one hand. For instance, a few years ago a fisherman on a Canadian sports-writing team in an international tuna fishing competition out of North Lake, Prince Edward Island, was doing fairly well— until he saw his monstrous eight hundred-pound opponent swirl near the surface. Scared white, the fisherman gave up his rod to an experienced saltwater angler. That simple motion excluded the fish from the tournament, of course, because under international angling rules the fisherman is disqualified if someone even touches his rod accidentally.

Another angler couldn't reel a fresh, twenty-five-pound-plus chinook straight into our boat, so he tightened the star drag of the reel until it locked up. That tactic might be all right for perch but when that big king took off again the snap of the breaking line sounded like a small explosion.

These stories are a small sampling of ways fish are let off the hook. I've seen many more over the years, most of them committed at one time or another by myself, but such mistakes often have a common denominator: a fisherman who doesn't know how to handle tackle under maximum stress. Since we all make errors in judgment, anyone can lose fish. Sometimes it's simply a matter of betting the wrong way.

On the Atlantic salmon streams I fish each year, for example, there are times when, in order to make the best fly presentation, it is necessary to put yourself in a position where it is impossible, because of bridge abutments or steep cliffs, to wade downstream after a fish. You bet on the chance the fish will stay in the pool. Sometimes they do, sometimes they don't. And when they don't, you often have no alternative but to throw yourself into the river and hope you'll hit a wadable section somewhere downstream before the ocean-bound salmon empties your reel of line and backing. One of my angling buddies has pulled this stunt so often he can now come out of the water with his hat and sunglasses intact, still puffing on his cigar.

No matter where you fish or what type of tackle you use however, there are some basic, big-fish fighting techniques that will give you a sporting chance to land that dream trophy.

Ideally, you should first put away every reel you own that has any kind of a slipping clutch or star drag on it, and fish a whole year with an old-fashioned freespool casting reel that doesn't mechanically cover up most minor mistakes. If you did that, you'd not only have a better feel for the fish and how much pressure you can exert on them without breaking off but, equally important, you'd know how to utilize thumb or finger pressure on a reel, a skill needed to put maximum pressure on a fish by literally "pumping" it into the boat even when you're using a reel with a slipping clutch.

Since few would quit using a favorite reel just because it has a star drag, it is important to establish how to set drag tension properly. A star drag is simply a slipping mechanical clutch that, once a preset pressure is applied to the reel spool, disengages the gears so that a heavy fish can take line out even though the angler is still cranking the reel handle. Simple. But ask the average angler how the drag should be set with, say, a 12-pound-test line, and I'll bet the answer would be Just under the breaking point, or about eleven pounds. The real answer is about 30 percent of your line test or, in this case, using the above-mentioned line as an example and keeping our mathematics as simple as possible, about four pounds.

The reason, and remember we're talking about reel-screaming fish in the heavyweight category, is simply that tension on a line is never constant. For example: Suppose a monstrous fish roars off with several hundred yards of your line. As the spool diameter shrinks from having

A light drag setting is vital when battling large fish such as this Michigan brown trout. As a basic rule-of-thumb, tension should be about one-third of the line's breaking point. (*Photo by John Power*)

less line on it, line tension rises way above the breaking point if you've set the drag at what seems to be a normal 90 percent. The smaller the diameter of the spool, the more force it takes to turn it. A fish that gives you a stop-and-start fight is also creating a problem because it takes far more pressure to start a reel moving than to keep it moving. But the real tackle-busting problem is water resistance.

If you give a big hard-running fish enough "belly" or arching line, it can break off even if you are knowledgeable enough, and cool-headed enough, to have thrown the reel into freespool when it took off. It's not unusual, for example, for big saltwater fish to break 80-pound-test line on a twenty-pound star-drag setting just from water resistance alone. That's part of the game. Imagine what a forty-pound chinook or even a twenty-pound rainbow trout can do to your lightweight mono!

A related experiment you should try at home is to tie the line of your favorite fishing outfit to any stationary object near floor level—a sleeping mother-in-law will do fine—and, after locking up the star drag so nothing gives, back away with the rod held in a high, nearly vertical fish-fighting position until you feel the rod is arced almost to the line-breaking point. Holding the rod in that position, loosen the star drag until line starts to release against the pressure of the rod. Stop right there! That's the clutch-release setting you should use when fighting a fish. If you then tie the line to a spring-type weigh scale and have someone hold and read the scale while you assume the earlier position with the rod, you should also find the drag release setting will be very close to 30 percent of the line-test rating.

All this is based, of course, on the assumption you have a matched outfit. A light line on a too-heavy rod will obviously break before the rod bends very far. The reverse situation of a heavy line on a lightweight rod will see the rod bend double, if not break, before the line gives. If not, your mother-in-law is going to wake up screaming blue murder.

Now let's go fishing. If you were on my boat for the first time, I'd probably ask you point-blank if you'd had any experience with big fish. Don't fudge on the answer. If your biggest fish was a three-pound bass, say so. Any experienced charterboat skipper will recognize your level of experience within thirty seconds of you picking up a rod anyway. Remember, he's not there to judge but to help, and it helps him to know these things in advance so he can alter his boat-handling techniques. Boat handling can make the difference between you losing or landing a big fish in deep water. In fact, that's how International Game Fish Association ultralight line-class records are sometimes set. If the boat's clutch burns out, you've had it.

Catching huge saltwater fish can be a unique game. On the hookup the skipper may slam his boat into high-speed reverse, roar in backwards on the still-unsuspecting fish until someone's close enough to grab the wire leader, and then slam a break-away or flying gaff into the fish. If it's done right, and with some luck, it might take all of three minutes. Sporting? Not really. Unless you're the guy grabbing the wire. That can get exciting. You also better be a good swimmer because sooner or later an irate fish is going to flip you right out of the boat.

But let's start with something easy, like a thirty-five-pound Great Lakes chinook salmon that's determined to make a quick visit to the other side of the lake. If you're not fishing for a specific IGFA freshwater line-class record, using lighter-than-normal lines, you'll probably be handling rods rigged with 16-pound-test mono. If you hook into a really strong fish, one capable of stripping a reel, all other lines will be lifted and, if the fish is still running, the skipper will change course to parallel the movement of the salmon. This simple boat-handling technique not only cuts down the water resistance created against the line by a fast-moving fish, but also helps you keep plenty of line on the reel. Once the salmon stops running, you'll discover you can't crank the fish into the boat. The star drag setting, at about five pounds, is simply too light. But never tighten the drag. Apply the pressure you need by placing a thumb against the reel spool. If you're fishing on your own boat with an open-face spinning reel, you can do the same thing by lightly cupping a hand around the spool. Combine the thumb pressure with a coordinated up-and-down rod movement and you'll be "pumping" fish like a pro, lowering the rod and reeling in the line you gain, applying thumb pressure as the rod is raised again against the fish, and then reeling in line as the rod is smoothly lowered. It's easy.

At one time, to digress a bit, I used to try to show customers how to pump a rod, a little extra bonus I threw in as part of a trip, knowing the importance of pumping in handling big, strong fish well and also knowing the process is a totally alien fish-fighting technique to the vast majority of freshwater anglers. But I quickly quit my outdoor classroom endeavors because of the high percentage of anglers who thought they knew how to handle fish and obviously resented being shown anything. There are three areas in which we all consider ourselves perfect it seems: driving a car, of course; making love; and, as I discovered, playing a fish. To even suggest imperfection of any kind is insulting, which is unfortunate. But as long as reels come with big handles most anglers will insist on using them as cranks. Why else would they be there? In fact, the cranking process is so ingrained among freshwater anglers I'm convinced a reel manufacturer could easily double annual sales just by putting bigger handles on its reels.

No one has ever written better or with more truth on the subject of pumping a rod than Harlan Major. Tucked away in his classic book *Salt Water Fishing Tackle* is a paragraph which could be beneficially repeated: "Too many fishermen think that pumping a fish correctly is as complicated as a problem of relativity, but it can be done with no more mental exertion than shifting gears in a car. It seems so difficult that over and over again you see fishermen at their fish-losing, line-breaking, gear-stripping method of hauling in fish. Fishermen are constantly asking for longer reel handles, so they can grind harder, and yet the most skillful fisherman I ever knew used only his thumb and forefinger in cranking his reel. The effort of pulling in a fish should be transmitted to the rod and not to the reel, which should be used (only) for storing slack line that has been gained by the rod."

All you have to remember is not to give the fish slack line by erratically dropping the rod faster than you're reeling line. Keep the rod bent against the fish. Its flex is designed to be used as a cushion to prevent line breakage by softening the power of a fish. You tire a fish by keeping near-maximum pressure on it at all times. Another general rule is that the more you baby a fish by applying less pressure, the greater the chances of losing it.

Maintain the light star-drag setting and, if the fish takes off again, which it will, just lift the thumb to avoid any possibility of popping a line.

Of course, as soon as anyone says, Always keep maximum pressure on a fish, you'll find exceptions to the rule. There can be times—such as when you want to get yourself in a better position to fight a big river salmon or West Coast steelhead—when you shouldn't apply any pressure at all until you're ready to start the fight. Normally, a fish doesn't react violently to being hooked until you start trying to do things to it, like yank it around. Migrant river fish especially will stay surprisingly quiet, hardly moving at all, until they feel the rod.

When a big fish gets below you in a river, it can put you in a no-win situation unless you get below it and use current and lateral line pressure to tire it out. One way to accomplish that is simply to release enough loose line into the current so it swings below the fish, creating a downriver drag so that, to get away from it, the fish will voluntarily move upstream to you.

Still another classic exception to the maximum-pressure rule is in handling a jumping fish close enough to the boat to create a straight pull. To avoid excess line pressure on the leap (and the possibility of having your lure pulled out), you "bow" to the fish, deliberately giving slack line by leaning forward and lowering the rod tip.

Angler fatigue can be lessened by using other parts of the body to take some of the rod-holding strain, such as tucking the rod handle under an arm. The open-face spinning reel is cupped by hand to increase line tension against a running fish when a light star drag setting is used.

Another problem in fighting big fish can be angler fatigue. Few anglers are capable of holding maximum tackle pressure against a fish with a fully bent rod for more than a few minutes. Arms and wrists give out, unless you're strapped into a special saltwater body harness. The solution is to use other parts of your body rather than just holding the rod by hand. Try tucking the lower handle against the underside of your arm. And why use only one hand? The reel-cranking hand is easily moved back and forth from reel to rod. Using a two-handed grip, you can lessen pressure against yourself by simply extending grip points. You have much better leverage against a running fish by dropping one hand close to the rod butt and grasping the rod with the other hand well above the foregrip. The leverage effect can also be increased by pushing down on the rod butt with the lower hand, relieving strain normally taken only by the other wrist.

Strangely enough, the biggest problem most freshwater anglers have is bringing the fish to the net. The general tendency when fighting a fish from the stern of a boat is to reel the fish too close to the rod tip, then, not wanting to give any line back, trying to lift the fish toward the net, a very effective way of losing a trophy. It's much simpler, and a lot easier on everyone's nerves, to leave about a rod's length of line between the rod tip and the fish and, by taking two or three steps backward, bring it headfirst towards the net. Or you can simply move forward and work off a side of the boat.

Just remember, if you're going to lose a fish, you're normally going to lose it at the last minute and close to the boat where some of the most violent, unexpected action occurs. If the fish wants to run, let it go. Either you do that or smash tackle—another good reason for a light reel-drag setting. A smart angler wants his biggest fish of the year making its wildest runs and highest leaps well away from the boat.

But the basic point is that having a better understanding of your tackle and using its full capabilities in fighting fish can't help but increase your angling pleasure and effectiveness, no matter how or what you fish.

13

The Compleat Netman

"That is the best fish yet taken, Ignatius," said the Professor;
"He will scale fully three pounds, and you landed him in two
minutes. . . . One should hold hard and kill quick."
　　　　　—James A. Henshall, Sport with Gun and Rod

If you ever want to see a charterboat captain's eyes glaze over from painful memories, ask about his biggest fish ever lost at the net.

　　You can imagine the scenario. People have paid reasonably good money to catch fish; you're billed as an expert, and expertise of any kind is worth money today, especially if it's backed up with thirty thousand dollars or more of boat and equipment. A big fish is soon hooked, proving right there you're worth every cent you're being paid. A happy, excited angler does his job well enough to get the fish near the boat, making various observations along the way such as "Wow, look at him go! Look at the size of the beast! I didn't know fish grew that large!" Then you step forward, net in hand, the Captain by God, best damn charterboater on the lakes—you've just proven it by finding a monster fish. Then, for any one of umpteen-dozen reasons—overeagerness, trying to reach too far with the net, a dangling lure catching on the net rim, the net snagging on a downrigger arm—you are forced to watch in slow-motion horror as a prize trophy slithers or slams its way free to disappear back into the lake.

For most of us this only happens once, usually early in our charterboating careers. That kind of humiliation leaves deep mental scars. It also provides an unforgettable lesson on the cost of carelessness. So we quickly become more firm about calling the shots, judging whether a fish is ready for the net and, if it is, not making a move with the net until the fish is exactly where we want it, even if that means playing psychological games with the angler to see that the fish is in a sure netting position.

Given a reasonably cool-headed angler who will follow instructions at the last crucial second or so prior to the moment of truth with a net, few fish should ever be lost at a boat. If a fish allows itself to be brought in too quickly, the angler is told the fish is still too "green," to ease off or get ready for a wild run. If the fish dives toward the boat, the angler should be prepared to let it go and shove the tip of the rod deep into the water so his line won't catch on the motors.

Netting fish like this twenty-three-pound chinook salmon calls for co-operation between the angler and the net-handler. The basic decision of whether or not a fish is in a nettable position must be made by the netman.

Big brown trout are notorious for coming in after the initial hookup without a struggle as though unaware anything is happening until they are alongside the boat, and then going crazy. I can remember a few rainbow trout also playing this game. The ultimate thrill, however, certainly from the viewpoint of any angler, is to have a freshly hooked giant chinook charge at the boat. Most anglers when this happens for the first time, no longer feeling the weight of the fish, think it has somehow gotten off. Many stop reeling. At such times, the close-in action is pretty exciting if the so-called lost fish suddenly comes roaring out of nowhere to put on a display of water-throwing aerial acrobatics off the stern. The worst situation with an inexperienced angler on the rod is if the fish just keeps going under the boat, of course. With everything happening so quickly, with so much loose line in the water, this can sometimes mean a break-off if the angler isn't quick enough, or lucky.

One decision to make long before any attempt to net a fish is whether other lines should be cleared. Losing fish in a tangled mess of fishing lines is almost as bad as losing one at the net. Any high lines, flatlines, or planing boards on the same side as the fish should come in automatically. If we're fishing deep with downriggers, unless it's obvious we've hooked an exceptionally large fish, I'll just raise lines on the angler's side of the boat, maneuvering the boat if need be to keep the fish away from other downrigger cables if the angler can't do it. When the fish are small, usually coho, no lines will be cleared at all. Why lose valuable fishing time resetting tackle? With coho being a school fish, there's a good chance lines left in the water will produce a second salmon.

As always, though, what is done depends on existing circumstances. For example, if it's the angler's first salmon, and boating it would obviously be an important moment, I'll not only raise everything to reduce chances of losing the fish, but throw the boat out of gear to let the angler gain an even greater sense of accomplishment by dueling the fish one-on-one. Keeping a boat moving at trolling speed while a fish is being played may cause an inexperienced angler to think his fish is a lot stronger than it is. But as a light-line angler, on the rare occasions I'm doing the fishing, a towed salmon is still a towed salmon and never offers maximum sport, not as I define it.

At other times, there are good reasons to keep the boat moving. If you're fishing in a pack you pick yourself a hole leading to open water so the fish can be played and netted away from the crowd, pulling whatever lines that need to be raised as you go. Stopping with lines out could result in sinking lures catching on bottom or floating lures becoming entangled with the fish near the surface. If lines are left in the water, and with a decent-sized fish kicking up spray behind the boat, the helmsman should at least ease off the throttle a bit. Even better, the fish-towing aspects of the game could be eliminated completely by running the boat in a wide circle, keeping the fish at its center, free of any effects of boat movement.

It's obvious that boating fish is made easier by having suitable gear. Nets large enough for big salmon just weren't available in the early years on the Great Lakes. Like everyone else I bought the biggest net I could find, which was still too small, and replaced it as even larger nets came on the market. Now, although the monstrous nets most of us use might make us look a little overgunned on most fish, there are always extra-big salmon to be caught that demand extra-big nets.

As a charterboater, the only drawback of the larger nets (and this gets back to little psychological games we're sometimes forced to play with anglers) is that many fishermen, seeing the cavernous bag of a typical net and its six- or eight-foot handle, consider any fish within ten feet netable. Maybe they're adding up arm length and any extra distance gained by leaning over the boat. But we can never use the maximum length of the net anyway. For starters, working out of the stern of a moving boat means the bottom of the netting has to be clasped with one hand against the handle, otherwise the base of the bag would float away, swirling over fish being brought to the boat and catching on dangling lures. Some boaters use a light elastic band to hold bottom netting against the handle, the net pulling free of the elastic once a fish is anywhere inside the bag. But by shortening up my grasp on the net, its long handle appears shorter and anglers tend to bring fish closer to the boat than they would if the net was stuck out as far as possible. It's reaching for fish, trying to use a net too far away from the boat, that gets most anglers with big nets in trouble and lets fish swim away free. If safe maximum reach is six feet, you patiently wait for the angler to bring the fish within half that distance, if you can, before making your move. And when you do move, you do it fast, always taking the fish headfirst into the net, letting go of the base of the netting as you thrust the net out to scoop the fish into its bag.

I think the bellwether sign for safe netting is the position of the fish's head. If the angler has the fish on the surface, with its head up, and can keep it moving in that position toward the boat, the fish is as good as on board. Even better harmony is achieved if the angler slackens line just as the net starts to be raised from underneath the fish. If the timing is right the fish will dive headfirst into the bag every time, almost netting itself.

When fishing alone, the easiest technique seems to be bracing the net handle under an arm while playing the fish into position or leaning the net in a convenient spot against a gunnel until it's needed. The most common one-handed netting mistake is using the wrong hand to wield the net. The net hand should be always closest to the bow of a moving boat so the fish is brought head-first into the mesh. Working off the port side, for example, with the rod in the right hand, the net in the left, unless a small fish is being brought straight in off the side of the boat, any attempt to net a fish usually results in it being netted tail first. This is always a dangerous procedure as the fish can use its tail and the weight of its body against the net to throw itself free. The second the fish is inside the net, the rod is set aside—usually just dropped—freeing the second hand to grab a forward portion of the net handle as it's being pulled toward the boat.

You'll discover in a hurry that few net handles can't be bent by trying to hoist big salmon aboard with a straight lift. There's just too much negative leverage. You have to use a hand-over-hand technique down the net handle until you can grasp the junction of the net rim and handle. Even then, you should support the far side of the rim with the other hand before lifting heavy fish.

Sooner or later, netting fish also leads to releasing fish, either because of the fish being undersized, unwanted because of species or chemical contamination, or because of closed seasons or daily species catch-limits. Whatever the reason, a question that needs to be answered is, How do we handle newly netted fish to minimize injuries? How do we ensure maximum survival after release? How do we know if a fish even has a chance of surviving?

Factors to consider before judging whether a fish is a potential survivor include the amount of stress the fish underwent during its struggle. How hard did it fight? How long did it take to boat it? At what depth was it hooked? Time of year is also important. Thermal shock may result from a fish being dragged too quickly from deep cold water into warm surface water. Most obvious of all is handling damage, something we can all do a great deal to prevent. Is the fish bleeding? How does it react when you hold it in the water hoping it will swim away? Even the species of fish involved should be considered, some fish apparently being more capable of survival than others.

Lake trout taken out of deep water in summer have long been considered the least likely to survive after being caught by an angler. We've always been told (in fact it's almost fishery management gospel) that taking a lake trout out of the depths too quickly results in its swim bladder, which regulates buoyancy, being unable to adjust fast enough to water pressure changes. Coming up, the trout's bladder balloons outward in the body cavity as water pressure decreases, making it physically impossible for the bloated fish to return to its cold-water environment. Sometimes the bladder will even burst because of such quick changes. In addition, lake trout face another hazard. As the body temperature of a fish is seldom more than two degrees warmer than surrounding water, quickly hauling a trout out of forty-degree water to surface water that can be as warm as seventy degrees can be equally fatal. However, the surprising results of a new Michigan Department of Natural Resources study show lake trout are far more capable of surviving such stresses than anyone has ever dared hope.

Because Michigan recently cut off early-spring lake trout angling and reduced daily catch limits from five to three fish a day after May 15, Great Lakes fisheries researcher Andy Loftus is wondering how many overlimit trout or trout accidentally caught out of season actually survive being returned to the lakes by anglers? Are the protective regulations really saving any fish?

To find out, Loftus has been clipping lightweight buoys on seventy-five yards of line to released fish and following the trout around. Out of forty-four lake trout taken out of up to 140 feet of water, forty fish reportedly survived initial stress. The only sign of discomfort was that some of the fish stayed near the surface for about thirty minutes, apparently readjusting air bladder pressure, before returning to deeper water. Even more surprising, of the four fish that died, one was deeply hooked, another's gills were damaged by an angler while being unhooked, and the third was almost drowned from being dragged behind a boat when a downrigger release failed to trip. The only unexplained fatality occurred in a live tank where Loftus had been keeping a number of the trout for longer periods of observation.

In equally contrary fashion, the fish most often thought of as being the toughest of the various species—coho and chinook salmon—are in reality about the most fragile in many ways. There can't be too many Great Lakes anglers who haven't had a salmon hit a deeply trolled lure, then rocket up to the surface, breaking line, and continue thrashing wildly about until it's so exhausted that it is an easy matter to bring a boat alongside and net it. I was on a boat working out of Port Credit on the north shore of Lake Ontario one morning when we spotted one of these fish, still flopping on the surface with someone's brand new Rapala in its jaws. Without needing to change direction or even slow down, we had a twenty-three-pound chinook on board before a line was even wet. If not found by anglers, such fish are frequently dead within hours.

The seeming fragility of salmon is even stranger when you consider all salmonids have a special duct leading from the swim bladder to the esophagus that functions to equalize rapid changes in pressure. It has to be the rocketlike speed of ascent without any expulsion of air that does the killing. Scuba divers face a similar problem, of course. Coming out of the depths too quickly without pausing to breathe or let the body adjust to changing water pressure causes what we call "the bends."

Physical exertion by migratory fish such as salmon and steelhead, who have lots of power and aren't reluctant to use it, can also drain oxygen supplies and create an overload of lactic acid in muscles and blood. This acid is a byproduct of substances the body uses to create energy. There are also individual differences in fish, some fighting a rod until completely exhausted from lack of oxygen, others giving up more easily (and more likely living, if released, to swim another day). I recall Mark Sosin and John Clark, authors of *Through the Fish's Eye*, citing experiments with coho salmon to determine specifically the percentage of lactic acid–related deaths. Fish taken by West Coast trollers were kept in live boxes for observation. Almost half of the coho salmon died. The biggest surprise was that similar tests on stream-caught coho failed to produce any fatalities. Why isn't known. One reason might be physiological changes related to spawning. Or stream fish might not fight as hard as free-roaming ocean fish.

Increased awareness of fish sometimes dying from exhaustion has ironically resulted in some finger pointing at light-tackle anglers who have been publicly criticized over their "sporty" methods of angling and the resultant prolonged struggles that kill far more released fish than necessary. As a light-tackle angler I think it's a bum rap. It's my observation that the intensity of fish reaction to rod pressure is directly related to the amount of pressure put on the fish. The harder you yank a fish around on heavy tackle, the harder the fish will react. The fight never lasts as long on heavy tackle, granted, but while it is happening the fish is paying a much higher cost in exertion and oxygen depletion than when involved in a much gentler, though longer, light-tackle fight. In addition, fish boated quickly on heavy tackle also seem to expend more energy by wildly flopping around. I also know from successfully releasing sufficient numbers of fish caught on light tackle in rivers and lakes that most salmonids can, and do, recover if handled properly.

One point that can't be argued is that the best of all ways to release any fish is to free it without taking it out of the water. The less a fish is handled, the less chance it will be unintentionally injured. Commercially-sold hook disgorgers or longnose pliers can be used to free single-hooked salmon lures from most small fish held within reach alongside a boat. Larger fish that must be netted can often be safely freed in similar fashion by leaving both fish and net in the water, raising the net just enough to bring the salmon or trout within easy reach.

Netted fish swung aboard are always handled the same way on my boat whether they are to be released or not because of a technique I use that gives maximum control of the fish with the least amount of damage to it, and minimum risk of the "hooker" (me) accidentally becoming the "hookee" while trying to manhandle big salmon. It's also the best way I know to all but eliminate fish injury by excessive squeezing or destruction of scales.

What happens is, as soon as the fish is on the floor of the boat, still in the net, it's all but totally enveloped in a large, wet towel. If I'm working alone, I'll put a knee or foot on the caudal fin or tail of the fish to control that end. A hand pressed down behind the upper gill prevents any flopping at the other end. At the same time, my right hand is clearing mesh from the lure and jaws of the fish prior to removing the hook with pliers I carry in a belt holder. If the salmon is big enough to make control difficult, I'll ask whoever is closest to hold the tail down with both hands. So far, using this method, I've only been injured once, getting a hook deeply imbedded in a hand when an angler, startled by the power of the fish, let go of the tail of an irate twenty-five-pound chinook at the worst possible moment. As soon as the fish is out of the way, either killed and in the box or back in the water, the towel is also used to wipe up any slippery fish slime on the floor, given a quick washing over the side, and returned to a corner of the stern where it'll be handy when I need it again.

Once a fish is in the boat, and anglers decide only then that the fish should be released, I'm not reluctant to make autocratic, Captain Bligh-style decisions. For example, visible bleeding means any legal fish is a "keeper" whether it's wanted or not. If necessary, I'll take the fish home or, if I don't want it, give it to one of a number of acquaintances who appreciate receiving fish occasionally.

Released fish should not be tossed back into the water and forgotten in out-of-sight, out-of-mind fashion, even though a shockingly high percentage of anglers do it this way. Who can't afford a few moments to increase a fish's chances of survival? Its first, most obvious need is to replenish a depleted oxygen supply, and this is best done by lightly holding the fish headfirst in the current caused by the moving boat so water reaches its gills through its mouth. When a fish is capable of swimming away, it will. You should also watch newly released fish closely once they do move away from the boat. Some fish quickly resurface in obvious distress. At this point you make the decision whether it's to be netted again and kept, or whether another attempt should be made to revive it. Incidentally, the normal routine of swishing a fish back and forth, forcing water into its gills, can harm a fish when water and surface debris are forced into delicate gill tissues from the wrong direction on each backward sweep. If you do it, at least do it gently.

Smaller salmon judged releasable can be carried back into the water by inserting a finger under the top of a gill flap, as long as you're not touching easily damaged gill rakers. The preferred method is to put them back while still rolled up in a towel. Larger fish are usually returned inside the net. These releases are a two-person operation that involves working the fish free of the mesh and gently holding it in the water in upright swimming position as your helper backs the net out of the way.

If a fish is big enough to be kept for mounting, the way it is handled on the boat is a major factor in how well it will look on a wall. Even the most skillful taxidermist will have trouble producing a lifelike mount if a few simple steps aren't taken when the fish is caught. Unlike wilderness fishing trips when you are many hours if not days away from home, Great Lakes fish are rarely far from a freezer, eliminating any need for field dressing. Until you can freeze them however, it's important to keep them moist in a flat position and carefully wrapped in plastic for the trip home. The usual practice of wrapping a fish in newspaper is a mistake if it's to be mounted. Newspaper not only leaves ink on the fish but, being absorbent, draws out moisture.

Most taxidermists report the greatest problem they face is trying to repair chipped or broken fins. To avoid such damage, the first thing to do on arrival home is to brace both sides of the fins with suitably sized pieces of cardboard stapled together or held together with paper clips. You might even pack the fins with cotton batting inside the cardboard to help keep the fins moist during the freezing and thawing periods. Wrap the fish in double-layered plastic garbage bags to prevent freezer burn and then freeze it until arrangements can be made to deliver it to a taxidermist. Taxidermists also say it helps them to recreate truer colors if you take a few color photos of the fish as soon as it's caught, preferably in the position you think you'd like it mounted.

14

Slow Day Tricks

The more I travel the less difference there is. . . .
—*W. G. Marflow*

The cycle of a charterboat skipper's year, like the life cycle of the fish we seek, is similar anywhere on the Great Lakes. A few background differences might exist, a particular species might be of more importance in one area than another, timing of major runs may vary, but angling methods—the business of catching fish—are basically the same.

Probably one of the greatest variations is accessibility of fish over a season, particularly in midsummer. An offshore angler in western Lake Ontario, for example, who can spend hours each day traveling to and from distant midlake fishing grounds, can't help but be envious at times of a counterpart in, say, Indiana, who enjoys superlative close-in fishing five months out of six, and in August, when Hoosier chinook may be difficult to find, there is always an excellent lake trout fishery not far away to produce limit catches.

There are other minor variations found around the lakes in tackle preferences, usually the result of a regional lure manufacturer successfully meeting local needs with a lure or lures not known elsewhere. Government stocking practices might also give one species of fish a prominent angling role not enjoyed anywhere else, such as Ontario's hybrid splake in parts of Lake Huron or Indiana's Skamania steelhead in southern Lake Michigan. But an angler who catches fish anywhere on the Great Lakes will do equally well anywhere else once local lake bottom-structure variations and seasonal fish movements are known. Geography and place names may change but the fish stay the same.

Carter Elenz, who has run his charterboat *Salmon Hawk* out of Michigan City, Indiana for five years, recently trading in his skipper's cap for a college degree in business administration, says Indiana's angling year starts as soon as the ice leaves in early March. From then until midApril limit catches of small coho are often taken by anglers flatlining body lures such as orange jointed Rapalas and red or chartreuse Tadpollys near river mouths and harbors. "As our shallow, southern end of the lake [Michigan] is the last water to cool off in the fall and the first to warm up in the spring, our area is a wintering ground for a good percentage of all the fish in Lake Michigan," Captain Elenz says.

"You also have to picture what our bottom is like to understand what happens. We have a different situation. From the shoreline out, there is a sandy bottom with a reasonable slope down to sixty feet about $1\frac{1}{2}$ miles offshore. At that point the 'Sixty Foot Shelf' starts where the bottom flattens until you're about $4\frac{1}{2}$ miles out and then it starts to gradually drop again. So we don't find any really deep water until we're a long way from shore.

"By midApril the bigger kings start showing up (with spawning smelt), most of the chinook being caught during the day with J-Plugs, Silver Hordes, Grizzlies, and Canadians off downriggers in thirty to sixty feet of water. The kings could be suspended anywhere from surface to bottom.

"May provides great fishing, with lots of coho (although they start moving north by mid-May or late May as the water warms); chinook fishing is good all month and we also start picking up lakers and steelhead. May is also the time we switch over from body lures [J-Plugs, etc.] to spoons, Northport Nailers, Suttons, and so on, usually in mixed colors like green-and-silver and silver-and-chartreuse. By June, we can be catching suspended lake trout in 80 to 120 feet of water plus some coho, chinook, and steelhead, although most of the chinook have also headed north by this time.

"I figure by June, everybody else's fish have moved back to their home waters and what we have left is primarily fish stocked by Indiana. June also sees us fishing back in the shallows for four- to six-pound coho salmon that have followed the alewife in close to shore; most of these fish are caught on orange dodgers and black or dark green flies with some silver mylar mixed in them.

"July, which used to be the worst month of the season, is now our best as our Skamania steelhead start staging off the rivers, usually first showing up in June and providing unbelievable sport during all of July. Given the right kind of water temperature, if we get a south wind that blows the warm surface water out, they'll be right on the surface. But usually they're caught flatlining in anywhere from twenty to sixty feet of water, mainly on orange Tadpollys and Rapalas. Size? Most will go ten to twelve pounds although we've caught them up to twenty-four pounds. Very few will be under ten pounds. They're just a super fish.

"In August, once the steelhead run is over we'll go back out into the deep water looking for chinook and, if they're not too plentiful, we can always catch lake trout. We've got clay under all our sand and there's one area called the 'Honey Hole' where there's about four square miles of bare clay that runs from about 95 feet to about 120 feet down that really holds trout. The guys [charterboaters] also all work together, they rely on each other, so there's not many days when anyone really has a lot of trouble catching fish. Then by the end of August, usually around Labor Day, depending on lake temperature, the chinook start showing up again."

Lake Michigan charterboater William Klemm, who operates the thirty-five-foot *Lady Carole-E* out of Benton Harbor, Michigan, starts his year with a mixed bag of springtime coho, chinook, steelhead, brown, and lake trout catches close to shore. Most of the fun comes from big brown trout each spring. (As always, you first have to know the structure of the lake bottom.) Offshore are three sand bars, he says, one 25 to 40 feet offshore under $2\frac{1}{2}$ feet of water with about 5 feet of water off its edge. The second bar, about eighty-five to one hundred feet out, is eight feet down with fifteen feet of water off each side. The third bar is about 150 feet out in 40 to 45 feet of water. The game is first to run lures off the inside edge of the first bar with planing boards and then, as the water warms and the season progresses, fish the second, slightly deeper bar the same way. As the lake becomes even warmer, he moves out to duplicate the system on the third ridge of sand. Eventually of course, the brown trout disperse into even deeper water and become more difficult to catch.

Summer offshore action is mainly centered on chinook in up to 210 feet of water eight to ten miles offshore. Captain Klemm favors various colored Hot N Tots, a big-billed diving lure fished three to six feet away from the cannonball. "I know a lot of guys run long lines" [off the balls] he said, "but I'm a firm believer that cannonballs are real fish attractors. Salmon will hear the noise [of a ball] going through the water, will come over and check it, and if the lure isn't there, if the fish don't see it, which they won't if the lure is running seventy-five feet back, they'll just turn away."

On a slow day he says he just starts digging into his tackle box. Favorite spoons include a green-and-silver Lucky Spoon and iridescent orange flutterspoons. When things really get tough, his highly imaginative aces in the hole are miniature dodgers he transforms into fishing lures. "What I do is take a tiny moocher dodger, maybe about 4 inches long and 1¾ inches wide, and drill two holes into the back end. I'll put a small O-ring into each hole, attach a small willowleaf spinner to each O-ring, attach a larger O-ring to the small ring and then add a No. 8 or No. 6 treble hook to the larger ring." He added, "I've tried single hooks on the dodgers but they don't work as well as the trebles for some reason, although I use singles on just about everything else." Captain Klemm also dresses up his fish-catching dodgers with strips of silver or gold prism tape. In late fall when the salmon are biggest, he'll use dodgers up to six inches in length.

Another trick Captain Klemm says is deadly on brown trout is to make a "bottom walker" out of a three-foot section of light brass rod. He wraps a circle in the middle of the tubing so the ends angle back in the shape of a V. A piece of hose is then stuck over one of the arms so its weight makes the V ride vertically in the water. A ringed swivel is attached to the upper arm for a leader-and-lure hookup. A medium-heavy rod line is then tied to the circle at the front of the "walker" and the rig is trolled behind the boat so it is bumping across bottom, stirring up swirls of sand. "Big browns love it," Captain Klemm says.

Captain Larry Scharich, owner of Reel Pleasure Charters operating out of the world-famous Michigan port of Manistee on Lake Michigan, also provides a fascinating account of his fishing year. "We start our fishing in the latter part of April and fish until the end of October. Our April fishing is mainly for brown trout with a few salmon also caught. May is mostly king salmon fishing with a few browns and lake trout also taken. June and the first part of July provide kings, lakers, and steelhead. From the middle of July on it's mostly king and coho salmon with quite a few steelhead in the fall.

"The spring fishing is mostly topwater fishing, mainly in the top twenty-five feet over varying depths. Baits used are mainly plugs (Rapalas, Rebels, Hot N Tots) and spoons (Nailers, Flutter Chucks, Krocodiles, Lighting Lures, and a couple that I make myself). Then it's mostly spoons in the summer plus cowbell–Wobble-Glo combinations for lake trout.

From late July through the first part of September it's dodger-fly combinations, spoons, and plugs (J-Plugs, Tiger Plugs, Silver Hordes). From late September through the end of October it's mainly spoons again.

"The depths we fish vary so much it's hard to say much about them except due to the change in weather conditions they can change daily. [Captain Scharich is referring here to preferred salmon water temperatures of fifty to fifty-five degrees Fahrenheit.] We might be fishing one hundred feet down one day then get a big blow from the north and be fishing on the surface the next day because the wind turned the water over and dropped the surface temperature to, say, forty to forty-five degrees. Also the reverse could happen with a big southerly blow."

Discussing slow days and how he handles them, Captain Scharich adds, "Sometimes through the latter part of June or early July, things will slow down, the fishing will be fairly deep and normal everyday fishing tactics may not work too well. It's on these days we'll go looking for colder water on the surface.

"We are fortunate that our area of Lake Michigan [south of Ludington to north of Frankfort] contains the deepest part of the lake. The deeper depths are accompanied by sudden breaks and a much contoured structure which creates strong currents—up-thermals, down-thermals, etc. These currents can cause the surface temperature to change as much as twenty degrees in a distance of only about one hundred feet or so of travel.

"These sharp surface temperature breaks are usually accompanied with a trash or scum line on the surface or sometimes on calm, warm days, a fog bank. These surface temperature breaks are great fish attractors because they stack up the microorganisms which attract the bait fish which attract the larger fish, etc. This also means the fish found there are usually feeding fish.

"Depending on the currents, the depth of water where this takes place might be anywhere from approximately 300 to maybe 800 feet, so the actual water depth is of little importance. All our fishing there is done from the surface down to about 30 feet or so. We use various spoons and occasionally a few plugs.

"When the right conditions are found, the fishing there [at the breaks] can be fantastic. The only drawbacks are finding these temperature breaks [they do not exist every day] and they are usually found about six to ten miles offshore. But there are many days we'll go looking for and find these conditions and turn an otherwise slow day into a limit or near-limit catch.

"Another exciting thing about this [thermal break] fishery is that you never know what you'll catch next due to the variety of species that are found together there. We've boated as many as six different species in one day: kings, cohos, lakers, steelhead, browns, and an Atlantic salmon."

Captain Bill Anhel of Gypsy Lady Charters, Troy, Michigan, who fishes Lake Huron from April to May and Lake Michigan from June to October says his major spring catches are six- to ten-pound chinook caught off planing boards and flatlines. His top spring lure is a No. 15 Bomber with an orange stripe on the underside of the lure. No. 3 J-Plugs and flutterspoons are also good bets when the water temperature starts nearing fifty degrees Fahrenheit.

Springtime fishing practices that Captain Anhel feels are important are:

1. Use the lightest line you feel comfortable with; I prefer 12-pound-test for my charters, he says.
2. Stay away from packs of boats. Early season fish are shallow and spook easily.
3. Run lures fifty to one hundred yards behind the boat.
4. Start trolling at the slowest speed which gives a natural action to the lure and increase speed periodically until strikes are obtained.
5. Tie body baits directly to fishing line with a loose-looped knot.
6. Use various sizes of weights tied three to six feet ahead of lures to vary the depth of your baits being run off flatlines.

Working out of Frankfort on northern Lake Michigan from June to October, Captain Anhel says, "Kings, cohos, and lakers make up most of the catch with steelhead and browns adding a little more variety occasionally. During summer months when the salmon action starts to slow down, running Tadpollies, Peanuts, and Little Guys behind cowbells and Whirl-A-Gigs will produce limit catches of lake trout.

"About midJuly the king fishing starts picking up again with flutterspoons and No. 4 J-Plugs taking most of the fish. Green, chartreuse, and silver are my best colors with black-and-silver Nailers taking many fish in early morning and late evening hours.

"In late August the coho start to school for their run up the rivers in October. Squids and flies behind size 00 dodgers take most of the cohos. These are run three to six feet behind the cannonballs. Silver and lemon-lime dodgers work the best for me."

Here are more tips Captain Anhel says will help take more fish:

1. When running dodgers, tune them by bending into an S shape. This will allow you to run them at various speeds. Use a leader length

[to fly] that is $1\frac{1}{2}$ times the dodger length. Tying the leader tight to the dodger will transfer more action to the fly.

2. Don't leave a fly down longer than twenty minutes if it's not producing.

3. Check lures for action alongside the boat to make sure they are working like they should.

4. Many times fish will be holding tight to a bank and will not appear on the graph. Trolling an S pattern and running the cannonball into the bank will often produce fish.

5. Run some lines above and below the thermocline.

6. Look for vertical thermal bars [scum or garbage lines on top of the water] and fish back and forth across these bars.

7. Experiment. Carry a variety of prism tape and magic markers to doctor up lures. It's amazing what color combinations will catch fish when nothing else is working.

8. Putting an 0-ring on the end of flutterspoons that attaches to your line will give them a little more action.

9. Vary lead lengths behind cannonballs. Even in deep water lead lengths can be critical.

10. Vary speed. Many fish are taken while changing speed.

11. Keep a log. Record all pertinent data for future reference. You may forget something that worked well in the past.

"These are some of the methods that have worked well for me in past years," Captain Anhel says, "but every new season brings new challenges. What worked well last year won't necessarily work this year. In my opinion the basic key to fishing success is experience, knowledge of the fish . . . and their environment and a willingness to learn and experiment. Nobody catches fish every time out so use those slow days to try new ideas."

Making a geographical switch to Ontario's exciting Lake Huron fishery, which seems to be getting better every year, here's what Captain Brian Moore of Hunky Dory Charters in Stratford, Ontario, has to say:

"Lake Huron has many different fish including rainbows, brown trout, splake, coho, pink, and chinook salmon. I fish out of Goderich and 95 percent of my catch is chinook. Whether it is just after spring ice-out or October, there are big salmon within reach. Sometimes they're relatively scarce but a few fish seem to hold to our area between the heavier migrations which pass by in May and June and come to stay in late July. It makes for a consistent fishery, ideal for my charter operation.

"It's pretty much a downrigger fishery although in April and May planer boards do very well early in the morning. Chinook, however, flee to the deeper water as the sun comes up.

"The fishery is good and getting better but we do have our slow days like everyone else. Some fellows really have trouble catching chinook though, usually the result of relying on the graph too much and ignoring [water] temperature. Ninety percent of the salmon will lie in the cold water under the thermocline and rise occasionally during the day to feed before dropping down to the forty-five-degree water.

"Often a graph will show many perfect hooks in the bottom twenty feet of water. However, the feeding salmon will be above these hooks and extremely active, showing up as faint lines or not at all. Many times a fellow will say, 'I ran my lures in the center of the school all day and didn't get a hit.' I'll ask if he took a [temperature] probe and he'll say 'That wasn't necessary. My graph showed me where they were.'

"If he was fishing in eighty-five feet of water he maybe fished the whole day seventy-five feet down in water under forty-five degrees where large concentrations of chinook were laying like suckers, motionless and looking good on the graph. On the same day I might find fifty-one- to fifty-four-degree water at fifty-five feet and this thermocline might be only four to five feet wide. I'm amazed by the number of fishermen who still ignore water temperature.

"You have to consider many factors because they all play a part," he adds. Considerations include water temperature, weather, water clarity, boat traffic, time of day, other fishermen's input, boat speed, currents, month, lure type, and color.

"Variety is the key; be flexible. If you always run a certain lure at a certain depth your success will be very limited. Chinook demand respect, experience, and know-how.

"I'm sure my 'slow-day' tactics are the same as those used in other areas but I'm glad to share them. Sometimes I'll lower the ball below the thermocline and then release the lure, allowing it to rise through the various temperature ranges. This tactic has put some big chinook in the box for me. This release tactic is especially effective just at sunset.

"Lake Huron has some tricky currents and sometimes it's hard to decide if your speed is right for the salmon. By zigzagging we constantly change lure speeds. If a fish hits the inside rod on a turn we know we've been going too fast. If it hits the outside rod on a turn we know they want a faster presentation.

"I'll also often put a sliding stacker [secondary lure] on a line, usually a flutterspoon, and let it run down the line to the spot where it starts back toward the ball. I find this method, which puts lures in slightly warmer water, gets me the odd rainbow and chinook in the five- to twelve-pound range.

"Of course I do the usual things on a slow day like vary lure size, color, body type and speed; use the VHF and CB to see if anybody has found an area or presentation that is working; raise lines and run to a totally new location; lengthen or shorten the distance between cannonball and lure. Another trick that really worked for me one day, producing chinook when no one else caught a thing, involved lighter lines and faster trolling speed. All the boats had been doing well until then with silver dodger–black fly combinations and everybody else stuck with the same rigs. I switched over to light lines, from 17 test down to 6, and starting trolling pearl J-Plugs at higher rpm. We took three fish that way, a four-teen-, an eighteen-, and a twenty-six-pounder.

"I fish for fun and along with these methods of getting fish on a slow day I have other methods that help fill the time and sometimes put fish in our box when every boat on the lake is empty. None of these methods has any reasonable explanation but they have all worked for me on more than one occasion:

1. I open my tackle box and say to my wife Gail, 'What looks good to you?' She says, 'That cute blue one with the big lip.' Sure enough the Hotspot lure, or whatever, gets me a twenty-pound salmon.
2. I find if you hold a soft drink in one hand, a sandwich in the other, and have absolutely no place to put anything down, a fish will hit.
3. Go to the washroom. Chinook can tell when you're least able to reach a rod and they'll hit then.
4. Don't stand and watch a rod. Kings only hit when you turn away. On rare occasions you'll turn back in time to see the rod pop.
5. Call the fish. It's an art. The call is 'Here fishy, fishy, fishy.' This call only works when you put your head in a bucket and hop on one leg. I didn't believe it either until I saw it.
6. Run a chum line or double chum line. When the lake is rough, clients will oblige."

On the American side of Lake Huron, Captain Bill Thede, who operates the Thumb Charter Service in Sebewaing, Michigan, says prime spring fishing is most generally enjoyed between March 30 and April 12. "Lake trout, coho salmon, chinook salmon are the main fish taken with an occasional brown, steelhead, splake, and Atlantic salmon being bonus fish. At the present time we are having to work under a new law . . . limiting us to not taking any lakers before May 15. That law, plus the

Charterboat Captain Bill Thede.

new limit on lakers from five to three [a day] has really put the stops on things. Before that we were able to fill the limits on board almost every trip out.

"Our lakers and salmon in spring come on smelt imitations—Rapalas, Rebels, Bombers—running along the shoreline to the deepest water [twenty-five feet]. During the spring fishing and late fall we count heavily on our planer boards. We run as many as three pair to the outside [as far as 150 feet out] of each side of the boat, plus, if we have the people to cover [2 poles per person] we set four downriggers and a flatline down the center [for a total of 11 lines].

"The planing boards take 50 percent or more [of spring fish) because of fish being spooky in the shallow water. We always run the deep divers

[Rebels, Fat Raps, Thin Fins] anywhere from ten pulls [a foot a pull] to twenty-two pulls behind the boards. We work the warm water coming out of streams and rivers or harbor mouths and warm water discharges, also any structure in those areas or down the shoreline. We are blessed with hundreds of rock reefs up and down the shoreline that shallow [up] to as little as four feet and drop off to twenty-five feet.

"Best colors in the spring are silver and gold with black backs, or chroma blue or chroma green with orange bellies. When the smelt run is over we find we have to change more to flutterspoons, Locos, and Nailers. We also find then that the lakers will start to take only lake trolls with a Wobble-Glo about eighteen inches behind, starting with mini-trolls and working up to the bigger-bladed long trolls as the water warms up. Some days, size 0 dodgers are better still, using Wobble-Glos in green, chartreuse, and chrome green.

"As we lose the salmon as the water warms up we concentrate heavily on lake trout during the summer months, although a few salmon are caught by running stacked lines above the lake trout lines.

"In August the salmon start to school up and we go back to magnum spoons, Nailers, G & Ws, and a few J-Plugs. Whites and blacks along with a few greens seem to do best. On August 15 our lake trout season closes so we get heavy into J-Plugs and running higher off the bottom trying to keep from catching lakers. By late August the salmon come in close to harbors and rivers and it's back to running planer boards or outriggers along with the downriggers. Most all the salmon are hitting J-Plugs, Grizzlies, and Producer plugs in whites, greens with ladder backs, or chroma green backs with chrome undersides."

Discussing slow days, Captain Thede says he always runs "with what generally works best for us, but I always have one or two setups down with different colors or lures set closer to, or farther away, from cannon-balls than normal.

"In the summer, on a slow day, a diving planer (Big Jon or Pink Lady) working down the middle anywhere from forty feet to one hundred feet back has saved the day.

"Probably the most useful two electronics on the boat are the B & C Combinator and the Loran C. The Combinator tells lure speed, temperature, etc., at the lure depth. This keeps us from working out of temp water and tells us if the lures are working right in case of any underwater currents. The Loran C keeps us on the fish when we do find them. We also watch our boat's surface speed on a digital to keep the right action on the lures we are running. I think correct speed to match the working lures is more important than what color or what lures are used.

"Another thing," Captain Thede says. "When fishing lake trout you have to be bumping bottom to do best, no higher than a foot above.

Now and then crank the rigger up one to three feet then reset to original position. This provides a lot of hookups. Lakers will follow trolled lures for miles sometimes before they hit. Speeding up or slowing down also works; anything to change the action sometimes does the trick. Also for lake trout—we are usually fishing deep, 70 to 120 feet—we have found the best releases to use are ones that have at least a five- to seven-inch leader cable on them [offshore releases], it makes it so much easier to detect a laker mouthing the lure. A lot of time we are able to see the pole bow, be able to take it out of the holder and have it release while holding the pole.

"I really don't think charter captains are that much better fishermen than anyone else," he says, "but they are on the water more and know from day to day where the best place is to go and what's working best. Here in the Thumb [of Saginaw Bay], everyone helps each other, a radio call will most always get you the information you need, not like some ports we have fished on Lake Michigan where they [charter captains] have their coded maps or messages. We feel no one person is going to catch all the fish; we all have gas costs and boat payments to make and helping someone else to take a skunk out of the box is what it's all about."

Captain Bill Smith is another lake trout angling expert. Bill, however, works the far eastern end of the Great Lakes system out of Henderson Harbor, New York, on Lake Ontario.

"For lake trout early in the spring," Captain Smith says, "we fish top water or slightly below the surface with downriggers. As you know, lake trout like water about forty-seven or forty-eight degrees and I try to find this [temperature] if possible. For top water I use a heavy lure like a Sutton spoon, usually an 88, and will run it 150 feet behind the boat. I use two topwater lines and two on the downriggers.

"In early spring the water temperature is about the same from bottom to top so one must look for the ledges and gravel shoals. Dragging a lure from ten-to-fifteen feet of water to around forty or fifty feet usually provides fish and once you find them they can be caught at that certain level for the day.

"Each day seems to be a little different and needs a different-colored lure. In shallow water, along with the topwater rigs, I use downriggers and try to keep the cannonballs four or five feet off the bottom. Lures are run forty or fifty feet behind the cannonballs.

"In deeper water, you can run lures three or four feet from the cannonball. If you use dodgers for deep water, put them four or five feet behind the cannonball and the lure about eighteen or twenty-four inches from the dodger. Always vary your speed."

Captain Smith's favorite lake trout lures include black-spotted silver Cleos as well as the Suttons. For brown trout he favors jointed Rapalas.

15

Why Not Fly a Kite?

The kite does two things. It lifts a moving bait so that it skips along the surface. . . . The bait being pulled by the kite follows a course parallel and to one side of the boat and avoids disturbance in the water.

—Harlan Major, Salt Water Fishing Tackle

I suppose I may as well openly admit right here that Gwynne and I use a boat in a slightly different fashion from most anglers. Our idea of a perfect summer day, for example, is to run offshore, boat a few fish, then, while chilling a suitable wine for lunch, pull tackle, switch the trolling motor off, and toss a huge truck-tire inner tube overboard before everyone manages to jump or dive over the side for a cooling midday swim. As I normally delegate myself to lifeguard duty, I have often witnessed other passing anglers or charterboat operators shaking their heads in obvious wonderment at our foolishness, seemingly not understanding how anyone could waste fishing time in such fashion. Although whether they came miles out of their way in the middle of the lake to see what we were doing, or simply to get a closer look at bikini-clad female swimmers clambering up the boat ladder is debatable. As a result, I doubt few anglers in our part of the lake were surprised in any way when they first saw a kite flying high above the boat. We were out there just playing around again. Or so they no doubt thought. Which is true—we *were* having a lot of fun. What they didn't know is that we were also catching fish.

For sheer, all-round angling fun, you might also want to try kite fishing, an old angling technique I've adapted for new use on the Great Lakes. Although it's hard to keep a kite a secret in any way, I've been quietly messing around with kites for five years now, experimenting with building materials, flying kites and fishing them, and as far as I know I still have the sky all to myself. To date, although I've proven only two things, I think the findings are of angling importance. One, there isn't an angler alive who doesn't have enough boy left in him not to become totally captivated by the fun of flying kites. Two, a kite is the most interesting way of all known angling techniques to catch Great Lakes fish.

Not that, as noted, there is anything new about it, except for my adapting kites for freshwater use. As a saltwater angler, I've been on many boats whose skippers have occasionally flown kites to bounce ocean baits across the surface for everything from giant billfish to bluefin tuna. Kites have been in common use for years off the coasts of both Florida and California. According to Harlan Major, a Catalina, California, commercial fisherman named George Farnsworth was the first North American angler to use a fishing kite way back in 1912. Farnsworth apparently got turned onto kites when local bluefin tuna suddenly refused to take lures trolled directly behind his boat. By quartering his boat into the wind and trailing a fishing line off a high-flying kite he was able to troll a bait well off to one side. In addition, he could for the first time bounce bait across the top of the water to look like live bait fish trying to escape a hungry predator. He was so successful, it turned out, his competitors, coming home empty-handed day after day, accused him of everything from refusing to tell them about his new secret fishing hole to buying his tuna. The following year, 1913, when his competition had caught onto his stunt, Farnsworth, still ahead of everyone else, handled a kite so well that a client, William Boschen, the inventor of star-drag reels, became the first angler to ever hook and land a broadbilled swordfish on rod and reel. Other big-game fishing centers where kites are popular today range from Bimini to the Bahamas.

What is more fascinating, to any kite flyer at least, is that use of kites for angling had its real beginnings, so history tells us, in the Malaysian Islands about 2,000 B.C., when natives figured out how to make kites of palm leaves sewn onto a framework of palm leaf nervules in order to fish offshore reefs either from shore or from canoes. Off the lower edge of the kite, they ran a baited fishing line that also acted as a stabilizing tail.

The author prepares a kite for launching on a day when the wind is right to utilize this unique Great Lakes fishing technique. (*Photo by Gwynne Wolfram*)

The kites were bridled by control lines much like ours. But knowing the difficulty of getting a modern kite to fly right at times, it's surprising to think of the amazing skills natives of British New Guinea and other islands had developed about four thousand years ago. I have still to see a modern kite that can be flown with the precise control they must have enjoyed in order to dap a lure in the pockets of a wave-lashed coral reef up to a quarter of a mile away.

How Malaysians even got kites into the air successfully from a beach lined with palm trees is a source of wonder alone. Great Lakes beaches were my starting point, a testing ground for my first homemade kites, and I can tell you a lot of things, all of them bad, about beaches that have trees or even sand banks close to them. But as someone once said prior to a total disaster, it seemed like a good idea at the time. Kites would be a simple way, so I thought, to get lures out to the edge of spring mud lines, which, by some quirk of fate, were consistently a few feet past my maximum casting distance from whatever beach I was on. But I soon gave up on all beaches that had trees in the background to disrupt air currents in any way; you need a smooth, uninterrupted flow of air to carry a kite skyward without it tumbling and spinning to the ground or water.

The late Harlan Major, obviously a veteran kite flyer as well as a knowledgeable saltwater angler, put it all together as accurately as anyone can when he wrote: "There is not much a man can learn from books about handling a fishing kite. After grasping a few principles, skill will only come by using the trial-and-error method, accompanied by much profanity."

Back in the old days of Farnsworth and, later, Miami charterboat skipper Bob Lewis, who popularized fishing kites in Florida, there were two distinct differences in how kites were rigged: California skippers ran kites off fishing lines, Florida anglers ran fishing lines off kites.

The original California style of attaching kites was to use a short strand of breakaway line to tie in a half loop on the heavier fishing line. The kite was run off the ultralight line so when a fish struck, impact broke the light kite-holding line, and the suddenly unattached kite, lacking line tension need to trap wind to hold it aloft, fell to the water for later retrieval.

Florida anglers took a slightly different tack. Their technique, now used just about anywhere kites are flown, uses a double-line system. The kite line is usually run off an old trolling rod and reel jammed into a rod holder just like we run Great Lakes sideplaners, except you should also tie a kite rod down with a safety rope. If you have a boat with a flying bridge it's often simpler, and certainly easier for the skipper, to run the kite off a heavy-duty saltwater reel bolted onto a convenient side roof strut. A secondary five- to ten-foot line is connected about fifty feet or so below the kite. At the end of this line is a butterfly-type release (early anglers just used a wooden spring clothespin) that holds the separate fishing line. When a fish hits, the line is pulled free of the holding clamp, the kite stays high and dry in the air (wet kites work about as well as wet dry flies), and the completely unencumbered angler is on his own to fight the fish.

My standard kite-flying routine, after snapping the kite line to the bridle, is to hold the kite rod over my head as high as possible so the kite can catch the cleanest wind I can find, even if I have to clamber up on the bow of the boat to do it. Kiters, incidentally, describe wind the same way anglers talk about moving water: if there's a smooth, uninterrupted flow, it's "clean," if it's being deflected or blowing erratically, it's "muddy" or "dirty."

If the kite wants to go, and most days a medium-sized kite won't behave unless you have a ten mile an hour wind, you slowly start feeding the kite line out, always keeping tension on it or else the kite will dipsy-

doodle into the water like a drunken pelican. Eventually, a swivel previously tied into the line fifty feet away from the kite will clear the reel.
(I didn't tell you about this before but, believe me, the swivel is there.)
At this point, with the kite fifty feet up in the air and, if all is well in the
universe, hanging there like a steady, well-behaved kite should, the reel
is locked so no line can come out and a short secondary line, prepared
in advance with a snap tied to one end and a line-release clamp tied to
the other, is snapped into the kite-line swivel. (This may start to sound
complicated, but it really isn't. No more than hooking up a sideplaner
or downrigger.)

So at this point we have the kite in the air and we have a short,
trailing line attached to the kite line with a lightweight line release on
the end of it close at hand. All that is left to do is clamp the fishing line
(with the lure trailing in the water behind the boat) into the release. Before
we do that, there is one simple but very crucial extra step. If we just put
the line into the release clamp as the old-timers did we're locked in;
there's no way except by adjusting the height of the kite by shortening
or lengthening the kite line that we can keep our lure exactly where we
want it in the water. Gusty winds could have it soaring high over the
water. But if we take a common, ordinary, everyday paper clip, insert
our fishing line into one end of the clip so it can run freely, and insert
the other end of the clip into the jaws of the release unit, all of a sudden
we can easily adjust lure position, no matter how erratically the kite might
be flying, by quickly reeling in or letting out line from the fishing rod
reel. Just take it easy when you're shortening line. A fast, jerky retrieve
can pull the line out of the release.

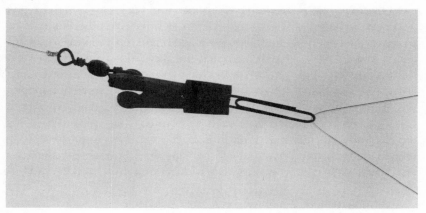

**A small paper clip in the rubber-tipped jaws of a lightweight alligator release clip allows
easy adjustment of line length to keep a kitefishing lure at the desired depth. When a fish
strikes, the paper clip pulls free and the clip slides down to the front of the lure.**

To complete the job (and for the first few times you might need an extra set of hands), you now let out kite line and fishing line at the same time until you think the kite is far enough away from the boat. Once the kite is in position, the control reel's freespool lever is put into lock position and a tapered piece of soft wood is used to wedge the butt of the kite rod securely in its holder.

Adjusting the position of the lure to the kite is equally simple. Although most saltwater anglers think kites are usable only for surface fishing, I run lures anywhere from just under the surface to a depth of twenty feet or more. Because of the higher angle of the line off the kite compared to a normal boat rod, a deep-diving lure without a sinker on the line in front of it will usually only hold about five to ten feet down, about where I want it as a near-surface attractor for steelhead or coho on offshore thermal breaks. (Active fish holding at a deeper depth are sought with other tackle.) The more line that is out, the deeper the kite-held lure will run, of course. An alternative is to lengthen the connecting line between the fish line and the kite line. This puts the lure deeper by decreasing the angle of the line from the kite.

But if I want to maintain an approximate ten-foot depth knowing, say, I need 150 feet of line in the water to do it, I'll have 150 feet of line in the water prior to hooking up to the kite, and mark the distance by tying a loop in the line and attaching a strip of brightly colored cloth. This allows an easy visual check of what's happening without having to watch the kite every second. If my bright flag is visible just above the surface, where I want it, everything's fine. If the flag is suddenly thirty feet in the air, I let out line to adjust for the higher-flying kite. If the flag can't be seen, I know the kite has dropped and I need to shorten up. I've also been wondering lately why I can't catch fish with the line marker. So I've been experimenting with oversized bright red and orange streamers as marker replacements, dapping the lures along the surface on a short secondary line. I have yet to catch fish this way. The next step, I think, is to put a small spinner in front of them. We'll see what happens.

It must be obvious by now that kitefishing is best enjoyed only on certain days. The greatest drawback, of course, is the need to have just the right amount of wind, even though you can sometimes trick a kite into flying with the forward speed of your moving boat. But there are also many days of bad wind or no wind during which a kite can't be used.

Although there are three basic sizes of fishing kites, an eighteen square-incher for high winds (called a storm kite), a twenty-seven-incher for medium winds, and a thirty-six-inch model for light winds, most saltwater anglers I know, and I've fallen into the same habit, just fly the medium-wind kites. If the wind isn't right, it's a lot simpler, and less frustrating, though not as much fun, to keep your lures well away from the boat via outrigger poles or planing boards. In fact, the first flexible outriggers were devised by California saltwater anglers to replace admittedly undependable kites as a method of skipping baits on the surface.

Another minor problem with kites is that with one in the air you can no longer wheel a boat around and chase a fish downwind in order to help a light-tackle angler retrieve line—not until someone cranks the kite in anyway. Dragging a drowned kite through water with a boat can rip cloth or snap struts. I take the boat to a sunken kite even when retrieving one by hand, rather than haul it through the water to the boat. Kites can create a surprising amount of drag, trapping and holding water better than many sea anchors. You also need an attentive angler doing nothing but tending the rod, adjusting or shortening line length as needed. But because our kite fishing system is so unusual, it's never a problem to get volunteers. In fact anglers usually insist on taking turns on the rod.

Still another lesson learned the hard way is that building what appears to be the simplest of all kites is not as easy as it looks. My first mistake was trying to use tightly woven nylon material that was totally windproof, not knowing you need porous cloth, cotton or silk, that will let some of the air pass through it. The next problem was that available wooden dowels never had the right amount of flex, they seemed to be either too light and would break, or too heavy and not give me the wind-catching arc or bend I needed. Balancing the sticks to the weight and wind-trapping ability of the kite material appears to be the real secret. I should have thinned down the heavier struts until I got the bend I wanted. Knowing commercially built fishing kites utilized fiberglass struts, I even came close to sawing up a few old glass fishing rods, but I abandoned the idea as too costly. In the end, not having found perfection, which I'd describe in a fishing kite as one which stays in one spot in the sky as though it was glued there, I wound up doing what I possibly should have done in the first place—buying factory-built kites from Florida.

Not that anyone should think the time and money spent building kites was totally wasted. I learned a lot about flying them. I also originated a few new swear words when the existing supply just didn't seem adequate—especially when trying to fly a kite in unmanageable surface air currents off land. At times, my suicidal kites kept smashing into hard ground faster than I could rebuild them. Rule Number 1: Always fly over water.

As with most kites, the cross line of the bridle is just a single line with a ring in its middle attached to a loop in each of the top corners so its length can be adjusted. The center line, also adjustable, passes through the kite material to link up with the top line at the ring. The struts, of course, are inserted into pockets sewn into each corner of the kite material. If the kite dives, it's telling you it's grabbing too much wind and either the center line should be shortened or the cross line lengthened. If it won't climb, it's doing just the opposite, spilling too much wind. In this case try shortening the cross line or lengthening the center line. If the kite jumps all over the sky, all the lines are too short. If the kite leans to one side, it's not pulling against the center of the cross line. Lengthen one side or shorten the other to even it up.

Despite occasional problems, given a day when a kite flies as it should—and it will if it's built right and it's given the right wind—there is nothing more enjoyable, or more different, to be found anywhere in the world of freshwater angling.

16

Safe Boating

The most dangerous boater is the skipper with between 100 and 500 hours of experience. In other words, the rank beginners and old pros aren't saddled with the dangerous, cocky overconfidence that often accompanies limited knowledge.
—Insurance Claim Statistics

A wise angler who ventures onto the Great Lakes in search of trophy salmon will quickly discover that safe seamanship starts at the dock, not out in the middle of six-foot waves.

OK, so you know you have lots of gas, the motor is running well, you have life jackets, a bailing bucket, and all the other common-sense items aboard. But the biggest safety decision to be made on any angling day is whether you go out or not. There are certainly many stormy days on the Great Lakes when the smartest, safest choice is to simply put the boat back on the trailer and go home. No fish is ever worth a dunking and inevitable loss of gear plus possible loss of life.

But what do you do on the in-between days, the days when you know the water is fairly rough but not too rough for the boat as long as conditions don't get any worse? Here most of us tend to gamble. We tell ourselves we won't go too far out. If we don't like it, if it gets worse, we come back in a hurry. Sounds reasonable. Especially if you and your family or fishing companions have come any distance, spending time and money to get there. Who likes to admit defeat, or that time has been wasted? The odds are just as good the wind and waves will flatten out instead of worsening. Or so we tell ourselves. But without VHF radio, which links you to fairly reliable, up-to-the-minute Coast Guard weather information, you're still guessing, and I've seen a lot of wet, frightened anglers making harbor—and helped pull a few of them out of Lake Ontario—who bet the wrong way.

Not that from a statistical viewpoint boating isn't one of the safest outdoor sports. But we also have to be realistic. And although Lake Ontario has yet to be hit by a major sport-fishing fleet tragedy—such as happened on Lake Michigan in the fall of 1967 when seven anglers died, another nineteen were hospitalized, and the wreckage of more than two hundred boats littered twenty miles of beach—the potential is still there. Another sad aspect of the Michigan incident, the worst on record, is that many of those anglers in their tiny boats sailed right by Coast Guard small-craft warning flags at harbor mouths, not noticing or understanding the meaning of the triangular red pennants.

So you start the day by checking weather reports, even if it's only a local newspaper or radio station prediction, to get some idea of what to expect. Drive a block or two out of your way, if need be, en route to the launching ramp to check the lake itself. Have whitecaps formed? How's the wind? How about cloud cover? Are the clouds fluffy, cotton-like cumulus, forecasting fair weather, or are they stacking up vertically, flattening out on top like black-bottomed anvils, which means problems? Once you learn to read clouds, almost a science in itself as there are twenty-seven recognized types of cloud cover, you have a big edge over any weatherman reading a state- or province-wide report prepared the previous day. Local weather conditions can, and do, change quickly.

Almost all commercial radio stations broadcast weather forecasts as part of hourly newscasts. More detailed and often more accurate weather data is accessible, however, by telephoning any Coast Guard office or your local airport. Coast Guard weather forecasts are also available on VHF/FM Channel 21 (161.65 mHz) and Channel 83B (161.775 mHz). In addition, a comparatively new radio network operated by Environment Canada's atmospheric environment service transmits weather information continuously on 162.475 mHz. A similar United States National Weather Service broadcast also operates continuously throughout most of the United States. All weather service radio stations in North America use one of three designated frequencies, 162.40 mHz, 162.475 mHz, and 162.55 mHz.

Other reliable weather clues you can count on include that ancient verse "Red sky at morning, sailor take warning / Red sky at night, sailor's delight." Another dependable short-range weather indicator is found in "When the grass is dry at morning light, look for rain before the night / When the dew is on the grass, rain will never come to pass."

There are dozens of such weather-telling signs. Rising smoke is a sign of high pressure and continued good weather. A nighttime ring of cloud around the moon predicts probable rain next day. But the real key is wind. Moving air currents carry the weather. Wind controls change. And although the effect of wind on water often depends on where you are—for example, a north wind might create no real problems on the Ontario side of Lake Ontario but could create chaos on the New York shore—the direction of wind and, more important, any shifting of wind, is vital knowledge to any boater on big water.

If the wind starts switching from northwest to northeast, or southwest to southeast, for example, expect trouble. Generally, fair weather winds blow out of the north, northwest, and southwest. From those compass points, the question is largely one of velocity. At 5 mph, you can feel the wind on your face. On the lake, expect small waves. At 10 mph wind velocity, waves will start cresting into whitecaps. At 20 mph, waves start throwing spray. At 30 to 40 mph or better, spray from waves, whether bouncing off concrete pier walls or off the bow of your boat is whipped away horizontally across the water.

The length of time the wind has been blowing and the distance it has traveled across the water can make a big difference. Waves created by surface friction between the wind and the water are one of two kinds: chop, or steep shallow waves created by brisk short-lived winds; and long larger waves from wind blowing steadily from the same direction for days. Long waves, resembling classic ocean swells, can be fun and quite safe, even in a small car-top boat. But that same boat can be in trouble quickly in whitecapped chop when almost vertical waves are coming at you close together, the second wave smashing into your boat just when the bow dips into the trough between them.

The traditional advice for this situation is to head your craft into the waves, easing off on the throttle to avoid excessive pounding, and try to keep calm. This is fine, but only if your home harbor is in the general direction your bow is pointing. I keep having horrible visions of weekend boaters blindly following "keep your bow into the waves" advice and winding up in the middle of nowhere, out of gas, and no help within miles. At that point, with no fuel left, all you can do is rig a bucket or open cooler on the end of your anchor rope and, using it as a sea anchor, toss it overboard to keep your drifting boat nose into the wind. You might also pray a bit.

Assuming you have power and know which direction you have to go to get home (unless, of course, there's a safe harbor that's closer) you have four basic options in a storm depending on necessary direction of travel. Stay into the wind, run with the wind or, if port is in a direction that would put your boat parallel to the waves, causing severe rolling and possible broaching, use the first two tactics alternately to zigzag your way home. The fourth option—anchoring—might be used in a last-minute attempt to prevent waves from washing your disabled boat up on a beach or rock shoal where it would be torn apart, although few pleasure boats carry a heavy enough anchor or enough rope to survive such a situation. The formula used to determine how much anchor weight will provide sufficient holding power under normal sea conditions is: 1 pound of weight per foot of boat. A twenty-foot boat needs a twenty-pound anchor. You also need a minimum 5:1 boat-to-bottom ratio of anchor rope. In 30 feet of water, you'd need 150 feet of rope. In a storm, your boat might, just might, hold with 200 feet.

To avoid taking on excessive water and a severe pounding, don't challenge waves head-on. Take them at an angle, anywhere from thirty to forty-five degrees depending on the boat and how it's loaded. You'll be amazed at how the ride will smooth out. Also, the higher the waves, the slower you should go. In really bad water, your speed may only be sufficient to maintain steerage.

Running with the waves, or "surfboarding," takes some practice on calmer days to do well. But if you have no choice but to try it for the first time under storm conditions, the basic principle is to get the nose of your boat just past the top of a running wave so you are riding its back and stay there by matching the speed of the boat with the wave. If you "lose it," and fall off either the front or back of the wave, be quick at the wheel to counteract the "yawing" effect of the following wave. With most of the weight at the stern of the boat because of motors, the normal tendency of a heavy sea is to sweep you sideways or "yaw" you around. If you do get caught in a trough, or "broached," accelerate out and around to get back up on a crest.

This surfboarding technique can provide an exciting, challenging ride—so much so that some of us venture out in bad weather to surfboard boats just for the fun of it. The most exciting spots are just off piers leading to river-mouth harbors, a situation we have at Port Dalhousie. Between normal rip created by river currents meeting opposing waves, the waves themselves, and previous waves bouncing every which way off the concrete piers, it's normal to have three huge swells coming at you at once from three different directions in such spots. Just stay with your original wave and maintain power, being quick at the wheel, as always, to counteract any broaching effects.

Other possible hazards in heavy seas include getting "pooped" or having an oncoming wave pour over the stern as a result of going too slowly. The opposite danger, the result of going too fast, is being "pitch-poled." When this happens the bow can bury itself into the trough or back of the wave in front of you. It doesn't take too much imagination to visualize what can happen next. If the bow digs in, and acts as a fulcrum, the next wave, if it's big enough and fast enough, can flip the boat upside down. You might describe it as a 100 percent wipeout.

Zigzagging home when you want to go, say, west against a north wind, only takes time and patience. Take a northwest tack, angling into the waves and, when you want to change direction, watch oncoming waves closely to time your turn. You'll often get a series of two or three waves much higher than the others, so watch for them. Get the boat around before you get slammed sideways, then angle downwind, riding the backs of the waves as much as possible. Just remember, especially if you have no visual contact with shore, your upwind tack will be much slower than downwind. In other words, if you want to head west, you can't zigzag fifteen minutes northwest and then fifteen minutes southwest and expect to stay on an over-all west course. You'll wind up miles south

Surfboarding a boat into harbor by riding the crest of a wave provides an exciting, challenging, rough-water ride. (*Photo courtesy of Outboard Marine Corp.*)

of your harbor. Double, if not triple, upwind running time. Once you can see shore, of course, you can adjust your zigs or zags to reach your destination. Just be patient, however. Don't spoil the day at the last minute. I remember one rather wild offshore salmon fishing trip in which I ended up deliberately taking the boat and its puzzled passengers well past the harbor entrance so that, once I turned to go with the waves, I had a straight surfboard ride to sanctuary. The other way, if I had made my turn at the harbor entrance where the seas were highest, the final, slam-bang run would have been in the trough of five-foot waves. Why get wet for nothing?

Marine fog is caused by warm, moist air passing over cooler water, conditions encountered in spring and fall, and particularly in September when you can be fishing far offshore. This is the time you will likely discover the importance of continually computing an everchanging picture of your approximate location in your head. If you don't, the situation will normally be summed up in three words: Where am I? You look around, seeing absolutely nothing (fortunately fog conditions normally mean flat water, why pile nautical problems up needlessly?), and feeling as though you're in the middle of the Atlantic Ocean. In short, failing to keep track of compass headings and running time means you do have a problem. Not a big one. Just an embarrassing one.

So what do you do? Fortunately, a lake only has four sides, north, south, east, and west, no matter how big it is, and if you came out of the south shore you line the compass up in a southerly direction and, wishing you had some sun to blame for your red face, head for the home port side of the lake. When you can see shore you may or may not recognize landmarks, depending on your knowledge of the lake. If you are still not sure of your location (do you go port or starboard?), all you can do is poke along the shoreline until you do recognize something. The only real challenge left at that point is to convince your passengers somehow, if you have any, that you knew where you were all the time.

Spring fogs should never present boating problems of any kind because the fish are normally close to shore. If you start trolling in a westerly direction, turning around and heading east will take you home. In the fall, if fish haven't congregated in specific spots prior to spawning runs and are well scattered offshore, I normally run a simple triangle course. If I'm taking a party out for six hours I know if I run a northeast trolling course for two hours, head west for two hours, and then fish southeast for two hours, I'll be right back on my doorstep. Or very close to it.

The key is to keep track of general direction and running time. If you're busy rigging tackle and you have a volunteer helmsman at the wheel, check the direction he's headed as often as possible. Some people find it impossible to hold a reasonably straight course. Also, get the best compass you can afford, use it, and believe it. There may be times when you'll think your compass has gone insane but do what it tells you anyway. Magnetic north moves, given enough time, maybe two or three degrees a year depending on what part of the world you're in, but for general freshwater fishing purposes—unless someone has unthinkingly put some form of metal, maybe a camera, tight up against the compass—north is still north and south is still south no matter what your twirling head says.

Going to a specific spot on a lake and returning, fog or no fog, takes you into the fascinating field of nautical charts, compass readings, plotting course lines, and mathematical formulations of speed, time, and distance factors. But whether you become involved in oceanic-style navigation largely depends on the size of your boat and whether you'll be doing any long-distance cruising. Knowing how to use navigational aids, whether you do the piloting yourself or buy a costly Loran computer to set the course for you, can always benefit any boater. At the very least you need to know what variously colored buoys mean, if only to stay off rock shoals. But most fishermen I know want to spend their time fishing, not messing around with a lot of charts. With the increasing variety of auxiliary gear already associated with Great Lakes angling, things are possibly complicated enough. And as an angler I know a good compass and commonsense will meet the everyday needs of almost any fisherman. On a normal day, you always have some form of land-based guide to get you home anyway. For those who are interested in advanced navigation, or think they might be, your local library will no doubt have a basic navigational book. If the subject is as fascinating as I hope you'll find it, the next logical step is to contact your nearest yacht club and inquire about power squadron training courses.

Some basic bits of offshore boating information it helps to have in advance (unless you like to be surprised by the huge knifelike bow of a fast moving ocean-going freighter charging down at you through the fog) are marine charts showing where the regular shipping lanes are in your part of the lake. Because of my location at the Lake Ontario end of the Welland Canal we're faced with a lot of heavy ship traffic, some heading northwest to Hamilton and its steel mills, some heading north to Toronto harbor, and others, the majority, coming and going to and from Montreal and the Atlantic Ocean via the St. Lawrence River at the east end of the lake.

I have one word of advice: Stay well out of their way. Never mind the "right of way" business. Under fog conditions, as a point of interest, no one has a right of way. Such legal niceties don't exist. And, anyway, why anyone would want to argue the question (common in the Vancouver area) with an unstoppable object that outweighs you a zillion pounds to zilch seems a little silly, to be as polite as possible about it. Insane might be a more accurate word. I don't consider myself a nervous person by temperament, but if you want to see a guy with all his sensory antennas working, just join me out in a shipping lane when visibility is bad. The only comparison I know of is backpacking or camping out in Montana or Alberta grizzly country. I get twitchy—call it survival instinct.

In most cases, marine laws governing basic boating rules are quite straightforward. In a meeting situation, where two boats are coming toward each other head-on, both are obliged to alter course to starboard or, more simply, to keep to the right. In a crossing situation, if the other boat is on your starboard side, you give way. If you're overtaking another boat you are simply obliged to keep out of the other boat's way until all danger of collision has passed.

Sailboaters are another matter. They almost deserve an entire chapter on their own. The best sailboat skippers are quite courteous. Too many sailboaters, however, based on my experience, aren't happy unless they can show their superiority over power craft. Their foolish arrogance, changing course to force us to change course, cutting across lines and similar nonsense, is largely based, I think, on that ancient bromide that sailing craft always have the right of way over power-driven craft. They don't. Once a sailboat is under power with its sails hoisted it is considered a power boat and must abide by power-boating rules. They have special privileges only in crossing situations. So do canoes and rowboats. But why argue? Anyone behaving erratically or without obvious thought is a potential danger whether he's driving a thirty-six-foot sailboat, another sport-fishing boat, or a football field-size freighter. So you try to stay well away from them. Throwing rocks or emptying a 30.30 caliber rifle into a sail is an absolute no-no.

In heavy fog I'll run a metal pie plate up a vertical outrigger pole as a radar reflector just to make sure any approaching ship knows I'm there. But freighter skippers as a rule, like some truck drivers on highways, expect you to move. You're smaller, faster, and more maneuverable. So you look a lot, and listen a lot. If the skipper of the freighter is following the rules, he's supposed to use his fog horn three times every minute but, as always, don't count on it. Big ships only follow fog rules, it seems, when there are other equally big ships in the vicinity. It all depends on whether you're the possible cruncher or the crunchee I guess. Tiny fishing boats, like fleas on an elephant, aren't worth consideration. This partially explains why a guy I know on the West Coast, after a confrontation with a Vancouver Island ferry, followed the ferry into dock, tied up, walked on board, asked for the skipper, and then punched him in the nose. Vancouver salmon anglers hold the questionable distinction of having put an ocean freighter up on the rocks a few years ago after a flotilla of tiny angling boats simply refused to move—although I think the freighter skipper must have been a novice making his first run. The basic rule still is "get out of the way or else."

I am also a self-confessed chicken when it comes to thunderstorms. When I see squall clouds forming (those black-bottomed anvils rising high in the sky I mentioned earlier) and hear the distant rumble of thunder, I'm on my way back to harbor long before bolts of lightning start brightening up the sky. When Zeus talks I listen. Although, statistically, it's amazing how few boats are struck by lightning. Certainly far less than might be expected. But the basic boating rule to "get off the lake" is still a good one.

Thunderstorms normally result from warm, humid air being pushed upward by a cold front, which can happen at any time, day or night, or by midday heat from the sun on the earth's surface creating updrafts, the reason so many summer storms occur in late afternoon. Such storms are normally accompanied by high winds and extremely heavy rainfall quite often preceded by a sudden calm. But how fast I jump depends on the location of the storm. If the storm signals are anywhere in the west, I pull up tackle and leave. Where we are, thunderstorms traditionally move east at 20 to 30 mph. If the clouds are to the south or the north, in either case over land, I normally keep fishing, but head toward home and maintain a close watch for any new developments. The east, with most of Lake Ontario's huge bulk of air-cooling water in that direction, I don't worry about. I can't remember a thunderstorm ever rolling in from the east, but always from a southerly or westerly direction.

Another statistic that should be of special interest to Great Lake salmon anglers in open boats is the significant number of drownings that occur because of people falling overboard, quite often while urinating over the side rather than using a container. I suspect the majority of these fatalities involve lone anglers, which raises an important point for anyone fishing alone. Although it's fairly easy to clamber back into a low-sided car-top boat if you fall overboard, a slick-sided, high-decked fiberglass cruiser is another story. Any time you're out alone on a bigger boat, always keep a length of knotted hanging rope tied to a center or forward cleat. It naturally needs to be long enough to reach the water, but not long enough to get fouled up with the props. With the knots in the rope giving you something solid to hang onto, and a loop tied in at the bottom end of the rope for a stephold, you can usually climb back on board fairly easily.

Back in the days I was bouncing around alone on Lake Ontario and leaning over the side in a tiny fifteen-footer to set downriggers, an old rough-water trick I used was to snap a short section of rope to an eye bolt conveniently attached to a gunwale and snap the other end to my belt. If you're going to go over the side of a moving salmon fishing boat, odds are good that's when you'll get wet. All it takes is an unexpected big wave hitting you the wrong way and throwing you off balance. It never happened but if it had I figured the rope would at least keep me in the boat. Another device available today is a "kill switch" similar to those used on snowmobiles that you could rig to your belt with a cord. Fall out and the engine stops. Last time I looked these switches sold for around ten dollars.

The technique involved in rescuing a man from the water is comparatively simple. If you remember the first basic rule of any form of aid—do no harm—you can hardly go wrong. Just don't go charging into a situation before thinking about what has to be done. If he's clinging to an upturned boat, the normal situation, come in slowly from the downwind side so the wind doesn't push your boat on top of him, and once alongside, cut your engines to eliminate any chance of injuring him with your props. Then either throw him a rope or, if he's close enough, grab him and haul him aboard. If he's been in the water any more than a few minutes, treat him for hypothermia. Get him into dry clothing or wrap him up in a cabin blanket or sleeping bag.

A rescue from another ship that is on fire is a lot trickier. Do it wrong, get too close, and you could wind up on fire as well. Always stay upwind. Stop for a moment and assess the situation. How bad is the fire? Can it be extinguished? Should you board to try it? Is there anybody in the water? Somebody could have been blown out of the boat by exploding gas fumes. If he's there, he may be badly hurt. Get him, even if a roped volunteer has to swim to him. If there are crew or passengers still aboard the burning boat and it's obvious the boat can't be saved, toss life lines to the non-swimmers. If oil or gas slicks are visible, do not, I repeat, *do not* instruct them to don life jackets. If they're wearing them, tell them to take them off. Any fuel floating on the surface near the boat could ignite with tragic consequences for anyone swimming on top of the water. If there's any chance of a surface fire, when they abandon the boat tell them to dive, stay under until they run out of breath, and swim hard. Move your boat so you won't drift toward the fire, cut your engines, toss life jackets to the approaching swimmers and start hauling them aboard. When everyone is safe, contact the Coast Guard by radio. They'll have an ambulance waiting for you at dock if needed. If you don't have radio, telephone them from the marina. They will send a craft out to tow the burned-out boat ashore.

If another boat is simply disabled, out of gas, or with a motor that suddenly decides to quit, any request for assistance cannot be ignored.

The situation might be reversed someday and it could be you in trouble. Distress signals range from arm waving (the proper arm distress signal is repeatedly raising arms slowly from legs to shoulder height, or else a passing boater might think you're just waving hello) to firing off an orange smoke flare. Most of us, incidentally, on seeing a boat dead in the water any distance offshore, will alter course without being asked to see if assistance is needed. There are times, however, when this good Samaritan attitude won't be appreciated. I've discovered the last thing lovers enjoying a cozy, romantic interlude want is company.

If you are asked for help, put bumpers out and approach from the downwind side if the disabled boat is of comparable size or smaller. In reasonably calm water you can rope the boats together while you do what you can to assist with gas or tools. If the disabled boat is a much larger craft and bobbing wildly in a rough sea, approach on the lee side, toss him a bow line, and maintain necessary distance to avoid any possible damage to your hull from the other boat banging against it. If your combined efforts can't get the second boat under way again, the next job is to tow him home. With luck, it'll be your marina. If his home port is a different, more distant harbor, take him to your marina anyway. Your responsibility is to ensure his safety, not provide a costly, time-consuming marine chauffeur service.

Theoretically, the line from his bow to your boat should be attached midship ahead of your rudder for maximum steering control, but I have yet to see a boat, excluding runabouts rigged for water skiing, where such a hookup was possible. You invariably wind up using a stern cleat causing the boat being towed to yaw or run off to one side, which means you proceed slowly.

The real secret of successful towing, and I have yet to see it mentioned in any book on the subject, is to adjust the length of the tow rope so that both craft are hitting waves the same way simultaneously. It makes for far easier control. Equally important, having one boat riding down a crest while the other boat is plowing into the back side of a wave is an easy way to snap a good rope.

In real heavy seas, you might also have to consider bringing the other boat's passengers aboard and cutting their boat loose rather than risking your boat, and everyone's lives, trying to bring an unmanageable, disabled craft ashore.

The bottom line is that a safe boater must always be conscious of the legal responsibility of command, an ancient, well-founded rule of the sea that applies on the Great Lakes as well as the world's oceans, no matter how small your boat. You are the captain. You are in command. Decisions to be made are your decisions based on your experience and knowledge. You are legally responsible not only for the safety of your passengers but anyone else affected by your decisions—and not just on board. For example, if you, while in control of your boat, allow someone to become intoxicated and watch him stagger off to his vehicle at the end of the day, guess who's liable to get stuck for a heavy portion of damages in any ensuing lawsuit if he has an accident on the way home?

These points are worth remembering the next time passengers lacking boating experience show up expecting a boat ride on a stormy day, and fail to understand (the water is quite calm at the marina dock) why you won't take them out into open water. Never allow anyone to sway a common-sense decision of any kind. In this case, stay where you are. You simply tell them, if need be, that if you go out one or two things will happen to them, possibly both. They'll either get seasick or scared stiff. And if by some chance they did like getting wet and banged around, you wouldn't enjoy it. With luck, if they have any boating potential, they'll not only hang around for lunch but help scrub decks. Which is a lot better, you'll admit, than knowingly inviting trouble on a big, storm-tossed lake.

17

History of Salmon

The salmon is the most unpredictable of fish. . . .
—George Frederick Clarke, Song of the Reel

By now I think most of us will agree that salmon are the ultimate angling trophy. Whether you're trolling tidal currents off Vancouver Island's Campbell River for giant fifty-pound kings, fly-casting for fresh-run Atlantic salmon on the scenic Margaree River in Cape Breton, or fishing the Great Lakes for high-jumping silvery coho, the game is the same anywhere salmon are found: to match angling skills and tackle against the world's top sporting fish. And if that isn't enough, at the risk of sounding like a highly prejudiced salmon-fishing fanatic (which I am), no other fish looks better or tastes better on a dinner plate.

Not surprisingly, the history of our salmon is as varied as their attractions to anglers. Although it has been argued for centuries whether salmon originated in fresh water or the ocean, most ichthyologists now accept the theory of freshwater origin. The fish were forced to adjust to salt water during the Ice Age about a million years ago after their riverine environment became largely frozen during periods of extreme cold, the

Two dory fishermen gillnet Pacific salmon near the mouth of the Fraser River in British Columbia in the early 1900s. (*Photo courtesy of Edna Ladner of Delta, British Columbia*)

ice killing off normal food supplies. It is conjectured that melt water from the massive ice fields significantly lowered the salinity of the oceans near shore, establishing a halfway situation where the salmon could make needed biological adjustments in order to become anadromous (capable of surviving in both fresh and salt water). No doubt adding to the transition was the fact that the ocean held huge supplies of forage fish.

It's hard to imagine much of Canada and the northern portions of the United States periodically buried by massive ice fields, as they were many thousands of years ago. The colossal movement of the ice sheets during successive advances and retreats—the bulk and weight of the ice capable of reshaping entire mountain ranges—created completely new oceans, lakes, and rivers. It is also possible under such conditions that fish once creatures of salt water suddenly found themselves trapped in freshwater areas. Previous freshwater fish may also have been thrust almost overnight into an ocean environment while others found themselves on the other side of the world.

There are five recognized species of West Coast salmon: sockeye, *Oncorhynchus nerka*; pink, *O. gorbuscha*; coho, *O. kisutch*; chum, *O.*

keta; and chinook, *O. tshawytscha;* plus *Salmo salar,* the famed leaper of the Atlantic. The question of which came first, the Atlantic or the Pacific varieties, has long been argued. (A sixth Pacific salmon, the cherry, *O. masu,* is found only in Asia.)

Dr. Ferris Neave, in a Canadian Fisheries Research Board paper, theorizes that the Pacific species are relatively recent offshoots of *Salmo salar,* the separation of *Oncorhynchus,* the Pacific species, occurring about one million to five hundred thousand years ago. Parent Atlantic stock, which had a much greater original range than now, likely wandered from the Atlantic to the Pacific Ocean via the Arctic prior to the creation of the Bering land bridge connecting Asia and North America.

Neave says shifting land masses that created the Bering bridge, leading to the original human settlement of North America by nomadic Asian hunters, isolated the Pacific population of salmon and resulted in the gradual development of the genus *Oncorhynchus,* which eventually dispersed over the entire vast Pacific rim. Neave also thinks *Oncorhynchus masu,* the cherry salmon found only in Asia, was likely the earliest offshoot of *Salmo salar* because of biological similarities including blood composition. Another branch of the family, trapped in western freshwater lakes, became what we now call Kamloops trout. Still other former members of the salmon family, steelhead trout, brook trout, and brown trout, although now given different scientific classifications, are all capable of spending part of their life cycle in salt water.

All Pacific salmon are morphologically alike in that they die after spawning. A small portion of mature Atlantic salmon, on the other hand, may return to their natal rivers two or three times to spawn. Another interesting link between Pacific salmon (*Oncorhynchus*) and Atlantic salmon (*Salmo*) is that despite now distinctive differences in appearance and life history, most members of both species still somehow return from the vast oceans to spawn not only in the same watershed of their birth, but often in the same area of the river in which they were born. Seagoing trout and char have shown the same remarkable characteristic.

The earliest mention of salmon in a scientific work is found in the *Natural History of Pliny the Elder,* written in the first century A.D. Pliny used the name *Salmo,* "the leaper," for the first time. "In the rivers of Aquitaine," he wrote, "the salmon surpasses all other fish." Many other references to salmon are found in English medieval writings, as in the eighth century Venerable Bede's *Ecclesiastical History of the English People* or Giraldus Cambrensis's twelfth century description of Wales.

The first known accurate account of the life cycle of salmon was reported in 1517 in the *History of Scotland* by Hector Boethius, principal of the University of Aberdeen, who no doubt spent time on the nearby famous salmon rivers Don and Dee. He wrote: "Salmon is more plentiful in Scotland than in any other region of the world. . . . Because the nature of this fish is strange, I will set down so much as I know hereof at this present time, as followeth:

"The salmon in harvest time cometh into the small rivers, where the water is most shallow, and there the male and female rubbing their womb one against another shed their spawn, which forthwith they cover with sand and gravel and so depart away. From henceforth they are gaunt and slender in appearance so lean they appear naught but skin and bone.

"The aforesaid spawn and milt being hidden in the sand . . . in the next spring doth yield great numbers of little fry but so nesh and tender for a long time, till they come to be so great as a man's finger, if you catch any of them you shall perceive them to melt and their substance to dissolve and fade even as it were jelly or as ice laid forth against the sun. From henceforth they go to the sea where within the space of 20 days they grow to a marvellous greatness."

The arrival of Europeans in North America triggered an even greater flood of enthusiastic reports of fisheries so huge and so numerous as to defy description. More than three thousand rivers and their tributaries from the Niagara River in Lake Ontario to the coastal streams of Newfoundland and Labrador, the Maritimes, and the New England states teemed with salmon. The earliest North American reference to these majestic fish, and their numbers, is found in the saga of Leif Ericson's voyage to Vinland in A.D. 995. Recounting his winter somewhere on the coast of Newfoundland he wrote: "There was no shortage of salmon there and these were larger salmon than they had ever seen before."

In 1497, John Cabot described the Grand Banks (off Newfoundland) as so "swarming with fish [they] could be taken not only with a net but in baskets let down [weighted] with a stone." In 1535, Jacques Cartier said the lower St. Lawrence River was "the richest in every kind of fish that anyone remembers ever having seen or heard of." Captain John Smith was equally enthusiastic in a report of New England in 1614. He found "no river where there is not plenty of sturgeon or salmon or both; all of which are to be had in abundance."

Nicolas Denys, writing of the Miramichi River in the early seventeenth century, says: "So large a quantity of salmon enters this river at night one is unable to sleep, so great is the noise they make in falling upon the water after having thrown or darted themselves into the air passing over the river flats [shallow rapids]."

Denys continues: "I found a little river which I have named Riviere au Saulmon [near Chedabucto Bay on Cape Breton Island]. . . . I made a cast of the seine net at its entrance where it took so great a quantity of salmon that 10 men could not haul it to land. Had it (the net) not broken, the salmon would have carried it off. We had a boat full of them, the smallest three feet long." He also reported salmon six feet in length.

One of the most interesting accounts of salmon fishing in more recent times was kept by Napoleon Comeau, a Quebec gamekeeper who, from 1865 to 1910, was employed by a few rich Montreal entrepreneurs to protect the Godbout River salmon fishery (two hundred miles east of Quebec City) for their personal pleasure. Comeau, who kept meticulous records, reports that the self-styled "Lairds of the Godbout," who only fished the river two or three weeks a year with rarely more than six "rods," caught during his forty-three years on the river 14,560 salmon averaging eighteen pounds each (or 262,080 pounds of fish). A typical two-week season in 1903 saw four anglers kill 543 salmon weighing a total of 6,334 pounds. Two hundred pounds of fish were smoked for transportation to Montreal; the remainder, almost three tons of fish, not counting the few eaten at camp, was left to rot.

The first mention of Pacific salmon in documented history occurred July 20, 1741, when German surgeon-naturalist George William Steller, who was with Vitus Johassen Bering's survey expedition of the north Pacific for Russia, found a quantity of smoked salmon in an underground Indian storehouse on Kayak Island in the Gulf of Alaska. Credit for fully recording all five species of West Coast salmon, however, goes to ichthyologist John Julius Walbaum in his *Artedi Piscium,* published in 1792. That same year, Captain George Vancouver first explored our northwest Pacific coast. At the entrance to Discovery Cove, across the Strait of Georgia opposite the mouth of the Campbell River, he encountered a band of Kwakiutl Indians drying huge racks of red-fleshed salmon on the beach. While rowing ashore for a closer look, history reports that one of Vancouver's crew, name and rank unknown, put a hand line in the water and, when a salmon struck, made angling history by likely being the first nonIndian ever to catch a salmon in Pacific Canada.

The dependence on salmon as food to various coastal Indian tribes quickly became equally important to other explorers and early settlers. A Canada Department of Fisheries booklet, *Canada's Pacific Salmon,* discussing the dependence of early natives on fish to survive, reports Indians "had many ingenious fishing methods and took an important crop of salmon. On the Columbia River they fished from large encampments, using dipnets, spears, hook and line, haul seines, jump baskets set near falls to catch the salmon falling back, and weirs or traps. They dried the fish, smoked them or made them into pemmican, both for their own use and for trade with tribes from other areas. It has been estimated that the Indians of the Columbia watershed may have taken as much as eighteen million pounds of fish a year."

Even better, from a white newcomer's viewpoint, salmon could not only be eaten but also sold. In time, salted salmon became almost as important as furs as a source of income. In 1830, for example, at Fort Langley the factor recorded obtaining fifteen thousand salmon from local Indians. The fish were cured in sixteen days, August 25 to September 10, and shipped out in two hundred barrels. The first commercial canning of West Coast salmon took place in 1864 at Washington, California, on the Sacramento River. By 1917, there were ninety canneries operating between California and Alaska. And although the present commercial West Coast salmon industry is now vastly reduced, primarily because of smaller fish stocks, it's still big business, worth up to $150 million some years in British Columbia alone.

The real modern-day story of sport fishing for salmon, overshadowing even coastal salmon fisheries in terms of angling popularity, is the successful introduction of Pacific salmon in the Great Lakes, creating a new, exciting, and more important, easily accessible sport fishery for millions of inland anglers. This dramatic establishment of a new resource, involving the large-scale fishery management efforts of seven American states and the province of Ontario, has transformed water previously thought "dead" or "dying" into the biggest, richest angling spree in fishing history. It has changed international tourist travel patterns, creating a multimillion dollar boom in boating and tackle sales and altering the lifestyle of most anglers living within an easy drive of any of the lakes.

Not that salmon were never found or previously stocked in the Great Lakes. When the first white settlers arrived, Lake Ontario supported the largest known freshwater population of Atlantic salmon in the world. But not for long. Land-clearing practices that led to heavy river siltation, poachers, pollution from tanneries and sawmills, and the building of dams all combined to destroy the fishery fairly quickly. By the late 1850s, Lake Ontario salmon were virtually extinct. In 1898, the last known survivor of a once great freshwater fishery was netted near Toronto.

In 1865, Samuel Wilmot of Newcastle, Ontario, built what he described as a "reception house," complete with water temperature controls and fish tanks. In 1869, his pioneer salmon hatchery work was recognized by the Canadian government. Ottawa paid him two thousand dollars, took over his hatchery, and put him on salary. In 1876, Wilmot was made Canada's first Superintendent of Fish Breeding. In 1873, the Ohio Fish Commission established a five-year chinook salmon stocking program in Lake Erie. Both it and a similar project in Michigan ended in failure, as did the Ontario program.

Another key player in the history of today's Great Lakes fishery, overshadowing all other early fish culturists, was Seth Green, a native of Rochester, New York, who earned the title "Father of Fish Culture in

Ontario's first coho salmon were transferred into tubs from a tank truck for stocking in the Humber River in the spring of 1969. (*Photo courtesy of Ontario Ministry of Natural Resources*)

America" by establishing the first commercially successful fish hatchery in North America at Caledonia, New York, in 1864. Green's credits include the first propagation of rainbow trout (*Salmo gairdneri*) in northeastern North America. He obtained his initial incubation stock from Campbell's Creek, a tributary of the McLoud River in California, in 1874. The resultant brood stock of rainbows from the Caledonia hatchery was planted in the headwaters of Caledonia Spring Creek and the Genesee River in 1878. By 1884, progeny of the Seth Green rainbows were first reported in Lake Ontario, reaching the lake via the lower Genesee River.

Green, a giant of a man with an equally huge beard, received part of the first batch of brown trout (*Salmo trutta*) eggs sent to North America from England in 1883, helping pave the way for the birth of dry fly fishing for trout as we know it today. Brown-trout fry from the Caledonia hatchery not only revitalized the Catskill fishery from which such early anglers as Theodore Gordon, George LaBranche, Emlyn Gill, and other notables developed unprecedented dry fly angling skills, but also helped establish important Canadian sport fisheries. The first brown trout ever caught by an angler in Canada came out of Lac Brule, Quebec, in 1890. The first Great Lakes tributary stocked with browns by the U.S. Fish Commission was the Pere Marquette River in Michigan in 1884 or 1885.

The big difference in 1966, when Michigan initiated the existing Great Lakes salmon fishery by planting its first batch of five- to six-inch-long Oregon coho smolts, was basically numbers (850,000) and a huge supply of forage food. The Great Lakes were so full of alewife, Atlantic herring that had moved into the Great Lakes via the Welland Canal, that annual die-offs were littering beaches with tons of rotting fish.

How well the combination worked is seen in the fact that the first coho caught unexpectedly in Lake Michigan ninety days after being stocked had grown from five to fifteen inches, and weighed $1\frac{1}{4}$ pounds, a phenomenal weight gain of roughly 2,000 percent in about twelve weeks. By early 1967, coho were being caught up to eight pounds in weight. By fall of that same year, anglers were taking salmon in the fifteen-pound class. At this point, an angling stampede started comparable to any gold rush. Former midwestern United States bluegill and walleye fishermen went literally crazy. One symptom: Hard-to-get West Coast coho lures were being rented, with plenty of takers, at five dollars a day. Motel rooms and rental boats were even harder to come by. By the spring of 1969, Michigan was planting four million coho a year and hundreds of thousands of chinook salmon annually. Similar programs followed in the other Great Lakes states and Ontario. The rest, we all know. With more hatcheries built, and even larger-scale plantings taking place every year, we now have the equivalent of an angling paradise right at our doorsteps.

Howard A. Tanner, a former Michigan Department of Conservation fishery specialist primarily responsible for the historic Michigan salmon stocking program—and undoubtedly destined for angling immortality—recalls the early days in *Sport Fishing USA,* produced by the Bureau of Sport Fisheries and Wildlife of the U.S. Department of the Interior to mark one hundred years of federal involvement in fisheries work: "Some of the background leading to this [salmon stocking] decision is extremely important," he said.

"International sea lamprey research and control [following the decimation of Great Lakes lake trout populations in the 1940s] and the lake trout rehabilitation programs were coordinated and directed by the Great Lakes Fishery Commission. On the United States side [of the lakes], these programs were carried out largely through contracts to the U.S. Bureau of Commercial Fisheries. The scourge of the sea lamprey after fifteen years of arduous labor [developing a selective poison to kill young lamprey in breeding streams] was, by 1964, coming under control. The international lake trout stocking program of the Great Lakes Fishery Commission had produced substantial recovery of lake trout stocks in Lake Superior. The first lake trout plantings were taking place in Lake Michigan."

Dr. Tanner added: "There were established traditions which led to the assumption that the Great Lakes fisheries, having always been managed for commercial harvest, would be returned to similar objectives.

"The newly reorganized Michigan Conservation Department, however, led a change in policy. Michigan had never before played a significant role in the fishery management of Great Lakes water, even though the State had 3,000-plus miles of shoreline and regulatory authority over 74 percent of the U.S. waters of the upper three Great Lakes. The State had the most to gain or lose in any Great Lakes fish management undertakings. The decision by its conservation department was to reorient all fish management of the upper Great Lakes to the development of recreational sports fisheries. It was this change in management objectives [putting sportsmen before netters] that led to the introduction of the now famous coho salmon."

In the late summer of 1967, when the first run of mature three-year-old salmon occurred off the mouths of the Manistee and Platte Rivers, anglers harvested fifty thousand coho averaging fifteen pounds in weight. Some fish topped the twenty-pound mark. Even more astonishing, a total of 312,800 fish were accounted for, representing an unheard of survival rate of 36.8 percent out of the original planting of 850,000 fish. Novice midwestern freshwater-salmon anglers, catching more than five thousand fish on several different weekends, had never before experienced that kind of trophy angling excitement. A fisherman's Valhalla had been created that sent massive reverberations into the other Great Lakes states and Ontario. And the future looked even more exciting. Michigan planted its first chinook that same year, 1967, which meant even higher quality angling was just around the corner in the form of larger (who could truly imagine it?) thirty- and forty-pound fish. "If Michigan can do it, why can't we?" sportsmen rightly asked elsewhere.

Two other species of salmon, pinks and kokanee, the last a subspecies of sockeye salmon, were introduced into the Great Lakes by the province of Ontario. In terms of success versus cost, the present-day

Great Lakes fish hatchery and stocking techniques have become as sophisticated as modern angling techniques. Here New York lake trout are stocked by helicopter in Lake Ontario near Watertown, New York. (*Photo by John Georg, New York State Department of Environmental Conservation*)

spread of pink salmon throughout the lakes has to be one of the most surprising chapters in Great Lakes fishing history. To start with, the whole thing was an accident. Ontario fishery officials didn't intend to put pinks into the lakes. The original stock of pink salmon was raised to fingerling size at Port Arthur at the head of Lake Superior in 1956 only to air-ship them north to Goose Creek (flowing into Hudson Bay) in hopes of boosting a native Indian fishery. After the aircraft left Port Arthur, hatchery workers discovered about 21,000 pink salmon fingerlings had been overlooked in the fish troughs. They dumped the tiny pinks into nearby Lake Superior and forgot about them. What chance did they have?

The following year, a Canadian Press report noted two pink salmon had been caught off the Manitou River and the Sucker River on the north shore of Lake Superior. Having only a two-year life cycle, spawning and dying every other year and rarely reaching more than 1.5 pounds in weight, the pinks were again forgotten until 1973 when a rainbow trout fisherman caught a pink in the Mindemoya River on Manitoulin Island, proving some of the original fish had not only reproduced but that their progeny, obviously increasing in numbers, were heading south. Heavy spawning runs of pinks were reported in 1979 at Wawa, Sault Ste. Marie, and Blind River. That same year, anglers began catching mature eighteen-inch pinks off Long Point in Lake Erie. By 1981, the fish were in Lake Ontario.

Ontario's kokanee salmon program, on the other hand, obviously designed to create a new commercial netting industry, was a costly flop. The province dumped millions of these plankton-eating salmon into the Great Lakes during the 1960s and early 1970s. Stocking figures show 5,748,751 kokanee were placed in Lake Ontario alone between 1965 and 1972. Even more were planted in Lake Huron during the same period. Finally, with no return rates evident, the program was terminated in 1972 as a failure.

18

The Lamprey Story

The most distinctive characteristic of the adult sea lamprey is the tooth-studded oral disc with which it grasps fish to suck out the blood on which it feeds.

—Canada Sea Lamprey Control Centre,
Sault Ste. Marie, Ontario, Lamprey Bulletin

All Jim Tibbles has to do is look out his office window to be reminded of sea lamprey control work waiting to be done. The brawling St. Marys River, visible from the Great Lakes Fishery Commission's Lamprey Control Centre in Sault Ste. Marie, Ontario, now holds some twenty million lamprey, the largest single concentration of these fish-killing predators to be found anywhere in the Great Lakes.

Dr. Tibbles, director of the Centre, says the reason St. Marys, the rocky outflow of Lake Superior, has never been treated with lampricide, a selective toxicant that kills only lamprey, is simply because there is too much water traveling too quickly for normal control techniques to work. The river has an average flow of 78,500 cubic feet of water a second (cfs), reaching as high as 127,000 cfs at times. So without some guarantees of success, the international control agency is reluctant to spend up to $4 million, the estimated cost of treatment, until it can be shown the costly lamprey-killing chemical TFM won't be harmlessly flushed out into

Lake Huron. Until then, lampreys capable of contaminating the entire Great Lakes system continue to thrive in the river.

One recent fight Dr. Tibbles won, however, was obtaining permission to start treating tributaries of Oneida Lake, part of the Finger Lakes chain not considered part of the Great Lakes drainage system. The commission's necessary approval of the project followed a 1984 study of Fish Creek, a tributary of Oneida Lake, linked to Lake Ontario via the Oswego River. Fish Creek was of special interest because it was one of the few remaining untreated streams in the Great Lakes system with a known large population of sea lamprey ammocoetes (the lamprey larval stage). The creek's average water flow and other related hydrological conditions also suited the proposed scientific study. Some 16,800 lamprey were collected and marked with a subcutaneous injection of latex dye and released. During the treatment of the river with lampricide, 205 of the 35,211 ammocoetes collected bore the latex identifying mark. By extrapolating this ratio, it was determined Fish Creek alone held an estimated population of 6,100,000 sea lamprey. The second stage of the study is now in the process of being carried out. It involves the recovery in Lake Ontario of tagged lamprey that were released in Fish Creek to prove to skeptics formerly blocking the project that Oneida streams are a breeding source of Great Lakes lamprey.

The overall success of the Great Lakes Fishery Commission's lamprey control work is still one of the happiest biological success stories to be found in North America, especially when you consider it only took the lamprey, a bloodsucking saltwater parasite with a 250-million-year-old talent for survival (making *Petromyzon marinus* even older than long-gone dinosaurs), less than fifty years to destroy the richest freshwater fisheries on earth. It's estimated that each 12- to 20-inch adult lamprey kills forty pounds of trout, salmon, or whitefish during its short, free-swimming career.

Today, as a direct result of the Commission beginning its lamprey control work in 1956—at a cost of about $7 million a year to maintain the fishery commission plus an additional $25 million of state, provincial, and federal funds each year to rear and stock approximately 36 million trout and salmon—we now have a still-growing sport and commercial angling bonanza worth an estimated $1.14 billion a year.

The history of the lamprey invasion of the Great Lakes began in Lake Ontario as a result of direct access to the Atlantic Ocean via the St. Lawrence River or the Hudson River–Oneida Lake–Oswego River system. The ocean links also allowed colonization of the lake by other saltwater creatures such as Atlantic salmon, American eel, alewife, and three-spined stickleback. One ironic note is that the same destruction of stream spawning habitat that destroyed the Atlantic salmon fishery may also have promoted lamprey reproduction. Some biologists believe the higher water temperatures created by current-blocking dams and denuded river banks, so fatal to salmon, created a more favorable environment for lamprey. Whatever the reason, the effects of overfishing, habitat destruction, and lamprey invasion caused Lake Ontario's fish stocks to decline in the late 1800s. As noted earlier, by 1900 Atlantic salmon no longer even existed in the lake.

Construction of the Welland Canal, bypassing Niagara Falls, which had previously blocked passage of lamprey into the other lakes, opened up the entire Great Lakes system to lamprey (and alewife, another prominent player) in 1829. However, with its slow-moving, often muddy and polluted tributaries, shallow, nutrient-rich Lake Erie apparently discouraged large-scale build-ups of lamprey populations in the new territory. The first adult sea lamprey wasn't reported in the lake until 1921, almost one hundred years after the canal provided easy access.

But like early pioneers crossing the inhospitable deserts of the Southwest to reach California, once lamprey reached the western end of Lake Erie, the other, friendlier lakes fell to lamprey in rapid succession. Not only did the deep, cold upper lakes hold clean-flowing tributaries in which lamprey could best spawn, but they also held an almost unlimited supply of prey species such as lake trout and burbot, both having the same water temperature preferences as lamprey. Lake Michigan became a new home for lamprey in 1936, Lake Huron by 1937, and Lake Superior in 1938. It is thought lamprey likely reached Lake Superior through the locks of the St. Mary's River the same way they gained access to Lake Erie, clinging to the hulls of freighters. How quickly hitchhiking lamprey can move around the lakes in this fashion is awe inspiring. Commission records show one Lake Huron lamprey tagged in Hammond Bay in northern Michigan was recovered in Lake Erie, about four hundred miles away, two days later.

Such ease of movement creates additional questions about the Great Lakes Fishery Commission's long-standing decision not to poison the fourteen major lamprey-producing streams that feed into Lake Erie, especially Cattaraugus Creek on the American side and Big Creek on the Ontario side, two of the lake's major lamprey factories. This situation is slowly changing as a result of growing public/political pressures. The fishery commission is now indicating treatment may start in 1988. But the commission has always publicly taken the position that few lamprey would ever be found in the warmest, most southern lake due to a limited number of suitable lamprey spawning streams. Increased stockings of salmonids by New York, Pennsylvania, Ohio, and Michigan (about 4 million a year) are proving it wrong, however. Lake Erie has now become little more than one huge free-lunch counter for lamprey. The lake is not only home of the largest-sized lamprey found in any of the lakes, but also the percentage of lake trout bearing lamprey scars is higher than sea lamprey wounding rates in Lake Superior in the 1960s when lamprey were equally uncontrolled there. The latest available data, from 1981, shows 57 percent of Lake Erie's larger trout (the study is broken down into five different sizes of fish) survived lamprey attacks, as compared to 43 percent scarring of the same size fish in Lake Superior in 1961. The ugliest aspect of the situation, dead fish, is difficult for anyone to envision in its entirety. Scarred or wounded fish are only those that survived an attack. One seldom sees fish killed by lamprey.

Back in 1940, however, the situation in the Great Lakes was a classic fox-in-a-chicken-house scenario. An extremely adaptable saltwater killer with no natural enemies was thriving as never before, with devastating economic results on commercial fisheries. Unlike most predators, including man, who'll voluntarily abandon a declining resource once it reaches the point where diminishing returns aren't worth the effort of pursuit, lamprey will keep killing lake trout until the last fish is gone. Only then will lamprey move to a less desirable environment or prey on less desirable fish. As a result, lake trout became virtually extinct in Lake Michigan and the main basin of Lake Huron. Trout catches in those lakes dropped from more than 11 million pounds in the early 1940s to less than 200,000 pounds by the mid 1950s, only fifteen years later. In Lake Superior, lamprey damage followed a similar pattern. Prior to 1952, Superior's annual lake trout harvest averaged about 4.5 million pounds annually. By 1960, the catch was down to less than 500,000 pounds.

At that point, the invader could no longer be ignored. Unlike its native cousins, the extremely abundant nonparasitic northern brook and American brook lampreys and the parasitic silver and chestnut lampreys that never became abundant, the sea lamprey was throwing off the entire ecological balance of the Great Lakes. Michigan initiated action in the 1940s, followed by Wisconsin and Ontario. The first scientific effort to learn hard facts about this exotic bloodsucking newcomer—where it was found, what its weaknesses might be—involved the building of a trap weir by Michigan biologists on northern Lake Huron's Ocqueoc River. In all the studies that followed, the conclusions were as evident as declining commercial fish-catch statistics: rapidly increasing sea lamprey populations were decimating the Great Lakes fisheries.

In 1946, the United States and Canada formed the Great Lakes Sea Lamprey Committee to coordinate the international studies, a move which eventually led to the creation in 1955 of the Great Lakes Fishery Com-

A Lake Ontario salmon is swung aboard author's boat with a king-sized lamprey still firmly attached to the hapless fish. These occurrences are becoming rarer due to U.S.-Canada lamprey control projects.

mission. The commission, which established its headquarters in Ann Arbor, Michigan, was given two basic jobs, to control sea lamprey and restore Great Lakes lake trout numbers.

With adult lamprey out of reach in the lakes, and disruption of the reproductive cycle the obvious place to start anyway, fishery workers first tried building mechanical barriers such as dams, weirs, and traps to prevent adult lamprey from reaching upstream spawning beds. Mature lamprey enter rivers to spawn between April and July, usually when stream temperatures warm to about forty degrees. Finding a site in riffled shallows with a sandy, light-gravel bottom, lampreys use their sucking mouths to move the gravel and stones in the streambed, creating a mound of gravel on the downstream edge of the hollowed-out nest. A single female will deposit an average of sixty thousand eggs, which are carried by the current to lodge in the piled-up gravel on the rim of the nest. Out of that number, a possible one thousand larvae hatch within ten to twelve days. Those that survive leave the security of their gravel crib a week or so later to drift downstream where they instinctively burrow in silty bottoms of quiet pools. They remain in the mud, feeding on microscopic water plants and animals for anywhere from three to seventeen years before entering the lakes as parasitic adults. Adult life span is between a year and eighteen months, the adults dying after spawning like Pacific salmon.

Another form of lamprey-blocking structure used pipe electrodes placed in the water to create a 115 volt electrical barrier. By 1960, some 162 of these electrical units were in operation on Lake Superior and Lake Michigan tributaries. But like the dams, which tended to get wiped out by floods or, when they did stay in place, encouraged lamprey to spawn below them, the electrical barriers also created problems, including the killing of trout and other native fish over six inches in length, a point at which fish become highly susceptible to electric shock.

In 1958, after four years of work screening more than six thousand different chemical combinations, a team of research scientists, led by Vernon C. Applegate at the U.S. Fish and Wildlife Service's Hammond Bay Biological Station on Lake Michigan, discovered what is still considered the ultimate weapon against lamprey, a compound that kills lamprey with little effect on desirable fish. This selective toxicant, 3-trifluoromethyl-4-nitrophenol (TFM), is still being used as the basic method of lamprey control today. In 1963, another chemical was added, 5,2'-dichloro-4-nitrosalicylanilide, or Bayer 73, which, when added to TFM, increased its strength to the point where dosages, and TFM costs, could be cut by almost 50 percent. (Bayer 73, by the way, if you're a trivia nut, is what your family doctor will usually prescribe to treat Great Lakes swimmer's itch.)

Having a safe, effective lampricide with the potential for controlling lamprey in all of the Great Lakes, the American Great Lakes states and Ontario then began in the late 1950s to rebuild once valuable fisheries by stocking millions of lake trout followed, in the late 1960s, by coho and chinook salmon. Both salmon species, as we now know, were introduced as alewife predators to help correct ecological imbalances in the lakes. But the fight against lamprey is still far from over. Any dreams of completely eradicating lamprey have long been shattered. Scientists now face the specter of lamprey not only developing resistance to TFM, but also becoming capable in time of spawning in open lakes rather than rivers. This last scenario, fortunately, is considered highly improbable.

Additional problems range from findings that TFM use is not as biologically safe as first thought, temporarily depressing stream insect numbers, to suggestions that lampricide might be actually improving chances of lamprey survival by reducing competition for food. Two U.S.

Fish and Wildlife Service biologists, Patrick Manion and Bernard Smith, have told the Great Lakes Fishery Commission that lowering the number of ammocoetes may give young lamprey that do survive a better chance to mature. As a result, nearly as many lamprey might grow up in a stream as could be expected if the stream were left untreated. Whether Manion and Smith were deliberately playing the role of devil's advocate is unknown. Reactions of other fishery scientists to their views are still extremely critical.

A probable result of reduced lamprey competition is seen in the Great Lakes, especially Lake Michigan where the average size of (better fed?) adult lamprey has jumped from less than 4.5 ounces in 1961 to more than 9 ounces. Inability to restore naturally reproducing lake trout stocks and disturbingly high ratios of lamprey-scarred trout (75 percent in parts of Lake Huron) also indicate lamprey are surviving much better than expected. Although lake trout have been stocked in Lakes Michigan and Huron since the 1960s, they have yet to spawn successfully. Whether the problem is lamprey predation or genetics (or a combination of both) is unknown. Trout do spawn in the lakes but no small fish are produced. Yet those same eggs, when taken to a hatchery, produce healthy fingerlings.

The same worrisome message was given in an international sea lamprey symposium held by the Great Lakes Fishery Commission in Marquette, Michigan in 1979 to pool the knowledge of eighty-eight of the world's top lamprey experts. Former Fish and Wildlife Service biologist Stanford Smith, and Ronald Morris, a zoologist at the University of Nottingham, England, concluded that "in the uncrowded stream environment, ammocoetes seem to be growing more rapidly, and transforming at a larger size, with a possible greater survival to transformation. Recently metamorphosed sea lamprey also seem to be growing faster, larger and healthier with a probably greater survival to maturity. Carried to the extreme, continued chemical treatments would eventually lead to a population of sea lampreys that spawned primarily in the lower areas of the streams with larvae that drifted into the lake shortly after hatching and completed their larval phase in offshore areas. If such selection were to occur, control by chemical treatment would, in fact, become impractical, if not impossible."

New defenses being studied include borrowing biological techniques used by entomologists to control insect pests by sterilizing and releasing large numbers of males prior to the mating season. Biologists at Hammond Bay are now seeking environmentally safe natural sterilants. Another possibility is chemically duplicating natural lamprey scent pheromones or finding other attractants to draw lamprey into traps where they can be removed from the rivers. Repellents could also be developed to discourage lamprey from entering prime spawning streams. Still another prospect is to genetically alter lake trout preference for forty-degree water, the same temperature preferred by lamprey, which is why trout are so heavily victimized. Equally "far out" is genetic alteration of sea lampreys. Hybridization with native, nonparasitic brook lamprey, for example, might produce a creature which, in brook lamprey fashion, would not feed as an adult. As brook lamprey become sexually mature, their digestive tracts degenerate; they spawn and die.

Equally effective lamprey controls may also be found in studies of streams not used by lamprey to discover why lamprey aren't using them. There must be some environmental factors involved that might, in the words of Stanford Smith, provide clues to new control measures. He believes, for example, that forest rejuvenation on some Lake Superior stream banks, and increased shade, have made the waters too cold for lamprey reproduction. Streams must warm up to at least sixty degrees for optimum survival of lamprey larvae.

Whatever the ultimate solution, all experts agree on two basic points: (1) using present lamprey control techniques, we'll always have lamprey with us, and (2) we have to continue what we're doing. There is, as yet, no alternative to the chemical treatment program. And without such controls we would have another total collapse of the fisheries.

19

The Future

We'll banish all sorrow
And sing till tomorrow
And angle and angle again.

—*Ancient Fishing Song*

I suspect future angling historians will categorize today's Great Lakes salmon fishery as one of the "golden periods" of angling, on a par with, say, the Catskill trout fishing era of Hewitt, Gordon, and LaBranche in the early 1900s, a time when the sun shone brightest, skies were bluest, and high-jumping fish came to a fly in pleasing, water-splashing quantity.

But considering the mind-boggling changes that have occurred in the Great Lakes in the last twenty years, any attempt to peer into the future, to predict what might happen in the next twenty years, can only be an imaginative exercise, however pleasant, with no real claims of infallibility. So much has happened so quickly on the lakes it is still difficult to grasp fully the extent of what has already occurred let alone what might happen in future.

The Great Lakes twenty years ago—discounting diminishing warm-water angling opportunities in places such as Long Point Bay on Lake Erie or portions of Lake St. Clair—were basically a polluted waste area holding nothing more than smelt and alewife, alien intruders that provided little sport except for spring smelt dip netters. Today, with smelt and alewife providing a rich food base for heavy-bellied, fast-growing salmon, our lakes and many of their tributaries provide angling thrills few, if any, of us could possibly have visualized a few short years ago. In fact our present fishery, in size at least, must almost equal that enjoyed by early white settlers. Who dared dream such a thing?

Even better, from a long-range biological viewpoint, the introduction of salmon is in some cases returning ecologically desirable predator-prey balances to the lakes' fish populations. Increasingly important social and economic values of the fishery have also helped create growing public awareness of environmental pollution, and the need for even more Great Lakes cleanup work. Because of salmon, and renewed interest in the lakes, the future quality of our lives, and our children's lives, appears much brighter.

One future aspect of the fishery that can be predicted with complete confidence, however, is that tomorrow's Great Lakes fish will be bigger, stronger, and better adapted to what is now a strange environment. Scientific advances in genetics alone—the ability to control, among other things, size, sex, and behavior of fish—although yet to be used to any great extent by fishery managers, may hold the key to some of the more exciting future changes in Great Lakes sport angling. As one example, who wouldn't want to tangle with gargantuan one hundred-pound fish? It's not a daydream. Importation of Alaskan Kenai River salmon for hatchery brood stock, the fish living seven years and often topping the one hundred-pound mark, is one way of doing it. There is also a wide variety of technology available to create finned monsters out of the local fish stocks we have now.

Two scientists at McMaster University in Hamilton, Ontario, Dr. Ronald Sonstegard and Dr. Tom Chen, are cloning rainbow trout growth genes and, by introducing extra genes in fertilized trout eggs, are confident they can produce genetically engineered, self-reproducing "superfish" that will top the one hundred-pound mark.

"Engineering a five-fold increase in growth could also mean that trout raised on fish farms will mature five times faster," Dr. Sonstegard says. It now takes 16 to 18 months for a normal rainbow trout to reach a marketable one pound size. The new fish would be ready for harvest in three to four months. Not stated, but implicit in the research, is that if 20 pound rainbow trout can be grown as large as 100 pounds, the same technique can turn normal 40 pound salmon into 200 pound fish! (A fellow charterboater, during a recent boatside discussion of the subject, shook his head in disbelief. "Good God," he said, "if they get into that we're going to have to start asking for danger pay to go out there.")

University of British Columbia fish geneticists have taken another approach to creating giant fish. They are manipulating the sex of unborn salmon by mixing control hormones with ripe eggs, a technique that is not only amazingly easy, but cheap. The original purpose of the research was to bolster the sagging income of commercial salmon anglers whose only real profit often depends on the sale of roe. The higher the ratio of hen fish in the sea, the better the chances of West Coast trollers being able to stay in business. From that point, it was a short step to the deliberate creation of both male and sterile fish, which is where the work becomes even more interesting from the viewpoint of a Great Lakes angler. A sterile fish with no sex mechanisms would theoretically stay in the lake and, by not spawning and thus postponing death that follows spawning, live an extra year or two, growing twice the size of the forty- to fifty-pounders found in the lakes now.

It would also be extremely easy, in theory at least, to manipulate the existing gene pool of Great Lakes salmon to produce above-average size fish just by selectivity. With fishery managers now largely relying on their own previously released fish stock for egg and milt sources, resultant genetic isolation will, in time, likely create a distinctive strain of fish, maybe even successfully self-reproducing salmon. But the process could be aided, and larger fish produced, by hatchery workers deliberately picking out only the biggest brood stock for reproduction. In most cases, the extra-large fish are salmon who stay in the lakes an extra year or two before spawning.

The value of selecting only the biggest and strongest fish for breeding purposes is best seen in the work of researchers at the Fisheries Center of the University of Washington in Seattle, where scientists have been using selectivity to develop "super salmon" since 1949. Basically, the researchers are stripping eggs from the biggest fish returning to their release point, laboratory pools connected by fish ladders to Portage Bay, and again, after more selective breeding and rearing, releasing only the hardiest fingerlings. The survival rate of the special fish, measured by returns to spawning areas, is reportedly thirty times that of fish used as brood stock without thought of size or vigor. The university's ponds boast a 60 percent survival rate, with at least 10 percent of the same fish, out of the quarter million salmon produced each year, surviving in the vast, often perilous Pacific Ocean and returning to spawn. Other work at the university has ranged from the development of improved hatchery fish foods, and increased growth, to interracial hybridization of specially selected rainbow trout with migratory steelhead (the steelhead crosses reach smolt size in about five months compared to the usual two years).

Another long-needed Great Lakes fishery management change is to alter man-made genetic weaknesses of the so-called "native" trout stocks.

Brown trout provide a classic example. These comparatively short-lived fish have been hatchery bred in North America for more than one hundred years for only one purpose, to grow fast in a stream environment. Put them in a big lake, as we're doing, and they are totally confused. Basic behavior mechanisms no longer exist. They even lose spawning capability. An alternative is to import longer-lived, bigger-growing "seeforellan" brown trout stock easily obtained in Germany or Austria.

Great Lakes hatchery lake trout strains are equally mixed up, although work now under way to "educate" fish to use suitable spawning areas by imprinting looks promising. Biologists at the University of Wisconsin–Madison Marine Studies Center, wondering why more than 40 million lake trout stocked in Lake Michigan since the middle 1960s have failed to reproduce—even though the fish were once native—now believe the basic problem is that the fish are not only being stocked in the wrong place, but at the wrong time. Research team leader Ross Horrall notes that lake trout, like closely related coho and chinook salmon, appear to become imprinted to their "home" territory early in life and, as adults, are drawn back to these areas to spawn.

Young lake trout stocked from piers or jetties where lake bottom and

Lake trout eggs nestle in AstroTurf prior to being incubated in traditional Lake Michigan spawning areas. It's hoped the newly hatched fish will become imprinted and return to the same shoals to reproduce naturally. (Photo courtesy of University of Wisconsin Sea Grant Institute)

water conditions prevented successful reproduction òn their return as adults are now being stocked by Wisconsin on offshore lake trout spawning reefs in Lakes Superior and Michigan. "Incubators" are framed layers of astroturf, the plastic grass used on football fields, that hold and protect the eggs until they hatch. Horrall's research also indicates lake trout should be stocked at an earlier age, another important reason for incubating fish on spawning reefs. "The critical imprinting period may be the first month after the eggs hatch," says Horrall. In other words, the standard technique of stocking fifteen- to eighteen-month-old lake trout is self-defeating if the purpose is to create a naturally reproducing fishery. Results of the Wisconsin work, being supported by the Wisconsin Coastal Management Program, the Wisconsin Department of Natural Resources, and the University of Wisconsin's Sea Grant Institute, won't be known until the fish mature and return to their place of birth to spawn in about 1988.

It is safe to assume much more will be learned about physiological capabilities and instinctual behavior of fish in the next few years. As often happens, research in one area of fish behavior leads to other findings of major importance. Two University of California biologists, Dr. Gordon Grau and Richard Nishioka, attempting to solve one of the biggest remaining mysteries—how ocean-wandering salmon find their way back to their home streams—may have solved another vital puzzle: How to know when hatchery-raised salmon should be released so that more of the young fish survive. Says Dr. Grau: "If they're not physiologically ready, in many cases their growth stops, they weaken and die."

The two scientists believe the key is a hormone, thyroxine, which triggers metabolic changes in young salmon. Thyroxine, found in all vertebrates, including humans, is a key agent in both brain and physical development. It is seemingly produced by salmon in greatest quantity within a day of a new moon. The simultaneous occurrence of a new moon and thyroxine "surges" was found after studying hundreds of salmon plasma samples. Grau, quoted in the *Los Angeles Times,* said: "If this works out like we think it will, it'll mean hatchery personnel will be able to predict migratory readiness by using a lunar calendar and not by complicated, time-consuming procedures such as blood enzyme studies" (or guesswork).

In the past, hatchery managers have largely keyed releases of salmon on visual signs such as scale loss, loss of interest in feeding, changes in weight-to-length ratios, and the congregating of fish at blocked raceway exits. Says Bob Rawstron, Assistant Director for the California Department of Fish and Game's anadromous fisheries branch, also quoted by the *Los Angeles Times*: "For fifty years we've been trying to figure out when to release young salmon. We've tried a lot of ways, some worked, some didn't. From the little data we've seen so far on this project [Grau's and Nishioka's], it looks promising." There is also some evidence thyroxine enables salmon to "imprint" scent of native streams, allowing them to literally smell their way back to their place of birth.

Although seemingly theoretical at the time, salmon homing studies done by renowned University of Wisconsin limnologist Arthur Hasler, whose discoveries in the 1960s of how salmon use odor to identify home streams during spawning migrations, have since proven to be increasingly important to fishery managers dependent on salmon returning to original release points. Worthwhile returns not only economically justify the stocking in the first place but are needed to obtain a fresh supply of roe and milt to repeat the stocking cycle. Hasler's classic experiment involved capturing salmon well upstream of a fork in a river. The fish were taken downstream below the fork and colored balloons were attached in order to track the fish, salmon from the left branch of the river trailing yellow balloons on the surface, right fork fish toting red. All unerringly chose the correct fork of the river. The next step, and the key to the experiment, was to recapture the same fish and take them downstream again, only this time Hasler plugged their noses with petroleum jelly. As he no doubt suspected, many of the salmon, not being able to smell, entered the wrong fork.

Today's stocking technique as practiced in Wisconsin and elsewhere, thanks to Hasler, is to imprint young salmon to a specific chemical odor—morpholine—in the hatchery. The salmon are then released in normal fashion. The year they are to return as spawning adults, the same imprinting chemical is "dripped" into desired rivers to attract the mature salmon back to the best spawning and harvesting sites. Controlled experiments, including telemetry tracking, have shown coho can be "called back" with the use of scent to any area within twenty miles of the original release site. Hasler's fundamental research, incidentally, provides a beautiful example of how theoretical fishery work at the university research level, although sometimes criticized by field workers and impatient anglers who want immediate results, often pays off big a few years down the road. When the "partnership" is working correctly, field workers and cooperative anglers gather fish population data for day-by-day management use, and university workers use the freely given information as a needed statistical base for long-range studies.

The question of what fish see is still a scientific mystery. This is rather puzzling, from an angler's viewpoint at least, considering the vital role vision obviously plays in piscatorial struggles for survival in shallow water. There has been much scientific work done on the physical structure of fish eyes. Scientists know, or think they know, what a fish should be able to see based on eye construction. There has also been a wide variety of research proving that fish can distinguish between various colors. But no one knows as yet (it would help to find a talking fish) how the brain of a fish interprets what it sees. When a sky-blue pink lure takes a lot of fish on an outing we tend to think, Man, do those fish ever love that color. In reality, squares could be circles—the fish could be seeing a particular color in a totally different way than we would; they could, in effect, be seeing a color we would not recognize.

It is also possible, if not probable, there are varieties of colors, some no doubt totally unpleasant to our eyes, that could be used on lures to improve their effectiveness greatly just because the fish could see them better. Remember the revulsive feelings most of us had as bass fishermen when purple plastic worms first hit the market? Yet the fish gobbled them up, and still do. Until science comes up with more hard answers, though, we will have to continue to experiment on our own, depending on the fish to tell us what they like by how often and how hard they knock lures free of our cannonball releases. But I still have a nagging feeling that some of the most revolutionary angling advances in making lures more visible to fish and increasing angling catches are still waiting to be discovered by a curious young scientist in a lab somewhere who, quite likely, will be working in a completely different area of research. (Among scientists, for seekers of trivia, these accidental discoveries are quietly but happily called "serendipity.")

Great advances are being made in the search for cures for fish-killing bacterial diseases such as furunculosis, which periodically wipes out the entire annual production of salmon and trout fingerlings in some hatcheries. One of the biggest, most active firms in this field of research, Aqua Health Ltd. of Charlottetown, Prince Edward Island, already has licenses from the Canada Department of Agriculture to produce vaccines for two bacterial diseases, vibriosis and enteric red mouth, and has applied for approval to market a furunculosis vaccine. Some of the vaccines are applied by spraying or immersing the fish, while others have to be injected.

In the future we will no doubt see even more advances in the development of highly sophisticated, increasingly powerful computers to find and track offshore fish. The direction in which the sonar industry is moving is easily seen in a unit now being introduced by the Lowrance Electronics Company of Tulsa, Oklahoma—the X-16—which has a depth capability of 8,000 feet, as compared to its predecessor's 2,490 feet, and can measure the water in 1-foot segments, a tenfold increase over the older X-15 model. This gives the new unit something like 32 million possible computerized range settings. Other firms, such as Techsonic

Industries in Eufaula, Alabama, makers of Humminbird fishing sonar units, are introducing CVRs, color video recorders that, like familiar TV sets, show bottom contours and fish in multicolored displays. Computerization allows everything from stop-action to zoom closeups.

Sonar transducers will be available that instead of just beaming sound impulses downward from the boat will make sweeping, circular scans to register fish all around the boat, not just between the boat and bottom. These units are being used now on bigger commercial fishing boats but are too large and too costly at the moment to be of interest to sport anglers.

Even more futuristic are the possibilities resulting from built-in sonar computer memories. The Lowrance X-16, for example, will record Loran-C navigational settings, printing coordinates on chart paper that will give you your exact location on the Great Lakes and, with a bit of map work, the compass reading needed to take you straight back to home port, even in fog so thick you can't see a boat length in front of you.

How about computerized sonar units someday being linked to your downriggers so your cannonballs and trailing lures are automatically lowered or raised to the same depth as newly registered fish? It should be equally possible, if you have a zillion dollars to spend, to link sonar computers to a boat's auto pilot system so the boat automatically keeps making trolling passes over the fish.

If you want to go really far out, in more ways than one, (this next prediction is based on the little known fact the Lowrance firm is big in the satellite business) it is also fairly safe to predict future sonar units may be incorporated with a space satellite system so that schools of fish in large bodies of water can be tracked via a satellite-sonar system from even a small boat. Far fetched? I don't think so. It's technically possible right now.

Computers will also unquestionably play a much larger role in the management of the future Great Lakes' fishery. As an example of what is being done, John Magnuson, Director of the University of Wisconsin–Madison's Center for Limnology, and his associates are using computers to establish mathematical models of lake fish populations. By feeding environmental data into a computer—the area of a lake, its maximum depth, pH, conductivity, and total size of the lake's watershed—the researchers can accurately predict the kind of fish community that can be found in the lake, depending on its geographical location.

The ability to look at the dynamics of a lake community on a computer screen and, by juggling data, predict the potential impact of management proposals, will be of great assistance in achieving an ecologically

balanced fishery, a necessity for meaningful, long-lasting farm pond management as well as management of the Great Lakes.

A great deal of work obviously must be done to coordinate stocking
programs of the various Great Lake states and Ontario based on forage
fish numbers, a perfect job for a computer once basic biomass data is
obtained. Continued dumping of millions of salmon and trout into the
lakes without knowledge of the full effects of such stocking on the food
chain suggests a future collapse of the fishery is very possible. On Lake
Michigan, where once tons of dead alewife washed up on lake beaches
periodically, it is a rarity to see dead fish now. Are too many salmon
eating too many bait fish? Are existing smelt and alewife populations
capable of meeting such predation pressures through natural reproduction? Are we slowly but surely killing the goose with the golden egg?
These, and similar basic questions, I have yet to see answered. But with
the help of computers, some urgently needed answers should be available
in the near future.

The probability of a general decline of the lower Great Lakes sport
fishery as salmon and trout slowly run out of food is of natural concern
to state and provincial resource managers. Even the normally mute Great
Lakes Fishery Commission is starting to act. Predator-prey issues were a
major feature of a commission meeting in Ann Arbor, Michigan, in March
1985. As Art Holder, head of the fishery section of the Ontario Ministry
of Natural Resources, noted in conversation, "It's a put-and-grow fishery,
not a put-and-take. They [trout and salmon] have to have something to
eat."

Richard C. Bishop, Department of Agricultural Economics, University of Wisconsin–Madison, writing on the economics of Wisconsin's
Great Lakes fishery in the 1982 to 1984 biennial report of the university's
Sea Grant Institute, summed the situation up this way: "The salmon and
trout fishery we have 10 or 20 years from now will depend on management of the forage base, stocking policies and lamprey control . . . A
large share of Wisconsin's $60 million annual benefits from sport fishing
rests on the continued viability of the forage base, particularly in Lake
Michigan. To ignore this fact is to risk having the trout and salmon fisheries
tumble like a house of cards."

Unmistakable signs of future fishery management problems already
abound. The most obvious ecological changes are found in Lake Michigan, the first lake to be stocked with salmon and still the most heavily
stocked water in all of the Great Lakes. Total salmonid (more accurately,
salmonine) plantings in the lake have increased from an annual average
of 3.4 million fish in 1965 to 8.6 million in 1969–72, 12.1 million in
1973–77, and 15.4 million during 1978–84, for a grand total of 215

million fish over a 20-year period. One result: A drastic decline in alewife numbers, the primary forage fish. It is estimated Lake Michigan's alewife population is now only 2 percent of the number that existed prior to the introduction of salmon, a 98 percent decrease. So it should be no surprise the average size of Lake Michigan salmon is declining.

Other changes in Lake Michigan include increased numbers of fish species formerly suppressed by alewifes such as chub, perch and, to a lesser extent, smelt. As yet, because of different lake habitat preferences, salmon have not made a seemingly predictable major diet shift to the other replacement food species, although some hungry salmon are now looking elsewhere for dinner. One 1984 Wisconsin study, based on two years of stomach samplings of sport angler catches in Wisconsin waters of Lake Michigan, showed chinook salmon have added yellow perch, sculpins, and even ninespine sticklebacks to their diets. Despite such findings, it's still hard to imagine once-proud salmon prowling shallow, weedy bays in search of warm water perch.

Strangest of all, but a good example of how inextricably life systems are interwoven, is a resultant ecological reversal of the standard biology classroom tenet that water quality controls fish life. Fish life, or lack of it, is now altering Lake Michigan water quality. With alewife almost gone, there has been a tremendous explosion of tiny animal zooplankton, which alewife fed on. The zooplankton, in turn, lacking a major predator, are literally gobbling up the lake's immense clouds of phytoplankton, even tinier vegetablelike creatures usually so plentiful they turn water a greenish color. The result: Decimation of phytoplankton is making Lake Michigan much clearer in terms of visibility. Formerly green-tinged water is slowly becoming more transparent.

Another factor worth considering in any discussion of future fish species composition of the Great Lakes is the ingrained leaning of most biologists to favor naturally reproducing species. Ideally, from their viewpoint, once some form of ecological balance is obtained in the lakes by knocking top-heavy smelt and alewife numbers down through predation (which was the only reason for introducing West Coast salmonids into the Great Lakes in the first place) and assuming increasingly stringent pollution controls continue, the costly and, to many biologists, "artificial" coho and chinook salmon fishery should take second place to regeneration of once-native lake trout populations and, in Lake Ontario, possibly Atlantic salmon. New York is now breeding Atlantics for stocking purposes. Ontario will likely stock landlocked Atlantic salmon from Maine. Also high on any future priority list will be steelhead and brown trout, simply because such fish, although technically "exotic," are capable of natural reproduction.

At the other end of the spectrum, no doubt canceling out rarely vocalized intents, if such exist, to rebuild a more natural, historically true fishery eventually, is the often quick response of American biologists to reasonable demands of well-organized sportsmen's groups. This obvious desire to give the public what it wants has been sometimes lacking in Ontario where anglers aren't as politically oriented as their American counterparts. Ontario fishery management funds also aren't related to fishing license sales.

The bottom line, however, no matter where you live, is that Great Lakes anglers want to feel the size and weight and excitement of big salmon. How much so is seen in the abrupt political demise of a former New York Department of Environmental Conservation commissioner who, for the very best of public health reasons, placed a ban on possession of Lake Ontario salmon and trout in 1976 because of high Mirex contamination levels in the fish. The resultant uproar from both anglers and tourist industry officials resulted in the possession ban being lifted the following year. Salmon stocking resumed in 1980 at a rate of about one million coho and chinook a year. In addition, a $10 million hatchery has been built by New York on the Salmon River. Similar costly expenditures, all keyed to production of salmon, have also been made in the other states bordering the Great Lakes, providing other major reasons why salmon (barring a total collapse of the food chain) will continue to provide angling thrills far into the foreseeable future.

More and more Great Lakes salmon angling derbies are turning over a portion of their annual derby profits to state or provincial angling agencies for specific salmon-rearing projects, the donations almost guaranteeing continued supplies of fish for their local waters. Other private organizations, such as Salmon Unlimited, based in Chicago, and the Bluewater Anglers of Sarnia, Ontario, on Lake Huron, are operating (or have operated) their own salmon-rearing hatcheries.

Also canceling out the many new forms of "machinery" and sophisticated electronic angling aids designed to increase future angling catches—and the increasingly critical "nonsporting" charges that are leveled against anglers even today by unknowledgeable observers—will be a definite trend toward lighter tackle and more sporting angling methods. Until recently, most of us have reveled in the comparatively new, exciting experience of catching big Great Lakes fish. Boating fish was of prime importance. Now, although we'll always have juveniles among us who confuse manhood with huge strings of dead salmon, a trend appears to be starting not toward catching fish (which is really not that great a challenge today) as much as to getting more sport out of the fish that are caught. Which is great. We've played the kid pigging out in the candy store. Now we're growing up.

New York State's Caledonia hatchery is typical of the new multi-million dollar fish-producing centers being built by the various states that border the Great Lakes. (*Photo by John Georg, New York State Department of Environmental Conservation*)

One of the surest signs this is happening is the growing number of fish I see anglers releasing every year. In most cases the released fish are "immatures" with another year or more not only to grow larger but possibly to provide additional sport for someone else. Another interesting change is the growing number of Lake Ontario charterboaters who now refuse to fish for lake trout. Because of the trout's longevity and resultant accumulation in its flesh of highly toxic chemical residues seeping into the lake from wastes such as ultradeadly dioxin buried adjacent to the Niagara River, a few of us have always been reluctant to rig for lakers or fish on bottom in areas we know they can be easily found. Apparently the message is spreading. While on a day's outing with charterboating friends working out of Port Credit last summer, there was not only the usual competition between the various skippers in setting tackle and downriggers on the boat, each fish caught representing so many points at the end of the day. But for the first time, anyone whose downrigger accidentally caught a lake trout had penalty points deducted, the trout being returned to the lake with such words as "Begone, you cancerous fish." On the other hand, the last newsletter I received from the Ontario Charterboat Association requested members not to call Ontario lake trout "glow-in-the-darks."

Some of the new tackle techniques to be employed might involve bouncing surface-skipping baits off kites, a freshwater game I've been having fun with on my own (see Chapter 15). Flying fishing kites and, if you really get into the game, building kites, is a highly entertaining challenge in itself. I have customers I swear get more fun out of flying a kite than catching fish. Are they reliving their youth? I don't know. And don't care. It's just a lot of fun guaranteed to take the worry wrinkles out of anyone's face. With the right kind of wind on an open beach, kites are also a great way for shorebound anglers to put lures in clean water at the edge of mud lines often beyond normal casting reach.

A few of us, and I think our numbers will grow, are also using fly rods loaded with 2- or 4-pound-test monofilament to flatline for spring salmon. An equal thrill is to hook a fall-run chinook in the thirty-pound class on a long, ultrasensitive rod and oversized single-action fly rod–style reel, the traditional West Coast mooching outfit. We deliberately leave the reel's antireverse click in the "on" position when we're fighting salmon with these rigs. The big reels have a unique sound. When one starts screaming against a running fish it is truly beautiful, soul-stirring music. Or so it seems to my prejudiced ears.

Better knowledge of fish habits will also present brand new angling opportunities. One example is provided by the still largely untapped close-to-shore fall movement of all salmonid species, including lake trout and Pacific salmon, when the fish are well within reach of a wading fly rodder patrolling a beach. Peak activity for a well-cast streamer is at dawn and dusk, although action is available all night long. The best sporting results are found in September and October before physiological changes associated with spawning slow down or terminate feeding. An interesting, although as far as I know, completely overlooked New York scientific study mentioned earlier, which found 50 percent of the diet of Lake Ontario rainbow trout is composed of insects, suggests another new fly-fishing opportunity: taking shore-cruising rainbows on a floating fly. I'm planning on using something big like a Grey Wulff salmon fly that will sit up and be twitched without sinking. Similarly, given the right kind of weather to venture out in a boat in winter, a few hardy anglers in my part of the country are discovering excellent, previously unknown shallow-water angling opportunities for brown, rainbow, and lake trout off sand bars near river mouths in December and January.

Increased angling fun will also come with greater public access to the fishery through stream improvement projects and construction of boat launching ramps and fishing piers. A classic example of bringing fish to fisherman is a cooperative Michigan-Indiana project to provide an additional thirty miles of high quality trout and salmon fishing in the St. Joseph River by building fish ladders at dams at Buchanan, Niles, South Bend, and Mishawaka. Construction of the passage facilities will allow Lake Michigan fish to move up and down a total of sixty-three miles of river through one of the more densely populated areas in the country. Tied in with the project, with the building of Indiana's new $1.5 million hatchery at Mishawaka, capable of producing 225,000 steelhead and 425,000 chinook annually, is the doubling of the number of fish stocked in the river. In the past, Michigan has been stocking about 640,000 trout and salmon in the St. Joe each year. The first major run of Indiana chinook should occur in the fall of 1987. Indiana's first release of Mishawaka steelhead should also return that year.

Where will it all end? We have accessible fish. We have the quantity of fish we need. The only real challenge left is to improve the quality of the fishery. And because each of us defines quality in slightly different ways, all of us having our own ideas on what constitutes a good outing, what the future holds can only be answered at a personal level. In the end, tomorrow's fishery will be what we make it.

Appendix

Angling Information Sources

Illinois

Department of Conservation. Division of Fish and Wildlife Resources, Lincoln Tower Plaza, 524 South Second Street, Springfield, IL 62706. (Brochures include *Fishing Lake Michigan, Coho in Illinois* and *Illinois Fishing Information.*)

Illinois Department of Commerce and Community Affairs. Division of Tourism, 620 East Adams Street, Springfield, IL 62701.

Waukegan/Lake County Chamber of Commerce. 414 North Sheridan Avenue, Waukegan, IL 60085.

Midwest Charterboat Association. 7320 North Bell Street, Chicago, IL 61645.

Illinois Charter Captains Association. P. O. Box 128, Elk Grove Village, IL 60002.

Waukegan Charter Boat Association. P. O. Box 946, Waukegan, IL 60085.

Chicago Sport Fishing Association. 25 East Washington Street, #823, Chicago, IL 60602.

Indiana

Department of Natural Resources. Division of Fish and Wildlife, 607 State Office Building, Indianapolis, IN 46204.

LaPorte County Convention & Visitors Bureau. 1503 South Meer Road, Michigan City, IN 46360. (April to October 24-hour Angling Hotline (219) 872-0031.)

Tourism Development Division. Box SM, 440 North Meridian Street, Indianapolis, IN 46204.

Michigan

Department of Natural Resources. Wildlife Division, Stevens and Mason Building, 6th Floor, Lansing, MI 48926.

Travel Bureau. Michigan Department of Commerce, P. O. Box 30226, Lansing, MI 48909. (Brochures include *Michigan, the Country's Greatest Fishing Waters* plus a list of all charterboat skippers. Out of state toll-free number: 1-800-248-5700.)

Waterways Division. Michigan DNR, P. O. Box 30028, Lansing, MI 48926. (*Michigan Boat Launching Directory.*)

Upper Peninsula Travel and Recreation Association. P. O. Box 400, Iron Mountain, MI 49801.

West Michigan Tourist Association. 136 Fulton East, Grand Rapids, MI 49503.

East Michigan Tourist Association. One Wenonah Park, Bay City, MI 48706.

Southeast Michigan Travel and Tourist Association. P. O. Box 1590, Troy, MI 48099.

Minnesota

Department of Natural Resources. Division of Fish and Wildlife, Box 12, Centennial Building, 658 Cedar Avenue, St. Paul, MN 55101.

Minnesota Office of Tourism. 240 Bremer Building, 419 North Robert Street, St. Paul, MN 55101. (Out of state toll-free number: 1-800-328-1461.)

Duluth Convention and Visitors Bureau. 1731 London Road, Duluth, MN 55812.

New York

Department of Environmental Conservation. Department of Fish and Wildlife, 50 Wolf Road, Albany, NY 12233. (Brochures of interest include *Great Lakes Fishing* and *Trout and Salmon Fishing.*)

New York Department of Commerce. Division of Tourism, One Commerce Plaza, Albany, NY 12245.

Lake Erie Salmon & Trout Association. P. O. Box 169, Dunkirk, NY 14048.

Rochester-Monroe County Convention and Visitors Bureau. 120 East Main Street, Rochester, NY 14614.

Greater Oswego Chamber of Commerce. 184 West First Street, Oswego, NY
13126.
Niagara County Tourism/Fishing Office. 59 Park Avenue, Lockport, NY 14094.
Orleans County Tourism Board. 508 Main Street, Medina, NY 14103.
Wayne County Public Information Office. 21 Butternut Street, Lyons, NY 14489.
Western Lake Ontario Charter Association. 2384 Peter Smith Road, Kent, NY
14477.
The Finger Lakes Association. 309 Lake Street, Penn Yan, NY 14527.

Ohio

Department of Natural Resources. Wildlife Division, Fountain Square, Columbus,
OH 43224.
Ohio's Department of Tourism will supply angling information through this toll
free number: 1-800-BUCKEYE.

Ontario

Ministry of Natural Resources. Fishery Division, Whitney Block, Queen's Park,
Toronto, Ontario M7A 1W3.
Ministry of Tourism. Communications Branch, 1200 Bay Street, 11th Floor, To-
ronto, Ontario M5R 2A5.
St. Catharines Chamber of Commerce. P. O. Box 295, St. Catharines, Ontario
L2R 6T7.
Information and Public Relations. City of Mississauga, 1 City Centre Drive, Mis-
sissauga, Ontario L5B 1M2.
Economic Development Department. City of Owen Sound, 808 Second Avenue
East, Owen Sound, Ontario N4K 2H4.
Georgian Triangle Tourist Association. 601 First Street, Collingwood, Ontario
L9Y 4C2.

Pennsylvania

Pennsylvania Fishery Commission. 3532 Walnut Street, P. O. Box 1673, Harrisburg, PA 17120.
Erie Tourist & Convention Bureau. 1006 State Street, Erie, PA 16501.

Wisconsin

Department of Natural Resources. Bureau of Hunting and Fishing, P. O. Box
7921, Madison, WI 53707.
Wisconsin Department of Development. Division of Tourism, Box 7980, Madison, WI 53707.

Select Bibliography

Applegate, Vernon C., and James W. Moffett. "The Sea Lamprey," *Scientific American* (April 1955).

Arnov, Boris, Jr. *Secrets of Inland Waters*. Boston: Little, Brown & Co., 1965.

Beeton, A. M. Personal communication with author, 1984.

Berkes, Fikret. "Ontario's Great Lakes Fisheries: Managing The User-Groups." Working Paper No. 19, Institute of Urban and Environmental Studies, Brock University, St. Catharines, Ontario, 1983.

Berners, Juliana. "A Treatyse of Fysshynge wyth an Angle." *Boke of St. Albans*. Westminster, 1496.

Bishop, Richard C. *Wisconsin's Great Lakes Fisheries: An Economic Perspective*. Biennial Report, University of Wisconsin Sea Grant Institute. 1982–84.

Cartier, John O. "The Coho Story: Carnival and Catastrophe." *Outdoor Life* (January 1986).

Cooley, J. M. Personal communication with author, 1985.

Craig, Robin E., and E. J. Crossman. "Genetic Variants in Canada of the Rainbow

Trout, *Salmo gairdneri,* called Golden Trout and Palomino Trout." *Canadian Field Naturalist* (July 1976).

Crowe, Walter R. *Great Lakes Fishery Commission: History, Program and Progress.* Great Lakes Fishery Commission, 1975.

Dawson, Blair. Personal communication with author, 1985.

Dobson, Hugh F. H. *Lake Ontario Water Chemistry Atlas.* Inland Waters Directorate, National Water Research Institute, Canada Centre for Inland Waters, Environment Canada Scientific Series 139. 1985.

————"Principal Ions and Dissolved Oxygen in Lake Ontario." *Proceedings, 10th Conference on Great Lakes Research.* 1967.

Downs, Warren. *The Sea Lamprey: Invader of the Great Lakes.* University of Wisconsin Sea Grant Institute, 1982.

Eckert, Thomas H. *Strategic Plan for Fisheries Management in Lake Ontario 1984 to 2000.* New York Department of Environmental Conservation, 1984.

Edgington, David N. "Great Lakes Eutrophication: Fish, Not Phosphates?" *The Future of Great Lakes Resources.* Biennial Report, University of Wisconsin Sea Grant Institute. 1982–84.

Falkner, N. W. Personal communication with author, 1985.

Fogle, Ned. Personal communication with author, 1985.

————"Surf Casting." *Michigan Natural Resources* (September/October 1984).

Francis, Austin M. *Catskill Rivers.* New York: Nick Lyons Books/Winchester Press, 1983.

Gibbs, Jerry. "Dr. Juice And His Amazing Elixir." *Outdoor Life* (June 1984).

Great Lakes Fishery Commission. *Sea Lamprey Management Program.* n.d.

Haig-Brown, Roderick, L. *Canada's Pacific Salmon.* 2d. ed. Department of Fisheries, 1956.

Hansen, Michael J. Personal communication with author, 1985.

Haynes, James M. "Finding Salmon and Trout in Lake Ontario." *Water Spectrum* (Spring 1983).

Haynes, James M. and David C. Nettles. "Fall Movements of Brown Trout in Lake Ontario and a Tributary." *New York Fish and Game Journal* 30, no. 1 (January 1983).

Heacox, Cecil E. *The Compleat Brown Trout.* Piscataway, N.J.: Winchester Press, 1974.

Hess, Richard. Personal communication with author, 1984.

Idyll, Clarence P. "Migrations." *Sport Fishing USA.* United States Department of the Interior, n.d.

International Game Fish Association. *World Record Game Fishes.* Fort Lauderdale. Annual Listing.

Kikkawa, Jiro, and Malcolm J. Thorne. *The Behavior of Animals.* New York: Taplinger Publishers, 1971.

Kitchell, James F. *Keeping Score: The Great Lakes Predator-Prey Game, The Future of Great Lakes Resources.* Biennial Report, University of Wisconsin Sea Grant Institute. 1982–84.

Kwain, W. Personal communication with author, 1985.

————"Pink Salmon Are Here To Stay." *Ontario Fish and Wildlife Review* (1978).

Lange, Robert. *Fisheries Management Plan for New York Waters of Lake Erie 1984–90.* New York Department of Environmental Conservation, 1984.

Larkin, P. A. Personal communication with author, 1985.

Lichorat, Bob, Mark Wenger, and Jim Winter. "Discover Salmon and Trout Fishing in Lake Erie." Environmental Resources Center Paper, State University of New York, Fredonia, 1982.

Lin, Leslie, Paul Nowak, and William Stapp. *The Sea Lamprey Story.* Ann Arbor: Michigan Sea Grant, 1981.

Lindquist, Wendy J. Personal communication with author, 1985.

Lauer, Thomas E. Personal communication with author, 1985.

MacCrimmon, Hugh R., and Barra Lowe Gots. "Rainbow Trout in the Great Lakes." Ontario Ministry of Natural Resources, Sport Fisheries Branch, 1972.

MacCrimmon, Hugh R., and T. L. Marshall. "World Distribution of Brown Trout, *Salmo trutta.*" Journal Fisheries Research Board, Canada, 1968.

Major, Harlan. *Salt Water Fishing Tackle.* New York: Funk & Wagnalls, 1948.

Martenhoff, Jim. *The Powerboat Handbook.* South Hackensack, N.J.: Stoeger, 1975.

Miller, John W. "The Ugliest Most Beautiful Fish." *Audubon* (May 1980).

Mottley, C. "The Classification of the Rainbow Trout of British Columbia." Progress Report of the Pacific Biological Station, No. 27, 1936.

———"The Spawning Migration of Rainbow Trout." Transactions of the American Fisheries Society, 1933.

Noltie, Douglas B. Workshop paper on Pink Salmon. Paper presented at 57th Annual Meeting of the Ontario Federation of Anglers and Hunters, February 22, 1985, at Sault Ste. Marie, Ontario.

Nunan, P. J. "Pink Salmon In Lake Superior." *Ontario Fish and Wildlife Review* (1967).

Power, John. Personal communication with author, 1985.

Ragotzkie, Robert A. "The Great Lakes—A Precious Resource." *Newsyear,* University of Wisconsin Sea Grant Institute (May 1982).

Raymond, Steve. *Kamloops.* rev. ed. Portland, Ore.: Frank Amato Publications, 1980.

Roule, Louis. *Fishes, Their Journeys and Migrations.* London, England: Routledge Publishers, 1933.

Spangler, G. R., and A. H. Berst. "Questions and Answers on Splake." *Ontario Fish and Wildlife Review* (Summer 1978).

Spurrier, John R. Personal communication with author, 1985.

Slade, John. "Spring Wading for Salmon and Trout." *Ontario Fisherman Magazine* (May 1984).

Smith, Peyton. "Fish Invaders." *Newsyear,* Wisconsin Sea Grant Institute (May 1982).

Smith, Thayne. Personal communication with author, 1984.

Stone, Livingston. *Domesticated Trout.* Cambridge: Cambridge University Press, 1877.

Teale, Edwin Way. *Autumn Across America.* New York: Dodd, Mead & Co., 1956.

Tibbles, James. Personal communication with author, 1985.

Van Covering, Jack. "Coho Crazy." *Sports Afield* (January 1968).

Voiland, Michael P. "Summer Netting For Lake Ontario Salmonids." *New York Sea Grant Bulletin* (April 1982).

————"Where They're At Is Where It's At." *Coastlines* 13 (December 1982).

————"The Rise of Lake Ontario's Charterboat Industry: Some Indications Of The Socio-Economic Impact Of A Developing Salmonid Fishery." Paper presented at the Annual Conference of the International Association for Great Lake Research, State University of New York College, Oswego, May 25, 1983.

Wagner, W. C., and T. M. Stauffer. "Three-Year-Old Pink Salmon in Lake Superior Tributaries." Transactions of the American Fisheries Society, 1980.

Wainio, Allan. "Pacific Salmon's Role in Lake Ontario." *Ontario Fish and Wildlife Review* (Winter 1979).

Walden, Howard T. *Familiar Freshwater Fishes of America*. New York: Harper and Row, 1964.

Wayne County New York Public Information Office. "Angler Survey." *1984 ESLO Trout and Salmon Derby Report* (November 1984).

Weeks, Edwards. *Fresh Waters*. Boston: Atlantic Monthly Press/Little, Brown and Co., 1968.

Wight, Harry, and Paul Vidal. *Fishing Lake Michigan*. rev. ed. Illinois Department of Conservation, Division of Fish and Wildlife Resources, 1983.

Winter, Jim. Personal communication with author.

Wooding, F. H. *The Angler's Book of Canadian Fishes*. Toronto: Collins, 1959.

————*Canada's Atlantic Salmon*. 2nd. ed. Department of Fisheries, 1956.

Wright, James E. Jr. "The Palamino Rainbow Trout." *Pennsylvania Angler* (March 1972).

Index

Some other fine fishing books
from America's Great Outdoor Publisher

Joe Humphreys's Trout Tactics
A systematic approach to trout flyfishing based on 80,000 hours of trout stream experience.
by Joe Humphreys

Learn How to Fly Fish in One Day
Quickest Ways to Start Tying Flies, Casting Flies, and Catching Fish
by Sylvester Nemes

Muskies and Muskie Fishing
How to Catch the King of Freshwater Game Fish
by C. H. Shook

Commonsense Fly Fishing
Practical guidelines that untangle the mysteries of fly fishing.
by Ray Ovington

Trout & Salmon Fly Index
Over 170 classic fly patterns: wet flies, streamers, nymphs, dry flies, salmon flies.
by Dick Surrette

Mastering the Art of Fly-tying
A hands-on guide to better fly-tying skills, including over 30 new and traditional fly patterns,
illustrated with 500 photos in color and black and white.
by Richard W. Talleur

Basic Bait Fishing
Mastering the baits, rigs, and techniques—in fresh and salt water.
by Ray Ovington

Tying the Swisher/Richards Flies
With hints and tips on how to fish them, with detailed tying instructions and step-by-step photos.
by Doug Swisher and Carl Richards

Naturals
A guide to food organisms of the trout.
by Gary A. Borger

Nymphing
An easy-to-use guide to identifying, tying, and fishing artificial nymphs.
by Gary A. Borger

Available at your local bookstore,
or for complete ordering information, write:
Stackpole Books
Dept. TS
Cameron and Kelker Streets
Harrisburg, PA 17105
For fast service credit card users may call 1-800-READ-NOW.
In Pennsylvania, call 717-234-5041.